Philadelphia Stories

EARLY AMERICAN STUDIES

Series editors: Daniel K. Richter, Kathleen M. Brown, Max Cavitch, and David Waldstreicher

Exploring neglected aspects of our colonial, revolutionary, and early national history and culture, Early American Studies reinterprets familiar themes and events in fresh ways. Interdisciplinary in character, and with a special emphasis on the period from about 1600 to 1850, the series is published in partnership with the McNeil Center for Early American Studies.

A complete list of books in the series is available from the publisher.

PHILADELPHIA STORIES

People and Their Places in Early America

C. Dallett Hemphill

Edited by

Rodney Hessinger

and

Daniel K. Richter

PENN

UNIVERSITY OF PENNSYLVANIA PRESS

PHILADELPHIA

Publication of this volume was aided by the
C. Dallett Hemphill Publication Fund.

Published by
University of Pennsylvania Press
Philadelphia, Pennsylvania 19104-4112
www.upenn.edu/pennpress

Printed in the United States of America on acid-free paper

10 9 8 7 6 5 4 3 2 1

A catalogue record for this book is available from the Library of Congress,

ISBN 978-0-8122-5318-4

CONTENTS

FOREWORD

Daniel K. Richter

Historian C. Dallett Hemphill died on July 3, 2015. Her passing came as a great shock to all those who knew her as a scholar, professor, editor, mentor, colleague, and friend. Most had no idea that she had been battling cancer on and off for years. Many of those who were aware of her struggle had no idea that the disease had returned with such a vengeance. And no one—especially those who knew her best—thought the end could be near. A person of such indomitable good spirits, we all believed, could never be defeated. She had taught at Ursinus College for more than a quarter of a century, published two distinguished monographs—*Bowing to Necessities: A History of Manners in America, 1620–1860*, and *Siblings: Brothers and Sisters in American History*—and served as editor of *Early American Studies: An Interdisciplinary Journal*, a publication she took to new heights of excellence. That professional track record alone left a huge void. But, formidable as her professional accomplishments were, the space that can never be filled is the one she created from her personal relationships in the Philadelphia scholarly community. She was a stalwart participant in the Friday seminars of the McNeil Center for Early American Studies, where she asked the wittiest and most insightful, but always supportive, questions. She went out of her way to encourage younger scholars, reading their work, cheering them up, and providing sage advice. All she spoke to somehow felt as if they were the only persons in the room who mattered to her.

Philadelphia Stories brings together the scholarly and personal sides of Hemphill's legacy. It also epitomizes the great loss her passing entailed, because she was unable to bring the project to completion. Its twelve brief biographies rest on deep scholarship conveyed with a light touch. Each subject was, like Hemphill, deeply embedded in the Philadelphia community, and she writes about them with careful attention to their human relationships. Two of them—Joseph Hemphill and Sarah Tyndale—were her ancestors. The papers of another forebear, Isaac Mickle, provide source material for several chapters. The borough of Trappe, where Henry Muhlenberg, subject of another chapter, spent much of his time, is just up the road from Ursinus College, where Hemphill inspired so many students. She frequently dispatched those students to internships there and at other sites associated with those whose lives she sketched. As always, Hemphill's scholarship is firmly rooted in her personal world.

Philadelphia Stories brings Hemphill's scholarly and personal connections together in another way as well. When her former student Rodney Hessinger discovered that she had left a nearly completed manuscript behind, he contacted me to explore the possibility of bringing the work to publication. One of us—or perhaps both of us simultaneously—hit on the idea that the best way to do that would be to draw on the collective expertise of Hemphill's many students and colleagues. We put out a call and were almost immediately inundated with a dozen volunteers, all of whom agreed to put the finishing touches on a chapter matching their own scholarly interests; their names appear in the table of contents. Under Hessinger's leadership, in May 2016 we convened a daylong workshop to agree on basic policies. Chapter editors would do their best not to impose their own voices, but to concentrate on filling in gaps, checking facts, standardizing citations, choosing illustrations, and polishing the prose in a way Hemphill would have done herself. Of course, judgment calls were necessary, but Hemphill left the chapters in good enough shape that the editors could fairly easily decide what to do.

Other parts of the manuscript required more direct intervention. Hemphill left behind only one complete draft of a section prologue—for "Declaring Independence: Three Revolutionary Wives." This draft made clear that she intended to draw out a few unifying themes for each section and to introduce readers to some of the scholarly questions it engages. Following that lead, Hessinger and I tried to make the prologues for Parts I, III, and IV do similar work. While we hope we have been faithful to Hemphill's vision and have incorporated some fragments she wrote, most of the words and ideas presented are necessarily our own.

The general introduction presented a different sort of challenge for Hessinger. The draft he was left to edit was reasonably complete and well-polished. But it began to lay out a broader vision for the project that we were unable to realize. Hemphill had apparently hoped to integrate the printed book with a digital mapping initiative that would plot various Philadelphia locations significant to the biographies in order to trace connections, sinews of community, and layers of meaning. From what we were able to determine from highlighted terms in the chapter drafts and from notes, digital files, and a few test images left behind on her computer, Hemphill had only begun to flesh out what she hoped to do. The maps that accompany each part—crafted by Erin Greb from data compiled by Stephanie McKellop—can merely hint at the special relationships Hemphill hoped to convey. It only compounds our sense of loss that we were unable to bring what surely would have been an exciting aspect of *Philadelphia Stories* fully to life. Still, we are proud to have been part of this collaborative effort to allow readers to savor the final work of an author whose own Philadelphia story we all treasure.

Philadelphia Stories

Introduction

Places and People

Why, with a city as rich in our national history as Philadelphia, do most of us only know about Ben Franklin and the "Founding Fathers"? Why do we visit only Independence Hall and the Liberty Bell? We've allowed ourselves to forget the fascinating stories of other people and their places, stories that can tell us much more about the colorful and complex history of America's first city. And yet these stories can be found and told.

This is not a new problem. In the 1840s, Philadelphia historian John Fanning Watson worried that people did not know which old house was that of colony founder William Penn. He noted the "popular opinion" that the inn known as "Penn Hall" was the house in question. But he pointed out that this was simply owing to its imposing façade. "The truth is," he asserted, "for many years the great mass of the population had dropped or lost" the location of Penn's House. Eager to retrieve it, Watson employed the primary sources at his disposal: he asked "old men about it." As historians do, he assessed and weighed the evidence he gathered: "Joseph Sansom, Esq. when about 60, told me he heard and believed it was the house at the head of the [Laetitia] court, and so also some few others; but more persons, of more weight in due knowledge of the subject, have told me they had always been satisfied it was the Old Rising Sun Inn, on the western side of the court." The latter location also matched Penn's instructions that his house face the harbor. Architectural evidence sealed the case for Watson, since the Penn house of "popular opinion" had not in Penn's time had an entrance on the main street.[1]

Watson wanted what he deemed the true Penn house to be purchased and restored "for future renown." This was a new idea in mid-nineteenth-century America, so he pointed to European examples, the preservation of the homes of Reformation leader Martin Luther and Italian poet Petrarch. Sounding like a latter-day tourist bureau official, he argued that "such things, in every country, every intelligent traveler seeks out with avidity." It took a while, but Watson prevailed, and the decrepit house was restored and moved to the city's Fairmount Park, where it stands today. Abandoned. Why the new neglect? Subsequent testing showed that this house was built in 1715, approximately thirty years after Penn supposedly occupied it. Oh well—it is still one of Philadelphia's oldest houses. This story shows how we continue to learn about Philadelphia's past. Also important is Watson's conviction that connecting past persons and remaining places could illustrate "the progress of our city."[2]

This book is the child of a marriage between Watson's old questions and new historical tools. Today Philadelphia annually attracts millions of visitors to its historic area, including "Welcome Park," which confidently marks the site of Penn's long-since demolished Slate Roof House, his second residence in the city. And yet the kinds of questions Watson asked persist if one takes the time to wander Philadelphia's streets, where countless old buildings sit amid new construction. Some walks present perennial issues, such as Watson's lament about the obstruction of views of the Delaware River by new development. In any case, for us, as for Watson, the face of the city preserves stories of the past that help us understand how we got to where we are today.

Although we now know much more about early Philadelphia—and profit, in many ways, from the knowledge—it is still the case as in Watson's time that the stories of many old edifices have been lost. Yet, like Watson, we can try to recover them. We cannot go about it the same way he did, by interviewing old people, but we have many more sources in their place. Some are thanks to Watson's generation, who founded the historical societies that have been gathering, cataloguing, and preserving documentary evidence ever since. Others are brand new, and among the blessings of modern electronic technology. The best tools at our disposal are, like the city itself, combinations of old and new, such as the digitizing of old maps and city directories that allow us to find people and their places and attempt to understand, with the help of the buildings that they inhabited, the past Philadelphias behind our Philadelphia.[3]

But the possibilities are not confined to new technologies. Archaeology, for instance, continues to yield insights into how we got to the present. Philadelphia was recently transfixed by one dig, as the firm excavating the site of "the President's House"—actually the home of Revolutionary financier Robert Morris that was loaned to George Washington and John Adams while Philadelphia was the nation's capital—unearthed a layer exposing the quarters of the first president's slaves. Twenty-first-century Philadelphia, with its Black plurality and tangled racial history, could not tear itself away from the site, and so a platform was erected for visitors to watch the dig's progress. Then a political battle ensued as to how the site should be interpreted for visitors. Conservative promoters of a laudatory exhibit on the first presidents fought liberal academic historians and activists seeking racial justice, who demanded that the trials and triumphs of the nation's "first slaves" be highlighted. The latter groups won, perhaps a fitting balance for a site that sits between Independence Hall and the National Constitution Center. While those two places justly glorify the "Founding Fathers'" achievements, the President's House exposes formerly hidden truths about Washington's evasion of Pennsylvania's abolition laws and the reality betrayed by the escape of some of his captives.[4]

While the Federal Constitution has endured, twenty-first-century Americans live in a world very different from that of the founding generation. Subsequent revolutions have extended political rights to persons previously excluded by virtue of their class, race, or gender identification. The newly empowered have wanted to recover histories not yet written because their actors were not, for most of the past, on history's more prolific winning side. And so, along with old and new tools, today's historians have new questions to ask of Philadelphia's past.

When one employs new technologies to look for people who have been forgotten, one finds not just individuals but networks. While Philadelphia's population grew rapidly in what was arguably its heyday, the century between the late colonial period and the Civil War, it remained a small town by today's standards, a place where inhabitants and visitors mostly encountered each other face-to-face. Even as construction spread slowly from the Delaware River on the east to the Schuylkill River on the west, the distance between these boundaries remained a comfortable half-hour walk. The same was true of the Northern Liberties and Southwark, the neighborhoods on the city's northern and southern boundaries. Early on, as the population hugged the banks of the Delaware, the city's first inhabitants would know each other by sight if not by name. By the end of the period, population growth had brought an unsettling anonymity, but the growth of institutions and organizations in response continued to link Philadelphians. It is difficult to trace the life of any member of a random group of Philadelphians without encountering one of the others, at church, in court, in a store, at a theater, or at a meeting. Thus although we may associate the Philadelphia of this period with individual Founding Fathers, scientists, or artists, the reality is that all Philadelphians lived not alone but enmeshed in groups, and traveling among the tight clusters of houses and public buildings plotted on the maps presented below.

The center of every individual's network, then as now, among both the poor and the powerful, were the household and the family. When Black, female, and working-class people gained access to the history profession in the twentieth century and began asking about their own pasts, the "new social history" of "ordinary people" that they pursued often had family and group life as its necessary focus, because the individual histories of their subjects had rarely been preserved. At this point, however, social historians' decades of recovery of the facts of everyday life of ordinary citizens have begun to allow the telling of individual stories. Moreover, they have elevated private life to an importance not previously appreciated. Initially, the scholars to pay most attention to private life were those investigating women's history; indeed, the assumption was that women were confined to private life, and that men were preoccupied with public life. But we now know that women shared the experience of events outside the home and that personal and family ties were important shapers of men's lives. We have come to understand that, even for Founding Fathers, the personal was political. Although their roles were different than women's, all men in this book were "family men." To the extent that the stories of these men have been told by others, the focus has been on their achievements on the public stage. These parts of their stories will be sketched here as well, but their personal lives are just as important to understanding their aspirations, motivations, and achievements, and thus will receive equal space. As with the President's House, the assumption is that all aspects of an individual's life are important. To tell stories of domestic relations and personal shortcomings is not to degrade people, but to humanize them. These stories are what we all have in common, can relate to, and can learn from.

Family ties both shape our lives and connect us. Some of these connections are lateral—linking some of these early Philadelphians to each other as in a network—but others cross generational lines. There are also connections over time between the characters and families described in this book. As with maps, new technologies have revolutionized what we can learn about family ties, through the use of such search engines as Ancestry.com. When combined, the networks and layers of past Philadelphians and their places can reveal even more of the hidden history of Philadelphia today.

This book begins with three men prominent in early Philadelphia religious life. One reason it does so is because of William Penn's early insistence on welcoming persons of different denominations to share Philadelphia with members of his own group, the Society of Friends, or Quakers. The coexistence and cooperation of these groups was an important feature of the city's early history that continues to shape it today. Another reason is practical: although many of the late seventeenth- and early eighteenth-century residences and commercial spaces of Philadelphia were destroyed in a wave of late eighteenth- and nineteenth-century construction, many of the city's first churches were spared, and remain for us to visit. The stories of these three men are also an important window on questions of immigration, ethnicity, and nationality, in that each man had to figure out a relationship between Europe and America, for his church if not for himself. Although very different in personality and lifestyle, all three men won over their respective communities, mostly through tenaciously living by their ideals—all the while constructing the modus operandi for a harmonious religious pluralism. This was not always an easy task, especially when the broad Protestantism that characterized a growing sense of Britishness in the rising empire was challenged by the existence of non-Protestant, non-English, or unchurched elements of the population. And then all three men were challenged by, but succeeded in coming to terms with, the American Revolution.

The first story is that of Quaker Anthony Benezet (1713–1784), who came to Philadelphia after his family fled religious persecution in France. He became a renowned schoolteacher, pacifist, pioneering abolitionist, and friend to all in need. He lived and worked near Fourth and Chestnut Streets, was a manager at the Pennsylvania Hospital, and was buried on the grounds of the Arch Street Meeting House. The second figure, Henry Melchior Muhlenberg (1711–1787), was a German immigrant and founder of the American Lutheran church. He was pastor in Philadelphia from 1761 to 1776, oversaw the building of several churches, and taught in the old Lutheran schoolhouse. In the process he befriended his Swedish counterpart and preached often at Old Swedes, Philadelphia's oldest church. He also served as an important liaison between the German community and Philadelphia's "English" political and religious leadership. His final home and local church can be visited in nearby Trappe, Pennsylvania. William White (1748–1836), our third man of faith, was born into an affluent Philadelphia family and showed religious propensities from an early age. He was educated at the University of Pennsylvania, ordained an Anglican minister in England in 1772, rose to the rectorship of Christ Church and St. Peter's, and lived all his adult life at 89 Walnut Street. White managed the delicate task of siding with the patriots during the American Revolution and guiding the birth of the independent American Episcopalian church, becoming the first American bishop. Taken together, the stories of these three men allow us to see how persons and faiths of European extraction came and worked together as a religiously and ethnically diverse Philadelphia became the capital of a new nation.

Part II turns to the stories of three women during the era of the Revolution. Their lives show an important but neglected side of the era of the Founding Fathers, important because they raise issues of power and autonomy central to the Revolution. The experiences of these three women show how even the most educated and affluent of Philadelphia's women had to struggle with a dependent legal and social status at a time when white men were throwing off their status as subjects. And struggle these women did.

Grace Growden Galloway (1727–1782) was an outspoken member of the Philadelphia elite and a poet. When her loyalist husband, Joseph Galloway, fled to England during the war, she remained behind to defend her property from confiscation. Her attempt to bar her Philadelphia doorway to patriot leaders did not succeed, but she remained and fought for her daughter's legacy. After her death, the substantial property she brought to the marriage was restored to her daughter; one historic home, Growden Mansion, still stands. Anne Shippen Livingston (1763–1841), called "Nancy," was a beautiful girl whose diary and letters tell a sad story. Living in the Shippen-Wistar House in Philadelphia after the British left the city, she fell in love with a young French diplomat. Yet she succumbed to family pressure to marry the wealthy but mean-spirited New Yorker Henry Livingston. After a period of abuse, Nancy left him, even though he made it difficult for her to see her little daughter, Peggy. Peggy eventually came to Philadelphia, however, and they lived the rest of their lives together. In contrast to Grace Galloway and Nancy Livingston, Deborah Norris Logan (1761–1839) had a happy marriage to George Logan, but even she was sometimes frustrated by his repeated diplomatic and political fumbles. As a girl, she heard the first reading of the Declaration of Independence from her family's garden fence on Chestnut Street (the later site of the Second Bank of the United States), but spent most of her life at her husband's family mansion, Stenton.

Philadelphia's central place in the politics and economy of the new republic made it the perfect arena for the subjects of Part III. These three men were largely self-made, and yet were able to contribute in various ways to the building of the city and the United States. Charles Willson Peale (1741–1827) was a wonderful painter. His many portraits of founding figures were the center of his famous museum in Independence Hall, and they now grace the Second Bank building. Stephen Girard (1750–1831) was born in France and came to Philadelphia as the captain of a trading vessel trying to elude British warships in 1772. He stayed and built a fortune as a merchant and banker. After the charter of the First Bank of the United States expired, he simply bought the business. At his death, the legacy he left the city for improvements and to build Girard College was so astounding that his will and biography were printed in the back of the city directory. For relaxation, he walked to and worked at the farm he called "the Place," in Passyunk. Joseph Hemphill (1770–1842), the son of a West Chester, Pennsylvania, farmer, told his father that his education at the University of Pennsylvania was legacy enough, and to divide any remaining inheritance among his siblings. He built a successful career as Philadelphia lawyer, judge, and legislator, and hosted political gatherings at both Strawberry Mansion in Fairmount Park and his townhouse across the street from Independence Hall. He was also a partner in Tucker-Hemphill China, the maker of America's first fine porcelain.

As Philadelphia grew in the decades before the Civil War, the city, like the nation, saw the emergence of bitter divisions. Owing to various factors such as its Quaker legacy and intellectual, economic, and cultural assets, Philadelphia was a hotbed of reform activity in these years; it was also home to a populace extremely hostile to reform, especially concerning race relations. Part IV concerns three individuals—a Black man, a white woman, and a working-class youth—who experienced and overcame the barriers imposed by virtue of their race, gender, and class. Not content with their own successes, these three, through different means, continued to fight the larger injustices of their time. Sometimes successful, sometimes not, their efforts shed light on issues that bedeviled the nation at large—and still do.

The Black man, Francis Johnson (1792–1844), was Philadelphia's foremost bandleader and a prolific composer of military band music and dance tunes. He was the first American musician to tour Europe, and Queen Victoria presented him with a silver bugle. Probably the first American to lead a racially integrated touring band, Johnson also experienced the rabid racism inflicted on successful Blacks. He performed often at the Musical Fund Society, for example, but he was denied membership. Sarah Thorn Tyndale (1792–1859) was the wife of an Irish immigrant and china importer and the mother of ten children. The building where their shop was located still stands at 707 Chestnut Street. As a young widow, she rescued the family's ailing business and soon became a wealthy reformer, patron of artists, and close friend of Walt Whitman. She attended and was lauded at the first women's rights conventions as an example of a successful businesswoman and "rescuer" of prostitutes. She summered at the North American Phalanx, a socialist commune in New Jersey. William Darrah Kelley (1814–1890), son of a poor Kensington widow, started to support himself at age eleven, first as an apprentice jeweler. He subsequently trained as a lawyer and rose rapidly in Philadelphia politics. Initially, he had a flair for the radical, promoting socialist writers and agitating for the common person. He gave many speeches at rallies at Independence Hall. Like Sarah Tyndale, he was active in the antislavery movement. He became a judge and commuted to his courtroom in Independence Hall after building a home called "the Elms" in one of the nation's first suburbs, in West Philadelphia. He then settled into a long career as "Pig-Iron Kelley," a pro-industrial-tariff Republican congressman from Pennsylvania.

This cast of characters was chosen because each is the subject of good stories that illustrate important aspects of America's political, social, economic, religious, and cultural history between the Revolutionary and Civil War eras. And each can be connected to visitable neighborhoods and spaces charted on the maps of Philadelphia and environs that accompany each part below. By setting the stories of these people in the places where they unfolded, I hope to add to a better understanding of the city—and America—today.

PART I

For the Love of God: Three Colonial Men of Faith

Prologue

We begin with stories of three men who shaped the city's diverse religious life. Philadelphia's jostling religious sphere is as good a place as any to start our journey, if only because William Penn so openly welcomed people of different beliefs to join his fellow members of the Society of Friends, or Quakers, in the colony granted him by King Charles II. Penn acted from a belief in freedom of religion forged from his own persecution as a Quaker in England. But he also embraced religious diversity for the same pragmatic reason that motivated many other founders of English colonies: he needed to recruit settlers to make a go of his venture. Europeans seeking respite from religious warfare born from intolerance were a major source of colonists in North America. Only a few founders like Penn (and Roger Williams of Rhode Island), however, actually embraced religious toleration—or rather, as they phrased it, "liberty of conscience"—in principle. In any case, the coexistence of various religious groups in early Philadelphia was an important feature of the city's early history that continues to shape it today. Through the lives of Anthony Benezet, Henry Melchior Muhlenberg, and William White, we see how people built networks across religious and ethnic boundaries to create movements for civic progress.[1]

Scholars disagree as to whether the relationships of early Philadelphia's many ethnic and religious groups were mostly harmonious or mostly embattled. Some stress the common spiritual goals that caused Christian leaders at least to try to surmount language and theological barriers. Others stress ethnoreligious distrust, especially as non-English immigrants from Northern Ireland and Germany began to pour into the colony in the eighteenth century. Naturally, religion and ethnicity intersected with politics to create ebbs and flows of cooperation and distrust. But the stories of the three men told here illustrate a middling position. Philadelphia's ethnic and religious groups both kept to themselves and worked together. To borrow an analogy often applied to later periods in American history, religiously and ethnically speaking, from the beginning Philadelphia was more of a salad bowl than a melting pot. That is, different groups mixed but only slowly melded, and often did so reluctantly. "Pennsylvania," as one shocked German Lutheran visitor observed,

> offers people more freedom than the other English colonies, since all religious sects are tolerated there. One can encounter Lutherans, members of the Reformed Church, Catholics, Quakers, Mennonites or Anabaptists, Herrenhüter or Moravian Brothers, Pietists, Seventh-Day Adventists, Dunkers, Presbyterians, New-born, Freemasons, Separatists, Freethinkers, Jews, Mohammedans, Pagans, Negroes, and Indians.... There are several hundred unbaptized people who don't even wish to be baptized. Many pray neither in the morning nor in the evening, nor before or after meals. In the homes of such people are not to be found any devotional books, much less a Bible. It is possible to meet in one house, among one family, members of four or five or six different sects.[2]

It is hard for twenty-first-century readers to appreciate how disorienting the ethnic and religious diversity of eighteenth-century Philadelphia could be. Of course, global travelers like Benezet and Muhlenberg had heard a cacophony of languages and seen all sorts of people on the cosmopolitan streets of London. There and everywhere else in the British realm since the time of the Glorious Revolution of 1688–1689, Protestants of all persuasions had enjoyed legal toleration—but that term usually meant literally to "tolerate" those who dissented from the state church, not to welcome them or treat them equally. So it was not diversity itself that was unfamiliar. What made Pennsylvania, and Philadelphia in particular, so disorienting was that no single ethnic group or religious persuasion held the levers of power, that no dominant group was in a legal position to *grant* toleration to less privileged communities who understood that they were minorities in a land controlled by others. Only in Pennsylvania in British America did Ulster Scots Presbyterians, Welsh Quakers, German Lutherans, German Calvinists, German pietist radicals, and countless others outnumber English Quakers, Anglicans, and dissenters who, thanks to William Penn, had no formal legal means to assert their religious superiority.[3]

Pennsylvania's Quakers and Anglicans had distinct advantages nonetheless. Thanks to William Penn, Friends had infused their values through every legislative and judicial institution in the province and continued to exercise power far beyond their numbers. Thanks to William Penn's sons' conversion to Anglicanism, the proprietary family, with its virtually unlimited control over land distribution, was able to confer substantial advantages on Anglican parishes, not just in the form of prime real estate to construct church buildings but in the form of revenue-producing properties that could support clerical salaries and other expenses. Pennsylvania was not entirely, then, bereft of something like a state church—or rather two differently advantaged state churches—but each spoke for a minority and lacked most of the usual rights and responsibilities state churches wielded elsewhere in the British Atlantic Empire. Perhaps nothing was more emblematic of the weakness of the Penn family's ability to impose its will on the province's institutional religious life than the story of the Quaker meeting house that William Penn insisted be built on the Center Square of his ambitious plan for the City of Philadelphia. Philadelphia Quakers duly built it, but almost universally refused to walk a mile or more from their homes along the Delaware to attend meetings there. By 1702 they tore the decaying building down and hauled the salvageable bits east to build a new edifice closer to their homes.[4]

But there was more to the Pennsylvania anomaly than who would fund meeting houses and pay clerical salaries (the latter, of course, did not affect Quakers, who had no paid ministers). In most of the British Atlantic world the state church—Anglican in most places, Presbyterian in Scotland, Congregational in New England—was responsible for countless functions that, thanks in no small part to the efforts of people like Benezet, Muhlenberg, and Smith, later came to be understood as secular. Parish officials doled out poor relief, oversaw the rearing of orphans, regulated marriage, policed morality, and ran schools. Churches also kept official records of births, deaths, and marriages. And they levied taxes to support all these activities. "In other words," one historian concludes, "priests, churchwardens, and overseers served as a layer of bureaucracy at the local level which counted, assessed, and taxed parishioners, as well as interacting with them regularly and sometimes passing on state pronouncements from the pulpit." Without such a bureaucracy, Pennsylvania lacked some of the most basic institutions of British government.[5]

Each of the three men studied here tried, in distinctive ways, not only to navigate the unfamiliar pluralism of Philadelphia but to fill crucial voids left by the absence of an established church. Anthony Benezet (1713–1784) emigrated to Philadelphia as the child of a Huguenot Protestant family of refugees from Catholic France. His efforts to create schools for girls and for African-descended people, to promote charity for Acadian refugees and others in need, to organize against slavery and for other efforts to improve society flowed from his profound commitment to Quaker values, not from any conscious effort to replace the bureaucratic and social welfare functions of a parish church. Yet they had that effect nonetheless, and laid the groundwork for the distinctive

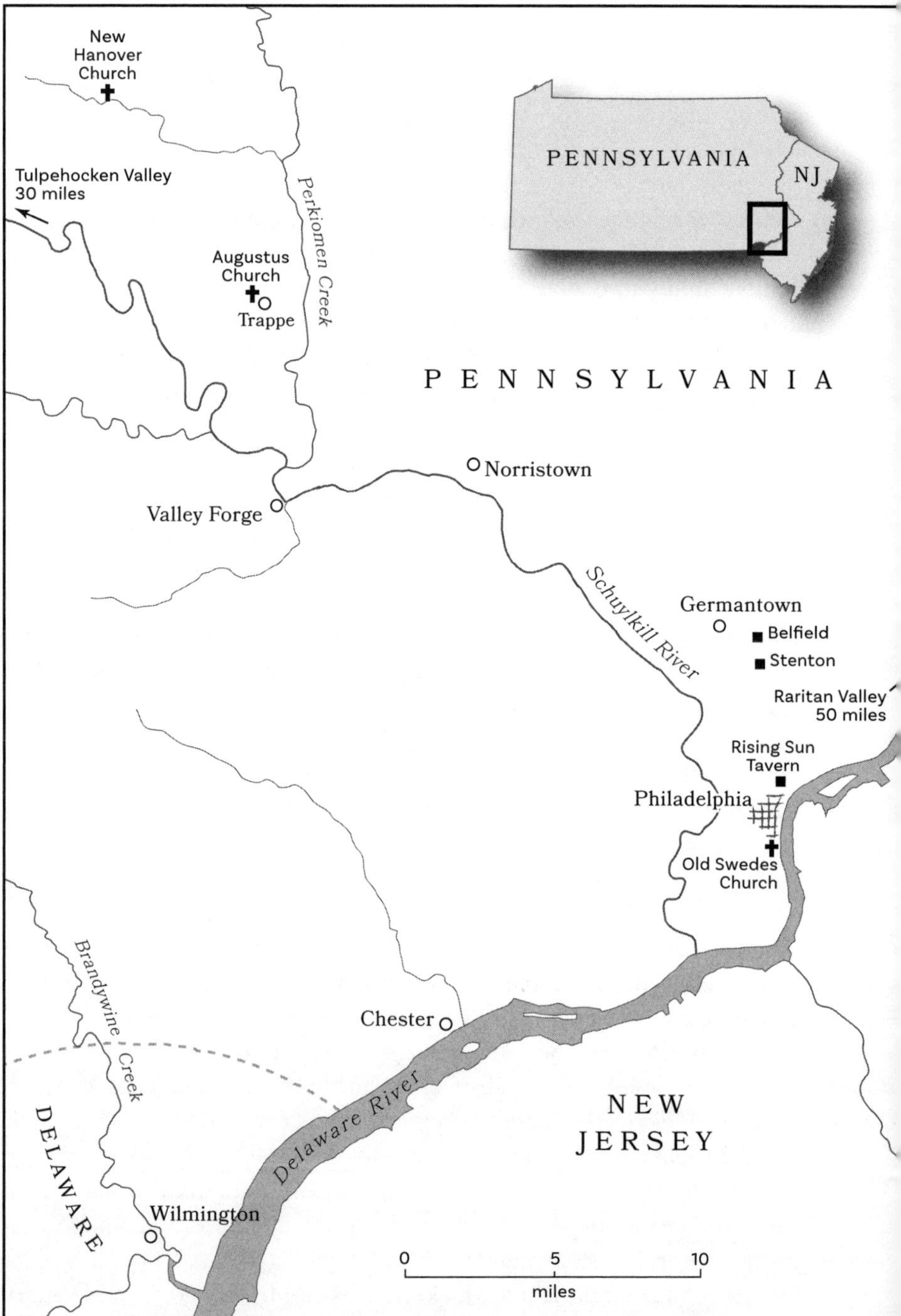

Map 1. People and Their Places: Three Colonial Men of Faith.

Philadelphia

1 Muhlenberg House
2 School for Black and Indian Children
3 Lutheran Schoolhouse
4 Former Lutheran/Reformed Church
5 William Smith's Academy/ College of Philadelphia
6 Friends Burial Ground
7 Thomas White House
8 Courthouse & High St Market
9 Future President's House
10 Episcopal Academy
11 High Street Jail
12 Laetitia House
13 London Coffee House
14 Anthony Benezet House
15 Pennsylvania State House
16 Friends School
17 William White House
18 Slate Roof House
19 Pennsylvania Hospital
20 Acadian Refugee Houses

A St. Michael's Lutheran Church
B Zion Lutheran Church
C Christ Church
D Friends Great Meeting House
E Friends Fourth Street Meeting House
F St. Thomas African Episcopal Church
G St. Joseph's Catholic Church
H St. Paul's Church
I St. Peter's Church

culture of voluntary organizations associated with more famous and more secular figures such as Benjamin Franklin.

Henry Melchior Muhlenberg (1711–1787) confronted Philadelphia's void in established religion more directly. A pastor dispatched from the headquarters of the pietist movement in the German city of Halle to impose order on the mostly shepherdless flocks of Pennsylvania's Lutherans, he came from a world of state churches supported by tax revenue. After he wrested control of Pennsylvania Lutheran congregations from the Moravian missionaries he regarded as heretics, he set about systematically building a set of voluntary mechanisms for financing clerical salaries, constructing churches, disciplining clergy, and standardizing liturgical practices. He did all this while building working relationships with clergy from other backgrounds and encouraging his fellow German speakers to acquire the skills they needed to navigate in an English environment without abandoning their identity.

Unlike the immigrants Benezet and Muhlenberg, William White (1748–1836), was a native Philadelphian born to wealth and the privileges of the Anglican Church, in which he took holy orders in England in 1772, before becoming rector of Christ Church and St. Peter's, both of which benefited from the Penn family's largesse. Yet the outbreak of the U.S. Revolution placed him in a situation very much like that of Muhlenberg. White's great achievement was to find a way to reshape the state-sanctioned institutions of Anglicanism into a new Episcopal Church adapted to the separation of church and state that prevailed through most of the new republic. All three men, then, not only found ways to live as members of religious minorities within a minority-majority city, but found ways to invent new institutions that would allow religiously and ethnically diverse Philadelphians not just to coexist but to prosper.

CHAPTER 1

Anthony Benezet

> Who could have lived a month in Philadelphia without knowing Anthony Benezet?
>
> —François Barbé-Marbois

Our stories begin with that of the beloved Frenchman who put the stamp of Christian charity on everything he did. If Philadelphia began as a Quaker city, no one embodied that spirit better than Anthony Benezet. But Philadelphia was not just home to the Society of Friends. Swedish and Finnish settler-colonists had lived in the area with local Lenape people even before William Penn established his "greene country towne," and Penn welcomed immigrants of different religious denominations from all over Britain, Germany, and France. As slavery grew in the American colonies, Philadelphia imported enslaved Africans as well. Benezet befriended all, and in this, too, he embodied early Philadelphia, or at least its better nature.

Benezet was in some ways a lifelong Frenchman—even though he left France as a child with his parents and four-year-old sister Marie Madelaine Joseph. He was born and given the name Antoine in Saint-Quentin in the northeast corner of the country in 1713, but his well-to-do Huguenot parents Jean-Étienne and Judith (de la Méjenelle) fled religious persecution before he turned three. They stayed briefly in Holland, then headed to England, where they arrived in August 1715. Young Antoine probably did not remember the flight, including a scare on the way to Rotterdam, when the family had to bribe a border guard to get out of France. The story goes that their guide proffered a gun in one hand and a purse in the other, declaring, "Take your choice; this is a worthy family, flying from persecution, and they shall pass." Fortunately the sentinel took the gold. Benezet remained as proud of this legacy of religious zeal and persecution as of his French ancestry. There was no going back for the Benezets. In Jean-Étienne's absence a royal court hanged him in effigy, subjecting him to civil death and the forfeiture of his property. Nonetheless, the family managed to prosper over the next sixteen years, owing to a network of mercantile connections in England. Surely one sign of family success was that Antoine, now Anthony, gained ten additional siblings. It is possible that the family joined the Society of Friends while in London; its teachings were not unlike those of radical religious groups in their old French neighborhood.[1]

In 1731, Jean-Étienne, Judith, and seven of their children came to America. They did not do so because of economic pressures, apparently, for Jean-Étienne (who became John Steven in England) quickly purchased two five-hundred-acre tracts and a large brick house in Philadelphia on Second Street, south of Race. The Benezets must have felt some comfort in that Philadelphia was already ethnically and religiously diverse and became more so over the course of Anthony's lifetime. Increasingly Scots-Irish and German immigrants joined the original Swedish, Finnish, Welsh, Irish, and English folk among the European settler-colonists; there were also other Frenchmen. Blacks were fewer than 10 percent of the population, but hailed from all areas of West Africa. Quakers predominated in terms of religious adherents, but Anglican, Lutheran, and Presbyterian congregations were growing; there were Catholics, Mennonites, and Moravians as well.[2]

Perhaps it was John Steven's business acumen that led the Benezets to move to Philadelphia at a time of economic growth and opportunity. The town was recovering from a recession in the 1720s, and the next thirty years saw the expansion of the trade that was the town's lifeblood. A good deal of building would result. When the Benezets arrived, the main public edifices were the Quaker Meeting House at High and Second Streets and the Court House at the head of the market sheds in the middle of that intersection. Wood structures abounded, although increasingly homes and shops were built of brick like the Benezets', and a few were substantial. Developed land, however, was still confined to a handful of blocks along the Delaware River. The Society of Friends had provided what little municipal direction and social services the town had seen thus far, but this was about to change as the population grew and became more diverse. Philadelphians began to display a habit of forming clubs and associations to meet various social and civic needs. There was plenty of scope for involvement on the part of newcomers. And there was plenty to do, as the mostly private efforts that had built the town thus far resulted in more taverns and dirty unpaved streets and alleys than the pretty stretches of brick construction and cobble-paved streets that would spread in the next generation.[3]

The Benezet home was located in what has been known as "Moravian Alley," which may reflect John Steven's connections with that group beginning in England. The Moravians, led by German nobleman Count Nikolaus von Zinzendorf, were an eighteenth-century revival of a suppressed Czech Protestant sect. Although John Steven attended Quaker meetings in Philadelphia, he had been acquainted with various Moravian leaders in England and was visited in Philadelphia in 1736 by Moravian Bishop August Spangenberg. Zinzendorf himself stayed with the Benezets when in Philadelphia in 1741–1742. And in the latter year Anthony's sister Susanna married Moravian missionary John Christopher Pyrlaeus. John Steven, Susanna, and two other daughters formally joined the sect in 1743. John Steven had already helped Pyrlaeus build a free school. Even earlier, he had supported an unsuccessful effort to establish a school for African Americans. Anthony's later commitment to educating the poor was thus a family trait.[4]

Anthony did not share the family zeal for Moravianism, as he either became or remained a Quaker. He did not seem disturbed by the religious diversity in his family. He was committed to religious toleration throughout his life. In 1748, for example, he and his friend John Smith paid a visit to Conrad Mathäi, the last remaining pietist mystic of the Kelpius community, who was living as a hermit along the nearby Wissahickon Creek. When Benezet's father died in 1751, Presbyterian Gilbert Tennent spoke at the grave. Anthony worked hard to help French Catholic Acadian refugees in Philadelphia in the 1750s, was interested in the teachings of the Native American prophet Papunhank, and even recommended a Chinese philosophical text—the Confucian *Analects*—to a friend.[5]

Benezet was less concerned with denomination than he was with specific beliefs. "Though I am joined in Church fellowship with the people called Quakers," he explained, "yet my heart is united in true gospel fellowship with the willing in God's Israel, let their distinguishing name or sect be as it may." He became friends with internationally famous Methodist preacher George Whitefield, and reported positively to a fellow Quaker on a 1770 meeting with the evangelist, "who appears in a very good disposition in meekness & universal love." Benezet was pleased to hear Whitefield's report on the desire for God that prevailed in England and Scotland, "even amongst those who have been zealous for the presbytery." While Benezet scorned the latter form of hierarchical church government, he believed "the Gospel must and will be preached to every creature under heaven, one way or other & it will prevail except [when] choked with covetousness, pride, the love of ease of self or lust of other things." Benezet stopped short of fully embracing Whitefield owing to the latter's waffling on slavery.[6]

Benezet could be critical of the practices of other denominations. When his sister Susanna planned in 1751 to join her Moravian missionary husband on a trip to England, Anthony and his brothers Philip and Daniel wrote the couple a letter stating their (and their mother's) objections. They did not think Susanna should leave her children behind and reminded her that she was not especially qualified for missionary work. Although loving in tone, the letter also characterized their other sister Judith's earlier trip among the Delaware Indians with her husband, Moravian David Bruce, as a "ridiculous jaunt." Perhaps indicating the real source of their disagreement, the brothers added the terse remark: "But Count Zinzendorf thought it proper, and therefore it must be complied with!"[7]

Benezet did not object to female ministry per se, because in 1736 at the Philadelphia Meeting he married twenty-two-year-old Joyce Marriott, who had been a Quaker minister for five years. The Friends recognized spiritual equality between the sexes, establishing separate women's meetings for business with important responsibilities parallel to those of men. The Quakers acknowledged and supported a good number of women who felt the call to travel through Britain and the colonies to speak at meetings. Since the Society had no formal, ordained ministry, women served in this and other capacities on an equal basis with men. Marrying Joyce likely solidified Anthony's commitment to Quakerism.

Anthony's and Joyce's marriage was happy, although the first years brought a measure of sadness in the loss of two babies. Mary, born in 1737, died before her first birthday. Anthony, born in 1743, only lasted six days. The Benezets had no more children. While Anthony never wrote about this, one wonders whether the loss and lack of offspring had anything to do with his becoming a teacher. He began in Germantown in 1739. Three years later, at twenty-nine, he became schoolmaster of the Philadelphia Friends School, the ancestor to today's William Penn Charter School.[8]

It had taken Benezet some time to find this calling. Brief stints as an apprentice in a counting house and then a cooper's shop in London in 1728 went nowhere. He failed at a manufacturing venture in Wilmington, Delaware, in the 1730s and languished as a proofreader for German printer Christopher Saur. Although his father, John Stephen, and brothers James, Daniel, and Philip were merchants, Anthony did not take to commerce. "I find being much amongst the buyer and seller rather a snare to me, as I am of a free, open disposition," he wrote to a friend; "I had rather be otherwise employed, and more retired and quiet." Benezet's distaste for the commotion of commerce is clear enough, but more telling is his recognition that he could not engage in the necessary dissimulation. All his life Benezet needed to tell the truth.[9]

Teaching proved the perfect outlet for his temperament and his brand of Christianity. Benezet wanted to set an example for others, and, in an age when many schoolmasters ruled by the whip, he was renowned for mildness. One day, for example, two boys put a live mouse in a pillory they had made and put it on his desk with the note "I stand here, my honest friends, for stealing cheese and candle-ends." Benezet shocked the class with his response. Rather than punish the boys, he observed that stealing was in the eyes of many a capital offense, and since they had not killed the mouse but instead more mercifully imprisoned it, he let them and the mouse go free.[10]

Benezet was notoriously kind to animals. He used to feed rats in his backyard as if they were chickens. When asked why, he responded that "you make them thieves by . . . starving them, but I make them honest by feeding them, for being so fed, they never prey on any goods of mine." Joyce and Anthony became vegetarians because they believed humans should not kill animals for food. Once, when offered chicken for dinner, Benezet commented, "What, would you have me eat my neighbors?" This eccentricity surely endeared him to pet-loving children.[11]

Benezet's concern for his students was quickly manifested in his request to the Philadelphia Meeting that a window be added to the dark and decrepit schoolhouse. He must have been delighted when the overseers decided instead to build a new building, near the old, at the southeast corner of Fourth and Chestnut Streets. It was close to the house at 115 Chestnut Street where he moved with Joyce in 1753 and spent most of his remaining years. Their dwelling was an older structure; it had been one of the first built of brick in Philadelphia.[12]

We get glimpses of Anthony and Joyce in the diary of his close friend John Smith. All three were on the Friends' "committee for visiting families" in 1747–1748, and they did just that, meeting and counseling with various members of the meeting. But schoolteaching and religious work still left time for socializing. Smith had the Benezets to dinners at his home and visited theirs. One August evening in 1748, Smith went to vote at the Court House at Second and High Streets and "then visited at Antho: Benezitt's, where were several agreeable friends." Indeed, many people visited the Benezets. Whether distinguished or poor, all shared alike in the simple hospitality described by a young Quaker, Jacob Lindley: "They had for dinner corn beef cabbage and Potatoes and for Dessert a huge Pye on an earthen Dish like those made for labourers on a Farm, the whole season'd with a most cordial hospitality & warmth of affection, truly characteristic." Like many other Philadelphians, the couple also took tea with friends, as when Smith noted that he "drank tea at E. Catheral's with A. Benezitt & wife

Figure 1. Anthony Benezet House, 115 Chestnut Street, Philadelphia, Pennsylvania (built ca. 1700). John F. Watson, *Annals of Philadelphia* (Philadelphia: E. L. Carey & A. Hart, 1830), 316. Library Company of Philadelphia.

& Sally Morris." The Benezets also attended Smith's 1748 wedding to Hannah Logan, at her family home called Stenton, where Benezet's student Deborah Norris would become mistress in the 1780s.[13]

Although Benezet was a very social person, he was not happy about all the alcohol his contemporaries consumed. Lindley, the young guest quoted above, was probably the first member of the Philadelphia Friends Meeting to speak out against strong beverage. In meeting, he had stood up at the back of the room, declared that he felt "oppress'd with the smell of Rum from the breaths of those who sat around him," and urged the Society to forbid its members to drink alcohol. His exhortation was little noticed, but Benezet went right up to him afterward to praise him and invite him to his home. There Benezet showed Lindley a pamphlet he was writing on the subject and asked him to add to it. The younger man declined, but must have been pleased when the pamphlet was published in 1774, entitled *The Mighty Destroyer Displayed*. In this way and many others,

Benezet influenced the prominent Philadelphia doctor Benjamin Rush, perhaps early America's strongest temperance advocate. Nonetheless Benezet did love tea, the era's other social drink. He claimed that three or four cups restored him nicely after a day of teaching, which is not surprising since he stinted on sleep.[14]

So the Benezets happily "tea'd" with many another Philadelphian. This shared social life was a sign of their good and strong marriage. A line from a letter to a friend with whom Joyce was visiting illustrates Anthony's affection, his respect for her autonomy, and his dislike of superfluity: "I would willingly write to my dear Wife but as nothing has occurred to communicate have nothing to say more, than, that much, very much Love dwells in my Heart towards her, & that I shall be very well pleased to have her with me, when consistant with her own Satisfaction & Peace."[15]

In 1750, Benezet began teaching Black children at his home in the evenings, for free. It is easy to overlook how revolutionary this was at the time. A "Mr. Bolton" had been arraigned in the Philadelphia court only a decade before for teaching Blacks. The only other attempts had been to instill religion, but Benezet taught his Black students the same lessons he gave to whites. His efforts paved the way for later Quaker support of a school.[16]

Benezet's work with Black children inspired a woodcut image, the only known representation we have of him. This lack of portraits was not for want of others' interest in his likeness, but his own modesty and consciousness of his plain looks. He was invariably described as small, and his face as marked with "strong features," or simply "ugly." No, no!" he protested when a friend expressed a wish for his portrait; "My ugly face shall not go down to posterity!" Yet all remarked as well on the stamp of peace and amiability on his face. His friend the French diplomat François, Marquis de Barbé-Marbois, wrote more neutrally that, in Benezet's old age, "white hairs were covered with a gray hat, with a turned-down brim. His worn face had a keen look."[17]

In 1754, Anthony resigned from the Friends School and opened a school for girls. Other Quakers had been teaching girls, generally alongside boys, but Benezet offered a more advanced curriculum, probably more advanced than any other school for girls in the colonies. In addition to reading, writing, and arithmetic, he taught English grammar, Latin, Greek, and French. He also used current events, as Deborah Norris (Logan) recalled, to "impress us with sentiments of truth, compassion, and charity." She also remembered how Benezet insisted on physical fitness, dividing the class into three groups and sending one at a time into a large room adjoining the schoolroom, "where abundance of means were provided for . . . recreation and exercise."[18]

Figure 2. "Benezet Instructing Colored Children." John W. Barber and Elizabeth G. Barber, *Historical, Poetical and Pictorial American Scenes* (New Haven, Conn.: J. W. Barber, 1850), 56.

While he taught many daughters of the elite such as young Deborah Norris, he cautioned them against fancy dress, and kept this up long after they left his care. His characteristic approach, at once stern and loving, was evident when he visited a newly married former pupil and found her dressed for a ball. "I should not have recognised my amiable pupil, but that thy well-known features and excellent qualities are not to be hidden by so grotesque and lamentable a disguise," he exclaimed. "Thy kind and compliant temper has yielded, at some expense to thy heart, to the opinions of others," he continued. "I love thee for the motive, though I cannot admire the evidence of it." Benezet's preaching of plainness in female dress was not simply a preference for Quaker custom; it was motivated by concerns for both charity and modesty. To another student he observed that "if every expense which might be spared is vainly wasting that which properly belongs to the poor, and every conformity to vain and foolish fashions is to please, and indeed often meant to allure, the wanton, what can be said in defence of the appearance of so many of our young women?"[19]

At times ill health forced Benezet to resign from school teaching, as he did in 1755 and again in 1766. Instructing girls like "Norris" (as he called her) must have been especially exhausting, because Benezet did not exactly slow down during the periods when not teaching. Instead he pursued other activities. He became an overseer of Philadelphia's free school and a manager of the new Pennsylvania Hospital, built just west of the settled area of the town at Eighth and Pine Streets. He fought against slavery and looked after refugees in Philadelphia, first from Nova Scotia (formerly French Acadia) and then from the Pennsylvania frontier during the Seven Years' War. Still, he could not bear to stay away from teaching for long and always returned to it. In the words of one biographer, "He loved children and they loved him." He resumed the girls' school in 1757 and, after nine months of rest in 1766, he started a school for poor girls, which he taught until 1782.[20]

Benezet added to his service as a teacher by publishing several spelling and grammar books and promoting useful education. After forty years of teaching, for example, he proposed a curriculum, that, in agreement with earlier proposals of his friend Benjamin Franklin, emphasized practical skills and eliminated the Latin of classical education. Benezet suggested that after pupils learned penmanship, English grammar, and "the useful parts of arithmetic, they should be taught mensuration of superfices and solids," preparing the way for mathematics. Boys and girls should "understand a short but very plain set of merchant accounts in single entry," and have "a general knowledge of the mechanical powers, geography, and the elements of astronomy, the use of the microscope," history, and, for "lads of bright genius some plain lectures upon anatomy."[21]

Whatever the subject, Benezet did not hesitate to teach the universal love that motivated all of his work. In the second edition of his *Pennsylvania Spelling Book; or, Youth's Friendly Instructor and Monitor* (1779), he asserted that "humble, merciful, and just souls are everywhere of one religion; and when death hath taken off the mask, they will know one another, tho' the divers liveries they wear here, make them strangers." No sect could object to the moral lessons the book advanced respecting the value of obedience, modesty, gratitude, charity, temperance, sincerity, benevolence, and religion. While no champion of empty rituals, Benezet did not hesitate to offer a Quaker version of the prevailing good manners of his day. He urged children to "sit in a decent composure of body and mind" in places of worship, "putting up your petitions to your heavenly Father, with an humble reverend disposition." After worship, they must "rise not up in a hurry . . . but respectfully pass along without pressing." At home children should be respectful of parents, affectionate with siblings, and kind to the "meanest servant . . . using the word 'please' where proper."[22]

After having taught Black children at his home in the evening for two decades, in 1770 Benezet helped to found a school for them, a first in the city. The school was a way of acting on his belief in racial equality and led to many Blacks coming to him for help. He had the same goals for Black boys and girls as he did for his white students: the cultivation of piety and morals and the inculcation of appropriate work skills. As he was getting older in 1770 and had his hands full with other activities, Benezet did not initially teach in this school, but he could not help putting his name forward when a vacancy came up in 1781. It was a good thing, as the school had suffered from the start from teacher turnover and irregular attendance. Benezet was overcommitted and the pay was low, but the cause was dear to his heart. He told Benjamin Franklin and other friends that the work "affords me much satisfaction, I know no station of life I should prefer before it." He taught the school from his home from 1782 until his death in 1784, and then ensured its perpetuation by bequeathing to it much of his estate on the decease of his wife, Joyce. Just as important, Benezet's experience with Black students enabled him to publish to the world that he could "with truth and sincerity declare that he has found among them as great variety of talents, equally capable of improvement as among a like number of Whites." This was novel, important, and influential testimony.[23]

Benezet's teaching had an important impact on the African-descended community in Philadelphia, as leaders such as Absalom Jones, founder of the African Episcopal Church of St. Thomas, and abolitionist James Forten had attended Benezet's schools. In 1787, Jones and other pupils of Benezet joined with African Methodist Episcopal Church leader Richard Allen, who had recently arrived in Philadelphia, to establish the Free African Society. This organization met for religious services and provided mutual aid in the Black community, holding meetings at the Quaker African school house, which Benezet had founded.[24]

Benezet's teaching career thus reflected his character, values, and affinity for working with women and African Americans. Interest in those without power pervaded his life. He is most known for his role in helping to launch the Anglo-American antislavery movement, but it is important to realize that his concern was grounded in local knowledge of "these difficulties which my situation amongst the Black People daily brings to my view," and his understanding that "the poor Black People's suffering originates in the Slave Trade." He was a crucial figure in the movement, mostly owing to his pamphlets on the subject and prolific correspondence with anyone he could interest in abolitionism, both in Europe and America. His correspondents included Granville

Sharp, Thomas Clarkson, and John Wesley, the founders of the British antislavery movement. They made much use of his writings. He was in frequent contact with his fellow Frenchmen of the Société des Amis des Noirs, who had his works translated into French. He also addressed the queens of France, Portugal, and Great Britain. Closer to home, he formed close partnerships with and greatly influenced Benjamin Franklin and Benjamin Rush.[25]

Benezet's antislavery activity began locally among his fellow Quakers, and the Friends' network helped him spread the message. Building on the earlier work of Philadelphia-area Friends such as William Southeby and Benjamin Lay, in 1754 Benezet and John Woolman wrote *Epistle of Caution and Advice, Concerning the Buying and Keeping of Slaves*, which Benezet presented to the Philadelphia Meeting. The reasoning was simple and powerful: "Now dear Friends, if we continually bear in mind the royal Law, of doing to others as we would be done by, we shall never think of bereaving our Fellow Creatures of that valuable Blessing Liberty; nor endure to grow rich by their Bondage. To live in Ease and Plenty by the Toil of those whom Violence and Cruelty have put in our power, is neither consistent with Christianity, nor common Justice." The Philadelphia Yearly Meeting considered and published the essay, henceforth discouraging Friends from holding slaves. In 1758, the yearly meeting began disciplining members who imported, bought, or sold enslaved African-descended people. Benezet turned the tide in favor of this measure when he stood up, walked to the front of the room, and, weeping, admonished the meeting with the plea: "Ethiopia shall soon stretch out her hands unto God" (Psalms 68:31). Slaveholding among Philadelphia Quakers subsequently began to decline (approximately 20 percent of Quakers owned enslaved people in the 1730s, 18 percent in the 1760s, and 7 percent in the 1770s).[26]

Friends thus first stopped buying and importing enslaved people, then Quakers freed the captives they held. But while Quakers retreated, others joined the slave trade, so that the decade from 1755 to 1765 saw many persons coming directly from Africa. Still, Benezet's campaign and other factors such as high Black mortality, an influx of white indentured servants, and an increasing number of runaways caused the proportion of enslaved Blacks in the city's population to decline dramatically, from 5.6 percent (1,481 persons) in 1767 to 2.2 percent (728) in 1775.[27]

Not only was Benezet against slavery and the slave trade, he also went further than other contemporary abolitionists in his belief in Black equality. He urged his fellow Quakers to help poor Blacks, especially the newly freed. Some responded, but most continued to regard "the oppressed Africans" as objects of charity rather than as equals in the meeting. Blacks were not encouraged to join, and those who attended generally sat separately. The result was that Philadelphia's Blacks gravitated to Methodist, Episcopalian, and Baptist churches, and then founded their own.[28]

Benezet strove to undermine racial prejudice. In addition to his effort to convince the world of Blacks' equal capacity for education, he set about to learn and write about Africa in order to challenge racist stereotypes and misconceptions. His resulting publications, like his antislavery testimony in general, were powerful because they were so well researched. He roamed the city's docks and interviewed Blacks he met working there. In addition to such testimony from African-descended informants, he pored over any available sources he could find in Philadelphia's libraries—from early travelers' accounts to scientific treatises. He was thus able to put together the most reliable African histories in the English language of his day, entitled *A Short Account of That Part of Africa Inhabited by the Negroes* (1762) and *Some Historical Account of Guinea* (1771). Participants in the slave trade vouched for the accuracy of Benezet's descriptions in his works such as *Observations on the Enslaving, Importing, and Purchasing of Negroes* (1759). A former British slave ship captain, Henry Gandy, wrote that on the basis of his experience, he could "confidently affirm that Anthony Benezet, and other writers quoted by him, are by no means exaggerated." Other antislavery activists in Britain and France relied on these works.[29]

In addition to African history and contemporary accounts, Benezet added the ideas of Enlightenment thinkers to the religious arguments against slavery of Quakers who preceded him. He tapped into the language of sensibility spread by new novels in circulation to touch the hearts and evoke feelings of empathy for slaves among his readers. He thereby took the concerns of predecessors among the Friends, mixed in persuasive arguments from various cultural currents, and helped start an international movement.[30]

So Benezet wrote antislavery letters and treatises and testified in meeting. He also worked face-to-face with fellow Philadelphians in the antislavery cause. He assisted in winning the release of a Black family kidnapped in New Jersey, stopping their progress south in Philadelphia. This event inspired the founding of the interdenominational Society for the Relief of Free Negroes Unlawfully Held in Bondage (the Pennsylvania Abolition Society), at a meeting at the Rising Sun Tavern on Second Street in 1775. Benezet became its first president. For years—from 1776 until his death—he visited slaveholding fellow Quakers as part of the Friends' manumission committee. His efforts to persuade them to give up their captive laborers were frequently rewarded, as when the Meeting minutes recorded, in Benezet's hand, that widow Esther House had set an enslaved person "free from bondage" in April 1776. While most Friends chose to emancipate their enslaved African Americans and remain members of the Society, Benezet and his co-workers also met with frustration as some members continued to drag their feet.[31]

Benezet did not rest in his labors, even after Pennsylvania became the first state to pass a gradual abolition act in 1780. In his final years, when teaching at the school for Blacks, Benezet was asked almost daily to help local Black families and did everything he could to bring attention to their cause. He pointed out that some enslaved people were "brought in this City to attend great men, members of Congress &c." Some of these were legally entitled, for various reasons, to their freedom "& look to us for protection." Benezet declared that he would feel Christian-duty-bound to do what he could even if they had no legal claim. He described others who were "torn children from parents & parents from children . . . to be sold in the Southward" into even worse circumstances than in Philadelphia. He grieved for some who, so distraught at their situations, took their own lives, "as was the case of a sensible french Negro, who from the most clear evidence was a freeman, & on whose behalf I had in vain requested a Habeas Corpus; redress being thus delayed & uncertain the poor fellow hung himself." Another enslaved man "drowned himself, as they were taking him down the river." Benezet strove to raise funds locally and in England to pay for legal assistance for these vulnerable persons. He prodded the Pennsylvania Abolition Society, which had not met during the Revolutionary War, to reconvene and take action.[32]

Benezet's work on behalf of the 454 Acadians who arrived in Philadelphia in December 1755 reflects many of his concerns. As Deborah Norris Logan observed, "He had a great and extremely natural partiality for his own nation" and therefore sympathized with his distressed fellow Frenchmen. After the outbreak of the Seven Years' War, these "French neutrals" were forcibly removed from Nova Scotia because they refused to take an oath of allegiance to King George, and they were distributed among the British colonies. They arrived in Philadelphia at just the wrong moment—soon after the French and their Native American allies had destroyed the British regiments led by Edward Braddock in in the contested zone then known as "the Ohio Country." The local populace was thus inclined to view the Acadians with suspicion and to fear that they would somehow join with Irish fellow Catholics to betray the province to the French. When word of Braddock's defeat arrived in summer 1755, a mob threatened to destroy St. Joseph's Catholic Church and was only turned back by a few valiant Quakers. Benezet was not at all bothered by working with those of another religious faith. He was happy to collaborate with Robert

Harding, the pastor of St. Joseph's, in helping the Acadians. (He would also work with Harding at Pennsylvania Hospital.) Benezet's charity and tolerance were by this time well known, which is why, in light of his ability to speak French, the Pennsylvania Provincial Council asked him to go aboard ship and see to the refugees' needs. He did and the Council provided supplies through him, demonstrating its confidence in his integrity.[33]

Benezet was typically energetic in this cause. He got wealthy fellow Quaker Samuel Emlen to donate land and had a row of one-story wooden houses built for the refugees on the north side of Pine Street between Fifth and Sixth. He continued for years to ask the government and individuals for money to help the Acadians, and persisted after public support ceased in 1762. With both frustration and a humble self-awareness, he confessed to his friend John Smith that he was "tired with begging, even of those who could spare a Thousand Pounds without having one Tear the less dropt on that account by their Heirs." He was trying to find someone to go with him in a door-to-door appeal, because he did not "think it prudent to go alone, being looked upon as an importunate solicitor." Potential donors were "apt to be soured at" his inability to make "allowances for other people's weakness" which, he admitted, "I am not always able to bear with Christian patience." As public charity waned, he taught the Acadians how to craft wooden shoes and make cloth from rags to secure a livelihood, and he helped to get their children into school. Often enough, he supplied the neediest among them out of his own pocket. One wonders what Joyce thought, when Anthony responded to her asking if he had seen some new blankets she had purchased. "Oh! my dear," he explained, "I gave them some evenings since, to one of the poor neutrals."[34]

The same heart that moved Benezet to feed and house Acadian refugees, to teach children normally deprived of education, and to work for the abolition of slavery and the slave trade also impelled him to campaign for better treatment of Native Americans, not a popular issue at this time of the Seven Years' War. The outbreak of this conflict led to the formation among concerned Quakers of the Friendly Association for Regaining and Preserving Peace with the Indians by Pacific Measures. Benezet joined and was several times appointed a trustee. He tried to publish the views and good intentions expressed by Indian leaders at the various treaty gatherings he attended, and he hosted a group of Friends and visiting Indians at his home in 1761.[35]

In 1763, when Native people attacked British settlements and forts in Pennsylvania and farther west, Benezet wrote to Sir Jeffrey Amherst, commander of the British forces, urging him to keep the peace by assuring the Indians that the English did not wish to drive them off their land, but only to settle peacefully among them. Amherst was unmoved. So too were European settlers terrified of Indian attacks. Before the end of the year, disgruntled frontier folk were on the move. In December the "Paxton Boys" murdered peaceful Indians at Conestoga (near Lancaster) and were marching on Philadelphia with a desire to kill Moravian-affiliated Indians who had been relocated to the city, supposedly for their own protection. The Paxton Boys and their many supporters were furious with Quakers like Benezet whom they accused of coddling and supplying the "savage" enemy. To the dismay of the Friends, those in power sought to mollify the unhappy backcountry whites.[36]

But Benezet did not give up. In 1774, when the First Continental Congress convened in Philadelphia, he met with many of the delegates to discuss the grievances of Indians. He continued to write pamphlets espousing their cause until his death in 1784. Writing to his friend George Dillwyn in 1783, he expressed his horror at another massacre of innocent Native people at Gnadenhütten in 1782, and his determination to confront "the prevailing prejudice in the back settlements against all Indians." He was concerned that "our experience of the fidelity & candour of Indians, when uncorrupted by an intercourse with disorderly White people, may not be buried with us, but communicated to such sensible, generous minded youth, who may improve upon it." In a treatise he was planning, he hoped to give a "careful account of that Melancholly Transaction, in as tender a manner to the perpetrators as truth will allow."[37]

Consistent with Friends' testimony against war, Benezet opposed military action while embracing the opportunities it presented to display human love, whether toward Acadian refugees or Indians. He thereby contributed to the American Friends' tradition of nonviolence and assisting those displaced and harmed by war. His abhorrence of violence impelled him to work against war with Britain after 1776. Various contemporaries describe conversations in which he deplored the resort to arms. He reprinted a pamphlet he had written in 1766, *Thoughts on the Nature of War*, and sent it to colonial leaders. He pointed out the incongruity of the principles of the American Revolution as espoused in the Declaration of Independence with the persistence of slavery. But Benezet's aversion to the war did not prevent him from helping those in need during the British occupation of Philadelphia in 1777–1778. Benjamin Rush recalled that "during the time the British Army was in possession of the city of Philadelphia, he was indefatigable in his endeavours to render the situation of the persons who suffered from captivity as easy as possible."[38]

Benezet must have been greatly relieved when Philadelphia was again in patriot hands and clearly delighted in the arrival of America's new French allies. He became a favorite of the French delegation. As the Count de la Luzerne exclaimed to a friend, "though Mr. Benezet has a small body—yet O! what a capacious soul he possesses." The friendship was mutual. When a fellow Quaker complained of the close bargaining the count had made over a house rental, Benezet defended his French friends, who understandably "did not love to part with their money for nothing." The French officers and diplomats were mostly aristocrats in silks, but this modest Quaker with the big heart charmed all.[39]

Well, maybe not everyone. There was one group of people who provoked Benezet's scorn: the miserly rich. In his view, men were to be Christian stewards of wealth, not "hoarders" for their own families. Upon hearing that a fellow Quaker had died leaving between forty and fifty thousand dollars, for example, he was incensed, considering it as disgraceful to their religious profession as if the man "had forty or fifty Thousand pair of Boots or Shoes in the house whilst the Poor were suffering in bare feet for want of them." He was particularly critical of fellow Quaker Israel Pemberton, whom Benezet criticized after his death in 1779 for leaving "60 or 70 Thousand Pounds" with "not a Farthing in charity." A story circulated of an exchange they had had in a Quaker meeting of business:

> Israel Pemberton rose & discoursed at some length on the inutility & danger of worldly possessions & advising the poor to be moderate in their desires & contented with their allotment. After he sat down, Anthony Benezet remarked that the advice of the Friend brought to his mind the recollection of a story of certain rats who were feasting on a cheese on the top shelf of a pantry, when a number of little mice, attracted by the good fare, were struggling hard to scramble up from a lower shelf to get their share & who kept scratching & scratching & jumping & jumping but could not get a bit. The rats, looking down on these poor starving little creatures, bid them to be quiet & contented & not make such a disturbance. Israel hung down his head & made no reply.

Yet when Benezet chastised him more directly on another occasion—for not taking "a proper care over his children"—Pemberton complained that it was "tiresome to hear Anthony always saying the same thing." This is as close as anybody ever came to criticizing Benezet, and Benezet actually remained on good terms with the Pemberton family. Everyone else praised him for practicing what he preached. Barbé-Marbois declared that "he carries his love of humanity to the point of madness." Benjamin Rush said similarly that "he seemed to possess a species of Quixotism in acts of piety and benevolence. He embraced all mankind in the circle of his love."[40]

Benezet was an influential Quaker, but not by preaching. He was not a public minister like his wife. His way was to talk with people in private. He spoke little at meeting and worried that some spoke too much. But he was active on various committees, served as an overseer, and was named an elder in 1751. These positions suited him, as they allowed him to visit others and them to come to him for comfort and advice. His characteristic tenderness softened the discipline he was bound to dispense—to all, that is, except the uncharitable rich.[41]

The Frenchman clearly preferred Quaker teaching over other religious doctrine and was occasionally critical of other denominations. He regretted Count Zinzendorf's control of the Moravians and his impact on the lives of his sisters in particular. But Benezet was open-minded to the good in other groups and the faults of his own. He lauded the Moravians, for example, for "allowing some of their members to dissent in the article of defensive war without casting them from under their religious care." For all his own pacifism, he thought the Quakers could learn from their example of tolerance.[42]

A famously busy person, Benezet got some respite, as well as most of his food, from gardening. When the space in back of his house proved too small, the Norris family set aside for him a large piece of the garden behind their nearby home. Deborah Norris Logan remembered fondly how he would often take tea with them after working in his beds. One wonders whether he shared a treat with his students that he described for his friend and fellow gardener, John Smith. He sent Smith a kind of Indian corn that, "when held over the flame for a few minutes in a warm shovel, will open its contents," that is, popcorn. The Norris house at Fifth and Chestnut, built in 1750 by Deborah's father, Charles, had grounds that would excite any gardener, with its "tiers of piazzas" and greenhouse where Charles Norris grew pineapples. In 1789, five years after Benezet's death, Charles's widow Mary Norris sold a part of the lot to the Library Company to erect its building. The plot is now home to the American Philosophical Society, which may stand on Benezet's old garden.[43]

The gardening is not surprising, for by all accounts Benezet hated idleness. He even denied himself too much sleep, observing that "such slothful indulgence" was inconsistent with "Christian fervour." When writing he would get up several hours before dawn. The garden was his relaxation. But this diligence and discipline were not those of a somber man. Benezet could find cheer in what others would bemoan. He remarked to a young friend that one advantage of losing memory in old age was that he could enjoy rereading books he had read in his youth but had since forgotten. "It gives me an advantage over thee," he said, "for thou canst find entertainment in reading a good book only once, but I enjoy that pleasure as often as I read it: for it is always new to me."[44]

Because he was energetic until the end, many were alarmed to hear of his final illness at seventy-one and hastened to visit and inquire after him. He succumbed on the third of May, 1784. The next day, James Pemberton wrote to his brother John in London: "I have now the sorrowful tidings to send thee of the decease of our valuable friend Antho: Benezet which occasions a general mourning among all Ranks of our fellow Citizens." James added that Benezet had been sick for a week but preserved his mental faculties to the end. He had shared a tender goodbye with Joyce, reminding her that "we have lived long, in love and peace." Pemberton described Benezet's last hours. He had stepped over from the meeting house to see Benezet, who asked him to take care of some pamphlets, "tho' he appeared then to be in greater pain of body than I had seen him, and his hands were cold; soon after which he lay quiet and went off with seeming great ease laying on his Couch in the outer room about Sunsett." Owing to the warmth of the weather, Benezet was buried the next evening in the old Friends Burial Ground, where the Arch Street Meeting now stands.[45]

In keeping with Quaker teaching at the time, Benezet's grave was unmarked. But his passing was not. According to Roberts Vaux, "the greatest concourse of people that had ever been witnessed on such an occasion in Philadelphia, was present; being a collection of all ranks and professions among the inhabitants; thus manifesting the universal esteem in which he was held." The throng included "many hundred Black people, testifying by their attendance, and by their tears, the grateful sense they entertained of his pious efforts in their behalf." These last mourners' gratitude likely increased when they learned that, as mentioned above, Benezet had bequeathed nearly his entire estate to fund the education of "Negroe, Mulatto, or Indian Children." Two codicils made further, and equally characteristic, bequests. He gave his library to that of the Friends Fourth Street Meeting, next to the school, "on condition that regular lists of those & the other Books be printed in order to make that Institution as profitable to our youth & others as may be." He also gave small gifts to his housemaid, to three French women, and to "Margaret Till an oppresst & much afflicted Black woman now in John Dickinson's service." He also gave two men "fifty pounds in trust for the use of a certain Society who are forming themselves for the relief of such Black People & other who apprehend themselves illegally detained in Slavery to enable them to employ lawyers &c." Benezet, in other words, took pains to see that his modest estate would continue the work he had done in life.[46]

Benezet's death naturally caused many to eulogize him. Perhaps French abolitionist Jacques-Pierre Brissot was the most eloquent. He asked: "Where is the man in all Europe, of whatever rank or birth, who is equal to Benezet? . . .

Who more useful to Society, to Mankind? . . . What author, what great man, will ever be followed to his grave by four hundred Negroes, snatched, by his own assiduity, his own generosity, from ignorance, wretchedness, and slavery?"[47]

Benezet was the quintessential Quaker, but he was not a big church man. He could not thus confine himself. He preached love and equality to the world. He wrote a short account of the Quakers in 1780, but it is dwarfed in importance by the volume of his writings on oppressed non-Quakers such as African Americans and Native Americans.[48] He did urge fellow Quakers to live according to their ideals of plainness and sharing but preferred either making such appeals personally or leading by example. He was a man of enormous charity, but worked to dispense it more to poor Catholics and other folk than to Friends. He was more likely to chastise fellow Quakers for their wealth. It is the universality of his vision that swelled his funeral train then and makes him a relevant model more than ever today.

CHAPTER 2

Henry Muhlenberg

> When there is only one hook in the house, everything is hung on it until it bends under the strain.
>
> —Henry Muhlenberg

When young Lutheran minister Henry Muhlenberg stepped off the boat onto the wharf at Philadelphia in late November 1742, he must have been thrilled. The trip from Germany—by way of London and Charleston—had been arduous. The journey is worth recalling, however, for his conduct along the way and his first steps in Pennsylvania reveal the man in microcosm. Muhlenberg was a bit of a complainer, but he took on challenges and was steadfast in pursuing them. He prized order and propriety, but did not run from disorder and contention. He was stern with the ungodly, but always loved children. As it turned out, his was just the right personality to win over the flock and put the Lutheran church in America on solid footing. At the same time, he helped lead his fellow Germans to a position of respect in Pennsylvania.[1]

Muhlenberg's first stop, a three-month stint in London, was rather enjoyable. Given his respect for hierarchy and proper credentials, he was pleased to receive a formal call to serve in Pennsylvania from Friedrich Michael Ziegenhagen, a Lutheran minister and chaplain for King George II. While waiting, Henry visited frequently with Ziegenhagen and worked on his English. The three-and-a-half-month sea voyage to America was less pleasant. The passengers suffered from illness and a lack of water. They were constantly afraid of Spanish attack. But Henry carried on as he did for the rest of his life—he preached, he tended the sick, he remonstrated with the captain and crew for their sinful behavior, and he gathered and taught the children on board. Although anxious to get to Philadelphia, he first headed south after landing in Charleston to visit Lutherans settled in Ebenezer, Georgia. That accomplished, he arranged passage on a sloop bound for Philadelphia, even though he was

Figure 3. Henry Muhlenberg (1711–1787). *Denkmal der Liebe und Achtung welches Seiner Hochwürden dem Herrn D. Heinrich Melchior Mühlenberg . . .* (Philadelphia: Melchior Steiner, 1788), frontispiece.

warned that the vessel was too dangerous. But it was the only opportunity available and Muhlenberg was determined to seize it. Sure enough, the voyage north was even worse than the ocean crossing.[2]

However pleased he was to reach solid land in Pennsylvania, Muhlenberg was surely aware that assuming his new role would be difficult. Already he had heard of Moravian leader Count Nikolaus Ludwig von Zinzendorf and his efforts to sweep Pennsylvania Lutherans into his fold. Accordingly, he spent his first days visiting the three congregations that had beseeched his Lutheran superiors in Europe to send them a minister, presenting them with his credentials and delivering sermons. In the process, he contended with an interloper in the form of an old German preacher, Valentin Kraft, and he confronted Zinzendorf. Muhlenberg's more impressive preaching and official credentials eventually prevailed with most members of these congregations.[3]

But winning over German Lutherans and reasserting orthodoxy among them was not Muhlenberg's only early task. He also had to assume a place in Philadelphia's ethnically and religiously diverse social landscape. Of help to him in this process was an old feature of that landscape, the Gloria Dei Church (later known as "Old Swedes"). Founded in 1677, this Swedish Lutheran congregation initially worshipped in a converted blockhouse but between 1698 and 1700 built a brick church that still stands. Although Gloria Dei was the home of a Swedish rather than German Lutheran congregation when Muhlenberg arrived, he was welcomed as the Lutheran minister at Philadelphia, in part because Gloria Dei was between pastors. Because the Germans had no church of their own, he was happy to deliver the first of many sermons there; indeed, he preached five times at Gloria Dei within his first two months in Philadelphia. On one Sunday he preached morning and afternoon, despite a case of laryngitis. "People want to hear something because it comes only every third Sunday and some of our members live four, five, and six miles from the city," he explained. "When there is only one hook in the house, everything is hung on it until it bends under the strain." Muhlenberg also established ties with those he would long refer to as "the English." He visited the resident Anglican minister, as well as the colony's governor.[4]

Most trying, initially, was his showdown with Zinzendorf. The count had only arrived the year before but immediately began trying to unite German Lutherans with the Moravians. He appointed John Pyrlaeus—Anthony Benezet's brother-in-law and a Moravian minister—as pastor to the Lutherans in Philadelphia, and soon gained a following among some of the area's Lutherans, along with control of their church records and sacramental vessels. But other Lutherans objected to this development and on July 18, 1742, they "dragged"

Pyrlaeus from their make-do church, a rented facility on Arch Street east of Fifth, which they shared with a German Reformed congregation. On December 30, 1742, just a month after arriving in the colony, Muhlenberg debated Zinzendorf face to face. Each asserted that he was head of Pennsylvania's German Lutherans. Zinzendorf argued that he had organized the local Lutherans and that Muhlenberg only confused matters by not recognizing this; Muhlenberg protested that he had official orders from Germany and a signed call to the position. The count tried to intimidate him, but Muhlenberg stood his ground. Zinzendorf was about to travel to Europe, so Henry wished him a "happy voyage. Good-by!" and ultimately won the day. Years later, it was Muhlenberg who would be acknowledged as the patriarch of Lutheranism in America.[5]

Henry Muhlenberg had come by his dogged persistence over long years of training in Germany. Born in Einbeck, in Hanover, in 1711, he had done well in grammar school and would have continued his education had his father not died suddenly of a stroke. Instead he endured what he considered "hard manual labor" in his midteens. He later wrote that he fell into bad company at this time and that his mother was too indulgent, but his scholarly propensity won out. He began to study in the evenings, first the organ and mathematics, then Latin and Greek. He went back to school. In his twenties he left home to take a teaching position that allowed him to continue his studies. This dedication must have impressed the townsfolk, for in 1735 they gave him a scholarship to the new University of Göttingen. Thus began a lifelong habit of supporting himself by combining several sources of income. Although he had received a basic religious education as a child, Henry did not become particularly pious until he came under the influence of Joachim Oporin, a theology professor at Göttingen. At twenty-five he began teaching at a charity school with some other students of religion. A year later he won noble patronage to study at Halle, the center of Lutheran pietism, a reform movement stressing personal faith over religious dogma. As he prepared for the ministry, Muhlenberg taught at Halle's renowned orphanage. He also studied the medicinal practices for which Halle was famous. Muhlenberg was getting ready to embark on his career, but he was not at this time contemplating a future in Pennsylvania. In fact, he wanted to go to Bengal in India. When that plan did not work out, he was urged to run a charitable school and orphanage in Grosshennersdorf, located in far eastern Germany. On August 24, 1739, he was ordained a Lutheran minister.[6]

Two years later, at age thirty, Henry was asked to go to Pennsylvania. The request came from Friedrich Michael Ziegenhagen, as noted chaplain of

George II, who was also the prince elector of Hanover. This meant the call came from the highest authorities, a fact likely to impress young Muhlenberg. Ziegenhagen was interested in the Pennsylvania mission because Lutherans there had been writing for the last decade, begging for a minister. There were three congregations in and near Philadelphia, totaling about five hundred people who were especially insistent in their requests, although they hesitated to promise a fixed salary. That was not an insurmountable obstacle because Muhlenberg was young and did not yet have a family to support. Besides, Ziegenhagen raised some funds. What did trouble Henry was the prospect of leaving his mother and siblings, who implored him not to go. But after searching his soul and seeking council as to God's will, he decided that he was willing.[7]

When Muhlenberg arrived in 1742 Pennsylvania had approximately 150,000 residents, and fully three-fifths were of German extraction. They lived throughout the colony, but mostly in clusters, and the majority were Lutheran. If they are considered together with the Swedish Lutherans, it is probably more accurate to call Pennsylvania a Lutheran colony at this stage than a Quaker one, although the Quakers still ruled. But mid-eighteenth-century Philadelphia in particular was a very ethnically and religiously diverse community; moreover the Lutherans were not organized. One reason was that they had come to the colony in different waves. Swedish Lutherans came to the area starting in 1638, nearly fifty years before the founding of Penn's colony. A succession of Swedish ministers presided over the congregation at Gloria Dei, among them John Dylander, who presided at Swedish, German, and English services between 1737 and his death in 1741. The few Germans who immigrated in the 1680s were mostly Quakers or Mennonites. They were followed by the so-called Palatine Germans between 1708 and 1720, which included German Lutherans and Reformed. One group settled in the Tulpehocken Valley, under the leadership of Conrad Weiser, Muhlenberg's future father-in-law. Between 1720 and 1730 came a more varied group; as with the previous waves, they were accompanied by few ministers. The years between 1730 and 1742 saw a sizeable increase in the number of Lutherans in Philadelphia. For a long time they depended on Gloria Dei for services, until the Rev. John Christian Schulze gathered a German Lutheran congregation in 1732. Religious faith was important to Germans, whatever their reason for immigrating, and Pennsylvania Lutherans lamented the lack of ministers, hence their letters to the authorities in Europe begging for more. Then young Henry Muhlenberg arrived, unannounced.[8]

The Philadelphia he encountered was hardly a town, much less a city. It was true that immigrants from Europe were pouring in, not only from Germany but from Northern Ireland as well, in almost equal numbers. These "Scots Irish" added Presbyterianism to the cultural mix. Many immigrants moved out to farm land in the countryside, however, and Philadelphia grew more quickly in density than breadth. Buildings still only extended westward to Fourth or Fifth Streets. West of this, in the northern neighborhood of Arch Street, was wooded. The unpaved streets were alternately dusty or muddy. While he must have been glad to get off the ship, Muhlenberg was not entering an organized and harmonious society. He knew no one and had to search out a local apothecary he had heard about in Georgia to help him find the Lutheran congregations he had been called to serve. This man told him that the local German Lutherans were following Zinzendorf or Kraft.[9]

Thus Muhlenberg had his work cut out for him. He had received a stellar theological education, had a fair amount of teaching experience, and had learned to fend for himself, but it cannot be said that he stepped off the sloop in Philadelphia a seasoned pastor. Yet he was challenged immediately to face down the clerical equivalent of quacks like Kraft and the even more serious threat from Zinzendorf. This required impressing and gaining the allegiance of the local Lutherans as soon as possible.

Meantime, Muhlenberg had to find a way to support himself. Despite their pleading for a regular and trained minister, the Pennsylvania congregations were not forthcoming with much of a salary. Soon they were hard-pressed with the cost of erecting church buildings. Further, in an effort to win people over, Henry did without baptismal fees and similar traditional payments. His first year was therefore difficult. His clothes wore out and he borrowed money to replace them. Fortunately, congregants were more forthcoming with food than with money. And, as he had in the past, Muhlenberg earned additional funds by teaching children and giving music lessons. In addition to helping him scrape by financially, these were sources of enjoyment for the lifelong complainer who nonetheless loved children and was a thoughtful teacher. Years later, for example, he grumbled one day that "he felt very weak and in pain" but, he added, "in the afternoon I had to instruct the young people, sixty-five confirmands in the church, and this made me well again." The music lessons also came easily, as he had a good singing voice, and enjoyed playing the clavichord.[10]

Muhlenberg had been called to serve a congregation in Trappe, another in New Hanover, and a third in Philadelphia. Considering that getting from one place to the other is a long commute even today, in the mid-eighteenth century, it was a severe challenge, especially in bad weather. On one early trip from Trappe to Philadelphia, for example, "the wind was strong and the two streams were so swollen that we had to swim them." The journey took all day. The locals thought it impossible for him to serve all three flocks. Not surprisingly, Muhlenberg immediately felt stretched thin. But he was determined to fulfill his call.[11]

He set about overseeing the construction of churches for these congregations—they had previously made do with borrowed worship space—first in Trappe, and then in Philadelphia. New Hanover already had a log church. Muhlenberg regarded church building as essential, noting, "If it is not done, the time would soon come when there would be no hope at all for our little Lutheran group." It took a while to locate a proper Philadelphia site; fortunately, just "before Easter the gracious God gave us a lot for the church in the center of the city." The church, called St. Michael's, was on Fifth Street at Appletree Alley, just north of Arch. It took time for the congregation to raise the funds necessary to complete the building; for a while members sat on pews made of boards perched between logs. These projects added an enormous burden of fund-raising and supervising construction, on top of Muhlenberg's normal ministerial work.[12]

But this was not all. Lutherans in Germantown wanted some of his time, and congregations in other parts of Pennsylvania, New Jersey, and even New York solicited his help in patching up differences and finding qualified ministers. The arrival in 1745 of an assistant, Peter Brunnholtz, along with two other young men who were to serve as teachers, was therefore a great help. It allowed Muhlenberg to focus on serving the country churches and to delegate the Philadelphia and Germantown congregations to his new colleague. Muhlenberg continued to supervise all, and he and Brunnholtz traded pulpits every month or so, but the new arrangement afforded much relief, and the two ministers worked well together.[13]

Perhaps it was the respite provided by Brunnholtz that prompted Muhlenberg to start a family, which he did by marrying Indian agent Conrad Weiser's eighteen-year-old daughter Anna Maria (also known as Mary), in April 1745. The young minister surely needed a household helpmate; moreover, he had already been falsely accused of improper advances by a young woman in his congregation. He had been exonerated, but likely felt a pressing need to remove himself from such suspicions. Muhlenberg made a wise choice of brides. Conrad Weiser became a great friend and important ally; more importantly Mary proved an excellent partner. After a few months in Philadelphia, the couple moved to Trappe, where they lived for fifteen years, until 1761. The next fifteen years found them back in Philadelphia, until the outbreak of the Revolutionary War in 1776. Henry and family then spent the war years—and the final decade of his life—back in Trappe, in a house near Augustus Church that can be visited today.[14]

Figure 4. Henry Muhlenberg House, 201 West Main Street, Trappe (Collegeville), Pennsylvania (built ca. 1750). Courtesy Historic Trappe.

The years of early marriage in Trappe were busy ones for the Muhlenbergs. In addition to serving his own congregations, Henry continued to travel to visit and help organize other Lutheran churches in the mid-Atlantic region. This was not easy. He frequently got sick or met with accidents on the road. He felt stressed by all his activity but fortunately had a strong constitution. Meanwhile, Mary had her hands full as their family grew. Son Peter was born in 1746, daughter Eve Elisabeth in 1748, Frederick in 1750, Margaretha in 1751.[15]

Although there was sometimes sparse communication with Philadelphia in winter weather, Muhlenberg went into the town on a regular basis and while there often mixed with other clergy. In 1746, he became good friends with German Reformed minister Michael Schlatter. He also preached to and catechized poor German indentured servants or redemptioners coming into the port. In the spring of 1748, he met with other Lutheran ministers to devise a common liturgy; that August, a synod was held in town, and the Lutheran Ministerium of Pennsylvania was born. May 1752 found him happily inspecting a new schoolhouse that still stands today at Fourth and Cherry Streets.[16]

Muhlenberg also worked with Benjamin Franklin in this period on an ill-fated project to establish charity schools for German children. Franklin and his allies had political objectives. They were defending the interests of the Penn family—the colonial proprietors—against the Quaker party that dominated the colonial legislature, and they were worried about the generally pro-Quaker German vote. They also feared the possible "Germanization" of the colony as a whole due to the recent influx of thousands of immigrants. Therefore they wanted to Anglicize German children through the schools. German printer Christopher Saur understood this and opposed the plan, but the more conservative Muhlenberg was interested in the benefits he thought Protestant British government offered to Pennsylvania's Germans. Muhlenberg also ventured to the newly constructed State House (later known as Independence Hall) in 1754 to take an oath of loyalty in the Pennsylvania court and thereby become a naturalized subject of the crown.[17]

The Philadelphia church became mired in controversy after the death of Brunnholtz in 1757 and unhappiness with the new pastor, John Frederick Handschuh. Its members pressed Muhlenberg to return and straighten out the mess. Although he preferred to live in the country, in the fall of 1761, he left the house in Trappe and together with Mary and their children moved into one on Vine Street. There were seven children at this point; an eighth had died soon after birth and three more would arrive in Philadelphia. The last was Emanuel Samuel, born in 1769, who died as an infant. The Muhlenbergs would have eleven children in all. Only seven would survive to adulthood, reflecting a degree of infant and child mortality not uncommon in the mid-eighteenth century. Indeed, Henry was constantly conducting funerals for the children of his parishioners, and was not infrequently summoned in the middle of the night to baptize a dying infant.[18]

The Muhlenbergs moved back to a changed Philadelphia. The skyline now had the dramatic spires that would grace it during the Revolutionary era, including the steeple on Christ Church, which at nearly two hundred feet was the tallest in the colonies. Pennsylvania Hospital had been founded, the first facility of its kind in the colonies. The streets, although still not paved, now had brick or flagstone sidewalks, and the main ones were lit at night by oil lamps. Other important changes were cultural. The town now had several newspapers to provide communication—and stoke debate. Quaker influence was declining socially as well as politically, and visiting theater troupes began to stage entertainments that Friends had discouraged. Although Henry loved music—thus the organs now ensconced in four of the churches, including his own—he, too, would have been happy with a quieter town.[19]

One of the reasons Henry and Mary preferred life in Trappe was that the city presented some child-rearing challenges. Henry had to punish young Peter, for example, for going out without permission and returning home late. The city offered worldly temptations to young men, such as the annoying (to Henry) custom of shooting guns on New Year's Eve (a practice that irks city leaders to this day). He would also complain of the noisy celebration of "the city's sports" at the news of the Stamp Act repeal in 1766. On the plus side, the city did present some educational opportunities. Henry quickly entered Peter into the College of Philadelphia (later known as the University of Pennsylvania) to learn Latin.[20]

Still, Henry must have been relieved when, in 1763, he was able to send Peter and next eldest sons Frederick and Henry Jr. to Germany to finish their education. As much as he missed the boys, he did not miss having to keep them in line. When describing a rash of juvenile delinquency in the hot summer of 1764, Henry must have been glad that his sons were not around to get into trouble. Yet Peter continued to worry his parents from abroad. First he abandoned his studies and had to be apprenticed to a merchant. Then he ran away from his master to join a military regiment. Peter arrived home in Philadelphia in 1767, whereupon Muhlenberg's good friend the Swedish Lutheran minister Dr. Carl Magnus von Wrangel took the young man into his home to complete his education in a sort of "private theological school." Peter finally determined on the ministry when von Wrangel, to Henry's great dismay, was recalled to Sweden in 1768. Through all this, the other two sons remained safe in Germany. Henry got news to them as he did to his Lutheran superiors, by taking a packet of letters to where merchants and mariners gathered—the London Coffee House at Front and High Streets—and putting it an outgoing ship captain's sack.[21]

In addition to being an easier place to raise children, the Trappe neighborhood, like its congregation, was more tranquil. In Philadelphia, Muhlenberg immediately found himself embroiled in contention. First there was a controversy over schoolhouse expenditures. He also had a difficult colleague in Handschuh. Henry thought his colleague's preaching was satisfactory, but grew depressed when Handschuh slandered his best friend von Wrangel and made snide comments to others about Muhlenberg himself. Muhlenberg continued to struggle with this man, and with himself over his ill feeling for him. Muhlenberg tried always to refer to him as a "good friend," despite the problems

Handschuh caused, such as the low attendance at church whenever he preached. Apparently Muhlenberg was not alone in his dislike.[22]

More than once, Muhlenberg claimed that church challenges were making him ill with worry, and expressed a desire to return to Trappe. Whether or not this was a performance, it succeeded in prompting church leaders and delegations of parishioners to urge him to stay in Philadelphia. Quarrels were reconciled and Muhlenberg managed to bring order twice with a new constitution. Yet the cycle of division and reconciliation returned with wearying regularity. When the country congregations periodically complained that they wanted him back, Muhlenberg was sorely tempted. He stayed because he believed he had a duty to stabilize the Philadelphia church.[23]

Contentions aside, the Philadelphia pastorate was a burdensome amount of work. Henry was so busy that he asked the church vestry to provide a house closer to the church and school. His Vine Street home was too far north, and the constant travel to visit parishioners was tiring him out. Even after he purchased a house closer in, he was forever zigzagging throughout the city to baptize ailing children, visit the sick, and fetch bodies for burial. When he was not out and about, numerous parishioners visited him. On a particularly busy day in 1763, he "had at least fourteen visits, one after another, from people of the congregation, this one complaining about something, that one inquiring, another quarreling, another delivering something or other, and so on."[24]

This aspect of his work involved Mary as well. She was the sort of ideal wife often referred to as a "help-meet" in the eighteenth century. Besides keeping house, Mary assisted Henry by talking to parishioners, taking messages, and accepting pastoral fees on his behalf. She also visited among his congregants, both with and without him. (In this they were not unlike the Quaker couple Anthony and Joyce Benezet.) Mary much preferred their life in Trappe, where she thought she would be healthier and he would get more rest. She did not acknowledge that household work was easier in the city, where she need not tend to a garden or livestock. She may not even have done much baking; Henry paid bills for bread deliveries. Nor does it appear that she made the family's clothing, because tailors and seamstresses were available to do that in the city.[25]

While Henry needed the income from baptisms, marriages, and funerals to support his growing household, he still declined to charge poor people; when he heard that one family had to borrow the shilling presented him for conducting a baptism, for example, he refused it. Sometimes parishioners paid him in kind, with food, or items like stockings and shoes. The church council provided firewood. This was not lavish support, and parishioners also periodically applied to him for alms. Henry complained of difficulty in making ends meet.

The situation did improve over time. By 1764, the church council voted on a salary of one hundred pounds for Muhlenberg as first preacher. This was reduced to ninety pounds at Henry's request, in order to raise the salary of the second preacher to sixty pounds.[26]

Another problem was simply that the congregation was growing too big. Even the burial ground adjacent to St. Michael's was full. By 1764, Muhlenberg was trying to get the congregation to buy land on which to build a second church. Two years later, after adopting and then abandoning plans for expanding St. Michael's, the congregation decided to buy a plot opposite the schoolhouse and began to build a new church, to be called Zion. Through these years, Muhlenberg, being Muhlenberg, continued to complain that he felt depressed, miserable, and sick. But he soldiered on, instructing children, baptizing babies, visiting the sick, and preaching. He gained an assistant in Christopher Emanuel Schulze, and this helped; then two other new preachers arrived from Germany. But new staff brought headaches as well as assistance as far as Henry was concerned, for he agonized over how to distribute the work of the Philadelphia church and school between the two new preachers and the two old ones.[27]

And Philadelphia was not his only responsibility. Henry needed to convene periodic Lutheran synods for the region, as he did in 1766 and 1769. These could leave him feeling very harried. He had to contend with staffing changes elsewhere, as when the Lancaster minister was called to New York, or when new ministers arrived and needed to be assigned to positions in Pennsylvania, New York, and New Jersey. Sorting things out often required that Henry visit these places, sometimes for weeks or months at a stretch. These forays outside Philadelphia increased in frequency in the 1770s. As always Henry complained of weariness; as always, he continued whatever activity was making him weary and worried about the congregations he could not get to visit. These trips were also hard on Mary, left at home with the children, and so she insisted on accompanying him and bringing their second-youngest daughter Maria Catharine (known as Mary or Polly) when he went to Georgia in late August 1774; they returned to Philadelphia in early March 1775. Henry hesitated owing to Mary's fragile health—she began having seizures in 1766—but on this matter she prevailed.[28]

The Muhlenberg family was still growing, only now not by birth but by marriage. In 1766, the year of her youngest sister's birth, eldest daughter Eve Elisabeth married Muhlenberg's assistant Christopher Emanuel Schulze. The other children were also assuming adult roles. In 1768, Peter got a position as assistant to the pastor of a Lutheran congregation in the Raritan Valley of New Jersey. Henry visited him there when making his rounds. Peter married in

1770, the same year that his younger brothers Frederick and Henry Jr. returned from Germany. They, too, became ministers, and soon preached in churches both in and outside Philadelphia.[29]

Accompanying the brothers from Germany was a new assistant for Henry, John Christopher Kunze. Kunze became indispensable to Henry in Philadelphia. They split all fees that came for pastoral services and Henry was grateful for his help. When Muhlenberg got sick in May 1771, he wrote that Kunze was "indefatigably diligent and conscientious in caring, meanwhile, for my official duties both at home and outside, which was a source of great comfort to me." Another Muhlenberg also appreciated Kunze; daughter Margaretha Henrietta married him within the year. Seventeen-year-old Henry Jr. also became a useful assistant to his father; in 1774, he became a third pastor in Philadelphia alongside Henry Sr. and Kunze. The Schulzes went to live near Mary's Weiser family relatives in the Tulpehocken Valley of Berks and Lebanon Counties, Pennsylvania, where Schulze became pastor of Christ Lutheran Church and several other nearby congregations. Frederick went to assist him before moving to a pastorate in New York in 1774. Muhlenberg did not record any significant conflict about these developments, so his children must have been happy to contribute to what was clearly in the making, at least for the time being: a veritable Lutheran family dynasty.[30]

The years 1775 and 1776 saw several turning points for Muhlenberg. On the one hand, they marked the peak of his role in American Lutheranism in that he was thought the best mediator for divisions among the Georgia Lutherans. On the other hand, his prolonged trip there required Henry Jr. and Kunze to run the churches in Philadelphia. While taxed by the responsibility—and Kunze's affliction with asthma—they managed. After his return, then, Henry decided to play more of an auxiliary role. He rented a house near the Zion Church and mostly just performed baptisms, marriages, and funerals. He gave any fees he earned to Kunze and young Henry, calling them the "regular pastors." He said he himself was too weak to continue to serve as such. Soon he would move back to Trappe.[31]

During his fifteen years as pastor of the Philadelphia congregation, Henry Muhlenberg had not only to work with other German Lutheran ministers but also churchmen of other nationalities and denominations. He invited all the local Protestant ministers to the 1769 dedication of Zion Lutheran Church, for example, and Anglican minister Richard Peters preached on the occasion. Muhlenberg must have been proud. Not only was the new church, which measured 70 by 108 feet, the largest in America; he must also have realized that by this time he enjoyed an international reputation.[32]

His closest relationship was with von Wrangel of Gloria Dei. The two churches had remained separate after an unsuccessful attempt to merge in 1744, but Muhlenberg and von Wrangel worked in harmony. Muhlenberg loved von Wrangel from the moment they met in 1760 and was forever reporting how much he enjoyed his friendship and conversation. The Swede often visited and spent the night and talked with Muhlenberg till late of religious matters. When Muhlenberg was burdened with disputes in his church, von Wrangel was an indispensable mediator and comforter. The two men also preached for each other. Muhlenberg was nervous about the first time he needed to preach in English at Gloria Dei to cover for von Wrangel when the latter was away, but von Wrangel quickly returned the favor by preaching to the German Lutherans in German. The men traded pulpits many times over the next decade; von Wrangel was especially helpful in filling in and preaching to the growing German congregations. Muhlenberg greatly appreciated the man and his valuable friendship, sometimes worrying that von Wrangel worked too hard, especially on his behalf. He wrote in 1764 that "I regret that this brave and good-hearted man, with all his own heavy official burdens and troubles, should be even more burdened and plagued by our German people." Sometimes the men worked together, ministering to the sick in Pennsylvania Hospital and the condemned in the High Street Jail. Muhlenberg was deeply saddened when his dear friend was recalled to Europe in 1769, and joyfully recorded receiving the occasional letter from him. Their correspondence was disrupted during the Revolutionary War but resumed thereafter until 1787, when Muhlenberg got word of his friend's death.[33]

While not as close as with von Wrangel, Muhlenberg was friendly with other religious leaders, especially the Anglicans. He considered the Anglican Church "our nearest and best friends," reflecting its closeness in ritual and doctrine, although he never considered joining with them as Lutherans in New Jersey and even those of Gloria Dei would eventually do. Relations with Anglican laity were not always smooth. When Anthony Benezet's brother Daniel asked Henry to preach for a sick minister at St. Paul's Church, the St. Michael's vestry objected. Muhlenberg had too many other pastoral duties. When the prickly Lutheran gadfly John Christopher Harwick filled in instead and kept the congregants squirming in their seats until 1:00 P.M., the city rumor mill mistakenly identified the long-winded preacher as Muhlenberg. Despite such setbacks, Muhlenberg developed warm relations with Anglican minister Richard Peters. They worked together to promote charity schools and visited each other in sickness and in health. Muhlenberg was also friendly with Jacob Duché, calling on him when he was ill and even visiting St. Peter's Church to try out its new organ in 1763. When two new German Lutheran ministers arrived in 1764, Muhlenberg promptly took them on a visit to these Anglican brethren. Friendly cooperation with the Anglicans (turned Episcopalians after the Revolution) continued to the end of Muhlenberg's life. In the early 1780s he and other German Lutheran leaders in Philadelphia worked with Rector William White on the problem of Episcopalian preachers appealing to the Lutherans for ordination as, lacking a bishop, American Episcopalians could not yet supply this need.[34]

The German Lutherans' relationship with Philadelphia's Presbyterians was more wary and depended on the individuals involved. Muhlenberg admired the Presbyterians for the growth of their churches and also the way they trained ministers. He objected, however, to their belief in predestination. Muhlenberg nevertheless worked to maintain good relations with Presbyterian leaders. In 1763 he noted that "my wife accompanied me to the Presbyterian church because the ministerium was holding synod and [Samuel Finley] the president of the Jersey College [later Princeton University] was preaching an evening sermon." The next day, Muhlenberg went with von Wrangel and "heard the Rev. Mr. Smith preach very edifyingly" He recorded visits to Presbyterian minister George Duffield, and also to the ailing Presbyterian leader Gilbert Tennent. When the latter man died, Muhlenberg referred to him as "the old, faithful servant of God."[35]

Muhlenberg was not alone in his efforts to work with other Protestant ministers. He noted that ministers of different faiths and nationalities attended Tennent's funeral. Similarly, when his colleague Handschuh died in 1764, Muhlenberg invited all the Protestant ministers in town to the funeral, and successfully asked Duché to toll the bells at Christ Church. Many of Philadelphia's church leaders embraced the popular itinerant Methodist minister George Whitefield. Muhlenberg met with Whitefield several times in the mid-1760s and went to hear him preach at St. Paul's. He lent benches from his church when Whitefield preached in the nearby Academy. And in 1770, Whitefield accepted Muhlenberg's invitation to preach at his capacious new Zion Lutheran Church. Muhlenberg also enjoyed many meetings with an assorted group that included von Wrangel and Duché for Bible study, or, as he put it "a devotional hour conducted by awakened English people."[36]

Philadelphia's Protestant ministers occasionally worked together to heal rifts in one of their churches. This happened from 1763 to 1764 regarding schismatic strife in the German Reformed Church. That Muhlenberg was asked to arbitrate was not surprising since there were some Lutherans involved in the division, but Anglican ministers Duché and William Smith also worked with Muhlenberg to help resolve the issue.[37]

Of course there were limits to this ecumenical bonhomie, whether for personal or doctrinal cause. As friendly as he was with von Wrangel, at times there were hints that Muhlenberg was jealous of Swedish Lutherans. He interacted little with von Wrangel's successor, Nils Collins. Muhlenberg let the "English Baptists" use his church for a conference once, but otherwise rarely mentioned them. He also rarely mentioned the Quakers. In part this was because the Friends did not have an ordained ministry for him to consort with, but he was not above slighting them, as he did in Handschuh's funeral sermon. He only mentioned Anthony Benezet once in his journals, recording that he wrote him a note in English as a favor for his Lutheran superior Ziegenhagen. But neither did Benezet mix much with non-Quaker ministers. As well liked as Benezet was, he, too, tended to socialize and work most among his co-religionists.[38]

Because they were contemporaries, it is instructive to compare the careers of Muhlenberg and Benezet. One would think they had much in common. Both were spiritually devout and deplored Christian factionalism. Both devoted themselves to the service of their countrymen in the "New World." Both loved children and teaching above all other activities. And yet the two men could not have been more different in their personalities and agendas.[39]

Benezet loved to seek out and aid his fellow Frenchmen, but their modest numbers meant that he would not confine his attentions to them alone. In contrast, Muhlenberg, despite his interaction with Anglo-American ministers, was almost wholly at the service of the large Pennsylvania German community. Unlike Benezet, Muhlenberg always described ministering to and interacting with "English" folk when not dealing with fellow Germans (whose ethnicity he usually did not note). Beyond collaborating with the leaders of other churches he occasionally met with political officials such as the governor, but he did so as the leader and representative of his ethnic and religious group. In Philadelphia, in particular, the English and German communities did not mix much. Muhlenberg occasionally attended or testified in court, either in connection with Lutheran church disputes or a German plaintiff or defendant. He did everything he could to help his fellow Germans succeed in their new environment. Along with encouraging English language instruction, he and Conrad Weiser and some others got a lawyer to compile a handbook with excerpts of Pennsylvania and English laws. It was translated into German and published in Philadelphia in 1761. But Muhlenberg did not want Germans to shed their culture. He was not as assimilated to English society as was Benezet, who had lived among the English from childhood. As befitted his status as the head of the German Lutheran community, Muhlenberg had a foot in both the English- and German-speaking worlds. He subscribed to an English newspaper, the

Pennsylvania Gazette, but spoke German at home. He was unapologetic about his love for sauerkraut.[40]

Muhlenberg generally attempted to give politics a wide berth, asserting that ministers should not meddle in such, but he could not avoid getting drawn in when the interests of his people were at stake. For his first two decades in America, Pennsylvania Germans generally supported the Quaker regime, grateful to have the religious liberty first guaranteed by William Penn. They also supported the Quaker party when it differed with the proprietors over taxation and policies toward Native Americans, because Penn's descendants threatened their access to land. But when the Quaker party went so far as to petition for a royal charter in 1764, Muhlenberg and other German leaders turned against them. The Proprietary party courted Muhlenberg as leader of the large German community, encouraging him to get the Germans to vote against the Quakers. Muhlenberg went along, considering as always which power would best guarantee German religious freedom and other rights. Most Germans were satisfied with the government as it was.[41]

But Muhlenberg's ambivalence grew with the work involved. In the fall of 1764 he was inundated with requests for administering communion and signing certificates of verification as required for naturalization, a prerequisite to voting. This was on top of all the translating and writing that he customarily did for his congregants. Muhlenberg lamented that he did not have someone to assist him with all this work that was "remote from the care of souls." But he could not compensate someone to do it, as he was not compensated for it himself. He did become somewhat politically engaged, however. He described the scene at the polling place and must have been happy that the German Lutherans helped elect a parishioner to the Assembly for the first time. This success notwithstanding, he refused to get involved when asked again to influence the German vote in 1765. With the movement for a royal charter a dead letter, Germans soon returned to their support of the Quaker party.[42]

Muhlenberg did not engage in charitable work to the extent that Benezet did. He worked very hard to serve his flock in religious terms. He would walk far to a baptism or funeral. He also gave alms as an individual. But he did not have Benezet's drive to overcome obstacles to helping others. While he usually lent assistance to the poor and ragged German redemptioners who needed to sell years of their and their children's labor to repay their ship passage to America, he sometimes told these groups that it was impossible for him to help. One cannot imagine Benezet doing the same. Muhlenberg supported the founding of the German Society in 1764 to assist new immigrants, but he did not take a leadership role in this venture as Benezet undoubtedly would have were he in the same position.[43]

Muhlenberg was also not as much a champion of Blacks and Indians as was Benezet. To be sure, Muhlenberg was no fan of slavery. When he first landed at Charleston in 1742, he was disturbed to witness enslavers' lack of concern for captives' souls. In the course of his ministry, he occasionally married or baptized Blacks, both enslaved and free. He also commented on the need for humane treatment of enslaved people when visiting Georgia in 1774. But Muhlenberg never publicly protested slavery or the slave trade, or even preached on the subject, and his sons Peter and Frederick both held people in slavery.[44]

His passivity was even greater regarding Native Americans. He recorded a lengthy conversation with an Indian chief he met while traveling in 1770, but that marked the extent of his curiosity. When commenting on frontier warfare, he inevitably referred to "savages" or "monsters." He may have felt torn on the issue, as many of the victims of Indian attacks on the frontier were his countrymen. He likely deplored retaliatory violence, however. In 1764 when his friend von Wrangel was part of the delegation of Philadelphia leaders who went to Germantown to confront the Indian-murdering Paxton Boys marching toward Philadelphia, Muhlenberg preferred to stay out of such matters. Unlike Benezet, his Christianity counseled forbearance, not activism. When a frontiersman urged him to send a circular letter to fellow preachers urging them to seek military protection against the Indians, Muhlenberg demurred. "I told him that we preachers could not permit ourselves to interfere in such critical, political affairs," he recalled. "Our office rather required us to pray to God the Supreme Ruler for protection and mercy and admonish our fellow German citizens to fear God, honor the king, and love our neighbor, etc."[45]

To be fair, Muhlenberg had far greater responsibilities to contend with than did Benezet. He was the chief intermediary between the English and the large German Lutheran community, and had to deal with all sorts of personnel issues and other contentions that Benezet did not have to worry about. The constant travel also demanded greater physical sacrifice than Benezet ever had to endure.

On war, Muhlenberg was both different from and like Benezet. He was not an avowed pacifist like Benezet, but he did try to stay out of the encroaching American Revolution. He had long felt an allegiance to the British Crown. He appreciated the Lutheran and German roots of the monarchy and was generally inclined to respect metropolitan authority. He was loath to cast it off. He tried, therefore, to remain neutral. But his oldest son, Peter, became a staunch patriot and left the ministry in 1776 to join the Continental Army.[46]

Henry, meanwhile, anticipating war, moved back to Trappe a few days after independence was declared. Frederick and his family soon joined him, fleeing New York. Henry Jr. and family came out from Philadelphia. Muhlenberg hoped that in Trappe he would be able to stay out of the war and keep his family from harm. He wanted to live a quieter life and to devote himself to writing and to teaching his grandchildren and other children, as well as conducting services in Augustus Lutheran Church. He was not fully successful. The house was crowded with children, grandchildren, in-laws, and servants; at year's end he noted that there were at times as many as twenty-two souls under his roof. Troops marched through the town on their way to join the Continental Army. Later they distressed the elderly pastor by quartering in the church itself. Political issues then arose that had to be addressed, such as the place of religion in the new state constitution. And Muhlenberg felt compelled to visit Philadelphia occasionally to preach and see his children who remained there. Kunze and Henry Jr. frequently needed help; Henry Sr. and Frederick did what they could to assist. Both church and family finances were a problem. Kunze found himself saddled with the quartering of paroled Hessian officers. The presence of these Germans fighting for the Crown was just another difficult twist of loyalties at this troubling time.[47]

There was simply no escaping the war. The family could hear cannons firing during the Battle of Germantown and saw countless refugees fleeing from Philadelphia in advance of the British occupation. Valley Forge was so close that Peter, who had been fighting all along, came to visit the Trappe house when it was already full of displaced family members. It is not surprising that Henry felt old and sick. Although he tried to stay neutral, it was increasingly difficult. The state demanded oaths of allegiance to the new government. Henry continued to feel vulnerable and was soon attacked in print. He anxiously looked for news from Philadelphia and lived in fear of attack. The churches in Philadelphia began to suffer physical damage as the occupying British used St. Michael's as a garrison and Zion as a hospital.[48]

The British withdrawal in the spring of 1778 brought a measure of relief, but challenges continued for Henry. He helped out in Philadelphia for a time, to give the Kunzes a chance to visit the country for a break. Although his children were grown, he continued to worry about them. Daughter Margaretha Kunze fell dangerously ill while pregnant in August 1778, and two months later her husband warned Henry that Frederick was about to leave the ministry. The following year, because Henry had been so rarely in Philadelphia, the vestry declared that his position as senior pastor was vacant and elected Kunze in his place. Kunze was embarrassed; the rest of the family was furious. Henry kept his cool but suggested that such a change would hurt the reputation of the church, so the vestry rescinded its action, allowing Henry to resign. Then Frederick was elected to the Continental Congress (in part because he knew both German and English). As with so many other things in his life at this point, Henry was ambivalent about his sons' career changes, but as they were of age, he acknowledged that they were free to choose for themselves. Still, he had hoped that Frederick would remain in the ministry.[49]

Henry was now in his late sixties. He had been slowing down more and more since the family returned to Trappe, and his wife's seizures grew worse. The family feared for her life when a fit caused her to fall into a pot of boiling beets and get badly scalded. The children helped out when they could, and Henry was in frequent communication with those in Philadelphia. But he spent more and more time at home in Trappe, reading and writing, working on his journals, and continuing pastoral duties at Augustus Church. He only visited Philadelphia occasionally, to help out for a few weeks and preach at Zion, to celebrate Christmas with some of the family, or to meet with a gathering of ministers.[50]

In 1782, with wartime disruptions at an end, for the first time in years Muhlenberg was able to communicate with Germany. In the meantime the independence of American Lutheranism had come about, and Henry's responsibilities waned considerably. The synod asked him to help compile an American hymnal, which was published in Philadelphia in 1786. He recommended a common order of service for all Lutheran churches but this would not be accomplished for another century. Still, in the forty years since his arrival in the colonies, he had put the church on firm footing. His sons were now on the main stage. Henry occasionally advised and mediated, but he no longer directed them.[51]

By 1787, he and Mary were feeble, and he was increasingly deaf. He continued to do a little reading and writing and performed some marriages, but he rarely preached. That spring, Peter's family moved in with them. Henry died in October, lucid until the end, though reporting increasing weakness; Mary and most of the children were gathered around him. He was probably at peace. His mission to organize Lutherans in North America was accomplished. Surely he was ready for a rest.[52]

CHAPTER 3

William White

Billy White was born a bishop.

—A childhood friend of William White

In April 1772, William White of Philadelphia was ordained into the Anglican priesthood by the bishop of London. He was twenty-four years old. Unlike Anthony Benezet and Henry Muhlenberg, White was a Philadelphia native. That his birth came six years after Muhlenberg's arrival in the city situates him squarely in the next generation. So does the fact that anointed as minister beside him was Henry's son Peter. The younger Muhlenberg had not rejected his father's Lutheran faith. He was ordained a minister of the Church of England for the simple reason that he had accepted a call to a parish in Virginia, and the Anglican Church was the established church in that colony. So he had to be ordained to fill the pulpit. But both his willingness to do so and his friendship with White are indicators that relations between Lutherans and Anglicans remained cordial.

White was a different person from Benezet and Muhlenberg in many ways. He was born in Philadelphia to a wealthy family of English ancestry. He never had to learn a new language or decipher a new culture to make his way. While Benezet was famous for his plain living, the White family was so affluent as to be famous for having an indoor toilet—most families' "necessary houses" were in the back yard. And yet despite the differences of generation and background, his story shares key elements with those of Benezet and Muhlenberg. First, although he was native born, his position in the Church of England created an enormous challenge at the time of the American Revolution. Should he, like many other Anglican ministers, remain loyal to the British nation and its church, oppose separation from the empire, and leave the colonies? Or should he, like many of his Philadelphia friends, support independence? He chose to stay, and it therefore fell to him, like Henry Muhlenberg, to negotiate a place in

Figure 5. Bishop William White (1748–1836). Oil portrait by Charles Willson Peale, 1788. Independence National Historical Park.

the new society for his denomination. Second, like Benezet and Muhlenberg, White served as a crucial intermediary between Philadelphia's diverse religious groups. Like Benezet, he strove to help the poor of all faiths. Perhaps most important, he was as mild mannered as Benezet and Muhlenberg, and this helped enormously when navigating controversy. Like them, White was much more inclined to make peace than wage war. Indeed, he might not have been able to pull off his most important achievement, the establishment of the first Episcopalian bishopric in America, had he not been so patient and well loved.

Though White was born into comfortable circumstances, he was just one generation removed from the immigration experiences of Muhlenberg and Benezet. His father, Thomas, had come to Maryland from England at age sixteen and rose in society through the determined accumulation of land. After his first wife died, Thomas White moved to Philadelphia, where he married widow Esther Hewlings Newman in 1747. They lived on the north side of High (now Market) Street, between Fourth and Fifth Streets. There William and his sister, Mary, were born in 1748 and 1749.[1]

William's penchant for his future career emerged early. A childhood friend remembered that he always wanted to play church, and preferred the role of preacher. "Billy White," she declared, "was born a bishop. I never could persuade him to play anything but church. He would tie his own or my apron around his neck, for a gown, and stand behind a low chair, which he called his pulpit; I, seated before him on a little bench, was the congregation, and he always preached to me about being good." She remembered, too, that once she "heard him crying and saw him run into the street, and the nurse-maid after him, calling to him to come back and be dressed" to go to dancing school. "He refused, saying, . . . I won't be dressed, for I don't think it is good to learn to dance. And that," his old friend added, "was the only time I ever knew Billy White to be a naughty boy." Just as characteristic was White's response, much later, when this memory was shared with him. He said that the story was true and that his mother gave up pressing him when she realized his aversion to dance, but he assured his questioner that he was "by no means opposed to others learning, if they like to dance."[2]

White said he was always religious, but said it "with humility, and with sorrow for innumerable failures, and for the having fallen far short of what was due to the advantages of early years." At sixteen, this early religious bent was confirmed by two events. The death of a friend occasioned questioning on his part, and then George Whitefield came to Philadelphia. White heard the famous evangelist preach "with great delight" and, like everyone else, was impressed by his "extraordinary elocution." Still, the serious young man was not inclined to admire Whitefield's emotionalism. "I found myself in no danger of becoming one of his converts," he recalled, for he feared that the "sudden impressions and violent agitations" wrought by Whitefield were generally fleeting. White later speculated that heated revivals actually had a negative impact on the number of converts over time. He was certain that such exercises were less successful than "a preaching not attended by the extravagances referred to." Yet White generously conceded the "general good intention" behind Whitefield's excesses. "Of his disinterestedness, and of his generous affections," he concluded, "there is here entertained no doubt."[3]

Seriousness about learning also showed early. White went to dame school as a young child to learn to read, and then began at the Academy of the College of Philadelphia (now the University of Pennsylvania) at age seven. It may have been there that he befriended Peter Muhlenberg. This was in the "New Building," built on Fourth Street south of Arch to accommodate the crowds that had gathered to hear George Whitfield preach in the early 1740s. Academically, White was ready to advance to the college at thirteen, but his father held him back. White, in retrospect, was grateful. He graduated instead in 1765, at seventeen.[4]

White had thus completed his college education by the time of the Stamp Act crisis. Both he and his father were sympathetic to the cause of the Whig resistance, but William was so caught up in his religious studies that he had determined to continue them. "I can tell you no news for I seldom stir out of Doores, and, as you know, our House is at some Distance from the Hurry of Business," he wrote to a friend in December 1765. "The Stamp Act furnishes Conversation for most People, but . . . my studies tend another Way." There was another distraction, however. "The Stay of the Young Ladies in Philadelphia often took me from my Business in Order to wait upon them," he admitted, "So that I have been obliged, since their Departure, to confine myself the more in Order to Retrieve my lost Time." White's comment is interesting for suggesting his preoccupations, and also reminds us that the hub of activity in Philadelphia was still along the Delaware River. In 1765, White could study in relative tranquility on High Street near Fifth. His mother's account book for 1770 provides a few glimpses into how White passed his time, with such entries as "Let Billy have to pay the Hebrew master £1," and "Took out for Billy, to pay for a book, £2."[5]

As he pursued his ministerial education, White worked with Philadelphia's most prominent Anglican pastors, Richard Peters and Jacob Duché, the same men with whom Henry Muhlenberg met for Bible study. In fact, private tutoring with these gentlemen was his only option to train for the clergy in the colony. In later life, White expressed his gratitude for their assistance, but was honest about their shortcomings. "There was in each of them," he confessed, "a singularity of religious character," which lessened their value as teachers. Peters's problem was seriously obtuse preaching, or, in White's more polite language, sermons that "were not always understood." White was somewhat mystified by this trait in a man "of an excellent education and of polished manners." Peters was, in fact, a powerful political figure, who served as a councillor in Thomas Penn's proprietary government, and was known as his most reliable negotiator with the Indians, as well as a canny adviser on politics, property, and appointments. Peters's experience was so wide-ranging and his political knowledge so deep that he seems to have neglected perspicacity in religion. One can sense the frustration of the young theology student in White's observations that "in social discourse, he could be exceedingly entertaining, on any ordinary, and on any literary subject. . . . Yet from the moment of turning the conversation to religion, he was in the clouds." The problem with Duché, in White's opinion, was vacillation; he changed his religious views frequently. He too, was well educated and amiable, but White lamented his adherence, first, to the unorthodox mysticism of the seventeenth-century Lutheran Jacob Böhme and the eighteenth-century Anglican William Law (the same thinkers Peters was drawn to), and then, after these ideas, his attraction to radical Swedenborgianism.[6]

In later life White said he was happy that, given how much he enjoyed the conversation of these two mentors, they did not lead him to abandon "what then, and ever since, I have considered as correct views of our holy religion." White got additional preparation by meeting on Sunday evenings and working with four other young ministers-to-be on theological exercises. They wrote out and delivered discourses on Bible history under the direction of the Reverend William Smith, provost of the college. Then they delivered these exercises in public, at the college, with Smith providing comments. This served to extend the men's learning, and also gave them practice in public speaking.[7]

Of course, being a young man, White could not study all the time, which might explain the role he played in helping a young woman elope with the painter Benjamin West. Betty Shewell was her name, and her brother had locked her up on learning that West wanted her to join him in England. The brother did not want her to marry the young artist, whom he called "a pauper." But White and some other friends sent her a rope ladder and a note through her maid, telling her a carriage waited around the corner to take her to a departing ship. The exciting late-night dash was a complete success. Yet even this White defended in a pious way, later claiming he would do it over again, for "God meant them to come together."[8]

In the autumn of 1770, White sailed to England to take holy orders as a priest. There he remained for two years, and for a simple reason: he was too young to be ordained when he arrived. The requisite age was twenty-four, and he was twenty-two. He also lacked another requirement, a degree from Oxford or Cambridge. This latter impediment was more quickly cleared, as White received a dispensation when he passed a qualifying exam with flying colors. His examiner said that his performance "would have been an honor to either of the universities." His diligent preparation had paid off. He was ordained a deacon that Christmas, but had to wait until April 1772 to enter the priesthood.[9]

This trip reveals more of White's connections with other people in this book. Apparently the young man knew prominent Philadelphia lawyer Joseph Galloway, husband of Grace Galloway, who wrote for him a letter of introduction to Benjamin Franklin, then in England. But this was a formality, as Franklin had been one of the gang assisting in Betty Shewell's elopement in 1766, and therefore already knew White. While in England, White stayed with his father's sisters. He was very fond of these aunts, and grateful that during his stay, they treated him with "truly parental affection." As he waited for ordination, he continued his studies and traveled though England with his friend John Benezet, Anthony's nephew, and a childhood friend of White. In London, he exchanged visits, enjoyed dinners, and attended the theater with Peter Muhlenberg and other Americans. When April 25 finally arrived, he and Peter and a third (unnamed) candidate dressed in gowns, took a coach to "the Lord Bishop's," and in a solemn ceremony at Westminster were duly ordained.[10]

As an adult, White suited the part he had chosen in life. Over six feet tall and with a benign face, he looked ministerial. When he was a young man, some female congregants thought him handsome. He never wore a wig although he did follow fashion so far as to powder his hair. Typical of his conservatism, he wore black silk stockings and knee breeches all his life, refusing to adopt the new fashion of trousers after the Revolution. (At home he always wore a silk dressing gown in warm weather.) He had a robust constitution that served him well as he ministered to his flock over the next six decades. At a time when sickness was common, he was hale until the very end. His health may have been aided by the fact that he was a hearty eater, although perhaps not by his reported penchant for butter. He slathered it on his mince pies and was said to "treat his bread as if it were furnished him for the sake of the butter that might be consumed with it." His doctor opined that if he were able to swallow nails he would probably be able to digest them.[11]

Returning to Philadelphia in the fall of 1772—again in the company of John Benezet—White likely felt less culture shock than earlier arrivals from London. The city was now the largest, wealthiest, and most cosmopolitan city of the British North American colonies. Its population would reach thirty thousand before the end of the decade. The city now had libraries, numerous clubs and associations, six newspapers, and the printers and paper mills to feed communications. Upon his return, White was invited to share a position as assistant minister of the joined parishes of St. Peter's and Christ Churches with his friend the Reverend Thomas Coombe, who had been one of the four young men of the Sunday evening theology exercises. Though he was still only twenty-four, White's family wealth allowed him to make a characteristically thoughtful gesture: he declined his half of the salary so that Coombe would receive the full amount. White was also able to begin a family the following year when he married Mary Harrison. William and Mary began married life in a house near

St. Peter's, at the southwest corner of Pine and Front Streets. They would have eight children.[12]

White was preoccupied with launching his ministerial career in the lead-up to the Revolution, but as it did for everyone else, the Declaration of Independence in 1776 prompted some soul-searching. The situation was especially difficult for the Anglican clergy, tied as their church was to the British state and to the king, for whom they had taken an oath to pray. White thought hard about the conflict, and in the end was swayed by his strong Whig ideals. He placed great stock in the constitutional principles of the Glorious Revolution of 1688–1689. He thought the traditional purview of Parliament and the limits on monarchy declared at that time had been violated by the recent acts of the British government, which "contradicted the rights which the colonists had brought with them to the wilds of America and were, until then, respected by the mother country." Accordingly, he took an oath of allegiance to the United States at the Courthouse. As he entered, an acquaintance was said to have made a hanging gesture, to suggest the risk of the classic punishment for treason that White was taking. As he came out, White supposedly acknowledged the sign. "I know my danger, and that it is the greater on account of my being a clergyman of the Church of England," he is said to have remarked. "But I trust in Providence. The cause is a just one, and I am persuaded will be protected."[13]

White explained in retrospect that this decision did not come easily. "Perhaps," he admitted, "had the issue depended on my determination, it would have been for submission, with the determined and steady continuance of rightful claims." But White was loyal to his fellow colonists as well, and "when my countrymen in general had chosen the dreadful measure of forcible resistance—for certainly the spirit was almost universal at the time of arming—it was the dictate of conscience, to take what seemed the right side." He was swept up by the political fervor that engulfed Philadelphia. White was now convinced "not merely of the injustice of [British] ministerial measures, but of the folly of them; indications of the utter ignorance of our country, and of the consequent incapacity for the governing of it."[14]

Still, White did not jump in with both feet. While Coombe, Duché, and Smith had, unlike Anglican ministers in New England and the South, preached sermons supportive of resistance to British tyranny, White had declined "to beat the ecclesiastical drum." When asked to preach before a battalion, he refused, saying he would not make the ministry "instrumental to the war." He continued to pray for the king on Sundays right up to the Declaration of Independence.[15]

White remained on the sidelines even after avowing the patriot cause. As the British advanced on Philadelphia in September 1777, he retired with his family to the Maryland home of his half sister and brother-in-law. His sister, Mary White Morris, also retreated there with her children. But then he heard that he had been appointed chaplain of the Continental Congress. Mary Morris had written to their mother that "Billy has been told that the Congress appoint'd him their Chaplain . . . but has not heard it yet from them, and begs it may not be mentioned." When informed officially, he accepted, saying he only did so in order "to be consistent in my principles, and in the part taken." Henceforth, he divided his time between his family and the Congress in York, Pennsylvania, until the British evacuated and all could return to Philadelphia. White remained the chaplain of Congress as long it was headquartered in the city.[16]

The tricky position White occupied, even with his reluctant engagement, is well illustrated by the fate of fellow Anglican Duché, who had expressed support for the rebellion beginning with his opening prayer to the First Continental Congress in 1774. The psalm for that day happened to be the thirty-fifth, which invokes God's help in striving with the enemy. John Adams recorded the strong impression Duché made on the newly gathered delegates. Like White, however, Duché was also tugged by loyalty to his ecclesiastical superiors in England. The outbreak of war caused him to doubt the wisdom of the patriot cause. In October 1777 he sent a plea to George Washington, urging him to end the war. This immediately made him unpopular in Philadelphia. At the same time, he strove to explain and defend in England his initial support for the patriot cause. He had left to do so in person by the time White and Congress returned to Philadelphia that December.[17]

All the other local Anglican clergy sailed as well, including Coombe, leaving White alone and the church in an awkward position. His congregation divided over the war; the vestry cooperated with the British when they occupied Philadelphia in 1778. Nonetheless, White was able to steer the church through the conflict. In April 1779, the rectorship of Christ Church was formally declared vacant, and he was elected to fill it. He agreed, but insisted that he would resign if Duché returned.[18]

The war years were not easy on Philadelphians, even wealthy ones like White. His father died in the fall of 1779. White lost a good deal of money during the war as well, because his debtors paid off their loans in depreciated

Continental currency. One such instance occasioned one of the few angry outbursts ever recorded of him. After a pair of borrowers had discharged their obligation in worthless paper, he questioned their honesty as they were leaving by calling out to his servants to be sure there were no silver spoons left out in the entryway while they were passing through.[19]

White also got caught up in the fight over control of the College of Philadelphia. The institution meant a lot to White: his father had been a trustee, he had gone to school there, and he himself had been a trustee since 1774. In 1779, however, the Pennsylvania legislature transferred the rights of the College of Philadelphia to a newly established University of the State of Pennsylvania and appointed new trustees. Apparently, the legislators feared that Anglicans were taking over the institution. White denied any such intent, even though he thought it a good idea for a church to have a school under its jurisdiction. He believed a political division—between the trustees and those, mostly Presbyterian at this point, who controlled the state government—was at work. The 1779 act was in his view a violation of the college's chartered rights.[20]

In view of this crisis, White thought it a good time to establish what he maintained the college had not been, a school where "youth, at least in the early stages of their education, may be instructed in the principles of religion, agreeably to the views entertained by the society in question." Accordingly, in 1785 he led the founding of Episcopal Academy. The school opened on Fourth Street south of Market (just up the street from the Friends School). This venture soon fizzled, however, when the college's original charter was restored in 1788 and the University of Pennsylvania was created anew in 1791.[21]

The war brought economic, social, and political upheaval of many dimensions, and White's status as wealthy Anglican leader did not shield him from all the storms. But his position and elite family connections also protected him from the much greater hardships of fellow Philadelphians who experienced—or lost husbands, fathers, and sons to—the hunger, disease, and wounds of military service, or those who simply suffered the adversity of wartime shortages, confiscations, and inflation. As brother-in-law to Robert Morris, White had entrée into Philadelphia's finest homes and entertainments. War's end found his sister Mary and Robert in what later become known as the President's House, since Morris lent it to Washington for his use after 1790 when Philadelphia became the nation's capital. This was one of the most highly taxed properties in the city. When Washington moved in, Mary White Morris and Robert simply relocated next door to what would come to be known as the Galloway house, an equally fitting space for Mary's famous hospitality.[22]

At war's end, White launched his life's true campaign and claim to fame, the founding of the Episcopal Church of the United States. The Philadelphia churches were ideally suited for this task, not just because they were between northern and southern congregations in a geographic sense, but because they occupied a middle position on issues of church government. White and his Philadelphia predecessors had neither revered bishops as divinely ordained as did their northern counterparts nor distrusted them as much as the southern Anglicans. White nevertheless had his work cut out for him. Among the difficulties were the post-Revolutionary distrust of what had been the British national church, the long-held prejudice of the colonists against bishops, the taint of loyalism on the part of both departed and some remaining church members, the dearth of ministers owing to wartime departures, and the lack of unity among the Anglican churches of the various states. Through extensive correspondence and many meetings, White worked painstakingly to reconcile all of these differences.[23]

The organization of the Episcopal Church of the United States was helped by the facts that the new republic was moving rapidly toward separation of church and state and that church law had never gained a foothold in the colonies in the first place. Yet a common Anglican liturgy and practices had long prevailed, and served to unite the churches going forward. Before the peace was even concluded, White published a pamphlet entitled *The Case of the Episcopal Churches in the United States Considered* (1782), in which he advocated strict separation of the church from any national state or party. While he proposed a modest hierarchy for episcopal government, he stipulated the equality of parish churches and that both clergy and laity should participate in all church councils. White strategically postponed the question of an American bishop until the outcome of peace negotiations. Conventions of the churches in Pennsylvania and Maryland affirmed these principles in 1783, but the question of a bishop remained the greatest hurdle to church unity. High-church northern Anglicans insisted on bishops, while low-church southerners opposed an episcopacy. White was caught in the middle, but finally succeeded in uniting his church through a brilliantly executed series of compromises. He was aided by his old teacher William Smith, now in Maryland, but it is surely because he was so well suited temperamentally that White was chosen the presiding officer at each of the successively larger meetings whereby U.S. Anglicans reconstituted themselves. A new constitution, drafted in 1785, organized the church by state, each with its own bishop, but the annual General Convention that governed the church would include lay as well as clerical delegates. Then, the

General Convention petitioned the English for consecration of three bishops, and Parliament obligingly enacted legislation removing any objection based on the independence of American candidates. In 1787 White was consecrated bishop of Pennsylvania by the archbishop of Canterbury in Lambeth Chapel. His old mentor and friend Jacob Duché was in attendance. He came home and continued to work on the American church.[24]

The New England churches only came into the fold in 1789. They finally abandoned an attempt to form a separate and more hierarchical denomination when two General Conventions of that year, thanks to White's skilled diplomacy, first created a separate House of Bishops and ratified the (more than a little irregular) Scottish ordination of Samuel Seabury as bishop of Connecticut, and then gave the House of Bishops significant power. White was instrumental until the end, playing a major role in revising the Book of Common Prayer, but still compromising, as by agreeing to the introduction of hymns, when he really only approved of the traditional psalms. With Seabury now at his side, White had set his beloved church on a sustainable path, with a governing body, constitution, book of prayer, and the means of ordaining priests and bishops in the United States. He is rightly known as the father of the Episcopal Church.[25]

White returned from England in 1787 to a new home, at 89 (now 309) Walnut Street. The handsome brick Federal-style structure was built that year. His wife, Mary, wrote loving letters while he was abroad, updating him on the progress of the house, but more importantly, on "the subject that I know will be most pleasing to you . . . the children, and to gratify you I shall be very particular." Mary loved the "noisy circle" with which she was surrounded, and was happy to relate the good behavior of Nancy, Betsy, Polly, Tom, and Bill, as well as their progress in school. Sadly, she could only report that "poor Henry [was] much the same as when you saw him." Reflecting the experience of many an early American family, the Whites would only move into their new home with six of their eight children, only three of whom—Elizabeth, Mary, and Thomas—would live to adulthood. "Poor Henry" had died at age three. An earlier son with the same name had lived only a year, and another infant had died at birth. Daughter Ann (Nancy) passed away at six, and most heartbreaking of all, namesake William, at thirteen.[26]

Mary had her hands full at home, then, while William was in England, and of course she fretted about the ocean voyages involved. Life was precarious. But she, like her contemporaries, was necessarily schooled to meet sadness and worry with resolve. "God only knows the pangs this separation has caused me, as well how great my struggles have been to keep myself from sinking under it," she wrote to

William. "I find I must in a double capacity" carry on as a parent, "turn my mind to a subject more agreeable, and indulge myself with thinking" about the homecoming of a husband "perfectly satisfied with every part of my Conduct."[27]

At that homecoming, the household over which Mary presided bustled in other ways. As bishop until his death in 1836, chaplain of the Senate until the federal government moved to Washington in 1801, member of the American Philosophical Society, trustee of the University of Pennsylvania, and wealthy gentleman, William White had the means and occasion to entertain political leaders and other members of the elite. Washington, Adams, Jefferson, and Franklin all dined at the White home. Archaeological evidence confirms that, unlike the simple fare offered by Benezet, sumptuous meals on Canton china graced the bishop's table. But like Benezet, and unlike Washington, the Whites relied on hired servants, not slaves, to cater to their guests.[28]

The Whites' house was grand and substantial. It had eight levels, including a wine cellar, a root cellar, and an ice pit. White had an impressive study, which his grandchildren had memorialized in a painting by John Sartain. His bedroom was unfortunately his alone for forty years after his wife's death, but his bed was equipped with a mosquito net, which, together with his penchant for cigar smoking, might have protected him during Philadelphia's multiple yellow fever epidemics. Perhaps most distinctive was the indoor privy. Of course servants had to empty it, which they did into Dock Creek, which ran behind the house. Because everyone else dumped their garbage there, even White's lovely home was not far removed from the dirt and stink shared with all citizens of eighteenth- and early nineteenth-century towns.[29]

White's family life was typical of others' in bringing him both joy and grief. He was never deprived, emotionally or materially. He was close to his parents and sister Mary, and the family was rich. In addition to his own position and wealth, William's close relationship with his sister bolstered his high position in Philadelphia society. Mary remained nearby, as she married Revolutionary War financier Robert Morris (for a time the wealthiest man in the city, although he died in debt). As the richest woman in Philadelphia for most of her married life, Mary Morris was always given the place of honor in social situations, a sign of the role of wealth in late colonial and early national America. It was her beautiful home that became "the President's House" when Philadelphia was the nation's capital. Visitors to the corner of Sixth and Market Streets today can see a reconstructed skeleton of the building, commemorating the lives of the enslaved people held captive there by George Washington.[30]

Embedded in circles of wealth and power, William's marriage to Mary Harrison was long and happy. He grieved deeply at her death in 1797 and never remarried. It was an especially trying year for White, as it began with the death of his thirteen-year-old son William. White continued to be surrounded by family and domestic comfort, however. After 1813, his widowed daughter Elizabeth and her two daughters came to live with him. She remained until her death in 1831. His son Tom had long lived in the house, and his wife, White's daughter-in-law, was its beloved mistress from 1806 until her death in 1814. Tom, with two daughters and two sons, remained with his father. In 1826, White also took in the five children of his recently deceased daughter Mary. So the household remained a full one. That White did more than support his grandchildren materially is shown in an 1828 letter to his grandson, George, about to go to sea as a naval midshipman. William urged George to avoid profanity and to pray daily, so as to avoid succumbing to the "sea of temptation."[31]

A man of regular habits his whole life, William must have taught his grandchildren much by example. He always dined at two and enjoyed his two glasses of wine (never more) while eating, with a cigar after. He often entertained guests but did not carouse. He enjoyed another cigar, a glass of sherry, and two roasted apples at night before retiring. He only overindulged in green tea, which he liked as strong as possible. He was an early riser and made his own fire until late in life. In the mornings, his children and grandchildren would find him in his study, next to his bedroom, at work at a small table to the right of the fireplace, seated with a book in his lap, or composing a sermon in his clear hand at a stand-up desk.[32]

White's longest professional engagement was as rector of Christ Church and of St. Peter's, for fifty-seven years (1779–1836). Christ Church, on Second Street north of High (Market) Street, was not only the tallest but one of the most beautiful and elaborate buildings in in British North America when its towering spire was completed in 1744. Shortly thereafter, St. Peter's was built at Third and Pine Streets to meet the needs of a growing group of congregants in Society Hill. Not only were these buildings themselves signs of change in the city, but, since the Christ Church steeple was funded and the land for St. Peter's donated by William Penn's descendants (now members of the Church of England), they also symbolized the end of Quaker hegemony in Philadelphia. Still, St. Peter's simple elegance was in part intended to appeal to former Quakers who, like the Penn family, joined the elite Anglican fold. Excepting the steeple, added later, St. Peter's appears today much as it did when White served it, with its classical lines, plain glass windows, and family pew boxes (built to retain warmth from portable foot stoves in winter). An interesting feature is the pulpit and lectern at one end of the church and altar at the other. Because

Figure 6. Christ Church, 20 North American Street, Philadelphia, Pennsylvania (built 1727–1744). *Birch's Views of Philadelphia,* Published by W. Birch, 1800, plate 15. Wikimedia Commons.

services were thus conducted at both ends of the church, the boxes were not later replaced with rows of pews facing in one direction as they were in many other churches.[33]

White was a beloved pastor. He was not, however, a great orator. He spoke too fast, a defect he acknowledged, but seemed unable to fix. A colleague observed that "in his delivery he was dignified, but without much animation, and entirely without action." Yet his parishioners remembered his services fondly. One recollected an exception to his general lack of movement while preaching, in that White used to walk up and down the aisle of the church when talking to children, and put his hands on and blessed the head of any child attending the service for the first time.[34]

White's success in all his endeavors owed most to his gentle demeanor and accommodating manners. This is tricky ground for his modern biographers, since the firsthand accounts are from his associates and reflect the romanticism of the early nineteenth century. In addition, because White did not write about private concerns freely with others beyond his family, it is hard, as one of his biographers observed, "to penetrate to the inner man." But even skeptical historians have concluded, as one did recently, that despite the biases and limitations of the sources, "one is still impressed with the unanimous praise given to White." Just as it was clear from childhood that he would be a minister, his benevolence and amiability were also evident throughout his life. He was a good boy, and became a good man. He was not often opposed or injured, but when he was, he was able to control his temper. Of his religious feelings, a colleague observed, "though calm and moderate, they were deeply seated, sincere, steady, serene." This was his general disposition, too, as his social and intimate relations were likewise characterized by mildness. "Throughout the whole," this friend asserted, "there was complete and beautiful consistency."[35]

That White did not come across as someone plagued with a sense of his sinfulness was attributed to his largely unblemished experience, but he was not sanctimonious or priggish. He saw no problem with participating in public festivities. His modesty and humility also contributed to his popularity, as did the moderation represented by his two glasses of wine with dinner and glass of sherry before bed. His manners put others at ease in his company. He was "tolerant and liberal" in dealing with those of other denominations or in taking controversial positions. As a result, William White had no enemies.[36]

Still, White did not often espouse ecumenical activity. There were exceptions. He joined with Roman Catholic reformer Mathew Carey and others in 1791 to establish the Sunday School Society. In 1808, he helped establish and served as first president of the Philadelphia Bible Society; he insisted that the Bibles the group distributed be given free of any comment or interpretation. In these doings he was certainly ahead of other Episcopalians who resisted interdenominational cooperation. White believed that every church should be treated with respect, but wished to "avoid all intermixture of administrations in what concerns the faith, or the worship, or the discipline of the church." He hoped that one day all could be united with God's help, and occasionally made gestures in that direction, but for the present was concerned that such efforts usually ended in strife. As someone who had expended enormous effort to get his fellow Episcopalians on the same page, he likely feared dilution or loss of what he regarded as essential doctrines.[37]

And yet strong testimony of White's religious toleration is left to us in a memorial by Unitarian James Taylor. As a member of a sect that was despised by many, Taylor prized his pleasant exchanges with the bishop. When Taylor asked White, as a trustee of the University of Pennsylvania, for assistance in getting the Unitarians permission to use a room at the school for worship, he found a sympathetic ear. "You are explicit & frank in avowing your differing from us, but we ought not to take this amiss," he said of Taylor's petition. "If you are nearer the truth than we are, & can set us right, we ought to feel obliged: but if we hold the truth, & we think we do, we shall keep our ground; for the truth must prevail." In sum, "You may do us good, but you cannot do us harm." On this as on other occasions, White was distressed by religious chauvinism. When the newspaper the *Episcopal Recorder* printed an article recommending that "the usual courtesies of life be withheld . . . from those who did not hold certain opinions," White assured the editor that he would cancel his subscription if like sentiments were ever expressed again: "What, must I catechize a gentleman, before I ask him to take a cup of tea?" Taylor also reported that when White heard some friends say that the Unitarians were not Christians, he retorted, "Not so fast, Gentlemen: suppose they were to take it into their heads to say that we are not Christians, & they have the same right to condemn us that we have to condemn them, what could we do or say, having set the example?"[38]

Indeed, White rejected religious absolutism of any kind, maintaining his own irenic faith. During the yellow fever epidemic of 1793, when some Philadelphians divisively and confidently ascribed the affliction to divine judgment, he asked how they could know that, "for by going a very little way into the country, there was perfect safety. But can divine judgements be thus easily escaped?" White believed it the duty of ministers to heal divisions, and for this reason he generally avoided politics. He thought "ecclesiastical politicians" were "the fomenters of strife." He always voted, however, and he presided at three large public meetings later in his career.[39]

The first was to promote the establishment of the American Colonization Society to help free Blacks emigrate to Africa. White's association with the colonization movement marked him as embracing an ecumenical (but over time, controversial) plan for manumission and repatriation of freedpersons to Africa. The society, founded in 1816, enjoyed widespread support from white southerners as well as northerners. Within a few years, African Americans in Philadelphia united against the society's increasingly racist portrayals of the dangers posed by free Blacks to the larger community. But White also had a history of making significant overtures to Black Philadelphians. He was a longtime member and supporter of the Pennsylvania Abolition Society. And while he initially opposed any separate church for Black worshipers (saying that such a move was marked by "pride" rather than necessity), in 1791, after a racist incident in St. George's Methodist Church, White amended his views. With

White's support, African American religious leader Absalom Jones changed his initial affiliation with the Methodist Church to join the Episcopalians in 1794. White conducted Jones's ordination as a deacon in 1795, and then ordained Jones as an Episcopal priest in 1806, despite his lack of Greek and Latin. But White conditioned the recommendation for ordination on excluding any delegates from Jones's church from denominational meetings "at present." St. Thomas's African Church attracted the most elite and largest congregation among newly founded Black churches of Philadelphia. But St. Thomas's suffered after Jones's death in 1816, as it continued to be excluded from denominational conventions until 1854, even after the church was led by a priest who met the language requirement. Still, White supported true independence for St. Thomas's; his was the only white denomination to allow an affiliated Black church genuine self-governance.[40]

The second political cause espoused by White in 1823 was to consider what measures could be adopted to support the Greek War for Independence from the Ottoman Empire, a project of both Christian import and expanding national identities among former colonies. White was the chairman of the Philadelphia Greek Commission. The third great political cause, which White joined in 1830, was to protest President Andrew Jackson's plan to remove southeastern Indians to west of the Mississippi, a brutal forced migration known as the Trail of Tears, which opened up twenty-five million acres to white settlement and slavery and horrified many Americans. White deemed all these causes consistent with his Christian ministry. In the last instance, he defended the apparent departure from his customary habit of steering clear of civil engagements by invoking the seriousness of the measure protested, and its violation of "the most imperious claims of justice . . . our humanity, and . . . the faith of the nation, often pledged to [this] helpless and unoffending people." His appeal was completely characteristic, urging listeners that, to prevent this harm, "every heart should feel, every voice should be raised, and there be put forth every energy, with moderation, but in such a direction as is the most likely to be efficient."[41]

While a consummate churchman and institution builder like Muhlenberg, White was more like Benezet in the scope of his benevolent activity. He was among the most active Philadelphians of his generation in philanthropic and reform causes. And like Benezet, he was much beloved for his generosity. White especially distinguished himself for his charity during the yellow fever outbreak of 1793. While his family, friends, and colleagues urged him to join the many leaving town to avoid contamination, he refused, although he sent his family to the countryside. He remained and ministered to the sick. He would continue to do so during subsequent epidemics, including the outbreak of cholera in 1832—when he was eighty-five years old. White's brave work during the 1793 outbreak might have been what caused George Washington to ask him how he might help during the following winter. Washington, whose presidency was spent in Philadelphia, wondered whether he might assist "fatherless children and widows, made so by the late calamity, who may find it difficult, whilst provisions, wood, and other necessaries are so dear, to support themselves." Washington wanted to remain an anonymous donor and so was happy to remit two hundred and fifty dollars when White offered to ensure that the funds would be placed "in proper hands."[42]

Most like Benezet's was White's work in 1795 to raise money to create a school for Black and Indian children under the sponsorship of Christ Church and St. Peter's. It was built on Race Street, between Fourth and Fifth. Five years later, he helped found the Magdalen Society, at the time a pioneering institution dedicated to helping prostitutes, or, as the society described them, those "unhappy females who have been seduced from the paths of virtue and are desirous of returning to a life of rectitude." He was the first president of the Philadelphia Society for the Alleviation of Miseries of Public Prisons, in the pursuit of which cause he worked with many Quakers who he also worked with in the Pennsylvania Abolition Society. In 1820, he founded the Pennsylvania Institution for the Deaf and Dumb, which still exists as the Pennsylvania School for the Deaf. He served as the school's president until his death.[43]

Until greatly advanced in age, William White led a serene and happy life. Protected as he was from the hardships most of his contemporaries experienced by his robust health and family fortune, his good works and kindly nature secured the additional blessing of everyone's esteem. And yet, even he was not immune to life's slings. A great trial came in old age and at the heart of his greatest achievement, when he was drawn as an septuagenarian into quarrels between high churchmen and evangelicals within the Episcopal Church in the 1820s.[44]

White had long tried to avoid division in the church, even if it meant keeping his own inclinations under wraps. He was by nature conservative, but many Pennsylvania Episcopalians were less interested in traditional liturgy. They wanted to be more like other Protestant denominations. White had worked hard to keep divisions from preventing the establishment of a unified American Episcopal Church in the 1780s, but now aggressive moves by the local low-church group forced White temporarily into the arms of the high churchmen. Those who held to the high-church side relied on the baptismal covenant and apostolic succession for bishops as the distinctive Episcopalian ecclesiology (and chanted psalms). Those who tended to the other side stressed adult renewal of faith like most evangelicals (and sang hymns rather than psalms). White believed deeply that efforts to dismantle the special characteristics of Episcopalian practice would be fatal to the church itself. In one speech he implored, like Hagar in the Bible, "Let me not see the death of the child!" He was so overcome with emotion that "it was some time before he could go on." But with characteristic grace, White managed eventually to recover his habitual equanimity. He did not in the end choose between the revivalists and traditionalists. Instead, he always appointed two assistant clergy, one from each persuasion. He thus avoided division, and was regarded as the beneficent patron of both groups, even long after his death.[45]

What upset White's colleagues the most was that the members of the reforming party were not content just to discuss practice; they also attacked White personally. One low-church clergyman claimed in a public meeting that "we all know that our Bishop is not a praying man." Some went so far as to doubt his personal piety on the grounds that he used silver forks at table. His friends asserted that these and other remarks made in a fight over the election of an assistant bishop in 1826 "savaged Bishop White." The attacks on his honesty and piety hurt him deeply.[46]

The other difficulty that White began to encounter in the 1820s was one that no one escapes: old age. In his mid-seventies, White had the desire and the health to continue doing all that he had been doing, as rector of, now, three churches and both bishop of Pennsylvania and the national church. Yet he no longer had the same energy that allowed him to do this when younger. White tried—he made several trips, for example, to visit churches to the west. But he simply was not as vigorous as in the past. Adding assistants did not improve morale, salaries, or leadership. Slowly, the vestry cut back on his duties.[47]

The 1824 visit of Revolutionary War hero General Lafayette to Philadelphia provided a little relief from the tumult and an opportunity to reminisce about old times. White got together with Lafayette frequently, both because he was one of the few remaining local citizens who knew the Frenchman from the war (another was Charles Willson Peale), and because he was involved in many of the associations and institutions that did the general honor. Ten years later, White conducted a memorial service after Lafayette's death.[48]

Although his age began to register physically, in his eighties White remained of sound mind. He continued to preach every Sunday and wrote occasional pieces for the newspapers. One such article registered his strong objection to the "unChristian" will of Philadelphia businessman and philanthropist Stephen Girard. White was concerned that in endowing and describing the future Girard College, Girard directed that no clergy be admitted to the campus and that no religion be taught in the curriculum. White thought this direction was dangerous to the prospective students and the city. Students' intellectual skills must be nurtured together with religious principles for guidance. He therefore pled with the city council not to accept the trust, signing his article "a Citizen of Philadelphia." White's plea was ignored by those who argued that the students could be taught religion, just not by clergy. White did not think this was Girard's intention, but this was the interpretation that persuaded the U.S. Supreme Court to sustain the will in 1844. Had he survived to see it, White would have been horrified.[49]

White remained in good health until the summer of 1836, his eighty-ninth. That June he fell ill and then recovered, but on the night of July 2, he had a bad fall and quickly declined. He died on July 17. He was mostly cogent until the end, and spoke to all who visited. He was aware of his situation, and serene. Because all knew of him and his final illness—and prayers had been offered in churches around Philadelphia on his behalf—his death did not come as a surprise. There was a tremendous outpouring of respect at his funeral. As a friend and colleague wrote, "On the day of his funeral, there was voluntarily a general suspension of business. . . . The public authorities, the various literary, charitable and religious bodies, the clergy and members of the different Christian churches, united in paying respect to his memory. And the good order and silence of the many thousands who thronged the streets, besides the great number composing the funeral procession, were a striking manifestation of the public sentiments. He was interred in his family vault at Christ Church, on Wednesday the 20th of July." In 1870, his remains were reinterred in the church chancel.[50]

PART II

Declaring Independence: Three Revolutionary Wives

Prologue

In Part II, we turn to three elite white women whose stories reveal the special challenges confronted by women at a time known for its liberating developments for white men. Bereft of the full legal and social power of male citizens, Grace Growden Galloway, Anne Shippen Livingston, and Deborah Norris Logan each confronted the stresses and innovations of a city in profound transition, often with no husband at their side. The women had to figure out what to do on the shifting ground of Revolutionary-era Philadelphia. And their range of choices was limited by societal conventions and laws that would be unfamiliar to us today.

The first of these obstacles was divorce law, which loomed large and foreboding to desperately unhappy people in the Quaker State. Until 1785, one had to appeal to the legislature for a divorce decree. The process was long and costly, and of course, frowned upon by one's neighbors. There were consequently no divorce cases from 1728 to 1766 in Pennsylvania. A handful were attempted during the Revolutionary War but it was not until the state passed a divorce bill in 1785 that women began to account for the majority of divorce petitions. The commonwealth loosened up the procedure by allowing the state Supreme Court to join the legislature in granting divorces. Pennsylvania was the first state to include cruel treatment as an acceptable reason for divorce, in addition to such traditional grounds as adultery, infertility, desertion, and bigamy. But the law remained mute on the subject of the custody of children. That issue was resolved on a case-by-case basis and the father had the advantage under English common law. Anne Shippen Livingston (1763–1841), called "Nancy," was very much affected by the marital constrictions of her time. Despite her love for a young French diplomat, her family pressured her into marrying the unpleasant and demanding Henry Livingston. She fled with her baby from her husband's Hudson Valley abode to her parents' home (the Shippen-Wistar House in Philadelphia), there to wage her battle for freedom and the right to raise her daughter.[1]

Another now happily vanished element of women's lives that significantly affected these three women is the concept of coverture. This tradition, which subsumed a married woman's legal identity under her husband's, meant that she could not control her personal property or earnings or act as a legal person on her own behalf. Her husband "covered" her, hence the term. But when it came to real estate, society's laws raised the lid. Trusteeships could be set up whereby property could be vested in a married woman's male relative. In the late eighteenth century, a simple contract could be made by husband and wife whereby some property remained hers to manage. Otherwise, the husband typically managed the property a woman brought to the marriage, but even he could not sell it. He could rent it out; he could cut wood on the land; but he could not "alienate" it without his wife's permission. We see this limited protection within coverture in the life of Deborah Norris Logan (1761–1839). She happily married George Logan, a man who did not properly manage his family's finances, spending significant cash to finance embarrassing one-man diplomatic missions to Europe. After he died, Deborah had difficulty paying her bills at Stenton, her husband's family mansion. Still, she did have protected assets, which had allowed her to use *her* ground rents and bank shares to relieve him of financial embarrassment when he lived.[2]

The doctrine of coverture has influenced how I tend to call the subjects of this book. As a compromise between then and now, in the chapters that follow, I will often refer to these women by their first names, whereas I often refer to the men in this book by their last names. In the eighteenth and nineteenth centuries, upon marriage these women would have mostly been referred to as, for example, Mrs. Galloway, assuming their husband's surname. To avoid confusion arising from these women's change of surnames at marriage, and references to their husbands, it has seemed best to refer to Grace Growden Galloway as Grace and Joseph Galloway as Galloway.

If coverture dictated that a husband spoke for the family and controlled its members, what happened to wives when Revolution occurred and each side punished the other for disloyalty? This brings us to another past practice called "attainder." During the American Revolution, lists of traitors were published (453 in all in Pennsylvania) and their property seized for the benefit of the state. Would a married woman be expected to follow her husband's political decisions? Could she make a claim to retain the property she had brought to the marriage? Here again, many of the states, including Pennsylvania, made a distinction between the traitorous man's property and that of his wife. As long as the wife separated herself from the husband by remaining in territory under American control, she had a chance to preserve her property for her children. Headlining every list of the "wicked and traitorous enemies of the United

States of America" was Joseph Galloway. His wife, Grace Growden Galloway (1727–1782), elected to stay in Philadelphia while her husband and only child fled to British-occupied New York and later to England. In order to maintain her claim to the substantial acreage that she had brought to the marriage, she spent four lonely years in Philadelphia, living a modest life in somebody else's home. She died there and so did not live to see some of her property restored to her beloved daughter, Betsy, including a mansion house at Trevose that still stands. Thus, some women succeeded in regaining their property, but the logic of coverture held fast for most. It would take a couple of generations before it would begin to be dismantled, thereby securing more of the promise of the Revolution for women. The struggles of their Revolutionary grandmothers are nonetheless part of that long story.[3]

These women's stories drive home an important truth: the American Revolution was incomplete, even for elite white women. To be sure, patriot leaders gathered wide support for the cause with talk of liberty and equality. And that talk has held out promise to women and Blacks ever since. But centuries of struggle have been necessary to turn that promise into reality. For African Americans, the ideal of equality was useful in securing the gradual abolition of slavery in the North. But it only led to new justifications for slavery in the South, where the invention of the cotton gin gave slave labor a new economic lease on life. For women, the promise of equality infused new discussions of marriage and divorce laws. But the chief constraint on white women's lives, the English common law of coverture, remained largely untouched by the Revolution. Taken together, the fate of women and Blacks means that for the majority of Americans, the Revolution entailed great promise but muted immediate impact.

That women like Grace Growden Galloway fought for their homes reflects another truth explored in these three chapters, namely, that women, especially affluent white women, were far more closely linked at this time to private and domestic spaces than to the public spaces we typically associate with men. Of course, men had domestic lives, as we have seen in the homes of Anthony Benezet, Henry Muhlenberg, and William White. But we have also considered these men's lives in the context of the religious, academic, political, and other public buildings where they were equally at home. It is harder to connect elite Philadelphia women with such public spaces. To some extent this was a matter of class and race; women of the middle and lower sort, just as concerned as their wealthier sisters with the lives of their families, could nonetheless more readily be found in shops, streets, markets, taverns, and jails. But white gentlewomen,

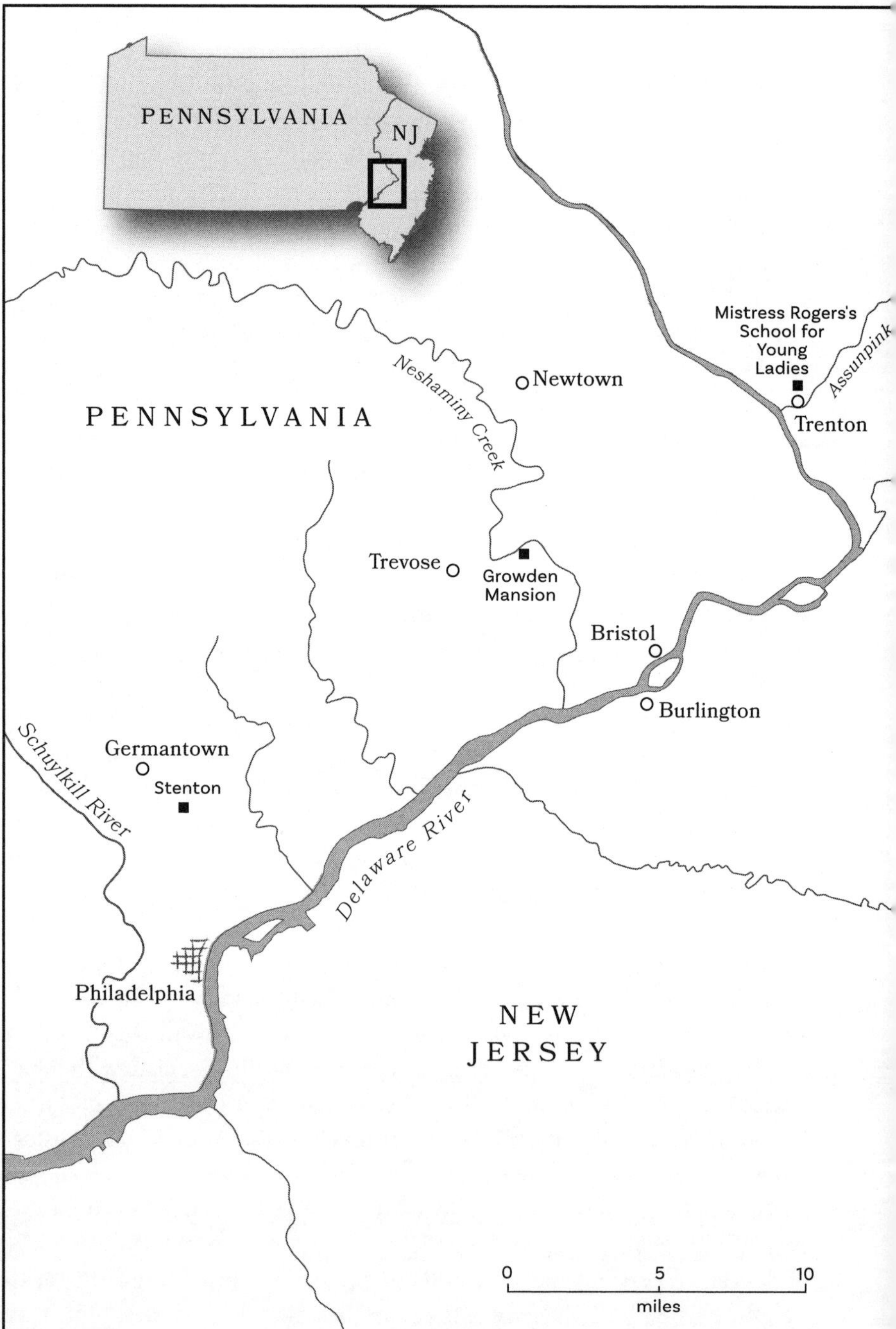

Map 2. People and Their Places: Three Revolutionary Wives.

Philadelphia

1 University of Pennsylvania
2 Galloway Mansion
3 Steadman Mansion
4 President's House
5 Episcopal Academy
6 Livingston House
7 High Street Market
8 Carpenter Mansion
9 Congress Hall
10 Pennsylvania State House
11 American Philosophical Society
12 Library Company of Philadelphia
13 Norris Row
14 Second Bank of the United States
15 Friends School
16 Morris House
17 Shippen-Wistar House
18 Powel House
19 South 2nd Street Market (Newmarket)

A Christ Church
B St. Peter's Church

as representatives and stewards of the family seat, made more fleeting visits to public spaces, mostly churches and shops. While their homes themselves could be centers of sociability where debates about politically relevant topics were common and even orchestrated by elite white women, they had to adhere to a set of social formalities that restricted their speech and behavior. Their family and social lives mostly unfolded in the mansions they lived in and visited. So telling their stories requires us to visit those mansions.[4]

CHAPTER 4

Grace Growden Galloway

> Mrs. Galloway . . . said upon the unpleasant occasion that others complain of being stripped, but for her part she had been *Pealed*.
>
> —Deborah Norris Logan

Grace Growden was unusual among the people of this book in that, while her parents were born in Pennsylvania, she was born in England. Her father, Lawrence Growden, was doing business there as a merchant when she arrived in 1727. The family, including a sister, returned to Philadelphia when Grace was six. Lawrence, then still in his thirties, was already prominent, not only as a merchant but also as a landowner and politician. He would serve in nearly every branch of the colony's government. He became in succession a member of the Pennsylvania Council, the Assembly (where he became Speaker), and chief justice of the Supreme Court. Clearly young Grace occupied a position at the top of Pennsylvania society, but we do not know much about her upbringing. Her later literary activities show that she was well educated. She wrote a religious poem at age fifteen that survives. It is possible that she exchanged pieces of verse with friends, as she received one at nineteen from "Philander," a common pseudonym in elite circles.[1]

Whatever her education, there was little question that the chief career of a woman of her station was to be a wife and mother. In 1747, at twenty, she was visiting her older and married sister, Elizabeth, in England and formed an attachment with a Mr. Milner, son of a customs receiver. But Grace lived at a time when economic status and parental approval still loomed large in marital decisions, especially among people with property. These factors were just beginning to be challenged by the idea that young people should make their own choices and marry for love. Predictably, Lawrence Growden thought Mr. Milner an unsuitable match, and ordered Grace home. She complied. Six years later, in October 1753, she married Joseph Galloway. Her father must have been pleased

Figure 7. Grace Growden Galloway (1727–1782). Oil portrait by Thomas Stokes, 1750. *Pennsylvania Magazine of History and Biography*, 55, no. 1 (1931), facing p. 32.

at this development, as young Galloway (he was just twenty-two) was a lawyer from a successful Maryland family. He had come to Philadelphia to finish his education and was admitted to the bar at eighteen.[2]

This was a "good" match; we do not know whether it was also a love match. Grace was four years older, but she was reasonably attractive. Joseph had converted from Quakerism to Anglicanism in order to marry her—they were wed at Christ Church—but he may have been motivated by social ambition as much as affection. Surely among Grace's attractions was the fact that Lawrence Growden had inherited substantial lands from his father and was one of the

Figure 8. Growden Mansion (Trevose Manor), 5408 Neshaminy Valley Drive, Bensalem, Pennsylvania (built 1683). Wikimedia Commons.

richest and most powerful men in the colony. Whatever their feelings for each other, Joseph and Grace clearly prospered. Joseph became one of the most powerful men in Pennsylvania in his own right, and one of the richest men in the colonies. When Lawrence Growden died, Grace inherited her father's estate at Trevose, which still stands today northeast of the city in Bucks County, along with other properties and an ironworks. So they got even richer.[3]

In 1770, the couple bought the Steadman mansion at Sixth and Market Streets in Philadelphia, right next to the Morris mansion, later called the President's House. It was a splendid brick house of three stories, built just nine years before, with elaborate finishes inside. Every room had beautiful moldings with pediments over every door. It was richly furnished with mahogany tables, chairs, chests, mirrors, and bedsteads. Ample china and glassware allowed for sumptuous entertaining, facilitated by three servants. Outbuildings included a carriage house and stables. The Galloways moved about with five horses and a coach, doubtless using them to get to Trevose, where they also spent time. Joseph's chief partner in Pennsylvania politics, Benjamin Franklin, often visited them there.[4]

The location of their Philadelphia mansion on the corner of High and Sixth Streets was convenient for Joseph, who as Speaker of the Assembly was often at the State House one block south. And yet although it seems hard to imagine today, when the Galloways bought it the house was at the western edge of the city. Most activity still hugged the blocks along the Delaware River, the commercial highway that sustained the growing town. Many of the city's most affluent families still lived along Front Street. The Galloways thus looked west to largely green and undeveloped land. That the area became the headquarters for the Revolution and founding of the new nation over the next thirty years drew many more important people to the neighborhood.[5]

Grace Galloway's comfortable circumstances help to explain her emotions and behavior later in life, when she met with reversals. She clearly thought herself a woman at the pinnacle of society. She was accustomed to a luxurious standard of living and expected to be served by others. In the turmoil of war the disappointment of these expectations would cause her grief. And yet she was not a stranger to unhappiness. Three of her four children died in infancy. This was not unusual but had to have been very hard for the young couple, especially Grace. It helps to explain the attachment of both parents to their surviving daughter, Elisabeth, or Betsy. And, however the parents' marriage had begun, Grace's poems reveal that it soon turned sour. One verse read:

> Dear Lolly attend
> The advice of a friend
> And never get Tyed to a man,
> For once you are yoked, Tis all a mere joke
> Of seeing your freedom again.

Other poems describe how Joseph's behavior had changed since their courtship; by 1759, Grace felt "Neglected Loathed Dispised."[6]

Years later, their daughter tried to explain these verses to her children, claiming "Your Grandfather was a good man, but your G[ran]dmother . . . had great sensibility." Grace might well have been more of a devotee than Joseph to the late eighteenth-century cult of sensibility or empathic feeling, but it is hard to see her as a weak victim. Both she and Joseph were known to have "imperious" personalities. This is not hard to believe since they had both grown up so privileged. Of course, once married, Joseph was supposed to hold the reins of authority and could circumscribe Grace's freedom. But perhaps her education, English experience, and age superiority leveled the typically uneven gender playing field a bit when it came to marital sparring, and maybe even fueled it.[7]

Unlike Grace, Joseph Galloway had the distraction from family sorrows offered by a busy political career. For twenty years between 1756 and 1776, he and Benjamin Franklin fairly controlled Pennsylvania politics. For most of those years, Joseph served in the Assembly; after 1766, like Lawrence Growden before him, he was Speaker of the House. Joseph became a member of Philadelphia's intellectual elite as well, as a member of the American Philosophical Society from 1769 to 1775.[8]

The year 1775, however, was a turning point for Joseph Galloway. Elected as a Pennsylvania delegate to the First Continental Congress, he tried to reconcile the disgruntled colonies to the Crown with his proposed Plan of Union. Not only did he not persuade his fellow delegates to adopt it, the Continental Congress expunged it from its record. Thereafter, Joseph Galloway's path diverged from his former compatriots. And, given the yoke of marriage, his decisions affected Grace's fate as well.[9]

At the end of 1776, with independence declared and the war begun, Joseph threw in his lot with the Crown and fled to the British camp in New Brunswick, New Jersey. From there, he joined the British forces in New York City and became an advisor to General William Howe. He wrote affectionate letters to Grace and Betsy, who had remained in Pennsylvania. At first he advised Grace to leave Trevose and have their livestock driven to forage in the woods, as he heard the "Provincials" were headed that way. Later, after he learned that a fellow Philadelphian, Colonel John Cadwalader, had graciously prevented the destruction of Trevose, Joseph advised Grace to return there with Betsy. The Galloways were separated for nearly a year, but when Howe captured and occupied Philadelphia at the end of 1777, Joseph accompanied him, and was appointed civil commissioner and superintendent of the police and the port. Howe occupied the house next door to the Galloways' home on High (Market) Street. The Galloways' reunion in Philadelphia actually took some maneuvering, because Grace, still at Trevose, found her way to town blocked by the patriot line outside the occupied city. Wartime conditions are reflected in the notes from Joseph to Grace during this period. They were written in minute handwriting on tiny strips of paper, doubtless because they had to be scrolled into a small object (a quill?) and smuggled through the lines. George Washington had no objection to Grace joining her husband; the sticking point was whether she could bring her furniture and other valuables with her. When Grace finally did come to Joseph, friends initially helped them furnish their home.[10]

Joseph proved a good administrator, but his ability would only make things more difficult down the road for his wife. Howe had effectively made him mayor of Philadelphia. He imposed strict curfews and other regulations on the city's residents. Naturally, everything he was able to accomplish for the British came at the expense of the Philadelphia rebels, and later, after the

British departed and Joseph with them, Philadelphia patriots had little sympathy for Grace.[11]

Yet it was probably not just Joseph's stance and actions during the British occupation that would turn Whig men of all ranks against his wife. Philadelphia's loyalist women earned the ill will of patriot leaders in their own right by welcoming the British. Not a few elite women reveled in the attentions of British officers and partook in lavish entertainments such as the Meschianza ball of May 1778. While the poor of both sexes would resent ostentatious feasting, congressmen who had evacuated to rustic York, Pennsylvania, and officers who had suffered with Washington's army at Valley Forge seethed at the news that Philadelphia maids and matrons were consorting with redcoats.[12]

It is not surprising, then, that Grace's future was being shaped during the winter of 1778 by an act of the Pennsylvania legislature (which had fled inland to Lancaster during the occupation), stipulating that loyalists had to face trial or risk forfeiting their estates. Soon Joseph was convicted in absentia of high treason, and all his property was confiscated. When the British withdrew from Philadelphia in June, Joseph followed, along with little Betsy. But Grace stayed behind. Like some other wives, she remained in Philadelphia in the hopes of preventing the seizure of property, especially that which she had brought into the marriage. Alone during these dramatic times, she began to keep a diary. It allows us to watch as she was forced to act on her own.[13]

The day after the British left, the Continental troops entered Philadelphia. The day after that, the artist Charles Willson Peale, now serving on a Revolutionary committee, visited Grace at the Galloway mansion. He broke the news that he had to take possession of her house for the state. Peale returned to follow up the next day, but General Benedict Arnold, in charge of the city (and living next door in the house just vacated by Howe), sent Mrs. Galloway his compliments and "assurance of protection." Two weeks later, however, Arnold told Grace "he cou'd do nothing on the Case." He would not be the last man to let her down.[14]

Grace's diary is an account of her desperate efforts to preserve her inheritance for her daughter. Every day she would list her visitors, and describe who was helpful to her and who was not. Clearly she expected assistance from Joseph's former associates. But while the Galloways' wealth and Joseph's role in Pennsylvania politics had given her a place at the pinnacle of society, the civil war that was the American Revolution disrupted these intertwined networks. Grace, like other elite women, knew and expected help from Philadelphia's leaders. She had no trouble contacting them. But over time, her diary entries became a litany of her claims of ill treatment by and loss of faith in various men. On June 27, for example, Colonel Timothy Matlack visited. "His behavior Convinced me there is no dependence on him," Grace concluded. She then "sent for Israel Pem[berton] but he would not come." She was especially disappointed in Chief Justice Benjamin Chew. "His high friendship is decreasing fast," she lamented. "I have no friends."[15]

Broken political alliances aside, it is not hard to see why the elite males of Philadelphia disappointed her, as she was not a pleasant damsel in distress. She would imperiously and repeatedly summon them and demand help. "I sent three times for [William] Lewise but he did not come," she pouted; "sent for ben Chew he came but . . . Acted far from a friend." That she had to work through men and try to get them to do things for her shows her difficult situation as a woman. But her plight only worsened, as she complained that "all the men keeps from me." She began to think that the men she importuned without success were more solicitous of fellow loyalist Rebecca Shoemaker. Shoemaker's husband had been an associate of Joseph's but was a Quaker, so she attributed this favoritism to the clannishness of Friends, who would "all Assist her but they wou'd let me fall."[16]

In fact, there were men, including Quakers, who reached out to or otherwise assisted Grace. Anthony Benezet visited to commiserate and offer comfort. She got legal help by hiring prominent lawyer William Lewis to look into her dower rights. But Grace looked down on these men, so keenly was she feeling her loss of status. She never referred to Lewis by his full name. Rather, he was "Lawyer Lewis" or just plain "Lewise" in her diary, as if to underscore the professional service relationship between them. He tried to help, but soon, as he gave bad news about her property rights, she grew disappointed with him as well. No wonder he failed to arrive at her beck and call.[17]

Grace was a fighter, but her moods swung with repeated defeats. All along, she assessed the social costs of her reverses. There were class variations in terms of how Philadelphians viewed and responded to her. Among the elite, some Whigs and Tories continued to get along, but the political gap grew as one went down the social scale. Of course, there was a revolution in progress, and one with social implications. Wealth inequality had been growing in Philadelphia for several decades and wartime privation only added to class resentment. The Galloways had undoubtedly attended General Howe's splendid entertainments next door while ordinary Philadelphians, prisoners of war, and even ordinary British soldiers suffered for lack of affordable food. The city was too small for folks not to notice. When the redcoats withdrew, the damage done by occupying troops was clear. The city was a mess; fences and furniture from churches and other public buildings had been burned for fuel, and garbage and waste were everywhere. At the same time that the middling and lower sort were feeling wartime deprivation, they were being radicalized by the conflict. Philadelphia's revolutionary leaders had rallied military and political support with slogans of equality as well as liberty, and had managed to win and preserve a state constitution far more democratic than Philadelphia's conservatives wanted. Those whom the elite had simply regarded as their inferiors before the war were discovering and asserting their social worth.[18]

Grace certainly felt these currents, but she did not comment on them directly. She was too outraged by what she perceived as the abandonment of those on her side. Although female friends continued to visit her, the disruption in her life was such that she felt only loss. She was bitter that no one stepped forward to offer her a place to stay if forced from her home: "No body offers to serve me or take Me in." She had a big dustup with a female friend. She was even angry at the British for not succeeding militarily. But she turned defiant, and was in good spirits when the committee came to inventory the estate.[19]

Joseph attempted to offer support, but wartime communication remained difficult. Again his letters took the form of tiny strips of paper smuggled through the lines. These notes could hardly comfort her in the face of news that swung from good to bad. At the end of July, Peale told her that she could stay in her home if she paid rent. A few days later, she received a letter from the Pennsylvania Council informing her that her estate was confiscated during Joseph's life. Then Peale came to tell her that she had to get out. When she told him that she had rented the house, he informed her that the Spanish ambassador had beaten her to it. Once again she called on friends for advice. She was happy to hear from Joseph, but there was little he could do from a distance.[20]

At the recommendation of her male counselors—for Benjamin Chew, William Lewis, and others did continue to advise her—Grace remained in her home. But she said the anxiety was making her ill. On August 20, Peale literally pulled her out of the house. At Lewis's instruction she had locked the doors, so Peale and his compatriots forced a back door open. Grace listed the men who dispossessed her along with their trades—"Smith, the Hatter & a Col Will, a pewterer in second street"—as if to emphasize their lower status. "I told them nothing but force shou'd get me out of My house," she recalled, but "Smith said they knew how to Manage that & that they wou'd throw my cloaths in the street." Retribution hung in the air as the men talked of ill treatment by the English and Smith "hinted that Mr G had treated people Cruely." Peale got her work bag and a couple of bonnets but the men refused to let her have her bed; this was not just a matter of comfort—luxurious bed hangings were important status objects at the time. When Grace repeated that she would not leave her own house voluntarily, Peale "said it was not the first time he had taken a Lady by the Hand." When he clasped her arm and began to escort her out, she grabbed the door frame and bid those assembled to take note that she was only leaving by force and not of her own accord. "Peel said with a sneer very well Madam & when he led me down the step I said now Mr Peel let go my Arm I want not your Assistance." He was, she proclaimed, "the last Man on earth I wou'd wish to be Obliged to."[21]

In a way, this climax brought some relief, coming as it did after days of worry about what was going to happen. Grace wrote to Joseph, "My Dear the fiery Trial is over I am forsed out of my house." For the time being she was with Joseph's cousins the Craigs. But with relief came anger. She did not pull any punches with Joseph. "I have No one to do any thing for Me," she informed him. "As to friends you have None." Indeed, on the eve of her eviction she had given full vent to her feelings in her diary, revealing the ways in which she blamed Joseph for both her current and past situations: "So much for Mr G['s] great friends he has not one who will go out of the way to serve him I am in hopes they will let me have my estate but that will be on my own Account No favour shown to JG or his Child: Nor has he a friend that will say one word in his favour I am tired with sending after a set of men that allways keeps from me when I most need them am vex'd." Along with expressing her anger, her claims show that she knew she had depended on her husband. They also suggest that she was learning not to. She was a proud and intelligent woman who had been constrained in the past to accept Joseph's superior legal and political status. She had not always been thrilled with that situation, but her social privileges and material luxuries made some compensation. Now robbed of those things, she was furious at Joseph for failing her. She vowed to show a "cheerful face," in spite of "the mortifications" she had met with. But she was afraid of a bad outcome. "We are ruined and I expect nothing but poverty and contempt," she confessed. "This I can bear but what is to be come of My Dear Child can I live to see her brought down?"[22]

Grace told Joseph that she would wait for his trial to see the outcome of their property situation. If all was lost she would come to New York. In letters back and forth in August and September, Grace and Joseph agreed that he should go to England, but they were at a loss as to what Betsy should do. Grace did not like the idea of a winter voyage and feared she would never see her daughter again if she accompanied her father abroad, but they did not know who could take care of her in New York while Grace struggled to recover their property in Philadelphia. Above all, she wanted to fight for her daughter's future.[23]

Joseph's letters were affectionate and supportive, but, not being able to find an appropriate situation for twenty-year-old Betsy in New York, he thought that she should go with him. Betsy herself said that if she could come to Grace or Grace to New York, "nothing on earth would induce me to go" to England. But she saw no alternative, as she did not think she could get through the lines to Philadelphia and did not want to stay in in Manhattan by herself. She hoped the separation would not be long. Grace grew increasingly despondent but struggled on. Despite her frustrations at her situation, her periodic outbursts, and the couple's prior disagreements, her letters to Joseph were generally affectionate. She wanted him out of the reach of his enemies. But she also asked him to sign over the estate to her when he left.[24]

Joseph and Betsy sailed to England in October 1778. Joseph might have been feeling guilty, for on the eve of their departure he wrote Grace that "I wish I could be with you in your profound distress and difficulties To comfort support and relieve or at least mitigate your Anxiety." He now entreated her to give up the fight for her estate, claiming that although a British victory in the war might regain it for her, "you never will obtain it fro[m] our enemies." Grace remained behind, thinking that if she left she would forfeit any claim to her property.[25]

Her feelings continued to vacillate. She felt neglected by those she thought friends and potential allies, but separate visits from Joyce and Anthony Benezet made her feel better. She was worried about money and was sad at walking home in the rain one day, only to see her old carriage go by, now confiscated and driven by others. Revealing her persisting sense of social superiority, she thought about what Betsy would say "to see her Mamma walking 5 squares in the rain at night like a common Woman." Because Philadelphia's streets were so dirty, riding rather than walking was a way rich women in particular displayed their wealth. But Grace soon grew inured to the sight of other people in her former possessions. That June, when she was out for a ride with a friend and they had to give way in the road to her carriage, driven by a Spanish don, she claimed that she "did not mind it." She was glad, moreover, about an alteration in her living situation. She moved from the Craigs' to the home of a friend, fifty-five-year-old spinster Deborah Morris, and this brought some comfort, especially as she now had a suitable space to receive her never-ending stream of visitors. "My good friend Morris was so kind as to let me have her front parlour and the chamber over it, she told Betsy. "The chamber is large and as good a room as I ever wish to have," while the parlor "is exceeding elegant." Betsy was glad because she thought Morris's house, on Front Street between Chestnut and Walnut, was in a better neighborhood than the Craigs'.[26]

At this point Grace's feelings about Joseph were mixed at best. News of the execution of two traitors brought relief that he had safely escaped such a fate, yet she worried over a report that his ship had been taken. The concern may have been more for her daughter, however, because Grace seemed more content without her husband. She may have been trying to bolster her own spirits in writing in her diary that she was happy, but then she went on to reveal what the separation was making her realize about her marriage: "as to Myself I am happy & the Liberty of doing as I please Makes even poverty more agreeable than any time I ever spent since I married but My child is dearer to me than all Nature & if she is not happy or any thing shou'd happen to her I am lost. . . . Indeed I am concern'd for her father but his Unkind treatment makes me easey Nay happy not to be with him & if he is safe I want not to be kept so like a slave as he allways Made Me in preventing every wish of my heart." In addition to past restrictions, she blamed Joseph for all the affronts she received in Philadelphia: "Every insolence I meet with from some of these low fellows makes me reflect on the little care he has taken to keep me from being insulted." When she tried to collect some rents, she learned that Joseph had received them in advance. "I find he conceals all he can from Me," she fumed. "Was it Not for My child I wou'd Never care anything about him for his base conduct to Me when present & his takeing no care of me in his absence has Made Me indiferant to him." By December Grace professed to be happy but for the separation from her daughter. She claimed to depend no more on men.[27]

She did have to attend to her own situation. She tried again to collect rent from various tenants and to have wood delivered from her properties. The New Year came and went, leaving her feeling ill and sad. She was sick over the next few months and kept to her room, although she continued to receive visitors. She worried over the lack of news from Joseph and Betsy and did not keep her diary during this interval. This suggests that the main purpose of the diary, conscious or not, was to record and vent about her wartime property dilemma. Finally, in March, she was relieved to hear that her husband and daughter had arrived safe in London. She also showed some signs of change. For the first time since she began to keep the diary, she mentioned having written some "verses," although she was not pleased with them. She also benefited greatly from a call from some Quaker women. At first she "was not well pleased with the visit." But she came to think "that as those good people came in great love to see Me I ought Not only attend to what they had to say but bring My Mind into a right frame to attend their Message." After the Friends urged her to pray to God for help to "wean Me from the things of the world," Grace felt "a New heart & soften'd . . . more than I ever was before." The encounter provided her "a pleasure beyond expression."[28]

Grace was always thinking about Betsy and anxious to receive letters from her or Joseph, but her state of mind was more affected on a daily basis by her political and social situation. She was challenged by the fallout of both her husband's loyalism and the revolutionary upheaval in class relations. Occasionally, she felt on guard about the family's loyalism when with her patriot friends. She may have been defensive because, although she did not express much interest in politics (aside from one loyalist poem), she never disavowed Joseph's position. She differed in this from some other women who were interested in politics and expressed their own loyalties. She clearly did not think of herself as a political being in her own right. And yet she refused to express allegiance to the American government, which, under the circumstances, was a clear political choice. She worried about rumors of the treatment of Tories. She occasionally erupted against the "Wiggs." Yet just as often she railed against the British, and confessed to herself that she abused the British Army because she could not publicly criticize her husband, the real target of her anger. Grace was simply more attuned to her social than to her political situation. It remained the case that while some of her affluent Quaker friends were loyalist or neutral, most were Whig, and this did not usually cause a problem between them. Grace and other privileged women had more to lose if the social elite crumbled under the weight of political division.[29]

Despite her complaints, then, Grace was not truly alone. She entertained visitors almost every day, a sign that other elite women and men shared her desire to pursue life as usual. But she frequently grumbled that although people came to take tea with her, they never asked her to their homes. She felt snubbed and complained openly about it. Her friends' reluctance might not have been solely political, for Grace could be sharp-tongued. She often said mean things about the persons she visited. She was also very demanding. When ill, she got angry at doctors she did not think were paying her sufficient attention. She hated that almost no one would lend her a carriage. She thought carriage rides were an important form of exercise and the only way for her to go visiting. Her erstwhile friends "knew My life almost depended on it," and she resented their failure to provide the mode of conveyance she deserved.[30]

The truth is that Grace Growden Galloway was a snob. She refused to visit or was cool to people she thought beneath her. She ridiculed those whom she considered "mock gentry" and was aghast at the social revolution the war was bringing on: "people are set Up whose Names were till Now Unheard of & some of the best fortunes lost & the owners forgot." The repeated instances of rude and impertinent behavior that she noted on the part of the many persons she deemed below her almost made her physically ill. She defiantly vowed not to put up with people who failed to "treat me as my Station in life requires." On one occasion, when she got "command" of her "spirits" she "Laughed at the whole wig party." Then she let loose with a bold statement of her current mood: "I told them I was the happiest woman in town for I had been strip[p]ed & Turn'd out of Doors yet I was still the same & must be Joseph Galloways Wife & Lawrence Growden's daughter & that it was not in their power to humble Me." Here she showed the traditional roots of her sense of identity as a wife and daughter who occupied her high social position by virtue of these male relations. And yet, as she continued, she revealed that she was coming into her own as a result of her experience of independence and was ready to assert social status by virtue of her own education and deportment, even if shorn of male-controlled property. "I shou'd be Grace Growden Galloway to the last & as I had now suffer'd all that they can inflict Upon Me I shou'd now act as on a rock," she declared. "I wou'd Never let these people pull Me down." She claimed that she could be happy with ordinary dress and furnishings, that "all that vext Me was that I shou'd be so far humbled as to be ranked as a fellow creature with such brutes." The speech must have been cathartic. Grace acknowledged that she had run on but was not sorry at anything she said, although her interlocutor "seem'd sometimes to wince."[31]

The only people who seemed to penetrate her sense of entitlement were the various Quaker friends and ministers who visited to comfort her. Of her neighbor Sally Zane she wrote, "there is something so honest & blunt in that plain woman that I prefer her company to most others," for "She stills my passions & Calms my soul." Although Quaker pacifism caused those who were not avowed patriots to be suspected of loyalism, the professed neutrality of many actually allowed them to reach out socially to both sides. And yet, while Grace took a great deal of comfort from such people as Zane and the Benezets, their visits did not change her feelings of betrayal by her wealthier peers. Her sense of social status prevented her from perceiving these true Friends as true friends.[32]

Another possible source of comfort is absent from Grace Galloway's diary or letters of this period. This was the sharing of reading and writing among a group of literary confidants. Unlike other elite women who managed to keep up this class-defining activity, the tumult of war brought a diminution of Grace's literary correspondence, which saddened her. Her mentions of composition were rare in these years, as when she said she was writing in May 1779 but was not pleased with her efforts. Even mentions of reading, as when she noted she had taken up *Arabian Nights* that June, are infrequent. Her legal struggles and the trials she perceived in the changing social scene distracted her from more creative pursuits.[33]

For Grace continued to worry about the fate of the family's properties. In March 1779, she learned that title to her Philadelphia home had been given to the trustees of Joseph Reed, the president of Pennsylvania's Supreme Executive Council. The Galloway house was now a sort of governor's mansion. An even greater blow was the news that came the following month, with updates over the summer, that her stepmother, "Mrs. Growden," was making a claim on the estate Grace had inherited from her father. Upset, Grace blamed Joseph for leaving her affairs in confusion. In June the culminating blow was to see "in Bradford's paper" that her estate was advertised for sale during Joseph's life. She was upset that none of Joseph's old friends would help her, but composed an articulate statement of her options and position regardless. That Trevose was ransacked and partially burned by the Continental Army must have seemed like par for the course of her life, given the misfortunes that plagued her at that moment. By July, she was tempted to give up the fight for her estate.[34]

Financial concerns exacerbated other worries. Although Grace had sufficient wealth never to feel the real wartime privations of many fellow Philadelphians, she did have trouble changing money and paying debts. Bad war news did not help. She did not generally chronicle the course of the conflict, but she noted that the English were defeated in South Carolina in June and expressed her frustration with British ineffectiveness overall in July. All she could do was to entertain the occasional visit from Philadelphia loyalists to commiserate over disappointing news. To top things off, she quarreled with her servant and then fought with her hostess, Debby Morris, whom she thought meddled too much in her affairs and betrayed too many confidences. Grace did not know whether to go to London or stay; she feared her health would not "bear a Voiage." By August she was so depressed about her prospects that even long-awaited letters from Joseph and Betsy did not raise her spirits. Hearing disparaging comments about her husband only made her feel worse. "It seems as if the world was in league against us," she lamented. "Oh how are we fallen."[35]

As summer 1779 turned to fall, Grace still felt low, but she was, fundamentally, a fighter. Writing her dark thoughts in her journal afforded some relief. Although she agonized over what to do, she did not give up. She laid out for herself the pros and cons of various courses of action and conferred repeatedly with "Lawyer Lewis," who ended up advising her to buy back her properties as they came up for sale. She strove, in the meantime, to prevent the purchaser of her estate from cutting down the woods. But difficulties continued, and she claimed to be losing hope, along with other Philadelphia loyalists. Some men were trying to help her but she did not fully trust them. She had joined with some other loyalists in legal defense but worried that her issues were neglected and wondered whether she should continue to waste money on lawyers.[36]

Just being in Philadelphia continually reminded Grace of her plight. One evening when she walked out to see fireworks in celebration of the French king's birthday, she was sad to see that they were set off in front of her "own house." and she "cou'd Not stand long to think that" it was now occupied by Reed in "JG['s] place." Sadness turned to anger when she discovered that a deed to her estate was in Joseph's name only and that he had sold some of the property she had inherited. Betrayal, she said, "I can bear from my enimies but to be deceived by a husband is two much." Sitting with Deborah Morris one evening, "feeling so low I coul'd not help sheding tears," she blurted out, "My ever Dearest Child what can I do for thee?" With regard to her husband, she added, "I have some affection for him yet I dispise & Abhor his vanity & baseness & am Now truly set against him yet I do not tell anyone." In the privacy of her diary, Grace confided, "I will never live with him more."[37]

As angry as she was with Joseph, Grace still wavered over whether she should go to England or stay in the hopes of regaining Trevose. She had not heard any news for some time and was concerned about Betsy. She was relieved when letters sent in March and April finally arrived in September, but the relief did not last long. Within a few days she was sick in bed, "Not well & . . . Not happy." The length of time it took for letters to cross had to have been an especial trial in her situation. Grace wrote to Joseph at the end of January 1780 that she had not heard from him since his letter of May. She did not know who to blame, but, whoever they were, "the base spirits, who with Unfeeling Cruelty can take from an Unfortunate Woman the only satisfaction which in her present situation she can receive namely the hearing from a Husband & an only child, must be too base & too low even to be ranked among the human species." She reported that her health had not been good and then got down to business, asking why he did not put it in her power to dispose of the property she had brought into the marriage of her estate. She described the division of her property with the hated Mrs. Growden, her various lawsuits, and which people had been good to her.[38]

In early March, ten months since the date of Betsy's last letter, Grace anxiously wrote to her daughter. She again detailed the division of her estate in case her earlier letters had miscarried. Then, in a postscript, she added that she had just received Joseph's and Betsy's letter dated August 21. It revealed that her husband was considering coming to Philadelphia, which Grace thought unsafe, and that her daughter was melancholic, which Grace found upsetting. Fortunately, in April, she received a loving letter from Betsy—dated February—that gave her much pleasure. Betsy had also sent her various items from England. Yet in the interval, Grace could only brood over her worry.[39]

Her letters to Betsy and Joseph at this stage contain curious contradictions. It was as if she wanted to assure them she was all right and at the same time convince them that she was utterly miserable. She said she was "in a state of nonexistence," but would not complain. She had remained in her room for months, but did not have enough time to write. She had lost everything and had no maintenance, but was bearing up and not in want. She had lost more than any other woman in Pennsylvania and needed a carriage badly for her health, but if she had one, she would never lend it to any but the poor and infirm. She was grateful for Deborah Morris's kindness, but she was in such a reduced condition that she did not want Joseph to bring her to England. In short, all was gloomy, but her spirits were good![40]

We must consider what these letters were. There was nothing reliable about this means of communication. Each party had to wait for a means of transmittal—word of someone traveling or a thoughtful sea captain inquiring as to whether there was something to take. Even then there was no guarantee of a letter's safe arrival. Clearly Grace suspected that her correspondence was being waylaid on purpose by Joseph's enemies. And then what if someone stopped by to say they were about to take passage for England and asked if she had any letters to send? Under time pressure, what should one say? If she was down or ill, would it alarm the recipient? How frustrating it must have been. "I am not satisfied with just letting you know the state of my health," Grace wrote to Betsy at one point. "My Soul longs for a more intellectual correspondence with My Only child."[41]

From the fall of 1780 to the fall of 1781, Grace's physical health began to decline along with her spirits. She ceased to keep a diary. She wrote to Betsy in October that it was hard to correspond when she had no freedom and few opportunities to send letters, that her health was getting worse and a voyage to England was out of the question, and that, because she had not received the things Betsy said she had sent, her daughter should not send any more. Grace was very down. She was still petitioning the Assembly and working on recovering her property but had no hopes; she did not think she would ever see Betsy again. She thought the war was coming to a crisis. The following month, Debby Morris wrote to Betsy for Grace, who was too sick to pick up a pen, although she seemed to be recovering. By December, however, Grace was writing her will. She left some specific items to Morris and to her nurse, and the rest of her property to a group of Philadelphia Quaker men, presumably in trust for her daughter. On February 6, 1782, Grace Growden Galloway gave up her fight.[42]

Several months later, Debby Morris wrote a long letter of condolence to Betsy and Joseph, not wanting to leave them in ignorance about how Grace had died. Debby listed the friends who had supported Grace and claimed that she "often acknowledged herself as happy as she could Expect to be stripped as she was & separated from you." She said she felt sorry for Grace and tried to accommodate her, adding that anything "Nurse could not doo, My Girls Did." Except for "little failures in Memory," Grace was "Sensible to the end." She had not wanted for money or anything else, but Joseph and Betsy were always on her mind. "I see myself Daily Wasting, all is over, I must go," she supposedly said as death approached. "I must Resign my D[ea]r Husband & Child, unto thy Allmighty Protection[;] Oh—my Good God, do for them as thou hast done for me." Debby thought Grace seemed easier after this profession. "About an hour before her Departure," Grace said of Joseph, "I loved him . . . But he Doant know how Ill I am or he would be with me."[43]

When death came, Grace met it "in a sweet easy mannor, much resign'd and Composed." She was in a "sweet sleep" as Debby "sat close by her" to "just Perceive her last breath." Those few friends whom Grace had wished to attend her last moments were also there, so that a "sweet . . . Sollemnity attended the awfull Scean." Debby was sure she died in peace. Grace was then "Decently Interrd as she Desired in our own Plain way, by her Dear little Babes as she used to call them"—the children who died in infancy—and "attended by a very large number of Fr[ien]ds & others." As Debby concluded, "all was done that could be don."[44]

From England, Joseph Galloway continued to fight to regain his property and for his right to return to Pennsylvania, but he did not succeed. He received a pension from the British after 1783. For her part, Betsy showed an intelligence and assertiveness that would have made Grace proud in corresponding with her Pennsylvania trustees over the next few years. She directed them to sell lands inherited from her grandmother to buy her father's confiscated share in family estates in order to preserve them. In 1790, Philadelphia financier Robert Morris and his wife, William White's sister, Mary, moved into the former Galloway dwelling at Sixth and Market Streets, allowing their own mansion next door to become the President's House. Joseph and Betsy continued to correspond with Philadelphia lawyers, to see if Betsy could inherit Grace's property. After Joseph died in England in 1803, the trustees got to work. Finally, the Pennsylvania Supreme Court ruled that the confiscation of Joseph's property for treason should not have affected the real estate of his wife. On his death, the husband's rights to that property lapsed, and so it belonged to Mrs. Galloway's heirs. Betsy Galloway thereupon inherited her mother's property. Grace's battle had not been for naught.[45]

Grace Growden Galloway was born to many advantages, but she shared with all women the reality that her gender brought lifelong constraints. No matter how intelligent and feisty, she faced real and psychological barriers, especially in terms of her unequal legal position as a married woman. She did not articulate any kind of gender protest although she did suggest in her private writings that marriage was a bad deal for women. And indeed, if a man chose to exercise his power, it could be. This is what Abigail Adams pointed out to John in her famous "Remember the Ladies" letter. If husbands were disposed to be tyrants, they could be, and Abigail wished men in power would address this as they made laws for the new nation. Since they didn't, Grace opted to channel her energies and intelligence into her social world and to preserving her estate for her daughter. Other women made other choices, but all shared the same challenge.

CHAPTER 5

Anne Shippen Livingston

Return to us if you don't find your husband alter'd for the better.
—Alice Lee Shippen

The ambitious young doctor and wife welcomed their firstborn, a daughter, at their Philadelphia home on the corner of Fourth and Prune (Locust) Streets, the place now known as the Shippen-Wistar House. It was February 1763, and the baby's future looked bright, descended as she was from two great colonial families, the Shippens of Pennsylvania and the Lees of Virginia. And yet, as she was a girl (whom everyone called Nancy), one could argue that her heritage was also a burden, since, like Grace Growden's, her parents wanted her to grow up to marry someone of high social status. Young people were beginning to seize more control over this decision in the revolutionary years, declaring independence from patriarchal authority and following new ideas about marrying a companion for love. But Nancy was subject to strong paternal pressure anyway. And in the end, she did not disappoint her parents. She married her father's choice, Henry Beekman Livingston, of a leading New York family. But in so doing, she consigned herself to a life of disappointment. The failure of her marriage stands in stark contrast to her fairy-tale courtship with the dashing French diplomat Louis Otto, one of the American Revolution's great romances. The frustrating thing to the modern reader is that she denied herself this love when she obeyed her parents' wishes. In that decision, and the fate of her marriage, lies another lesson about marriage in a time of revolution.[1]

Nancy was born just a year after her parents had met and married in London. Her father, William Shippen Jr., was completing his medical training there, and her mother, Alice Lee, had moved there after the deaths of her parents. Having returned with William to Philadelphia, Alice named her daughter after her best friend in London, Ann Home. Two years later, another baby arrived,

Figure 9. Shippen-Wistar House, 238 South Fourth Street, Philadelphia, Pennsylvania (built ca. 1750). Wikimedia Commons.

Nancy's brother Thomas. They may have been close as children since they were very close in youth. Their tie likely strengthened in the face of the deaths of six other babies that followed; like many other colonial brothers and sisters, they clung together as the sole survivors in their nuclear families. We can only imagine the impact of those deaths on their mother—Grace Galloway certainly would have had some idea.[2]

As children in Philadelphia in the late 1760s and early 1770s, Nancy and Tommy were eyewitnesses to the early years of the Revolutionary crisis. They were well positioned since their Virginia uncles Richard, Arthur, and Thomas Lee soon made the Shippen home their Philadelphia headquarters while serving in the Continental Congresses and during the war. Uncle Richard made his resolution for independence in the State House while staying with the Shippens.[3]

The larger Shippen family was certainly caught up in the war, though not always to unanimous praise. Alice joined other women in the Ladies Association to collect money to make shirts for the soldiers, a successful but unconventional campaign deemed ridiculous by loyalist women like Grace Galloway. William served the Continental Army as a physician and medical director-general, but not without even stronger criticism. He was accused of and tried for mishandling funds and supplies. He was acquitted, but suspicions remained. And Nancy's cousin Peggy famously married patriot-turned-traitor Benedict Arnold. So the family was deeply invested in, and somewhat divided over, the Revolution.[4]

Yet Nancy seemed untouched by politics, in part owing to her gender and age, but also because personal inclination and her education steered her interests elsewhere. By 1777, the fourteen-year-old was ensconced at Mistress Rogers's School for Young Ladies across the river at Trenton, New Jersey. In a loving New Year's letter to her mother she bemoaned the separation from family members who had left Philadelphia and headed for the South. (Tommy was at school in Maryland; William with the army as chief physician.) Nancy was hardly separated from the war herself, since General Washington had just turned the tide the week before with his surprise attack on the Hessians encamped at Trenton. Somehow Mistress Rogers managed to shelter her charges from the battle just outside their door.[5]

The family considered it all-important that, despite the war, Nancy attended to her education as a young lady. Even Tommy asserted that he wished "to see you shine." Alice assured her that "much depends on your being improved"; she, too, wanted Nancy to "shine" in the future. Alice stressed needlework and "the graces," and asked Nancy to "tell me how you have improved in holding your head & shoulders, in making a curtsy, in going out or coming into a room, . . . walking and setting," behaviors that "contribute so much to a good appearance that they are of great consequence." This was not the only opinion among elite Philadelphia women at the time; some believed that their daughters' intellectual training was most important, even during wartime. Judging from her later activities, Nancy herself preferred her work in music, English literature, and French to embroidery and deportment. She would eventually suggest that her formal education had been deficient.[6]

Alice herself did not just prize exterior shine in Nancy. She believed the most important goal for a young lady was to attain certain character traits, among them humility, patience, and industry. Like other genteel parents, Alice was not above promising presents for good behavior: "I have sent for some very pretty things which I can either bestow upon you or dispose of in another way if you should not answer my expectations." As if to prepare Nancy for future crises, Alice urged her to acquire the virtues of duty and obedience in particular. "Do remember my dear," Alice wrote: "the sweet peace that flows from the consideration of doing our duty to all with whom we are connected."[7]

At first, Nancy appeared to have mastered the other ornaments better than duty and obedience. Back from school in 1779, the sixteen-year-old was a handful. "Sweet peace" was certainly elusive as she and Alice "had high words," possibly over Nancy's dress. William intervened, reminding his daughter of the family's chief social goal and his view of the means to achieve it. "Your dear Mamma knows better than you & . . . it is your duty to obey her cheerfully always, although it may sometimes seem hard," he insisted. "She loves you and wishes to make you one of the finest women in Philadelphia." That Nancy had already attained this goal is suggested by another line of Dr. Shippen's letter, a teasing—and manipulative—reference to the fact that Colonel Harry Livingston had already begun his suit: "Yesterday I dined at General Greenes & at 3 oClock who should come in, guess." Livingston "looks mighty well & I never will consent unless you try to be very clever too & deserve him," Shippen continued. "I wont tell what he said neither till your Mama writes me you are a good Girl."[8]

No matter that he was over ten years older than Nancy. No matter that his own family bemoaned his selfish and immoral behavior. Henry Beekman Livingston was an officer and had earned praise for his conduct in the war. Far more important in securing William Shippen's favor, however, were his family name and assets. As if to prepare bait, Alice Shippen reminded Nancy that summer that "you must put on your best looks . . . be sure you hold yr head up & don't carry the children about yr shape wont bear it." But September 1779 brought the arrival in Philadelphia of something bound to distract Nancy from the task of pleasing Livingston, namely, the utterly charming French legation.[9]

This genteel and sociable group installed itself just a few blocks away from the Shippen house in the Carpenter Mansion at Sixth and Chestnut Streets. Having renovated the house and gardens, the men promptly set about ingratiating themselves by visiting and entertaining elite Philadelphiams. Their manners and titles must have dazzled the young woman. The new French minister was the Chevalier de Luzerne; he was accompanied by the first secretary, the Marquis Barbé-Marbois. Closer to Nancy in age was Luzerne's personal secretary, Louis-Guillaume Otto. Recently a student of law in Strasbourg, Otto resembled Nancy in romantic temperament, love of the arts, and good looks. The two quickly became friends. Within weeks he was visiting and composing music for her and the two were trading poems. They were also exchanging affectionate notes.[10]

Louis was clearly smitten. One poem declared:

She is the joy of my Eyes, she is the pride of the place,
Within my fond heart shall her dear Image reign. . . .
Reason and Pashion both bow at her Shrine
And she captivates Hearts, or at least has wone mine.

Nancy, as appropriate to her sex, was more coy, but managed to make her reciprocal appreciation clear. They contrived to "meet" regularly when he began to take a daily walk by her house. One evening, he described for her the scene of the family at tea as seen through the parlor window. He pictured himself, "standing before the window" wishing that he was the object of the absence of mind he observed in her, who, appeared, however, "*as lovely as an Angel.*"[11]

Otto was obviously thinking ahead when he declared that "you are a lady that would make a great noise in France." He added, "I studied your conduct since I have the pleasure of knowing you, nothing escaped my watchfull eye." She evidently passed the test, since he was compelled to tell her that "I adore you more than ever." Despite the increasing passion of his notes, the two had to observe the proprieties of the day. They managed to be close to one another when they frequently played the harpsichord together. Louis was delighted to proclaim that "very often I think I understand you when you look at me or when you press my hand in yours."[12]

When she looked back in old age, this year must have seemed a dream to Nancy. It was filled with visits, parties, dinners, and dancing, much in concert with the cosmopolitan French officers who arrived in Philadelphia in the fall of 1780 with the Comte de Rochambeau's army. For they, like the French diplomats, were as charmed by Miss Shippen as she was with them. Major General the Chevalier de Chastellux himself immediately took note, proclaiming of the ladies who "decorated" the scene at the first party he went to that "among them Miss Shippen, daughter of Dr. Shippen . . . claimed particular distinction." In another sign of consensus on her beauty, at her cousin Anne Willing Bingham's wedding, Nancy was partnered with the high-ranking Vicomte de Noailles. Chastellux soon penned a picture of Nancy and Otto after attending a tea party at the Shippens: "Miss Shippen sung with timidity, but with a pretty voice. Mr. Ottaw, Secretary to M. de la Luzerne, sent for his harp, he accompanied Miss Shippen, and played several pieces."[13]

Nancy was a beautiful girl in a society where a woman's fate depended on her marriage. The situation was thus as fraught with danger as it was productive of pleasure. This was especially the case at this time when, among those who prized respectability, a young woman was increasingly responsible for preserving her own chastity before marriage. Nancy was surely aware of this, since it was the major theme of the fashionable new novels imported from Britain. Her behavior and writing display all the signs of thorough steeping in the language of sensibility promoted in those books, often tales warning young women of the perils of seduction. Unfortunately, she was as headstrong as she was romantic, and risked displaying the behavior most warned against, that of the flirt, or coquette. Fortunately, young as he was, Otto was not as impetuous as she. And his actions show that his delicacy of manner was not superficial; it emanated from his character.[14]

Otto refused to let Nancy do anything that would harm her reputation. Indeed, he seemed to have more care for Nancy than did her own parents. Although he and Henry Livingston were obviously both courting their daughter, William and Alice seemed not to object. Dr. Shippen wrote Tommy of a Thursday evening: "Otto & Nancy playing Harpsichord together. . . . Mr Otto visits Tuesday & Saturday—Col. Harry Livingston often." A couple of months later, he mentioned "your sister who has Otto & Livingston contending for her smiles." But Otto urged caution. When Nancy confided that she feared she had encouraged Livingston out of vanity, Otto wrote her a fanciful letter posing as an old lady confidante and warned her that any man so trifled with would want revenge. Having entertained Livingston thus far, she could not now disillusion him or show preference for another without inciting his anger. Her only recourse, according to "Milady Old-fashion" (Otto), was to appear so disagreeable and flighty as to lessen his ardor.[15]

Perhaps Otto's concern for her reputation was motivated by the fact that he was in love in earnest. He claimed to have trouble expressing himself to her, but the occasional awkwardness of his adopted English only made his passionate love letters the more affecting: "I had never so great a desire to please and never I felt so much my inferiority." Charmingly, he begged her to write more in return: "I have only a small collection of small notes, written in very small paper. . . . These notes send you an humble petition for some sisters to keep them Company. Would you be so cruel as to refuse your own children?"[16]

The danger in the situation mounted as William Shippen began to express a preference for Henry. He spelled out the situation for Tommy: "Nancy is much puzzled between Otto & Livingston. She loves the first & only esteems the last. On Monday she likes L—& his fortune. On Tuesday evening when O—comes he is the angel. L—will consummate immediately. O—not these 2 years. L—has solicited the Father & Mother. O—is afraid of a denial. In short, we are all much puzzled. L—has 12 or 15,000 hard. O—has nothing now but honorable expectations hereafter. A Bird in Hand is worth 2 in a bush. They are both sensible. O—handsome. What do you think of it?" Alice, on the other hand, favored Otto's suit, perhaps because she recognized how much the two cared for each other. But patriarchy prevailed as Dr. Shippen began to restrict Otto's visits, much to the latter's dismay. The Frenchman's letters became more ardent: "My whole life will be entirely devoted to you, and all my happiness shall consist in giving you proofs of my tender attachment." But she failed to respond. Disconsolate, he left town for a few days. It worked. When he returned he won her consent to marry him. Otto was overjoyed. "Was it a dream my dear Nancy? or did I really hear you pronounce that heavenly *yes*!"[17]

It might as well have been a dream, for William intervened. He made Alice tell Otto he could not see Nancy for four days, and then promptly used those days to engineer a reversal and Nancy's acceptance of Henry. At first, Otto, still aglow with his victory, was perplexed but determined to get through the forced separation. Then he became suspicious. Suspicion turned to cold fear when he made his customary walk by the Shippen house on day two and saw Nancy and Livingston in the parlor, he holding her hand and looking happy, and she, he observed in agony, "seem'd to be very happy" herself. Otto wrote, begging for an explanation. On day four, Nancy wrote to confess the truth.[18]

Otto was heartbroken. It was a few days before he could respond. He could not understand. Nancy had seemed so sympathetic and encouraging. She knew their "Caracters," and that "there is no happiness without love." His feelings ran from confusion to anger. Echoing the new ideas in circulation about the importance of marrying for love, he could "not see for what reason in this *free*

Country a Lady of sixteen years who is handsome enough to find as many admirers, and who had all the advantages of a good education must be married in a hurry and given up to a man whom she dislikes." For some time, he had not believed their own union possible, but ever since her assent, he had been consumed by thoughts of her. Grief led to resolve. He begged her to "Be my Friend as you was before and let me believe that I occupy allways a part of your heart as much as religion and decency will allow you."[19]

Nancy married Henry at Shippen House on March 14, 1781. At her request, her father accompanied her to her new home at Rhinebeck, New York. Of course, he could not stay long. And her unhappiness began almost immediately. Henry could not control his jealousy and anger. Since he knew she had loved Otto, he suspected her every move and motive, even though she gave him no cause. Nancy and Otto had had no contact or communication since her marriage. The sole bright spot was that she became pregnant almost immediately. But this did not appease her husband—it only stoked his suspicions—much less did it suffice to give them common ground on which to build a marriage.[20]

That she was unhappy is hinted in letters from her father that July, since he assured her that it was her duty to fix things: "Much is now in your own power & conduct," for the happiness of both families "depend[s] in some measure on you." Despite his patriarchal manipulation of her marriage choice, William's view that it was up to the woman to fix an unhappy marriage was widely shared, even among those who touted marrying for love and companionate marriage. So Nancy probably agreed with him and did her best to win Henry over. William's ample instructions for how to do so, however, show no deviation from his long-standing social aspirations for her: "Have you returned the visits you owe to your kind neighbours[?]" he asked. "I shall be much disappointed if you are not called one of the most polite, affable, good-humor'd Ladys on the Hudson, and one of the most notable, careful & affectionate wives." Remember, he said, that "you never look half so well as when you smile." and that "if you encourage your natural good temper, tis calculated to make every body happy around you & love you." Above all, "never forget that it should be your first care to please & make your husband happy. . . . Show the world you have all the good qualities of a Shippen & of a Lee without one of their bad ones."[21]

Henry had been a problem from youth. His mother, widowed family matriarch Margaret Beekman Livingston, indulged and worried over him, although she knew he was not of good character. Everyone knew it. His army career had been checkered by his impetuosity; while it made him brave, it also made him insubordinate. He finally left the army in 1779 when he was passed over for promotion by men he considered his inferiors. Still, "the Old Lady" had a soft spot for her wayward son. Perhaps that, along with Nancy's beauty and grace, was what inclined her to like the young wife from the start. Nancy often stayed at her home.[22]

That Nancy had not succeeded in winning her husband over became clear that fall, when he forbade her to return home to Philadelphia to have her baby, despite her parents' ardent wish that she do so. She tried to persuade him, and begged her parents to come to her should she not prevail. At last, perhaps coaxed by his mother, he allowed Nancy to travel home in October. The day after Christmas, she gave birth to little "Peggy," named after her mother-in-law. Nancy doted on her "angel child."[23]

Doubtless all the Shippens would have preferred for her to stay in Philadelphia, but Nancy had to return to her husband. We cannot know how she fared over the next year and a half, as no records survive from that period. But things cannot have gone well, because the marriage was not healed. At some point she learned that, although their daughter was Harry's only legitimate heir, he had had several children with other women. While propriety mandated that she be silent about these transgressions, she was horrified to hear that he planned to gather all his children together in one house. In addition, he may have become physically abusive. In any case, by spring 1783, she had resolved to leave him, a drastic step for a woman at this time with few alternatives to marriage and with legal custody of her daughter belonging to Henry. In April, she and baby Peggy returned to Philadelphia.[24]

Nancy began a journal at this time. Its literary quality confirms her allegiance to the sentimental culture of her era. Indeed, she was fulsome in her praise of "sensibility," and reported reading sentimental novels like Samuel Richardson's best-seller *Clarissa*. Like the authors of those novels, she gave fanciful names to the chief characters in her journal (William Shippen was "Lord Worthy"). Some have suggested that Nancy was comforting herself by romanticizing her fate, but it is more likely that she was trying to figure out her own situation in light of the sentimental code of her generation. She ended the diary not when her predicament was solved, but when she had resigned herself to it, perhaps a harbinger of the loss of faith in sensibility in post-Revolutionary America.[25]

At the outset, Nancy was fatalistic about her marriage choice ("the die is cast—& my life must be miserable"), but she sought consolation in that she had obeyed her parents. This was a theme in sentimental literature. Since the new fashions of individual choice and marriage for love made picking a husband a perilous matter for a young woman whose fate would be determined by that move many authors advised girls to seek parental advice. Whether she was active or passive in accepting her father's choice at the time she did so, in her diary she portrayed her decision as a conscious one, and took comfort in "having conform'd to the will" of her parents "in the most important action of her life." Nancy was also content that now at least her father saw the "consequences of my unhappy choice." Significantly, she initially wrote "his unhappy choice" and then struck out "his" and substituted "my." At some point, possibly later, she took responsibility for her decision to follow her father's advice and marry Henry Livingston. Still, she was comforted that her father now saw that he had given bad advice. Indirectly, she continued to blame him too.[26]

Nancy's chief consolation at this time was her daughter. She worshipped little Peggy, and loved spending time dressing her, covering her with kisses, and hearing others compliment her. She saw company and visited a bit, but was largely indifferent to these activities. She could hardly have been indifferent when she ran into Otto and he praised her baby. But she simply and circumspectly declared him a "good man!" for doing so.[27]

As Nancy settled back into life in Philadelphia, her moods varied. Hearing from Henry—"Lord B" in the journal—was always discouraging. "He still continues to persecute me with his reproaches," she recorded, "God knows that I do not deserve them." At other times she was her old self, sociable and anxious to appear well. A large dinner party at the imposing Powel house on Third Street proved "a most delightfull Evening." She spent the better part of a day preparing, and was satisfied that the mirror "told me I look'd well." Reflected there was the twenty-year-old, "dressed in pink with a gause petticoat—and Elegant French Hat on, with five white plumes nodding different ways—a bouquet of natural flowers—& a white Satin muff." Her continued immaturity and confusion are registered in her response to meeting Otto there, who told her "what I believed—that I look'd like an Angel—shall I confess that I felt pleas'd to be approved of by him? Why? Because he is my sincere friend—& was once (O happy time!) my lover."[28]

Of course Henry Livingston would have felt vindicated were he to witness this encounter. Nancy expostulated just a week later that she had been "miserable all day" from having received a letter from him, that "now you say I left you because I loved another." She was furious that he accused her of infidelity, maintaining that "nothing but your being jealous, & treating me ill in consequence of that jealousy, shou'd have tempted me to leave you." It is hard to see how the two would ever be able to overcome the combination of Henry's toxic temperament and the reality of Nancy's past preference for Otto.

Even though Nancy and Otto were innocent of any real sin, neither could she pretend to be blameless for preferring him still, at least now that she had left Livingston territory.[29]

Nancy clearly had to work out where she stood in the tangled mess of her marriage. Her mother urged her "not to murmur but be resigned to the will of providence." Meanwhile, Nancy began transcribing the Marquise de Maintenon's famous advice to women on marriage. Some lessons echoed her mother's insistence on resignation to her fate: "Do not hope for perfect happiness; there is no such thing in this sublunary state." The female "sex is the more exposed to suffer, because it is always in dependance: be neither angry nor asham'd of this dependance on a husband." It was vain to "hope that your union will procure you perfect peace: the best Marriages are those where with softness & patience they bear by turns with each other." Nancy also transcribed Maintenon's expectation of an emotional disconnect between man and wife, sadly still a stock-in-trade for advice writers today; to make the marriage work, the woman had to show a sensitivity missing in her husband:

> Do not expect the same degree of friendship that you feel: men are in general less tender than women and you will be unhappy if you are too delicate in your friendships. . . .
>
> Do not hope to bring back a husband by complaints, ill humor, or reproaches. The only means which promise success, are patience & softness: impatience sours & alienates hearts: softness leads them back to their duty. They are naturally tyrannical; they will have pleasures & liberty. . . .
>
> Do not examine whether their rights are well founded, let it suffice to you that they are established. They are masters, we have only to suffer & obey with a good grace.[30]

Nancy agreed with de Maintenon's description of men, but could not bring herself to accept her views of a woman's role as wife. She subscribed to the more recent "companionate" view of marriage: "I cannot agree . . . that Women are only born to suffer & to obey that men are generally tyrannical I will own, but such as know how to be happy, willingly give up the harsh title of master for the more tender & endearing one of Friend," she insisted. "Equality is the soul of friendship: marriage, to give delight, must join *two minds*, not devote a slave to the will of an imperious Lord."[31]

Clearly, Nancy was wrestling with her own predicament—she was unable to see a potential "Friend" in "Lord B." She was also contending with continued paternal pressure. Ever concerned with securing the family's status, one morning, she wrote, "Papa told me . . . at breakfast that I must send my darling Child to its Grandmamma Livingston." This "was for the future interest of my baby, that its fortune depended on the old Lady's pleasure in that particular—beg'd me to think of it, & be reconciled to it." The next day, her mother asked her what she had decided, and Nancy said she would not part with Peggy if she could possibly avoid it. But Alice told her that William "had determin'd that the Child shou'd go at any rate—that he cou'd not be answerable for the Childs losing her fortune." Nancy "cried all the time she was speaking."[32]

Among other things, Nancy appeared to be struggling with resentment of her parents. On a morning visit, she was "much affected at a little anecdote" she heard "of a young Lady who was sacrificed to the avarice and ambition of her parents to a man she hated—& her death was the natural consequence of her misery." The woman "had a soul form'd for friendship . . . & she died a melancholy victim to the Tyranny of her friends & the tenderness of her heart." Nancy found "it . . . a painful consideration, that the happiness or misery of our lives are generally determin'd, before we are proper judges of either." Painful indeed. She could not bring herself to condemn her parents directly (her "friends" in the older sense of the word as one's family relations). She clung to the fact that she had dutifully obeyed them. Nor could she admit fully to her own guilt in making the wrong choice, and forsaking the "friend" (in the new egalitarian and sentimental sense) she had had in Louis Otto. She preferred to point to her youth at the time that she was pressured to decide.[33]

She spent a lot of time "caressing & playing with Peggy," but she never complained of the burden of child care. Nor did it prevent her, if she chose, from sewing, reading, or visiting. It is clear that she had the help of servants like "Betsy," whom she sent out one morning "with the Child to give it an airing." But as the time approached when she was supposed to part with her, Nancy spent more and more time with her little girl. She also began to consider how her daughter should be educated. Here again, we find quiet condemnation of her own upbringing as Nancy hoped that "in some particulars" Peggy's education "may differ from mine." As she copied down "Some Directions Concerning a Daughters Education" in her diary, we see what she wished to change. She included "never use any little dissembling arts, either to pacify her or to persuade her to anything" as well as the need to "inculcate . . . SINCERITY." Was she admitting to her father's manipulation and her own fault in not following her own heart? Religion, industry, order, and health were on her list of important matters; deportment and appearance were not.[34]

Despite these reflections, Nancy's near hysterical response when little Peggy fell ill in the spring of 1783 shows her continued immaturity. She must have exasperated her father with her frequent calls upon him to attend the child. A friend's suggestion that country air might benefit the baby made Nancy think more favorably upon the idea of taking Peggy herself to her grandmother's in New York. She even began to think that seeing his lovely little girl might soften Henry and help them reconcile. She set off, after a teary farewell to her parents, in early summer, writing that her mother insisted, and her father agreed, that she "return to us if you don't find your husband alter'd for the better—don't let your love for our sweet baby tempt you to throw yourself into Misery." Nancy's hopes began to falter when she did not hear from Henry as she approached. She went on to his mother's and was received with "affection"; Nancy was sure that Margaret Livingston cared about her. Margaret wrote to her son, and told Nancy his reply: that "he continues Obdurate—will not come & see me & his dear infant—continues to repeat his false suspicions & to be jealous of me." Margaret also told Nancy she thought "it will be impossible to live happily with him." After a few more attempts to communicate, all with the same "resentful" response, Nancy returned to Philadelphia, miserable at leaving her beloved eighteen-month-old behind, though "under the care of an affectionate & prudent Grandmother."[35]

Otto wrote to console her that she had done the right thing by trying to reconcile, and that it had brought to "your Side those few who had been prejudiced by misrepresentations." He urged her not to be miserable and "avoid the world," as such a conduct "would be a proof of guilt." But neither should she "appear quite unconcerned." Instead she should adopt that "decent and reserved Behavior of which you are perfectly mistress and which is the only ornament of innocence and Virtue." Again Otto was giving voice to the new ideas about women's proper conduct. A wife should try to reform her husband, but such was not possible if he was so immoral as to be immune to her influence. She could take comfort in having made the effort.[36]

As usual, Otto was giving Nancy the benefit of the doubt. But she did not fully merit his confidence that she had learned from past mistakes in regard to coquetry. She managed to restrain herself from acting on her feelings toward him, although she was always happy to see him and very sad when he left on a trip home to France. But she was not above dallying with others. She took the devotion of her friend Bushrod Washington for granted, for example, praising his looks, manners, and conversation, and allowing him to visit and write and to escort her to various events. "He very often favors me with his company," she noted, "of which I am extreamly fond." After one ball with "Mr Washington my partner," she wrote that "I believed I looked well at least my Partner told me so." She was not acting with the caution and reserve that Otto had recommended.[37]

Despite Otto's efforts to console her, Nancy still pined for her daughter and wrote often to Margaret, begging for news. Margaret assured her that little Peggy was healthy, "the sweetest and best tempered Child in the world, and as happy as an Angel." Although Nancy had asked how Henry was disposed toward his daughter, one wonders how she felt at reading Margaret's reply that "her papa is very fond of her and she of him." Nancy worried when she heard Henry was in Philadelphia and had come by the house to see her, wondering what she would do "if he comes and forces me away." Implying past abuse, she fretted that "I really think my life will be in danger from his jealousy and unmanaged passions." Her concern only grew as weeks passed with no news of Peggy. She was elated when, finally, a letter came or someone reported having seen her in New York.[38]

Buoyed by the periodic reports that her child was healthy and beautiful, Nancy's spirits began to improve. She reported more socializing in the form of visits, teas, balls, dinners, card games, sleigh rides, and various other outings. She did not even appear bothered by a few unpleasant letters from Henry. These are revealing, however, when compared with those she had sent to him. Both husband and wife accused each other of mistreatment; both claimed to be injured. When she rejected an imputation of misconduct on her part in a long letter accusing him of irrational jealousy, he replied, "In your last you were pleased to Misconstrue some Words, rather meant as a Caution than an implication of guilt—I should have given you this satisfaction sooner, had I not conceived myself injured." It is hard to know what had really happened between them, although other parties agreed that he was a volatile man. It is clear that these two would never have been able to live peacefully together.[39]

Paradoxically, Nancy got along better with her parents when she was dejected than when her spirits were high. Her moods vacillated over the winter of 1784, and, when down, she appreciated her mother's wise counsel. But they also clashed. Nancy resented her mother's finding fault with her one afternoon, and they "got to very high words," for which Nancy felt at fault. Reconciled the next day, she was happy, began to plan a party, and praised her father in particular for having the "sweetest disposition in the world." It was not long, however, before Nancy and William clashed over her late hours. Just turning twenty-one, Nancy did not behave, and they did not treat her, like an adult. Her mother interposed, for example, to make Nancy turn away gentlemen callers on Sundays. After they fought, Alice sent Nancy to her room. When her parents corrected her, she pouted or cried and complained in her diary, but she always complied. She wondered when the day would come that she could be "free and uncountrould" and periodically tried to assert her independence, but she did not really seem to want to escape their power. She declined to go to a ball at the French minister's one evening, "at my Papas request," even though she had wanted to attend. But she did not trust herself: "It was certainly prudent not to go; how happy am I to have a wise parent to judge for me."[40]

Relations with her parents were also tried that spring and summer, when, after a brief visit to New York City, where she stayed with a Livingston sister-in-law and saw Peggy (who, not surprisingly but painfully, did not know her at first), Nancy returned home to find that her father had rented a smaller home and expected her to go to the country to care for her mother, who was in poor physical and mental health. Nancy hated being in the country, especially as her mother kept insisting she was about to die, only to recover each time. The situation was a little improved by visits from a friend named Louisa and her uncle Arthur Lee, but Nancy was much happier on the occasions when she was able to come into town. Finally, in the fall, her father relented and let her move back to Philadelphia, "as Mamma is so fond of solitude & I am not."[41]

Otto had returned to France in July, while she was still in the countryside. They did not see each other before he left, and Nancy professed to be glad as "it wou'd have affected me too much." He felt the same way. He wrote that he was consoled at having "constantly acted according to the strictest rules of propriety," which he thought "gives me an unquestionable right upon your friendship." He hoped that she would write.[42]

Nancy was happy to be back in town, where a more active social life and mornings or afternoons spent shopping with her friend Louisa helped pass the time between what really mattered to her, namely, reports of Peggy's well-being. But she continued to worry about her very depressed mother, and grew bored. Doubtless she was happy to receive fanciful and friendly letters from Otto in France, now signed "John Waittoolong," and written from "the other world." But she left off keeping her diary, not thinking there was anything worth recording.[43]

Nancy resumed the diary in February 1785, because of what she thought was a hopeful event. In January, Henry Livingston, in Philadelphia on business, had asked her to meet with him to discuss a reconciliation. Nancy agreed, hoping that this would lead to a reunion with her child. But her dreams were dashed in early March when her refusal to agree to some terms she found unacceptable led Henry to write that he was leaving "this Fatal Place" with "an almost Bursting Heart." He begged her to pardon any offenses on his part, which he insisted were "without intention, or premeditation," and claimed that "tho I feel myself Cruelly Injured, my Heart will never allow me to complain." Nancy showed the puzzling letter to her father, who at last agreed that "it will never do for me to return to my inflexible husband."[44]

Nancy resumed her domestic and social pursuits but left off the diary again, until, in September 1785, she had something worth noting: Louis Otto's return to the United States as a diplomat in the French Embassy. This distressed her, as it caused her to think how she might have been happy had she waited until he was established in life, while now that he was, it was too late, and "I be wretched in the reflection of what I have lost." She began to neglect her domestic duties and seek distraction in socializing, but to no avail. As this displeased her father, she vowed to keep more at home but was still miserable. All, she thought, would be better if she were not kept from her little girl. She did wish for a formal separation from her husband, but learned in October that this had fallen through. Meanwhile, she was disturbed at reports that he was selling property and otherwise depriving "his wife & lawful heir" and "throwing" what should belong to her "away on miserable undeserving objects."[45]

Soon Nancy heard that Louis Otto had married her friend and relation by marriage Eliza Livingston. Nancy wished them happiness, but this must have been occasion for rueful thoughts during the monotonous months that followed. Fortunately her spirits were revived that fall, by funny letters from Tommy, pursuing legal studies in London, and even more, by the news that Peggy was coming to spend the winter with her. While Nancy was too busy to keep her journal at this time, in letters to Tommy, Dr. Shippen indicated that everyone was delighted with the little girl, and he gave Nancy credit for her "management" and improvement. Peggy was "universally admir'd and makes herself very agreeable." She was "held up as a model for all little misses." They were all sorry to see her return to her New York relations that spring. Clearly the visit had restored Nancy's spirits as she resumed entertaining in June 1787, including hosting General Washington, in town for the constitutional convention, several times for tea.[46]

At year's end, Nancy learned of the death in childbirth of Otto's wife, Eliza. When she wrote to condole him, Otto appreciated the friendship and interest "of a heart so full of its own sorrow, that there seemed to be no room left for those of a Stranger." Over the course of 1788 he continued to write, finding her friendship a great balm to his grief. He thought that her sorrows had improved her. It is probably fortunate that he did not come to visit her in Philadelphia as he sometimes considered doing. They were both too vulnerable. They could barely contain their feelings within proper bounds in their letters, Louis exclaiming that "I am constantly checked by the apprehension of saying too much or too little—too much for you to read; too little for my feelings."[47]

Nancy had disagreed to terms Henry initially proposed for a separation agreement in 1785, deeming them injurious to both of their reputations, but by 1787 she had reconsidered and was ready to try again. Two years later, separation was still pending. Nancy was ready to agree if Henry promised to contribute to Peggy's support and education. Meanwhile Nancy considered trying to obtain a divorce and consulted with her uncle Arthur Lee about it. He hardly took her seriously. The reality was, as a married woman "covered" by her husband's legal identity, she had no legal ground to stand on, and the Revolution had brought only limited gains in a few places for women seeking divorce. Arthur advised her that it would have to be by a special act of the New York legislature. He told her who the best lawyers for the job were. Nancy's mother-in-law, Margaret Beekman Livingston, pained at her son's terrible behavior, was fully supportive. Unfortunately, the legislature was not sufficiently moved by what Margaret Beekman called Nancy's "oppressed innocence," to grant her the divorce. Nancy would not be freed until October 1789, when Henry obtained a divorce in Connecticut on the grounds that she had deserted him.[48]

In the meantime, a tragedy unfolded in Henry's relationship with his mother and her heroic support of Nancy. Margaret reminded Nancy that "I am a Mother and every misconduct every Sin and Immorality recoils upon my heart and makes it Vibrate with ten fold force." Describing Henry's behavior with little Peggy the few times he had seen her, Margaret wrote that it "was so cool . . . that I felt the utmost pain." It was clear that Henry's efforts to get custody of Peggy were simply because Margaret had excluded him from her estate while including her granddaughter. He vented his rage on his mother and threatened suit. For a time, Margaret sent Peggy to live with Nancy, for fear that Henry would seize his daughter if she remained in New York. Then the little girl went back and forth, spending the early spring of 1788 with Nancy, the summer months with her grandmother, and the winter of 1789 back with her mother.[49]

Margaret supported her daughter-in-law's effort to get a divorce even when Nancy's own parents abandoned her to side with Livingston. The latter three demanded that Nancy appear with Peggy in the judge's chambers. Margaret knew Henry would simply seize the child and was furious at the Shippens for their "sordid interestedness." But she counseled Nancy, as their daughter, to try to overlook their failings. Margaret agreed with Nancy that Peggy should remain with her in Philadelphia, asserting that "were I to take her tomorrow he would take her from me the next day till I give up her Estate to him. When that is accomplished I suppose he will never care a straw where she is—in the meantime at my age, being near 69 years . . . I am not fit now . . . to encounter the salleys of his turbulent temper." Margaret even sent Nancy forty dollars for her legal expenses. "My heart is pained for you; when will your troubles end," she wrote. "He says he has proof of your infidelity before marriage & after" and "says he will publish Mr O . . . and . . . the treatment he has received from his own family" in marital troubles. "Oh what a malignant heart has he, unhappy man, got." Margaret commiserated. "Keep up your Spirits. Pray to God to give you grace and strength." Both Margaret and Louis Otto cautioned Nancy to be very circumspect in her behavior given the scandals Livingston was spreading. Louis also assured Nancy that the rumor he was to remarry was false. Peggy remained with her mother for some time and then returned to her grandmother. All the while Nancy and Margaret consulted extensively by letter as to the progress of her education. They did not always agree as to specifics, but they were of one mind as to its importance. Peggy also assured her mother of her progress by writing, as well as of her affection, ending one note, "If you did but know the love I feel for you."[50]

Margaret Livingston's support meant everything to Nancy, and thus she felt abandoned for a time when Margaret reconciled with her son in 1790. Margaret wrote that "a great change has taken place in the Cols Life and conduct . . . and it is his wish, joined with mine, that Peggy shall return to me." This came on top of the news of another abandonment: Otto was indeed going to remarry—his neighbor Fanny de Crèvecoeur. He had waited long years for Nancy, but if she married him she would give up all hopes of keeping Peggy from her father. Nancy understood, but now she would be deprived of the balm of his loving letters.[51]

This must have seemed like the end of their story, and indeed, Nancy stopped keeping her journal at the end of 1791. She noted in her last entry that "it is certain that when the mind bleeds with some wound of recent misfortune nothing is of equal efficacy with religious comfort." Her sad love story was truly over; and she no longer received any benefit from keeping the journal. Religion was more consoling now.[52]

At least Margaret Livingston's support was soon renewed, for mother and son were again at odds in 1792. For the next two years, Henry continued to try to get his daughter away from his mother and Nancy. For a time, Margaret decided to send her to live with people she trusted, under an assumed name. Peggy wrote notes to reassure her mother, indicating the growing strength of her attachment: "I'll find a way to see you with out putting myself

Figure 10. Nancy Shippen Livingston (1763–1841). Oil portrait in locket by Benjamin Trott, ca. 1796. Smithsonian American Art Museum, Gift of Natalie Brooks Sears Shippen and William Brush Shippen, 1999.87.1.

in danger don't be afraid." Now in her early teens, Peggy continued to move back and forth between her mother and grandmother. When with her, Nancy continually apprised Margaret of Peggy's progress, and Margaret sent funds to pay for it. Educating her daughter was a source of great satisfaction to Nancy. She devoted all her attention to it and derived some consolation, since "in contemplating her I seem to live my youth over again." Indeed, she could have been describing her old self when writing Margaret that "I have the pleasure to tell you that our dear girl was much admired at a Ball." (Peggy had written her grandmother of her dancing lessons, with seven other girls "of the neighbourhood," including "Bishop Wm White's daughters.") Nancy also wrote her brother Tommy that Ann Bingham, the leader of Philadelphia society, had taken Peggy to a few balls and was "very attentive to her." And yet, Nancy strove to give Peggy a better education than she had had, assuring Margaret that "our dear girl makes the most astonishing improvement under her new master who teaches her french & as a favor geography & arithmetic & will very soon teach her Italien." In addition, Nancy taught Peggy housekeeping skills. Despite this contentment, both Nancy and Margaret lived in perpetual fear that Henry would make good on his threats to "bear her off."[53]

In the spring of 1797, Peggy made her own move, deciding to go to Philadelphia to live with her mother permanently. She gave up the comforts and loving circle of her adoring grandmother and aunts, potentially renouncing the promised fortune. Just sixteen, she began a quiet and retired new life with her mother. This has been described as a sad ending to their story, but in fact, it was the victory both had striven for. Moreover, her granddaughter's departure notwithstanding, when Margaret Livingston died in 1800, she left Peggy a large bequest. Two decades later, in 1819, Peggy and her mother were living at the Livingston House, 346 High Street. That they were very comfortable is paradoxically revealed in a newspaper story about an armed robbery of their home in 1822. Nancy and Peggy were surely frightened at being tied up while their home was rifled, but a gold watch with diamonds, a variety of necklaces and other jewelry, and sumptuous bedclothes were amid the plunder. Henry Livingston, in contrast, died nearly penniless and in debt in 1831. He was eighty-one. Nancy followed, at seventy-eight, in 1841, and Peggy, still unmarried, in 1864, at eighty-two. Unfortunately, by this time much of her fortune had been stolen by swindlers taking advantage of her religiosity. Still, their primary wish to be together was again fulfilled when she was buried in her mother's grave.[54]

Some view Nancy Shippen's story as one of the tragic consequences of a young girl's indoctrination into a system of patriarchal power. But I think history tells us that women's lives were more complex than that. Nancy certainly struggled—with her father's venality, her mother's passivity, her husband's hypocritical jealousy, and her own slow-to-mature superficiality. But she was not just a victim; she was a whole person. She might not have said so directly in her sentimental journal, but her actions did. In leaving her husband and educating her daughter she asserted herself to shape her life. Unfortunately, the Revolution had not given her new powers to do so. American legislators did not stay true to their rhetoric of liberty and equality when it came to reviewing the laws of marriage and divorce. They were as much captive to the gender assumptions of their time as anyone in this story. Only the hindsight of history shows us that change was possible, just painfully gradual.[55]

CHAPTER 6

Deborah Norris Logan

> Oh dear Reader! When an hundred years shall have flown what would thee not give to see things as I behold them now!
>
> —Deborah Norris Logan

As we have seen, the American Revolution did not alter the legal underpinnings of women's inequality in marriage. What did this feel like for intelligent and educated women who were as aware as their husbands of the new thinking about equality that accompanied the Revolution? We know there were plenty of unhappy marriages like those of Grace Galloway and Nancy Livingston. But it appears that even the good ones, like that of Deborah and George Logan, were hard on women. And yet this generation of women did not protest their position as women. They lacked the necessary feminist consciousness. It would take dissatisfaction with the new ideology of "woman's sphere"—the pedestal offered women as if to compensate for their exclusion from politics in the new republic—for them to act on a shared sense of grievance as women. But how did wives cope in the meantime? In Deborah Logan's case, a combination of avoidance, the outlet of writing, and appreciation of what her husband did offer allowed her to live with the era's constraints.

Deborah Logan was not without advantages. She was born in October 1761 in the beautiful home her father built on Chestnut Street, just half a block east of the State House (later Independence Hall). She lived there with her mother, Mary Parker Norris, until she married; her father, Quaker merchant Charles Norris, died when she was four. Deborah loved the house and gardens and preserved their memory long after they were torn down and replaced by the Second Bank of the United States, which stands on the site today. An old drawing shows that the three-story brick Norris mansion was imposing. It dominated the block and was renowned for the greenhouse out back. "Debby," as she was known, remembered walks with her brother, Isaac, and their nurses in the garden, a showpiece laid out in symmetrical square beds, intersected by gravel and grass walks. In a poem, she invoked its importance in her childhood play, recalling, "I knew each walk and every valley green . . . With every haunt for sports from side to side." She probably went through the garden to get to Anthony Benezet's school for girls around the corner.[1]

Young Deborah was "full of spirits," and Benezet, who tailored his approach to the character of each student, found that the best way to keep her in line was to appeal to her sense of honor. So he put "Norris," as he called her, in charge of the class whenever he had to leave. She had many fond memories of Benezet's teaching, and credited him for her clear penmanship. When it ended, however, she was not sure she had made the most of her schooling, so she continued to read on her own in her father's ample library.[2]

Deborah Norris continued to gain polish as well, because her mother was educated herself and good at attracting company. Since they were just down the street from the State House (she could see its steeple from the parlor window, over the garden's willow trees), Deborah met all sorts of people in the mid-1770s, including members of the Continental Congress and most of the signers of the Declaration of Independence. She was a vivacious girl who enjoyed socializing with a circle of other young Quakers. She was popular and enjoyed her friends' esteem. When Peggy Rawle asked Sally Wister not to show Deborah her letters, for example, fearing they would look silly to Deborah who wrote so well, Sally responded that of course Deborah would never make "ill-naturd remarks" about them.[3]

We don't have any painted images of young Deborah, but we do have word portraits. During the British occupation of Philadelphia in 1777–1778, when Sally Wister's family relocated to Hannah Foulke's house in North Wales, she and Deborah wrote back and forth, giving us a glimpse of the Revolution from the perspective of two teenagers. When Deborah mentioned the British presence, she did so between reports of the visits and spats of mutual friends, quotes from popular British poet Alexander Pope, and her gladness at hearing that Sally's siblings had recovered from an illness. Since both girls had been schooled by Benezet, the letters, with their scattered references to embroidery, novels, various works in Latin and French, and the *Lady's Magazine*, in addition to Pope, give us a sense of their education. Not surprisingly, they reveal above all a circle of girls with an avid interest in young men. Sally was sure Deborah would be fascinated by her descriptions of the American officers quartered near the Foulke's farm, including her admiring sketch of a young Virginia slaveholder. The imagined responses she ascribed to Deborah were not staid or prudish, but teasing. And Deborah's letters to Sally did often jest. One comment combined humor and gossip: "I am amazed that Miss Stocker is called a Beauty," Deborah wrote. "We have a chance for it now, I think."[4]

As the war continued, so did Deborah's interest in courtship. At one point she apologized to Sally Fisher that she had "no matrimonial intelligence to send thee." As late as May 1780 she confided to Sally that "indeed my dear it seems to me that we shall neither of us marry; but for reasons rather different, thee from not having an offer thee approves, I, from having no offers to disapprove." But then George Logan appeared in her parlor that fall, just returned from medical training in Britain. Deborah told Sally that "we will call him Altamont" (after a young nobleman in a popular tragedy), that he had visited for tea, was "agreeable," and had entertainingly described his recent travels. By December, Deborah was getting teased about him, writing that "he is a great Beau here No wonder when we have such a scarcity but seriously I think him very agreeable, And should be very much obliged to the World if it would spare its Conjectures."[5]

That Deborah assigned George a romantic pseudonym was typical practice among educated youth at the time. She was an avid subscriber to the vogue of sensibility or empathic feeling encouraged by the popular new novels. She wrote that her mind was "agitated with very tender sensibilitys" over the illness of an aunt. On news of the recovery of one of Sally Fisher's aunts, she gushed: "How sweetly amiable and pleasing is sensibility, how beautifully does it gild and add lustre to other accomplishments; like the sun beam to the trembling dew drop! These were my reflections when I read that part of thy letter which Concerned thy Aunt."[6]

How did this emphasis on feeling affect Deborah's attitude toward courtship and marriage? Her comments about matches being made around her hint at her own views at a time of change in marriage making. She must have thought economics a proper consideration (as they always had been), since when one wealthy acquaintance married a man of middling rank, she noted that "almost every body wonders at her choice." She herself thought she would be "mortified with having it Universally thought I was too good for the Gentleman." "And yet," she added, "he may be a very good sort of man," indicating that class was not the only thing that mattered in making a good match. Romantic love was beginning to be regarded as an important ingredient, and Deborah approved the trend. Although another friend had married secretly after a rapid courtship, causing concern, Deborah noted: "She appears happy [and] their happiness is romantic, to one who's brain is as much turned that way as mine, it is not disagreeable."[7]

Deborah and George did not tarry themselves, for by February 1781, just a few months after his first appearance in her parlor, they were engaged. Her self-deprecating comments to girlfriends notwithstanding, Deborah was not acting for lack of other possibilities. One gossip commented that "Doctor Logan will have a prize in her—their intended marriage will much disappoint one of the same profession, by what I have heard." Perhaps the short courtship was good, since some women expressed apprehension about the fateful step of marriage, even though there were few alternatives. Deborah insisted that she did not share the general contempt of spinsters, so perhaps she did not feel compelled to marry. Her father was long dead and George's parents had both died while he was in Britain, so the two were more or less free to make their own choice. Deborah surely consulted her mother, but Mary Parker Norris was not likely to object. Mothers tended to be more favorable to romantic over economic considerations than fathers, and she must have known that the literature of the day had endorsed the growing trend of children choosing mates out of affection rather than parents doing so for economic reasons. Not that Mary Norris would have complained on the latter score, since, like Deborah, George was descended from one of Pennsylvania's most eminent families.[8]

Deborah's comments on courtship indicate that she was looking above all for an agreeable companion, and in fact George and Deborah personified the ideal mates—virtuous and moderate, tender and affectionate—that newspapers and magazines had begun to extol. When they announced their intention to marry at meeting on July 27, 1781, a friend remarked approvingly that "he must be entirely insensible to every delicate and refin'd sentiment if he does not feel the most tender attachment for her, she is indeed a lovely girl." Deborah's looks and manner were not just admired by her girlfriends. The French diplomat the Marquis de Barbé-Marbois was captivated when he met her at Anthony Benezet's, and described her as "beautiful as an angel." He loved her subdued Quaker style, She "dressed with neatness, simplicity, and . . . elegance," and "her hair had not been tortured by the coiffure." Instead, "it was drawn back behind her head without powder and covered with a little gauze cap" that complemented "a grey satin dress." In sum, he insisted to his correspondent, "the charms of Mademoiselle Norris are all her own, and she owes nothing to art."[9]

George Logan was as much a catch as she was. He was of medium height; his portrait shows a handsome face. He was the grandson of William Penn's powerful secretary, James Logan, and had inherited Stenton, the house James Logan had built just outside town. George was born and lived there until his teens, after which he spent some time at school in England and then as a merchant apprentice in Philadelphia. He had gone back to Britain at the start of the Revolution for medical training. The timing of his move is not surprising given the ambivalence about the war of the pacifist Quaker elite.[10]

Deborah and George must have known each other before George's departure for Edinburgh. The Norrises and Logans were part of a fairly self-contained Quaker social group. Indeed, theirs was not the first Norris-Logan marriage, since his aunt Sarah Logan had married her uncle Isaac Norris. Moreover, as a boy George had attended the Friends School, around the corner from her house, and his apprenticeship was also very near. They must have crossed paths or at least seen each other at Quaker Meeting. But Deborah, only fourteen when he left, might not have caught the twenty-two-year-old's attention. She did not take long to do so at nineteen, when he returned. The Meeting approved the match and the pair were married at the Friends Great Meeting House in September 1781. Forty friends and relatives gathered afterward to celebrate at her mother's home.[11]

Despite his training and interest in medicine, in coming home to war-battered Stenton George grew interested in agricultural reform and threw himself into farming. In 1785 he became a founding member of the Philadelphia Society for the Promotion of Agriculture. His new bride supported his desire for self-sufficiency and home manufacture in her own work. Considering the report that he only toned down his penchant for fancy dress at the time of his marriage, however, it is possible that his turn to homespun was actually influenced by Deborah's taste for simplicity. That taste must have stood her in good stead since the paper money George had inherited was nearly worthless at war's end and Stenton needed many repairs. Although Deborah was able to bring some beautiful pieces of furniture with her when the couple moved in, she could no longer continue to live in the luxury of her youth. Nevertheless, the couple set to work and apparently lived in great harmony at Stenton, where Deborah soon bore and they reared three sons with the fabulously sentimental names of Albanus, Gustavus, and Algernon.[12]

Deborah loved Stenton and left wonderful poetry and journal entries describing her daily routine, the turning of the seasons and their associated tasks, and the reception of fascinating visitors. George Washington was among them. A farmer himself, he came out to see George's experiment in gypsum-fertilized clover—manifested in George's initials grown into the lawn. Deborah was charmed by the way Washington took her "little boy on his knee," and her baby in his arms, "with commendations that made their way immediately to a mother's heart." Ben Franklin visited in the early years, as did many other American and foreign statesmen. Her favorite, Thomas Jefferson, was a frequent

Figure 11. Stenton, 4601 North 18th Street, Philadelphia, Pennsylvania (built 1723–1730). Stenton House Museum and Gardens.

guest in the years he was in Philadelphia. Dinner and teatime conversation in these early years of the new nation must have been wonderfully interesting, especially in the precious days of the late 1780s before party divisions took hold.[13]

Stenton was certainly a handsome place to entertain. Deborah admired the beautiful symmetry of the brick house, with its three-story facade, two windows flanking the wide door on the first floor, six windows in a line on the second, and three dormer windows in the pitched roof on the third floor. The front door opened onto a center hall which gave way to the formal "best parlor" on the left. Here George's portrait hung over the marble fireplace. On the right was "Papa's parlor"—George Logan's office. Behind it and the stairway was the dining room, the site of formal entertainment. In its corner stood a small desk, Deborah's "winter writing establishment" (perhaps because it was out of the way of other activity and near a big fireplace). The dining room gave out onto a covered porch leading to the separate two-room kitchen. Across the hall from the dining room was a bedroom that Deborah used in old age. Upstairs were two small nurseries and two large bedrooms, including one which served as her summer bedroom, and then her library in widowhood. Almost parts of the house, to Deborah, were the different trees seen and smelled from the upstairs windows. She loved the way the light filtered in through them.[14]

So comfortable was she at Stenton that Deborah seldom went to Philadelphia—usually only to run errands and visit close friends and kin. She attended the Friends Yearly Meeting there each spring. This was also the occasion for an annual house party at her cousin Sarah Dickinson's. When she did visit the city, Deborah noted its change and growth. The southwest corner of the Norris house lot was sold in 1789, and the new "Library Hall" built there. Long the home of Benjamin Franklin's Library Company of Philadelphia, it is now, in a mid-twentieth-century reconstruction, the home of the American Philosophical Society. Soon the northwestern end of the garden was portioned off for the building of five beautiful townhouses on Chestnut Street that became known as Norris Row. In 1818, when her childhood home itself was sold, Deborah would go "take leave of the dear Old House." The parlor awakened memories of her mother. A few months later, she noted that the house had been leveled to make way for the Second Bank of the United States; on another walk she watched the building get under way. Besides the loss of the home of pleasant memory, Deborah must have been struck at the way her old neighborhood evolved from a largely residential into a commercial area in the decades after the federal government moved out in 1800. In addition to the new bank, shops and manufacturing establishments were replacing old homes and boarding houses. By 1819 she wrote that "such is the improvement in some respects, Alteration in others, that I felt like a Stranger in my native City." Home was Stenton.[15]

Just as clearly as she loved Stenton, Deborah loved George. She sang his praises throughout her *Memoir of George Logan,* published after his death and a period of deep mourning. The challenge is to get underneath the loyal professions of marital harmony to the actual marriage. How did this bright and vibrant (Anthony Benezet and Sally Wister would have said mischievous) young woman experience their union at this complicated time in the history of Western marriage? As cultured young people, Deborah and George would have imbibed the new fashion that husbands should be sensitive and feeling companions to their wives. And yet the centuries-old common-law tradition of coverture, wherein wives were subordinated to their husband's legal identity and authority, as well of control of property, held fast. How did these contradictory cultural currents affect the Logan marriage?[16]

Like other women of her time, Deborah Norris underwent a clear change of status and experience in marrying. She altered her behavior to suit. Gone was the gay and playful girl who gossiped with her female friends. She was now George Logan's devoted wife and soon a busy mother. Ten years into their marriage, Deborah's sister-in-law Sarah Logan Fisher confirmed that Deborah had succeeded in conforming to the feminine ideal of the time. Sarah asserted that "My sweet Sister is the humble Dairy maid, the domestic housewife, the Affectionate wife, the tender Mother, the improving Companion and Friend, and when in publick Company, the most accomplished lady that ever graced a circle." Deborah might have made it look easy, but this was actually a difficult role to perform. Despite the chatter in the postwar press about equality and friendship in marriage, the small print insisted that if there was conflict, it was up to the wife to defer to the husband. Thus the new ideal of equality did not supersede patriarchy, but accommodated it. Ideal marriage in the new republic was a complex mix of mutuality and wifely submission. Deborah made it her business to appear to fit the mold. She was not alone. Even the most educated and politically aware women of the time, with equally good marriages—Mercy Otis Warren and Abigail Adams come to mind—did the same.[17]

The new ideal of marriage granted some influence to the wife. Marriage was now seen as a school for the morality and virtue necessary to sustain a republic, wherein the educated and virtuous wife would have a beneficial influence on her husband's character. In a poem she wrote several years before George came on the scene, Deborah had encouraged her female friends to look within for moral guidance, not to men, who were often "the slaves of vice." She went so far as to insist that women had "equal if not superior Qualities" to men. Perhaps these ideas, also encouraged in popular literature, gave Deborah satisfaction in her role as wife. In fact, no one considered George a slave to vice or even questioned his virtue. Maybe this reassured Deborah that she had chosen wisely and was doing a good job as a "republican wife."[18]

Yet neither Deborah nor George ever hinted that such an influence was at work in their marriage. For one thing, it required a receptive husband. George was no unfaithful scoundrel like the impervious villains of the new seduction novels, but he seems to have had a deaf ear to Deborah's guidance, especially in matters political, where he was sorely in need of it. And there was nothing she could do about that. In fact, politics might have made him impervious to her advice. Although Revolutionary-era thinking about government as a voluntary contract had sparked discussion of egalitarian marriage, after the Revolution there was more emphasis on the bond formed by the granting of consent. Just as citizens delegated authority to their elected representatives, so did the wife consent to that of her husband. George and Deborah seem to have thought along these lines. But this had to have been a challenge for her, given her prior conviction of women's "equal if not superior Qualities."[19]

George's letters to Deborah reflected the mixed character of ideal late eighteenth-century marriage. At times he expressed an egalitarian affection and respect for her judgment. Announcing his imminent return from a trip, he declared that "I hope to have the . . . pleasure and inexpressible happiness of meeting you *my best Friend* & our dear little Son." But after pledging to "omit giving any instructions respecting our affairs at Stenton, having great confidence in your judgment," he proceeded to tell her to hire some help. This pattern of expressions of confidence in her decision making diluted by specific instructions continued years into their marriage. When he went to Europe in 1798, he made arrangements to leave her power to sell any property in his absence, should she deem it to his advantage "or your ease and happiness." Yet, he told her to "procure as much as possible the company of your Cousin Dickinson" and "attend to the Education of the Children." Son Albanus, whom "Mr Patersons family speak well of," should visit the Patersons in Philadelphia and, "during the summer vacation might accompany you to Jersey, or visit it himself." Algernon was to keep a journal, which George expected to be "*full & correct.*" And he gave her further instructions about farmhands and other business.[20]

It was not just when he was far away that he felt a need to instruct her. From nearby Lancaster he wrote, "On receiving this Letter, if the road will admit visit Philada: spend two days with our Uncle & in visiting your friends, take our Children with you." She was also "to visit Mrs. Smith" and "tell them Mr. Bingham is applying to the Legislature for an act of divorce on acct: of his daughter." To be sure, George was on the legislative committee to deal with this matter and needed information, adding, "*Write to me immediately on this subject.*" But did he need to specify that she was to spend two days with their uncle and in visiting her friends and should take the children with her?[21]

Some letters were entirely solicitous. "Pray my dear Girl make use of the advantages I gave you in placing my affairs in your hands, to make yourself as happy as possible," he wrote from England. "Keep all the servants as I left them, or change them for such as may be more agreeable to yourself," but "neglect nothing or no expence that may contribute to your *own health.*" Occasionally, he took pains to consult her views, as when, anticipating a Christmas recess from the state legislature in 1799, he suggested that she summon the boys home from their school in New Jersey so the family could spend a week together. But, he added, "I suggest this plan merely for your information & consideration should it not meet with your full approbation, it is not to be executed."[22]

Yet at other times, especially early in their marriage, he could be downright preachy. When visiting his brother in Virginia in 1783, George urged her to "keep good company" while he was gone. Soon after he repeated the instruction to seek the company of her "superiors," explaining that she was young and her manners not yet formed. He then added that she should stick to her books and cultivate her mind, else on his return he would spurn her. One wonders how Deborah—the sassy girl in whom Benezet saw leadership ability, the avid reader who continued her education in her father's library, the cultivated daughter of Mary Norris who charmed French diplomats—took this instruction. Not infrequently, George's requests come across as peremptory: "Please to send to my friend Tench Coxe *immediately* 50 copies of my last publication." And he always addressed his letters to Deborah—in accordance with his legal status as head of the family and owner of the premises—to "Dr Logan, Stenton, near Philadelphia," even though he, Dr. Logan, was the one actually sending them.[23]

While George could be condescending, Deborah played a role in shaping their marriage through wifely self-subordination. She left no records of ever challenging his authority and appears to have asked for his guidance. "I have this moment received my Dear Girls letter of Friday," George wrote in 1802. "I am sorry she should be perplexed a moment respecting our affairs." He then gave her his typically ambivalent advice, underlining for emphasis his instructions on what to do regarding their tenants, then concluding, "However you must judge for the best." He signed "Your best friend, Logan." And yet, in a nonconfrontational way, Deborah did what she wanted. George regularly asked her to come be with him in Lancaster, or, later, Washington, D.C., for example, and she never did. After a while, his requests on this subject became almost forlorn, as when he wrote, "Our friends Jefferson & Madison are well, they regret very much your not coming on with me. Several Members are accompanied with their wives."[24]

Deborah preferred to remain at Stenton while George pursued his political ambitions. This was not owing to a desire to remain with the children, since from an early age the boys were away at school. Given the course of his political career, she may have stayed at home to preserve their marriage. For her devotion was put to the test when George turned politician. Time after time, he engaged in projects that brought enormous criticism. Deborah always stood by him, despite doubts about his decisions. Perhaps Stenton provided a refuge for her and ensured that they would meet mostly on private and domestic ground.[25]

To begin with, in 1791 George was read out of the Friends Meeting for supporting the militia and distancing himself from the Society. This must have been painful to her, as she continued to attend Meeting by herself. Soon, his concern at what he perceived as a conservative Federalist counterrevolution during George Washington's presidency led him to a new activism, startling to many observers. Newspapers described him "like a Bedlamite escaped from the cell, brawling in every tavern against the government . . . and endeavoring to excite disturbances and tumult." Deborah's old friends thought this development must be a trial to her, but she put up a brave front. Like everyone else, she could not perceive the emergence of what we today take for granted as a legitimate two-party system. She disapproved his public criticism of Washington, but did not make a fuss. Then, as an avid—some would say rabid—member of the Jeffersonian Democratic opposition, George took it upon himself to go to France in 1798 to negotiate for peace at a time of great international tension. He was vilified as presumptuous or even treasonable by the Federalist press; Deborah herself deemed his quest "romantic." Congress responded with "Logan's Law," barring private citizens from entering into diplomacy with foreign powers.[26]

In her posthumous memoir of George, Deborah described his every step in France and included extracts from his letters, to vindicate him and his motives. But she seemed embarrassed by his actions. She did not hesitate to describe her anxiety at the time. "I could not help being appalled with a sense of the difficulties which he would have to surmount and the clamour which would be raised upon his departure," she wrote. "I was as completely miserable as I could be. . . . But I found it necessary, by a strong effort, to control my feelings."[27]

Although her letters as a young woman had dwelt more on courtship than the Revolution, the postwar matron was deeply interested in politics. The interest had been latent rather than acquired from her husband, since her mother, Mary Parker Norris, had long been keen on politics and young Deborah had sometimes indulged in political discussions with friends. There is no question that, in 1798, Deborah was intensely aware of the political dangers of George's "mission." Given the newly passed Sedition Act, the threat of his being named a traitor was real, and she noted several times her doubts that he could behave so perfectly as to be free from any accusations by the other party on his return. He was not a careful man, and she confessed in the *Memoir* that she "hardly dared to hope that he, 'who certain of the weight,' often disregarded 'the impress' of what he said and did, had been so cautious that spies and enemies would not be able to pick out something to accuse him of which they would deem criminal."[28]

Her anxiety only intensified during his absence. A Federalist friend warned that Stenton might be searched for incriminating papers. The Federalist newspapers kept up a barrage of attacks, even naming her. Jefferson visited her and advised her to show herself publicly, so as not to appear ashamed. She took his advice and went into Philadelphia, although it was not easy, as even old friends expressed their surprise at seeing her in public. The Federalist press, meanwhile, dropped nasty insinuations about what she and Jefferson did on his visit. That the Republican papers lauded her as the virtuous wife of a patriot did not suffice to quell the pain inflicted by the rumors.[29]

This was not the last of Deborah's trials as politician's wife, however, as George served in the Pennsylvania legislature from 1798 to 1800, followed by a term in the U.S. Senate. Although no one doubted that he was a good man at heart and sincere, he generally failed to impress his peers. Abigail Adams, for example, thought "Logan seems more fool than Knave." And then, Logan's Law notwithstanding, George took himself to England in 1810 to try to soothe the tensions that would ultimately lead to the War of 1812. Despite the obvious failure of this second private diplomatic mission, Deborah defended him again. But you can read her misgivings between the lines. Indeed, the *Memoir* chapter that recounts "Dr. Logan's Peace Mission to England" opens with this observation: "He declined a re-election to the Senate, which he might have obtained, and which I had reason to regret he had not accepted, as it furnished reflection and employment to a mind so devoted to the best interests of his country and of society that they appeared peculiarly his province, and that mind seemed to refuse to occupy itself with interest in less important concerns." If only he were safely ensconced in Washington, she seemed to hint, he would not have gotten involved in this second unsuccessful foreign mission. An avid newspaper reader, she must have been mortified at the way he was pilloried in the press.[30]

Fortunately, that was the last of his overseas adventures. But George, although clearly not a careful or savvy politician, continued to have an irrepressible zeal and energy to do what he thought was right. Deborah never doubted his motives, but she was by far the greater realist. The next year, for example, she wrote to her daughter-in-law that "Dr Logan has left home this afternoon upon another visit to Washington his uneasiness of mind on the prospect of Public Affairs is the inducement, I participate in his Anxieties, yet I wish he could leave things more, to this he says if it was a common time he would, but he thinks the Public good so much at stake that he makes it a matter of conscience to do what he can to save his country from an Abyss which he sees open to receive her if she deviates from the path of wisdom."[31]

Soon Deborah began to keep a diary that confirms her own interest in politics as it opens with a stream of comments on the War of 1812. Although she shared George's Republican leanings, she did not mince words about her disappointment in that party's leadership of the nation, referring, for example, to "the frightful imbecillity apparent in our Rulers." By January 1815 she was noting that "It is now talked of that both Parties will join to represent to the opiate besotted [last word crossed out] President [Madison], that his Resignation of his office is indispensable for the Public Good." Though always supportive of George, this was not a woman without strong political opinions of her own. Deborah also had her own work at this time, as she embarked on the huge task of transcribing the James Logan–William Penn correspondence and other historical manuscripts that she had found at Stenton. Interestingly, "Dr. L," as she generally referred to him, is not often mentioned in the diary, even though he was now home most of the time. When she did mention him, she hinted at reservations about his political behavior. When Thomas Jefferson wrote George to complain about his publishing one of Jefferson's private letters, for example, Deborah copied the letter and added, "I must own I am of the same opinion, and told my husband so on this occasion." But she quickly backed off from criticizing George, adding that he acted "without ever deviating from his accustomed truth and sincerity."[32]

Deborah was just not inclined to criticize George, or at least was not going to leave any criticism for posterity. She loved him, and sometimes wrote sweet vignettes indicating how much she enjoyed being home alone with him: "At home all day and uninterrupted by company. Dr. L and myself spent it comfortably together, before a good fire in his parlour." On another occasion, she noted that after tea "we sat in the twilight meditating, as if by consent—Dr. Logan took his flute, the air he play'd was in unison with my mind." He was clearly a loving husband. When she got ill on a trip, for example, "my dear Dr. Logan who was very attentive and uneasy about me" helped her to get "so much better, as to go on." She repeated this praise when she fell sick on another trip, asserting that "nothing could exceed the kindness of my dear Dr Logan, he watch'd over me with the anxious solicitude of a mother over her darling babe, and took neither Refreshment nor sleep till he saw me better." Needless to say, she appreciated his attentions.[33]

Deborah was certainly not going to criticize George in the travel portions of her diary, written to be shared with others back home. At most she was tongue-in-cheek, as when she described meeting a lady from New York: "I saw Charlotte eyeing Dr Logan very attentively and when he left the room she observed that his Phisiognomy and the make of his head bespoke a decided and remarkable character, and turning to me she said, 'Mrs Logan when your husband takes a Resolution to do anything, can he be diverted from his object?'" Winking to her niece back home about George's famous stubbornness,

Figure 12. Deborah Norris Logan (1761–1839). Oil portrait by Charles Willson Peale (1816). Stenton House Museum and Gardens.

Deborah added: "you may guess at my reply to this question." But she would not criticize him outright.[34]

Did she censor herself? She was so smart, so well educated, so interested in politics. By contrast, truth be told, he was a bumbler, if a well-intentioned one. He somehow managed to be both rigid in pursuit of his ideals and wildly inconsistent. The newspaper accounts of his diplomatic and other ventures contained far more scathing criticism than praise. How did this feel to her? She was not always happy, but she left no record blaming him. In her diary, she would write things like "to describe what has been the state of my mind of late, is a thing I cannot undertake" followed by words crossed out. Deborah and George were different in her desire to stay at home and his restless adventures in the public sphere. She sometimes went out with him to visit neighbors or to go to Philadelphia. They took an annual summer trip to New Jersey. But she loved above all else to be alone at Stenton, and often noted this right after he left the house. Diary entries like that for April 21, 1817, for example, are common: "Dr L., Algernon, and Debby went to town to meeting. I was left at home, agreeable to my own desire, and have been very tranquil and happy by myself."[35]

Deborah found "seclusion and quiet" essential for her favorite activity, writing. Because "Dr. L almost continually inhabits the Library, and I hate to be asked what I am writing," she complained that she could not write there. She lamented one day that she had not had time to compose a letter because "I cannot write agreeably to myself unless alone." The next sentence was heavily crossed out. Indeed there are very many passages crossed or cut out of her diaries. And although descendants may have been responsible for removing some pages, the cross-outs look like hers because they use similar ink to the entries and are consistent in style. They suggest that Deborah wrote, and then heavily censored, her own thoughts. Expecting the diary to be read by her descendants, she was not going to leave behind any expressions she thought inappropriate. Yet Deborah clearly used the diary as an outlet for her emotions before editing them to create the model she wished to leave behind. She had a great deal to say that she soon erased. Her feelings must have been complicated. The strikeouts often followed mentions of unhappiness that are not explained, pointing to some sort of struggle for Deborah. It might have been about her sons, or had some other cause or mix of causes. But it is likely that some of it described frustration with George, or even accounts of conflict with him.[36]

Despite mixed signals during George's political career, there is no doubt that the strength of Deborah's love for him grew over the course of his long final illness. It is painful to read her daily accounts of the ups and downs, not only of his health but also of that of her beloved niece Debby Norris, who lived with them. Deborah noted in March 1819 that she had been uneasy for several months about George's ill health, and was busy caring for him. But at first she was hopeful of his recovery. Three months later, she described the change his illness had wrought in her life: "constant attendance in the Chamber of my poor husband has prevented me from having much recourse to my Pen or noticing what is passing in the world around me." Although she claimed to be "happy if I can contribute to his welfare and comfort," she also noted that she could "do very little besides waiting upon and nursing him," implying that she could imagine doing other things. She grew exhausted by worrying about and caring for the two invalids, and gave horrifying accounts of the bleedings and mercury purges that her niece's doctor prescribed. Autumn came, and George and Debby were still sick. Again Deborah quietly noted her sacrifice: "In this situation of things I cannot chuse what my occupations shall be, but must put off employment that would be gratifying to myself to attend to duties." Deborah was not going to say more about this at the time, but later comments about true happiness being found in things intellectual and her being "famished as to intellectual food" suggest what she was missing during these long days in the sickroom.[37]

By the end of the year, Deborah began to lose hope about George's survival. She noted that "Dr L is better as to his health, but his constitution has undergone some shock which causes me to dread that he will soon leave us." George tried to make it easier on her. "Our own family continues in a distressing state but Dr Logans mind is happily quite calm," she reported a month later. "Never shall I forget the kind and grateful manner in which he received our attentions and the expressions of his affectionate attachment to myself. It has left a feeling of pure and holy tenderness which can never be effaced." George could not shield her from the obvious, however, and by February she wrote, in despair: "My husband's weakness is fully apparent it is increasing, and I cannot conceal it from myself."[38]

Deborah's days continued to revolve around the two invalids, keeping her from spending time "as agreeably to myself as I might . . . but it does not signify to complain." The only thing that comforted her was that George's thoughts had been turning to God. "A great change has taken place in many of his sentiments," she wrote; "in short . . . he is a Christian." By early April, the end was in sight. "Oh it is utterly impossible to describe the chaos of distress and care with which I feel myself surrounded" when faced with the realization that her "beloved husband will die." Anguished to "see his failure step by step," she wondered how she could "part from one who loves and values me as my beloved Dr Logan does?" Finding that "no words can express my feelings of tenderness, respect & unutterable love towards him; he seems nearer and dearer than life itself." In addition to appreciating his love, she also expressed her own. She felt tenderness and respect, even if she found it hard to put her own love into words. Naturally the idea of losing him caused the outburst, but her feelings had grown in depth and complexity. Confined to his bed, he could no longer embarrass her; confined to his bedside, she had the chance to repay his devotion to her. Her nursing may have absolved feelings of guilt about, even in his time of need, her desire to be alone to read and write.[39]

In his final days, George stopped taking food and was occasionally delirious, but calm. He knew the end was coming. Deborah and their two sons were at his side when he died on April 10. Then her emotional floodgates burst: "Oh my best loved and dearest earthly treasure, in thy loss; and in the severing of a union of nearly forty years, I feel that the world has nothing more to offer me since I have lost thee!" Having bemoaned her lack of time to write during his long illness, now she wrote, "I never found my pen so inadequate to express what I have felt."[40]

Deborah grieved for George for a long time. Through the summer she was busy attending to Debby and receiving visitors, but felt lifeless. "All my pleasant days were come—and gone," it seemed to her as she came home to an empty house after Meeting. '" She tried to get back into her domestic work but wrote that "there is no describing how lonely and miserable I am." Part of her grief seems willed, as when she noted after receiving visitors that "I reproach myself for being capable of feeling a temporary cheerfulness." She appreciated visits of sympathy best when friends would speak highly of George. But still, months later, she continued to note her unhappiness and the "void in my heart," or "a sense of loneliness . . . that nothing in this world will ever erradicate."[41]

Aware that George was constantly in her thoughts, she reflected that the anniversary of the death of their son Gustavus was not so painful as it once was and wondered why she could not accept this in her present situation. Instead, in September she marked their fortieth wedding anniversary and wrote that they had lived together "thirty nine years, seven months and three days . . . in a most happy union." In sum, "to look back it appears like a dream. What else is life?" After a while, she claimed to be tired even of recording her grief: "It is not worthwhile to note my own miserable sensations," she wrote, although she continued to do so. And this is only what we can read today, for she crossed out and cut out very many passages from the diary for the six months following George's death. Did she erase even greater effusions of grief? Did she give voice to more complicated feelings—regrets, or emotions of which she was not proud? We cannot know.[42]

Gradually, the pain began to ease. Deborah found some distraction in a nasty epidemic that swept through the neighborhood that fall, as she had much to do to assist her neighbors. She was also helped by the project she gave herself of writing her memoir of George. This was just the ticket for her. It involved historical research and writing. It allowed her to indulge her passion for politics—difficult now since her sons were not interested. It allowed her to think about and record the story of her beloved husband. But it also allowed her to shape that story in such a way as to refute any of the criticism that had been launched against him, and maybe to embellish his reputation a bit. Indeed, writing the *Memoir* allowed Deborah to create a George Logan that she could spend the rest of her life with. It was painful at first. She said she began "without animation, without spirits or pleasure, scarcely with sense or capability," but it contributed to her starting a new life on her own. Reminiscing may even have brought some pleasure. By November, she describes a day "alone in my dear Dr. Logan's parlour and not without my pensive enjoyments."[43]

Thus, after several years of mourning and depression, the fog lifted. Deborah lived for almost nineteen years after George's death and seemed to take a new lease on life after 1825. Inwardly, she pursued spiritual completion in preparation for death. But this could not quell her natural curiosity about other people. She herself was clearly interesting in old age, as she continued to attract visitors to Stenton. She loved spending time with her grandchildren, especially her granddaughters. She developed close relations with a number of young women (some kin, some not), some of whom lived with her for a time. She enjoyed their companionship. They must have loved hers, and her wise counsel.[44]

When not housing or entertaining young relations and other visitors, she pursued the history that she loved. For as her allusions to missing her writing while nursing her patients suggest, she had discovered her true calling in 1815 when she stumbled upon that cache of James Logan manuscripts in a closet. She considered the organizing and copying of these papers her most important work, although she also wrote and published, anonymously, a number of newspaper articles, biographical sketches of the founders, obituaries, and poems. She simply loved to write, often getting up early and settling down to it—in the dining room in winter, surrounded by plants, her dogs, cat, and pet birds; or in her upstairs library in the summer. Her work in preserving the manuscripts was of incalculable value. The Historical Society of Pennsylvania, founded at this time and then housed at the American Philosophical Society, made her its first honorary female member in gratitude. She modestly dismissed this achievement, just as she declined to publish her longer works during her lifetime. But one cannot help but think that her investment in writing was an act of self-preservation. She seemed to know we would be reading her "an hundred years" later, and to secretly want it that way.[45]

Given her expertise, visitors began to come to Stenton in search of historical information, especially John Fanning Watson, the Philadelphia historian, who began to call upon her in 1823. The two built a strong friendship in talking about the past, revealed in his constant references to her in his *Annals of Philadelphia*. He must have been thrilled when she gave him an old cane chair that she had found in the attic and had repaired for him. William Penn had given it to James Logan. Watson reciprocated, giving her a box made of four "relic woods," namely pieces of the "Penn treaty elm" and three other historic trees and buildings. Once again, however, Deborah Logan had to bite her tongue in embarrassment over the men in her life, for although she enjoyed Watson's visits, she was mortified about the many errors she found in his history. She nevertheless remained a loyal supporter publically, and when she died in 1839, Watson wrote a glowing obituary.[46]

But just as much as Watson needed her help, she needed him to talk history with. The older she got, the more she venerated the past. She might also have depended on him to get the stories out. Of course this was frustrating. Although she never said so, her mortification at his errors implies that she thought she could have done a better job herself. She, who as a proper Quaker woman only published anonymously, would have censored the thought. She had even refused the Historical Society's request to publish her *Memoir of George Logan* in 1825, although she allowed it to circulate. Still, it is hard not to imagine her thinking she might have written a better book than Watson's. In the confines of her diary, she regularly expressed pleasure when editor Robert Walsh published one of her pieces in the *National Gazette*.[47]

Nonetheless, Deborah continued to be hampered by her dependence on men, for despite the family's former prominence, George Logan did not leave her very well off. This came to light just a few months after his death, when she wrote that she was "very unhappy and fatigued with a thousand cares and distresses—among other things I doubt that my income is sufficient to maintain this large family in the way that we have been used to live." She did not want to deny anything to her ailing niece, and concluded that she knew "not what better to do than to use a decent economy, go into no new expenses that I can avoid," and trust in God. There was little else she could do.[48]

Ten years later, she was still perplexed. One day, after someone had come with a bill she could not pay, she wrote that "it is a weary life that I lead now." She then linked her present situation with George: "I have walked down to the enclosure and seen the verdant turf that covers the resting place of my beloved husband, and have more satisfaction in thinking that I parted with my last ground rents and Bank shares to relieve him from such kind of embarrassment as I now feel, than I should have in their reservation for myself—I rejoice that I promptly and willingly gave them up, and made his mind easy on such a score." The next sentence, heavily inked out, does visibly begin with "But." She may have been referring to property he sold to pay for his diplomatic ventures. In any case, Deborah continued to fret when presented with bills she could not pay.[49]

Actually, Deborah had not been completely alone in the decade after George's death, as her son Algernon still lived at home and did much to help manage her affairs. But when he died, she was truly alone. Her grief equaled that at George's death. In October 1836, now in her mid-seventies, she wrote, "I feel the loss of my beloved son in all things, and at present a kind of derangement of everything which he used wisely to control, has taken place, nothing seems to go on right. I feel my own inability to manage my affairs. I want help, essential help." But for all her dependence on men, Deborah clung to a degree of independence in holding on to Stenton. She only let her eldest son, Albanus, and his family move in and take over in the last months of her life. Perhaps, in her old age, she was learning to distrust female dependence on men. She began urging the young women around her to take steps to protect their own property before marrying.[50]

Financially vulnerable, never challenging domesticity, Deborah Norris Logan was nonetheless a full person intellectually. Consider her obituary, written by Albanus's wife, her daughter-in-law Maria Dickinson Logan: "Richly endowed by nature, with talents and genius of the highest order, and intellectual capacities surpassed by few, yet her well-regulated mind, conscientiously and faithfully attended to the performance of every duty, even to the minutest relations of domestic life, diligently laboring to redeem her invaluable time." Deborah's "heart was formed for love and *enduring friendship*," and "none more enjoyed the refin'ed & elevated companionship of congenial minds." The obituary ends with praise for her religiosity. What it does not do, beyond mentioning in the first line that she was the "relict of the late Dr. George Logan," is say anything about her husband. Of course Deborah survived him by many years. In so doing, she showed to others, if she did not observe it herself, that there was life for Deborah without George Logan, despite her doubts after his death.

In fact she was able to live her own life because she had already carved out a space for herself in her thirty-nine years with George Logan. He may have been a fool in the minds of some, but she chose to dwell, not without struggle, on his idealism and love. Given the circumstances, she was probably smart to do so. What would she have gained besides marital strife had she not opted for submission? George was no more likely to have been receptive to a wife who openly contested the gender roles of the time than was John Adams. Even these smartest of wives of the Revolutionary era, with the most caring and well intentioned of husbands, had to find other ways to cope with the gender constraints of their time.[51]

PART III

Striving to Succeed: Three "Self-Made Men" in the New Nation

Prologue

Most famous for birthing American political freedom, Philadelphia would also help lead America to growing economic independence. And this pairing was not incidental. As most Americans knew, Jefferson's invocation of "life, liberty, and the pursuit of happiness" was a slight rewriting of John Locke's appeal to the rights of man to "life, liberty, and property." Philadelphians would pursue property with remarkable energy in the decades following the Revolution. In colonial Philadelphia, economic dependency was a fact of life. British merchants and officials helped establish a flow of unfinished colonial goods to the British metropole, products that were to be re-exported to the colonies and the rest of the world when finished. And Philadelphia society itself was typified by patterns of economic dependency with servants, apprentices, and slaves composing much of the city's workforce. Late eighteenth-century Philadelphians started to cast aside these forms of economic bondage with hopes of rising in the world. But access to these opportunities was not equally available. The three figures in this part highlight some of the ways it was possible to achieve economic freedom.

The potential for riches was manifest in the rapidly growing city. While three decades after independence Philadelphia would be overtaken by New York City, it nonetheless experienced exponential growth. Shortly after independence, census takers found that about thirty thousand people inhabited the city. By the time of the Civil War, over half a million people called Philadelphia home. This rapid swell in population was fed by two major streams: foreign immigration and domestic rural migration, both groups seeking upward mobility. The labor market of Philadelphia became more dynamic as older forms of bound labor were abandoned. While in the middle of the eighteenth century almost one-half of all laborers were bound as indentured servants, apprentices, or slaves, by the end of the eighteenth century the use of unfree labor had collapsed. The benefits of this change were notable. Inspired by Philadelphia's own Revolutionary rhetoric, workers staked a claim to greater personal freedom. No longer did they have to live under the roof and obey the paternalistic demands of their masters. However, the shift toward wage labor also had serious difficulties. Changing labor practices were coupled with a growing capitalist economy. Masters were freed of the obligation of providing food and shelter, as labor became one more resource to be bought and sold on an open market. This could mean that some jobs, particularly unskilled ones, could not provide a living wage. Nonetheless, many chased the opportunities of the growing city. With shrinking available farmland and an increasingly competitive global grain market, young adults from the countryside took their chances in the city. And they came from Europe too. In particular, Germany and Ireland, experiencing economic and political crises, launched seekers of the American Dream to Philadelphia.[1]

The ideal of the self-made man was first and most forcefully advanced by the most famous of Philadelphians, Benjamin Franklin. Anticipating the experience of other migrants in the decades to come, Franklin had broken free of bound labor, fleeing apprenticeship from his domineering brother in Boston to seek his fortunes in his adopted city. It is not surprising, then, that Franklin would emerge as the model American. During the early republic Franklin's *Autobiography*, often coupled with his *Way to Wealth*, became the premier guide to self-made men. But Philadelphia's story is not just Franklin's story. In fact, his story was not even his story. Historians have shown how Franklin constantly recast his image to meet the expectations of his audiences. His record on slavery provides an example. While later in life Franklin would claim the mantle of abolitionism, thereby standing for Black economic self-determination, Franklin had spent most of his adult years profiting from slavery. So it is worth our while to consider the lived experiences of other noted self-made men, in order to get a wider view of the myths and realities of this archetypal American story in the era of capitalism's first major expansion.[2]

As an artist, Charles Willson Peale never amassed great personal wealth. But he did become famous. Like Franklin, he paid close attention to self-presentation. With a keen eye for dramatic displays, he was perhaps America's first great showman. First rising to prominence as a portrait artist, Peale would help establish "Peale's American Museum," a storehouse of biological wonders, including the skeletons of two mammoths he excavated from bogs in New York. Stephen Girard *did* amass great personal wealth, more than Franklin could have hoped to imagine. Girard is estimated to be the fourth richest American of all time. Working up the ranks, he landed in Philadelphia as a ship captain. Hampered by a British ship embargo during war, he relaunched his mercantile pursuits on land. Orchestrating the exchange of goods across the globe proved quite profitable, but renewed protectionism eventually drove Girard into banking, which is where he made his largest fortunes. Joseph

Hemphill, the least remembered of these three men today, was nonetheless well known in his own time, including by both Peale and Girard. Provided by his father with an education at the University of Pennsylvania, Hemphill then rose on his own to greater heights as a lawyer, judge, and congressman. He would cap his career by helping establish the production of American porcelain, serving as the chief financial backer and partner in the Tucker and Hemphill Company.

While the rags-to-riches ideal became a touchstone of American character, it also invited criticism. In fact, as early as the 1830s, French visitor Alexis de Tocqueville took stock of the psychic toll exacted by a nation full of people competing with one another. He suggested such competition could shrink the soul: "It is strange to see with what feverish ardor the Americans pursue their own welfare; and to watch the vague dread that constantly torments them lest they should not have chosen the shortest path which may lead to it." But these three men don't seem to have been driven by fear, nor do they seem to have thought only of their own self-advancement. Instead, they seemed to embody an expansive spirit unleashed by independence. In this, they exemplified another side of Benjamin Franklin, his restless spirit of volunteerism, his commitment to living "usefully" in service of others. Perhaps this civic spirit was first prompted by the absence of an established church and the void it left in social services and public works. But the commitment to volunteerism was given further emphasis by the very project of democracy. Only a prosperous and educated citizenry could be entrusted with self-government. These men would leave a legacy of civic-minded pursuits that have left a lasting imprint on Philadelphia.[3]

Put another way, these men were just as notable for their participation in nation making as in self-making. While political theorists and historians have sometimes posited that nations are "imagined communities," built on myths of shared origins or cultural stereotypes, when we look at life on the streets and in the homes of Philadelphia, we can see that Philadelphia operated as a real community, as a web of personal relationships. Though Philadelphia was rapidly growing, the people we will come to know in the final half of this book, just as those in the first half, knew and worked with one another, helping to create a shared identity. One of the key ways they did this was by partnering together to build the country in quite material ways. Whether they were making art, like portraits and china, or building roads, houses, and colleges, the nation became manifest in the growing material environment of the city.[4]

In paintings still displayed in American museums today, Peale helped create an American pantheon of founders. Stepping out of the studio, he created a

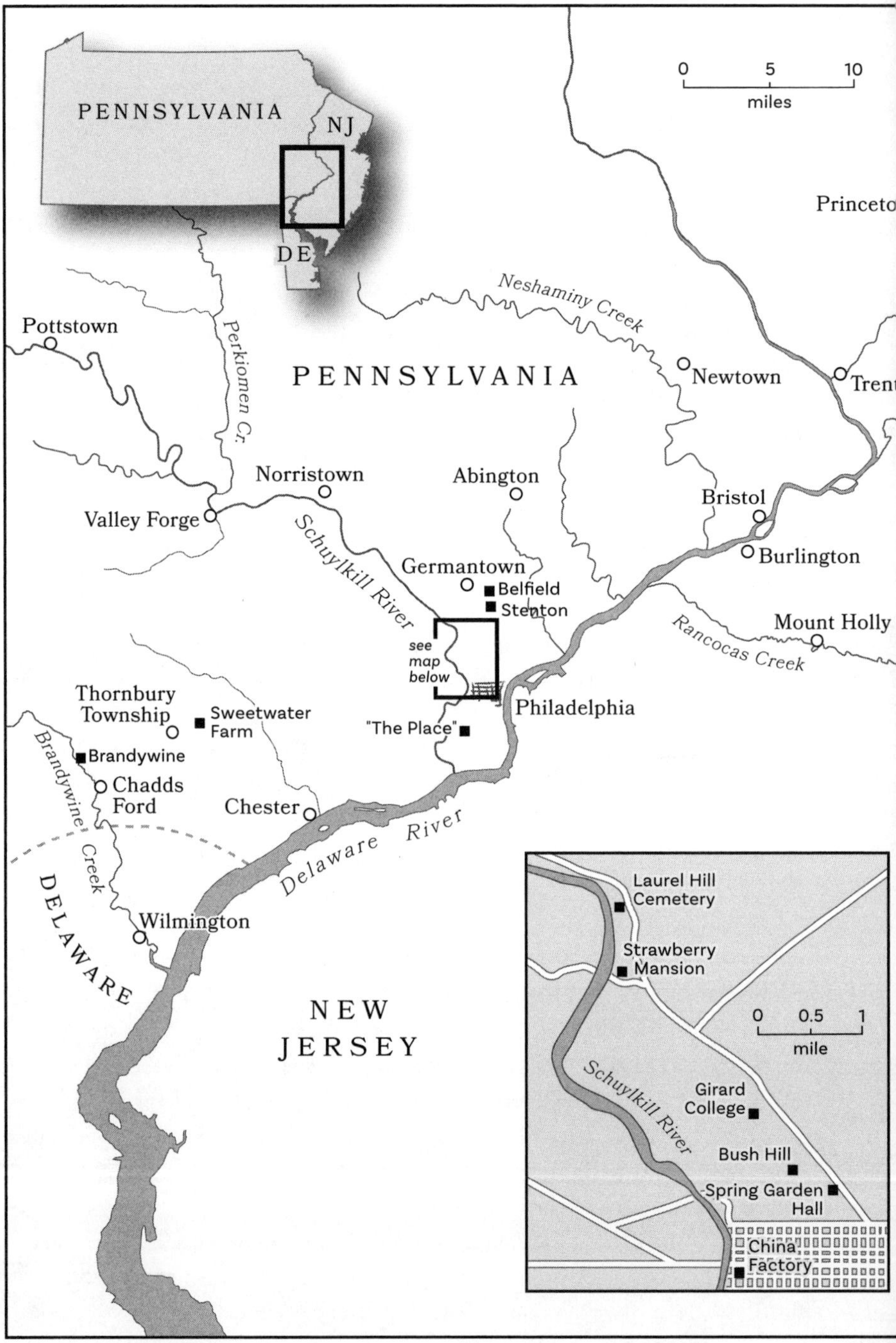

Map 3. People and Their Places: Three "Self-Made Men" in the New Nation.

Philadelphia

1 Christ Church Graveyard
2 Girard House
3 China Factory
4 High Street Market
5 Walnut Street Theater
6 China Factory
7 Arcade Building
8 Court House
9 Pennsylvania State House/ Independence Hall
10 American Philosophical Society
11 Library Company of Philadelphia
12 Hemphill Townhouse
13 Custom-House
14 Girard's Bank
15 Merchants' Exchange
16 Holy Trinity Cathedral Cemetery
17 City Debtors' Prison
18 Pennsylvania Hospital
19 Girard's "Philadelphia Rows"
20 City Alms House
21 South 2nd Street Market (Newmarket)
22 Peale House and First Museum

A St. Augustine's Roman Catholic Church
B Christ Church
C First Presbyterian Church

series of public art displays, celebrating significant events such as the return of Lafayette to Philadelphia. Countless Philadelphians would tour and talk about the wonders in his museums. Thus, he created a set of shared experiences that helped bond Philadelphia as a community. Girard's civic spirit was expressed through philanthropy. He gave generously during his life, supporting a wide range of institutions, including a Widows' Asylum, volunteer fire companies, public schools, and Gallaudet's school for the deaf. To the despair of his relatives, at death he left most of his inheritance to Philadelphia. He endowed the city with works projects and a school for orphans, known today as Girard College. Joseph Hemphill's dedication to the public and nation building was first expressed as a lawmaker. Serving in both the U.S. and Pennsylvania legislatures, he left his mark on the country by tending to the nation's legal and transportation infrastructure. As a Federalist early in his career, he helped establish the independence of the judiciary by protecting judges from political firings. Later, as a Jacksonian, he broke from his party by supporting the development of transportation networks. In later life he would leave a different sort of legacy. The wares of the Tucker and Hemphill Company would fill the homes of Philadelphians; many of them can be found at the Philadelphia Museum of Art today.

The British American colonies had been quite fragmented. In fact, those colonists who traveled were more likely to voyage to London than to neighboring provinces. They had very different economies, religious practices, and settlement patterns. The rice fields and plantations of South Carolina looked nothing like the family farm villages of New England. Historians have often wondered how a country composed of such disparate parts could come together as a nation. It is not surprising that Philadelphia, a pluralistic community from its very origins, would be central to knitting the larger nation together. These three men, while climbing the social ladder, built a material and cultural legacy for their country. In helping establish the terms of the American Dream, they helped produce a unique American identity.

CHAPTER 7

Charles Willson Peale

Idleness of all things is most disagreeable to Peale.

—Charles Willson Peale

Although he became famous over the course of his long life, Charles Willson Peale, the man who painted Deborah Logan—and, it almost seems, everybody else—was born in 1741 in decidedly humble circumstances. His father had fled a forgery charge in England, and served as a schoolmaster in Chestertown, Maryland. Peale insisted his father was "truly a good man," and well respected, though "his Income was low; as is too generally the Case with Teachers." In any case, Charles Peale the father died in his forties, when his son was only nine, and his widow, Margaret, was left to care for their five children "by her Industry alone."[1]

Like many another colonial widow, Margaret Peale moved the family to the nearest city (Annapolis) and began work as a dressmaker. Fortunately, a former student and family friend, John Beale Bordley, took the mother and children under his wing. Young Charles learned the basics at school over the next four years, and then, at thirteen, was apprenticed to a local saddler. Looking back, Peale praised his master's practice of paying him a little for work done "overtime," which Peale thought a good spur to diligent labor. But he criticized himself for spending his first earnings on a watch and a horse, rather than saving them: "To possess such property appears to be the too prevailing passion of American Youth." Here as elsewhere in his autobiography, Peale elaborated on his life story to instruct others, not unlike his contemporary Ben Franklin, whom he sometimes quoted. Peale hoped "that the overflowings of his heart on some such occasions in the course of his History will not be without its use." At the same time, he was painting word portraits—in the third person—of his curious, ambitious, and restless self. When the watch broke, for example, he decided to "try if he could not save the expense by repairing the watch himself, and in this attempt it may easily be immagined that he did the watch but little service, however by this essay, he acquired knowledge of the principles of such Machines."[2]

Restless also describes Peale's initial pursuit of his first wife, Rachel Brewer. He was just seventeen when he met her on a visit to her brother, a friend, and soon "Our Amorous youth," as he styled himself, began to call often. He thought her very pretty. Years later, he described her as an aging artist would, as small and fair, with long dark brown hair "which hung in curling ringlets, on her long beautiful white neck." With "her face a perfect Oval, she had sprightly dark Eyes, her Nose strait with some few angles, such as Painters are fond to immitate." Appreciating her modesty, affability, and piety in addition to her good looks, Peale pressed his suit, "having no greater wish than becoming the Husband of so fine a Girl." Unfortunately, he pushed too hard. After proposing, he pulled out his watch and gave her an hour to decide. When she refused to answer, he said good-bye. Chagrined, he made an equally quick and equally unsuccessful bid for another young woman, and then decided to reapply himself to his work. Not long after, he ran into Rachel in Annapolis. When he lamented the cause of his absence, she "informed him that he was precipitate, and that the manner of his treatment of her, did not deserve an answer." Chastened, the overardent swain begged her forgiveness and resumed the courtship. But still he could not slow down, and asked her to give him "a decisive answer" when he visited the next Sunday. Either Rachel decided she had made her point, or she was worn down by his pursuit, for, when Sunday came, "she finally agreed to accept him for her intended Husband." At least she did so in full knowledge of his irrepressible enthusiasm. Nor did he let up, as, now accepted, "let it hail, rain or blow, no weather deterred him from crossing South river & a Creek every week to visit Miss Rachel Brewer."[3]

Surely Rachel's caution was warranted since he was at this point only eighteen and still had two years to go in his apprenticeship. Given the circumstances, Charles leapt at an offer from his master to shorten the term by four months if he would take over the shop while the latter made a trip to Bermuda. He was soon crushed, however, when the master changed his mind about both the trip and the shorter term. Ever impetuous, and knowing that the original indenture had not been properly registered, Charles threatened to quit unless the saddler kept his promise. His master agreed.[4]

Charles was eager to finish his term because this would allow him to get married, and because he had long felt restive, "confined to the same walls and the same dull repititions of the same dull labours." He rejoiced in "the sweet, the delightfull sensations attending a release from a bondage of 7 Yrs. And eight months." Of course, work itself was not ended, as he now had to find a way to support a wife. While blessed when a friend of his father offered him twenty pounds to buy materials to set up his own saddlery, Peale made the mistake of letting his former master talk him into taking on a hundred pounds' worth of stock on credit. Peale thus began "in difficult circumstances." Nevertheless, he and Rachel were married in January 1762, and she came to live with him at his mother's house in Annapolis. He had not yet turned twenty-one; she was just seventeen.[5]

To support his new family and pay off his debts, Peale threw himself into the making of saddles and took on other jobs as well. He helped a carriage maker with upholstery. He began to make and repair watches and clocks. He also did some silversmithing, "such as making Buckles, Buttons, Rings &c." But he found it difficult to sell his saddles for cash as Marylanders were increasingly able to buy them on credit. Peale discovered a new line of work by accident. Visiting the rooms of an acquaintance while on a trip to buy leather in Virginia, he noticed the "miserably done" paintings executed by this man. Peale reflected later that "had they been better, perhaps they would not have lead [*sic*]" him to think he might do better, and thereby "smothered this faint spark of Genius." Instead, the occasion made him remember "that he had a great fondness for Pictures from his early youth, as when a School Boy, used to draw paterns for the Ladies to work after. He also now and then amused himself by copying a print, with Pen & Ink." After enjoying Milton's *Paradise Lost*, he attempted a picture of Adam and Eve. And when an uncle died, his grandmother had pushed him to "draw his picture from the Corpse." These memories unleashed, Peale was seized with the "Idea of making pictures."[6]

He tried a landscape, then a self-portrait. Soon he was painting his wife, his siblings, and a friend. These efforts were praised and led to a commission for the portraits of a local couple, for the sum of ten pounds. "And this gave the first idea to Peale," he wrote, "that he possibly might do better by painting, than with his other Trades, And he accordingly began the Sign painting business." Peale's descriptions of his start show just how much of a beginner he was. When he went to Philadelphia to buy paints, he realized he did not even know the names of the different colors, much less which he should buy. Accordingly, he found a book about painting in a shop and spent several days studying it before completing his purchase and returning home. Back in Annapolis, he made a deal with one of the few painters in the area, John Hesselius, for instruction. In return for a saddle, Hesselius agreed to let Peale watch him paint. He also executed half a face and asked Peale to complete the other half. Peale learned a good deal from this session, which "infinitely lightened the difficulties in a new art."[7]

Peale also made his first foray into politics at this time. Together with other tradesmen, he joined "the Sons of Freedom" against the "Court" party of the proprietors and their cronies in the highly contested Maryland election of 1764. Instantly, he was hauled into court for debts owed members of the Court party. To escape imprisonment, he was forced to leave Rachel, now pregnant, and flee to New England. Peale blamed himself for his quandary. It was not that he had wasted time and money in "Taverns, or any other kind of Extravigances." He had worked hard. But he had taken on too many different pursuits and thus "allowed himself no time for reflections of any kind. He did not seem to regard the future, being wholly occupied with the present." Or so he felt looking back from old age. In Boston he met John Singleton Copley, the sight of whose "picture-room" was to him "a great feast." But Boston not seeming to promise any business, he headed home. But he could not remain there for more than short periods, owing to continuing threats from his creditors. He finally got a break in the form of a group of wealthy sponsors who sent him to England for further artistic training. There he received encouragement and advice from fellow American Benjamin West, and strove to master "the whole circle of arts," including modeling and casting. He spent three years there, returning home in 1769.[8]

The venture had been valuable, but Peale was glad to get home to Rachel, especially since their baby, James, had died in his absence. He was happy to gather the family under one roof, including his mother and brothers St. George and James. He taught his brothers to paint and they all "lived in the utmost harmony together," inspiring Peale to begin a famous group portrait. To help support the family and retire his debts, he took advantage of a number of commissions in Philadelphia, and gradually persuaded Rachel to move there. In May 1776, he rented a house on Arch Street near the river, not far from Christ Church, which he began to attend. The family had moved in time for him to hear, along with Debby Norris, the Declaration of Independence being read in the State House yard.[9]

Peale found lots of painting business in Philadelphia. With the onset of war, officers wanted to pose in uniform and many people wanted miniatures for loved ones. John Adams toured his painting rooms at this time and admired what he saw, although he was sure Peale was not as good as his Boston fellow citizen Copley. He nevertheless described Peale to Abigail as ingenious, as well as friendly and affectionate.[10]

Although far from warlike, as Adams noted, Peale caught the patriotic fever. He had espoused the American cause from the start of the conflict with Britain. Now he joined the Philadelphia militia and was soon elected lieutenant of his neighborhood unit. Peale spent a great deal of energy "mothering" his command, at one point making moccasins from a couple of cowhides for his shoeless men. He was at Trenton and the Battle of Princeton, while his family fled, temporarily, to quarters he had arranged at Abington, northwest of the city.[11]

Once back in town, he found himself involved in politics. Peale was a radical and supported the very democratic Pennsylvania constitution of 1776, opposing any alteration, especially while the British were marching on Philadelphia. He was active among the radical Whigs, and was soon called upon for a variety of political duties. This suited his "busy, active Character" to a T. It also made him vulnerable to arrest once the British succeeded in occupying Philadelphia in the fall of 1777, so he kept on the move, in part by going back and forth between the army (soon at Valley Forge) and his family, which fled to new quarters outside Philadelphia. He rode through Trappe a few times in the course of these movements, and therefore contributed to the parade of wartime traffic in front of Henry Muhlenberg's home.[12]

Although he was happy to support the cause, some of Peale's political duties were unpleasant. First, he had to visit and put on parole men suspected of loyalism, and some of these were old friends. In the fall of 1777 he was appointed to the Council of Safety charged to secure the property "of such Citizens as had joined the British Intrest." The redcoats' evacuation of Philadelphia in June 1778 made it possible for him to begin this "very disagreeable office." It was thought expedient to start with the most important cases first, and this is what brought him to Grace Galloway's door, since Joseph Galloway had been the leading local official for the British. In his autobiography, Peale described finding the house locked on his second visit, and, after seeking authorization from Revolutionary authorities, breaking in by a back door. He thereby truncated his description of the process of evicting Grace, which, actually took a number of visits. Peale tried to mollify Madam Galloway, by bringing Benedict Arnold's elaborate coach to receive her and fetching her bonnet and work basket from upstairs. But she scorned his efforts. When he offered to help her into the carriage, she told him he was the last man on earth from whom she would want a favor. She spurned his arm and got in by herself, threatening to sue.[13]

While it was a way to serve and also to profit (he was supposed to get a 5 percent commission on sales of forfeited property), Peale hated this work. He was able to quit in 1779, when he was elected to the state legislature. By this time, he had become fully embroiled in the intense political strife between radical Whig defenders of the state constitution, such as he and his friend Thomas Paine, and conservatives, such as financier Robert Morris, whom the radicals thought were profiting from the war. Peale attempted, not always successfully, to keep a damper on outright violence between the groups. In any case, his election to the assembly was part of a sweeping victory for the radicals. He even shifted adherence from Christ Church to the First Presbyterian Church as befit his radical allegiances.[14]

Peale was not so discriminating in his true vocation, for all the while he was busy painting Revolutionary figures of all parties. He painted prominent men of science and the churches, too, including Henry Muhlenberg and William White. Soon he had enough portraits of notables to build and open a gallery at his new family home at Third and Lombard Streets. The skylit sixty-six-foot-long gallery that adjoined the house was the first such building in the United States, and with its forty-four paintings of Revolutionary leaders, arguably the first American museum. The scope of his body of work was distinctive compared to other American painters. Because the colonies and infant United States lacked sufficient patronage for large history paintings or landscapes, most artists earned their living by painting portraits for those sufficiently affluent to thus commemorate their family lines. Peale received commissions for a number of such portraits. In addition, he is known today for some more complex and playful paintings of his family and himself in his museum. Yet the bulk of his work consists of the portraits of the leaders of the day, lined up side by side in his museum.[15]

The need to pay for this new home and the recognition that painting was the only way to do it, as well as his dismay that politics inevitably earned him enemies, made him resolve not to run for reelection to the Pennsylvania Assembly. He would likely not have been successful anyway, given a resurgence of the conservatives. Despite his decision to quit direct political involvement, Peale remained connected to politics through his art. His Revolutionary paintings were not confined to the mostly head-and-shoulders portraits of leaders. Many more Philadelphians saw his various efforts at public art in the cause. In 1780, he made a double-faced effigy of traitor Benedict Arnold, which, along with a figure of the devil, was paraded around the streets in a cart, publically mutilated, and burned. The following year, news reaching Philadelphia of Cornwallis's surrender at Yorktown, Peale covered all the windows of his house with transparent images of Generals Washington and Rochambeau and other scenes from the war. Lit from behind at night, they created quite a spectacle, and attracted a large crowd. He would produce these large transparent paint-

Figure 13. Charles Willson Peale (1741–1827), *Self-Portrait with Angelica and Portrait of Rachel* (ca. 1782–1785), Museum of Fine Arts, Houston.

ings on various occasions over the next several decades for the State House and other buildings.[16]

Peale's biggest such effort was the Triumphal Arch commissioned by the Pennsylvania Assembly to celebrate the signing of the peace treaty with Britain in 1783. He was proud of the result: three painted wooden arches the width of Market Street, decorated with columns, statues, and festoons of flowers, the whole forty-six feet high. It had been a huge undertaking. Unfortunately, the spectacle began with fireworks that were set off too close to Peale's varnish- and oil-rich transparent paintings; the whole thing caught on fire and was quickly consumed. Nancy Shippen had thought it was going to be a "grand display," but instead "the Explosion . . . was the largest bonfire that was ever seen in Market St." Peale himself only escaped by jumping from the back of the structure, suffering fractured ribs and burns that kept him in bed for several weeks.[17]

The injury was for a good cause. The new nation that was being born had little in the way of common traditions and symbols to bind its different parts and peoples together. With different religions, nationalities, and even languages in the mix, ingredients for incipient nationalism were sorely needed. "Invented traditions," such as parades and festivals commemorating aspects of the Revolution, would play a big role, and Peale would be the first important provider of décor. In his countless images of Washington, use of classical imagery, and Latin mottoes such as the one over the ill-fated 1783 arch—which translated as "By divine favor a great and new order of the ages commences"—Peale helped shaped America's self-image.[18]

Unfortunately, this was the beginning of an era of difficulty for Peale, though he met every setback with his characteristic optimism. Lying in bed with his burns covered with various ointments, he remarked on the lesson learned from his servant boy, also burned. The latter, left to himself while the family attended his master, simply splashed his skin with cold water from the well. Peale cheerily noted that the boy's healing much faster than he did proved the superiority of cold water for burns. Peale's greatest difficulties, as ever, were financial. He did not get fully reimbursed for the expense of building and rebuilding the Triumphal Arch. The government was also slow to pay him the commissions earned by his Council of Safety duties. People did come to see his gallery. Nancy Shippen visited with her brother, Tommy, and other friends in 1783; she visited again with friends in 1786. George Washington toured during the constitutional convention and sat for one of the many portraits Peale would paint of him. But Peale still needed to make more money. He thus tried to replicate a project pioneered in London: moving picture spectacles. These consisted of a series of decorated tableaus with moving parts and sound effects. The subjects ranged from a scene of Market Street changing from day to night to the dramatic naval battle between the *Serapis* and the *Bonhomme Richard*. Unfortunately, these shows did not bring the desired income. Peale's problems were compounded by the general postwar recession, and a decline in his portrait commissions as wealthy Philadelphia conservatives, miffed at his politics, favored competing painter Robert Pine.[19]

Financial need was surely an incentive for Peale's next venture, but the form it took was a natural outgrowth of his restless curiosity and democratic tendencies. At the suggestion of his brother-in-law, in 1786 he decided to add natural history exhibits to his portrait gallery and turn it into a museum. This was an age of science and the educated had striven to put America on the map by locating and classifying American species. Elite figures had long shared their "cabinets of curiosities" among themselves. But Peale proposed to throw his collection open to the public, for a modest admission fee.[20]

Friends began to present Peale with specimens that required preservation if they were to last; so he threw himself into experiments in taxidermy. Since "he had no acquaintance that could give him any instruction how . . . he had recourse to Books." Through trial and error with various techniques and preservatives—some fairly toxic—he gradually succeeded. This and the study necessary to arrange and classify the specimens ate up time he might have spent painting, and thus he remained in economic straits. Peale rationalized that his museum would be a benefit to the public, and, eventually, to his family. The reality was that his enthusiasms carried him away from the steady pursuit of earnings. In a moment of self-knowledge, Peale noted that while the museum as yet brought little gain, "the gratification which every new object produced in the mind of an enthusiastical man, is all powerful."[21]

It was not that he cared little for his family. In the midst of these labors, for example, when he realized his sister was dying, he secured portrait commissions in Maryland that allowed him to spend time with her. Unfortunately, Rachel, pregnant for the eleventh time, caught cold on this trip, and her health steadily worsened. The difficult decade was capped by her death in April 1790. Rachel had been Peale's patient and loving partner for twenty-eight years. Peale was bereft, and sat with her body for three days before allowing her burial across the street at St. Peter's Church. In later years he explained that he knew of cases when people were declared dead prematurely, and this was why he did not bury her right away, even though he admitted that it was clear in her case that "the powers of nature" were drained.[22]

This devotion notwithstanding, the fifty-year-old Peale was soon in search of a new wife. In May 1791, he married twenty-six-year-old Elizabeth de Peyster of New York, whom he met when she visited his museum. Peale had been struck by her maternal quality on this first meeting, and his impression proved true as his children took to her from the start. The affection was mutual. Peale later recalled that he urged her to go to her family in New York with their baby during the yellow fever epidemic of 1793, but she insisted it was her duty to care for his children in Philadelphia. While the majority of Philadelphians left the city under this scourge, the Peales did not. Charles did take the precautions advertised in the newspaper—keeping his family at home, sprinkling the rooms with vinegar, and periodically shooting off a gun indoors. Betsy still came down with the fever, but Peale nursed her back to health. He claimed not to have undressed or slept more than snatches during the two weeks of her illness.[23]

Betsy proved a good partner over the next two decades, as Peale left off painting to expand his museum. Not only did he continue collecting native specimens everywhere he went, often with the aid of sons Raphaelle and Titian; he soon began exchanging duplicates for European specimens with a variety of individuals and European societies. To put the museum on firmer footing, in February 1792 he invited a group of prominent men, including William White, to serve as trustees on a board of visitors. Peale hoped that these men would help him get government support owing to the educational qualities of the museum. He wanted it to become "a great National institution." After a number of meetings, however, he found that gathering the group had taken more time than warranted by the results.[24]

Meanwhile, the museum on Lombard Street grew. In addition to the long skylit gallery, Peale added a smaller room for the moving picture exhibits and bought the lot next door for the museum's growing menagerie. The house was typical of others on the street in combining work and family space; such was the case with the baker, grocer, and coach maker who were his neighbors. Manasseh Cutler of Massachusetts was charmed by the museum when he visited in 1787. He liked the historic paintings and portraits and was awed by the many animal specimens artfully arranged in natural scenery. He described the pond filled with stuffed fish and waterfowl, "all having the appearance of life," animals large and small "in the thickets and amongst the rocks," and trees "loaded with birds—some of almost every species in America." Cutler doubted that "Noah could have boasted of a better collection," and marveled that Peale's specimens "were all real—and finely preserved." As the collection grew, and encouraged by the American Philosophical Society (to which he was elected in

Figure 14. Philosophical Hall, which housed Peale's Museum, 104 South Fifth Street, Philadelphia, Pennsylvania. Wikimedia Commons.

1786), Peale adopted a more formal Linnaean classification and separation of his specimens. He exhibited many of them in glass cases arranged below his paintings (for one thing, he could not keep visitors from touching the arsenic-filled objects). But the space was increasingly cramped. Peale purchased property on Third Street south of his home and asked the legislature for a grant to build a building there. He was refused. But a friend mentioned that Philosophical Hall, the American Philosophical Society building adjacent to Independence Hall, was becoming available. Peale secured an advantageous ten-year lease.[25]

Peale moved his family and museum from Lombard Street to Philosophical Hall, still standing on Fifth Street, in 1794. In typical Peale fashion, "to take the advantage of public curiosity," he made a show of the move itself. He got all the boys of the neighborhood—"as Boys generally are fond of parade"—to march between the old and new museums with his artifacts. This amused them and advertised the new museum. Peale patted himself on the back for thus saving on moving expenses, and claimed that the boys succeeded in bringing "all the Inhabitants to their doors and windows to see the cavalcade."[26]

The family's now vast array of exotic and domestic live animals was settled into what became a popular little zoo in a fenced enclosure behind Philosophical Hall. All except, that is, the bald eagle, who lived in a cage on the roof. This bird was so friendly with Peale that it would "utter cries expressive of its pleasure on Seeing him" approach the building. The zoo was practical in that it provided future specimens; as the animals aged and died they became fitting subjects for mounting inside the museum. These included, eventually, Peale's friend the eagle, still perched to greet visitors today—though now in silence—among Peale's paintings in the Second Bank of the United States. Some animals did not make it into old age. When a bear broke into the cellar of Philosophical Hall in the middle of one night, terrifying the family, Peale entrapped it there and shot it the next morning. Then he went to the cage and shot its mate. They were soon mounted together.[27]

Needless to say, Peale loved all these new projects. In later life he claimed that he was happy to jump into anything that might be for the public good, but he clearly enjoyed losing himself in his endeavors, whether staring into a bush for hours on an insect-collecting jaunt or writing pamphlets on such varied topics as a new way to make wooden bridges or how to preserve one's health. He recalled that "his next hobby horse on which he rode as hard as on health or on bridges was that of curing smoky Chimnies," which led to his getting a patent for his improvements on fireplaces. Peale was not alone in these interests, as other Americans were also advancing transportation and mechanical improvements at the end of the eighteenth century. But Peale was surely among few—Franklin and Jefferson come to mind—in the breadth of his interests. His wives must have been good-humored to accommodate his ever-changing passions, especially when few brought significant remuneration.[28]

Activity was a drug for Peale. He turned to it to relieve boredom, and also to endure grief. Hating the time wasted in traveling, he always tried to have something to do, employing one protracted trip to Baltimore to make brass screws to extend the length of his drawing pencils. When his son Titian died of yellow fever in the fall of 1798, despite Charles's diligent effort to nurse him back to health, the grieving father tried to cope "by keeping himself constantly employed in making necessary things" about the house, painting new portraits, and nursing others. Peale had been proud of eighteen-year-old Titian's talents and application in taxidermy and painting; he thought the young man would make the museum great through his collecting efforts. It was a heavy loss. Titian's death occurred while the family was in New York, where Peale worked on installing six of his efficient fireplaces in the almshouse and one for his father-in-law. In addition, he "painted 14 Portraits & 5 miniatures, preserved near 30 Animals of different sorts besides his labours with the sick." Peale concluded that he could leave New York "saying that he has not been a lazy man."[29]

All this activity notwithstanding, Peale needed to find a way to make more money. He began a series of lectures on natural history, based on museum specimens. Once again, attendance was such that "he did not get all the advantages he expected." Yet Peale always looked on the bright side. He asserted that these lectures "made him a gainer in the end, for they encreased his knowledge." It was "his sincere opinion" that the study of animal species "must elevate in the mind to a most exalted Idea of the wisdom manifested in the variety of forms," all contributing to "the universal harmony of the world." This was not just Peale justifying himself in later life; he wrote pages at the time describing his awe at the perfection of the system that showed "the wonderful hand of an allwise & providential power!"[30]

Peale's next venture did pay off, both intellectually and financially, for it would contribute to knowledge of the mastodon and eventually draw in visitors to the museum. After reading newspaper reports of the discovery of mammoth bones in a New York swamp, he determined to go see and describe them for the American Philosophical Society. He ended up buying the bones and the right to dig up the remainder. After securing a loan from the society, enlisting President Jefferson's aid in getting a pump from the navy, and gathering supplies, he embarked on the enormous task of draining the pond in which the initial bones were found. Through trial and error over the course of a week, he and his workmen contrived a wheel to pump out the spot with buckets, but this was only the beginning of their work, as they had to battle the ever-encroaching mud to get at the bones. Peale being Peale, he got some young onlookers to walk the wheel pump for free, and when he woke up with a sore shoulder one morning, marveled at how lucky he was to have to labor for a living, for walking the wheel himself made the pain and stiffness go away. The lessons learned in this experience expedited the collection of two other sets of bones at other bogs nearby. After returning home to Philadelphia, Peale and his workers delighted in the jig-saw puzzle exercise required to fit the first mastodon skeleton together and fill in gaps with wood or papier mâché. This skeleton went on display at the museum. Upon completion of a second, sons Rembrandt and Rubens set off to exhibit it in New York and London, but not before having an unusual celebratory dinner for twelve, within the skeleton.[31]

In 1802, the Pennsylvania state government having relocated (temporarily it turned out) to Lancaster, Peale was granted use of the upper story of the State House/Independence Hall for his museum. In addition to the mammoth, another new attraction was the "physiognotrace," a silhouette-making machine invented by Peale's friend John Hawkins. Peale set his slave Moses Williams to work making the silhouettes. Moses did well, producing nearly nine thousand silhouettes in his first year, and netting $700. This convinced Peale that Moses could support himself, a requirement for manumission under Pennsylvania's gradual abolition law. Peale accordingly set Moses free. The twenty-seven-year-old promptly bought a house on Front Street and moved in with his new bride, Maria, formerly the Peales' cook.[32]

What else did visitors encounter when they climbed the State House stairs to the museum? They arrived, first, at the center hall, which contained instruments for demonstrations of electricity and later would be the performance site for a variety of chemical and other experiments. Thus scientific education, one of Peale's main goals, began from the start. It continued in all the remaining rooms, where thousands of animal specimens were identified by Linnaean classification and their Latin, English, and French names. The "Quadruped Room" contained displays of larger animals grouped in natural settings. Here one saw specimens from North America, such as a bison, an elk, and a grizzly bear, as well as more exotic animals, including a great anteater, a sloth, a llama, a musk ox, an orangutan, and many monkeys. The main gallery, the Long Room, which ran across the front of the building, contained, along the south or back wall, 140 glass cases in which over a thousand birds were mounted in natural poses against painted backgrounds. Above the cases were hung a double row of Peale's portraits of famous Americans. On the north-facing wall, tall glass cases projected into the room between the windows. These held an array of smaller items, such as insects, minerals, shells, and smaller fossils. Microscopes were mounted above the smallest specimens, to continue the scientific engagement of the visitor. The final room was the Marine Room, with displays of larger shells and a variety of fish, amphibians, and snakes. Three rooms in Philosophical Hall displayed the mastodon skeleton (with that of a mouse at its feet, to show the scale), other archaeological finds, and recent inventions.[33]

The museum came into its own in the new setting and enjoyed its years of greatest success. That it was lit up at night was another popular novelty. But all these positive developments were offset by a great loss, as Betsy Peale died in childbirth along with their last child, in February 1804. William Shippen was among the doctors called to this final difficult delivery, but their efforts were fruitless after the infant son, too large to be delivered, caused Betsy's uterus to tear. She expired as a last-ditch surgery finally extracted the boy. Peale mourned her as a loving wife, especially lauding her mothering of his older children by Rachel. One comment gives a glimpse of what she had had to put up with: "Although there was a disparity of years between them, yet they lived together in much harmony for many years, and when the expences of erecting a Museum called for all the funds that he possessed added to his constant manual labour, which consequently deprived him of the means to live in a more fashionable stile which accords with the Idias of a youthful mind, and are attra[c]tions to bring togather more wealthy and gay visitors, these are illusians that do not often produce the happiness attached to such associations." Peale went on to describe the requirements of true happiness, ending with the "virtue of forgiveness." The passage is cryptic—does it hint of early disappointment on Betsy's part with his demanding and eccentric lifestyle?[34]

Peale resolved to do everything he could to raise their children, including a son named after the deceased Titian, to become "good and useful members of society—If I cannot give them riches, at least I shall endeavor to make them deserve well from those connected and interrested for and with them in whatever situation chance may place them." In fact, Peale had always been an engaged father. His fond hopes for and interest in his children began with his naming them after famous artists at birth. He then included and trained them—boys and girls alike—in his various artistic, collecting, and museum pursuits. Daughter Sophonisba even joined some hunting expeditions.[35]

As his sons attained adulthood, Peale tried to set them up in various ventures, whether by dispatching Raphaelle and Rembrandt on tours to exhibit the mammoth, sending Raphaelle on a trip to Virginia to make silhouettes, accompanying Rembrandt to Washington to paint portraits, funding a later European trip for Rembrandt by commissioning him to paint portraits of famous Europeans for the museum, painting portraits himself in exchange for cotton for Franklin and for the second Titian's mill, or getting Titian appointed assistant naturalist for a western expedition. Rubens, meanwhile, learned to manage the museum when his father was absent, and pleased his father by mastering type composition for the small printing press Charles had purchased (both to do museum printing and "that his children would thus acquire a knowledge of the printing business which might be advantageous to some of them"). The children generally went along with their father's plans, even if they did not always succeed at their endeavors.[36]

Of course Peale missed Betsy, and claimed to be reminded of her by "an hundred objects daily." Characteristically, he dealt with grief by burying himself in work. He tried, unsuccessfully, to sell his polygraph, or copying machine, and was turning back to painting, inspired by the success that Rembrandt was starting to have in this line. But a distraction occurred in the form of Hannah Moore (a Quaker cousin of Deborah Logan's), whom he met when she was having her silhouette made at the museum. After a determined courtship, she consented to marry him in August 1805. Charles, as usual, was in a hurry, "seeing no reason to delay a business which had been well considered, and finished would enable him to attend to manifold labours in the City." Still, he was sensitive to her needs, insisting that his children write to welcome her and cooperating in a successful campaign to persuade the Society of Friends not to expel her for marrying him, a non-Quaker. Charles was delighted in Hannah's attention to his younger children and found her "the most affectionate of Women." His only complaint was that she refused to kick her habit of taking snuff.[37]

Peale's older children were marrying and becoming more independent, and he wanted to retire to the countryside to pursue longevity and the rustic life. So he gave up management of the museum to Rubens, also thinking it would make the young man more ambitious. He then retired to Belfield, a farm he purchased in Germantown, with Hannah and the younger children. But this did not slow him down. He decided to take up farming, though he had no experience of it. He tried to learn from managers and neighbors, and admitted that his "farming was not economical"; still, he enjoyed making "machines for very many uses." As always, his inveterate optimism carried him through disappointments, at least in retrospect, as when he thought he needed to make some contraption to keep the door to the milk house shut, to keep it cooler. He worked on this, but meanwhile the butter was not good, and then he learned from a tenant's wife that the milk house needed to be open and airy to make good butter, "and thus he was relieved from his difficulties of making contrivances to keep the door closed. And the butter much improved." He thought himself clever in cutting down weeds before they went to seed rather than pulling them up by hand, despite the sore arm he got in doing so, until he discovered to his dismay that this only made their growth more profuse. "Thus he experienced a double mortification, a sore arm and a loss of labour. But Perseverance was his motto," and soon he was trying another idea. He had also turned to building and then tinkering with his mill. Peale admitted that these various experiments were "great follies . . . except that while contriving and making them it afforded him amusement." Then the garden "became his hobby-horse," including various ornaments inscribed with moral sentiments on the walks. A "hobby-horse" of a different sort was his bicycle—also called the "fast walking machine" or "pedestrian accelerator;" that the seventy-something-year-old made and used for exercise. All the while, he continued painting. When Deborah Logan visited his painting rooms at Belfield with her niece in 1815, they admired three portraits just recently finished. Three years later, she gave in to her family's repeated urgings, and sat for her own.[38]

However vigorous, Peale worried about the disposition of the museum at his death, and sought to have it taken over by the state or the city. These efforts unavailing, he traveled to Washington in 1818–1819 to try his luck with the federal government, stopping in Baltimore to see the museum his son Rembrandt had started there. He soon learned that Congress would not take over his museum either; he would end up incorporating it to prevent dissolution by his heirs. Still, he came back with fifteen paintings of politicians—including President James Monroe—for his gallery. He was proud of his continued ability to paint in old age. He also returned having seen perhaps the first North American velocipede (another early type of bicycle), and promptly commissioned a Germantown blacksmith to make one for himself, which he and his grandchildren then rode around the streets of Philadelphia, to the amusement of onlookers. Then, back at Belfield, he gloried in his ability to work all day helping to build a milldam.[39]

Peale's luck gave out in the summer of 1822, when, after having ridden his velocipede hard to Germantown to complete an errand and be back in time for dinner, he fell ill. He gradually recovered from the fever over the space of five weeks, under the constant attention of his children and nieces (Rubens hardly left his bedside). But he suffered the loss of Hannah, who fell sick soon after him. She had not, as had Peale, refused the administration of calomel or salts of mercury; perhaps this more violent treatment hurt more than it helped. Deborah Logan wrote her obituary.[40]

Indeed it was an unlucky time for all. The Panic of 1819 had triggered a severe depression. Small businesses were hit especially hard. Rubens Peale headed to Baltimore to try to revive Rembrandt's failing museum, and Charles moved back to Philadelphia, boarding with the newly married Titian, to resume charge of the Philadelphia museum. To help restore his finances, he began to make porcelain teeth (after years of experiments with animal teeth and ivory to supply family and friends). When Rubens's Philadelphia house proved difficult to sell, Peale bought it himself and fitted it up for painting and teeth making. He labored prodigiously over the latter, trying to make protodentures that would be comfortable and lasting, but profited little, because he was not satisfied with the results. His children urged him to do work that was less taxing and more remunerative, but he was drawn to such projects he thought promised good for humanity. In any case, Deborah Logan thought the eighty-year-old still quite vigorous when he visited her in the spring of 1822. She later remarked: "I think I never saw any one wear quite so well." He had rented out, and then sold, the farm at Belfield.[41]

The year 1824 brought a welcome period of celebration in the form of the triumphal visit and tour of the Marquis de Lafayette. Anticipating the old Revolutionary hero's arrival in Philadelphia, Peale, as on like occasions in the past, prepared transparencies to adorn the museum windows in the State House. When Lafayette arrived in the city, Peale wrote to invite him and his party to make a private visit to the museum. Peale did not record the tiff that occurred between him and the event planners, whereby he was left out of all arrangements for the visit. The City Council had ordered the museum closed on the day Lafayette was to process to the reception on the first floor of the newly renamed "Independence Hall," but Peale advertised tickets to watch the procession from the museum's windows. This annoyed the planners, who wanted to preserve the dignity of the occasion. The day of the celebration, only his family gathered at the windows, and then came down to watch from the stairs as the elderly general entered the building. Noticing Peale, Lafayette strode across the hall to embrace his old wartime friend before any of his handlers could respond. Lafayette insisted on Peale's attending the reception and other events, and visited both the museum and Peale's studio at home.[42]

Peale must have been gratified by this chance to relive old times with a Revolutionary compatriot, as he was entering a phase of old age that psychologists today call "life review." He had started on a series of self-portraits in 1822, including the famous *The Artist in His Museum*, and then, in 1825, his autobiography. Some have suggested that Peale wrote about his accomplishments in an effort to deal with a traumatic event in his personal life. This had been the case when he penned an earlier fragment in his fifties. The trauma of 1825 was something he barely mentioned in his memoir, the death of his eldest son, Raphaelle. Indeed, Peale made no mention of Raphaelle after the latter had reached adulthood. Family letters hint at a stormy relationship that Peale declined to discuss in his autobiography. Still, the evidence is fragmentary, leading to contrary speculations as to what had been the matter. Some have gone so far as to suggest that Charles slowly poisoned Raphaelle out of jealousy over the latter's painting talent; others assert that Raphaelle, an alcoholic, was his own worst enemy. In any case, Raphaelle's life was a mixed success in the conventional sense, although Charles's brief mention of Raphaelle's premature death at fifty included the son's consolation to his father that he died content knowing that he "never did Injury to any man." Charles's brief mention is telling: "He has to record the death of his eldest son Raphaelle, the talents of whom have been mentioned in a former part of this history, and he will only say that he died at a premature stage of life, and that he possessed a heart of universal benevolence." The terse "he has to record," and "he will only say," nevertheless speak volumes about the pain of this relationship.[43]

This was clearly a time of reminiscence and self-assessment for Peale. In addition to the self-portraits he also painted a fond likeness of his brother James reading by lamplight. In compiling his autobiography, he worked closely from the diaries and letters that he had kept faithfully from his youth. Indeed, he often simply extracted from them, leading to many awkward transitions. Peale was thus confident that he was telling things like they really were and reminds us that he was not simply working from a perhaps faulty memory. As the irregular mentions of Raphaelle demonstrate, however, he avoided discussion of family problems and disputes. His editors also suggest that he shaded the truth on occasion to avoid hurting others. His refusal to relate the tiff over Lafayette's reception shows that he did not care to rehash conflict or blame others, even to defend himself. Endearingly, he did identify many of his own "follies," even if he did not explore their literal and emotional expense for others, especially his wives and children. His resolutely secular tale avoided such introspection.[44]

Although Peale did not complete or publish his autobiography before his death, he clearly wished that it would be read by and be useful to posterity. He knew that the efforts of his pen could never equal those with his brush, and struggled with the prose and organization of his memoirs. When he sought his friend Deborah Logan's help, she was candid, and approved his plan to get help with the editing. She thought that the work contained "materials which if dressed to advantage would be quite entertaining," but "of the style . . . it is to be hoped alteration and correction will both be bestowed upon it before it is given to the public."[45]

Deborah's main concern, however, was that she thought he was too easy on himself regarding his part in the Revolutionary-era confiscations. Logan admired her "old friend" Peale and enjoyed his visits and conversation. She also thought him remarkably vigorous (the eighty-six-year-old walked the five miles out from the city to Stenton to dine with her). Nevertheless, on his Revolutionary activities, she was his toughest critic: "I knew beforehand what part of his public conduct required the most apology, and I believe, that a good natured man as he is, must often have reflected in himself severely for having been the principal executioner of severe decrees upon the wives and families of those Tories who had left the city with the British army: taking possession of their forfeited estates etc.—which occasioned many scenes of severe distress—and which nothing, not even party excitement, ought to have induced him to have taken a part in." Deborah complained that "the author has got over this as lightly as he could, but it would have been better more fully to have avowed that this part of his conduct had been the occasion of deep regret to himself (as I am sure it must)."[46]

Peale was not able to finish the autobiography, or attain two other late-life goals: one, of remarrying and reestablishing his own household (Titian and his family lived with him at Rubens's old home on Walnut Street); and second, of moving the museum to larger and more commercially viable quarters in the fashionable new Arcade building being erected on Chestnut Street. The eighty-six-year-old swain fell ill when returning home from a courting visit to a New York widow, and the museum did not move to the new building until six months after his death in February 1827.[47]

Although he did not bring these final projects to completion, or indeed many others over the course of his long life, Charles Willson Peale was surely an early American success story. Those who enjoyed his public art, visited his museum, or chewed with his teeth certainly appreciated his efforts at the time, although the government at all levels maintained a laissez-faire response to his appeals for support. On hearing of his death, Deborah Logan was sad to note that he also failed to reach another goal: that of living to one hundred. But she was sure that "his love of the arts and zeal for their promotion will cause him long to be remembered." And she was right; generations of Americans since have certainly been the richer for the legacy of his wonderful paintings.[48]

So what was the secret to the success of this self-made man? Surely Peale's incessant curiosity and hard work were crucial elements. Not only was he hyperactive; just as important were his perseverance and positive attitude. It bears remembering that his success was not always or even often apparent at the time. His life was a struggle. He never stopped working, but he enjoyed every minute. At one point he rather piously observed in his autobiography that "I hold it as a divine favour that we are required to gain our support by the sweat of the brow, and I do solemnly aver that no man can enjoy happiness without he practices some useful employment." But he mostly came across, in the words of one biographer, as a perpetual boy.[49]

Although Peale died in 1827, his museum, the nation's first, would continue to be a must-see attraction for some time. He would love the fact that his paintings now hang less than a block away from where they were first displayed, in the Second U.S. Bank building—on the spot where Debby Norris's house stood, with the beautiful gardens where Anthony Benezet tended his vegetables.[50]

CHAPTER 8

Stephen Girard

My actions, must make my life.

—Stephen Girard

Compared to Charles Willson Peale's perpetually sunny outlook, Stephen Girard's was partly cloudy, and sometimes downright stormy. And yet he was early America's foremost success story—at least in terms of wealth—and one of the United States' greatest citizens, in terms of wealth given away. His life story illustrates some of the risks and possibilities of the early American economy. His choices for the use of his fortune after his death still shape the city today.

Like Anthony Benezet, Girard was an immigrant from France. Born in Bordeaux in 1750, he was the second (and first to survive) of ten children and the eldest son of Pierre Girard, a decorated sea captain engaged in trade with the West Indies. His later home of Philadelphia might have reminded him of his birthplace. Both had narrow streets of brick houses near the waterfront of a large river (in the French case, the Garonne) well inland from the ocean. Étienne, as he was called in France, did not have an easy childhood. The house was crowded, as four brothers and four sisters followed him. He was blind in his right eye from an accident in early childhood and was teased for its fish-eye appearance. He thus became a bit of a loner.[1]

Young Étienne was educated at home and then, at ten, began work in his father's mercantile office. It was there that he began to learn how to conduct long-distance trade. But tragedy struck when his mother died two years later. His relationship with his father turned turbulent. So it was perhaps to everyone's relief when he went to sea at fourteen as a *pilotin*, or apprentice officer. This was a challenging and thorough training in all aspects of seamanship, covering the functions of sailors and officers alike. The teenager continued this apprenticeship through several more voyages. It was probably for the best since the family situation did not improve. Pierre remarried when Étienne was seventeen,

Figure 15. Stephen Girard (1750–1831). Etching by Albert Rosenthal based on oil portrait by Bass Otis. Library of Congress.

and the boy disliked his stepmother. Moreover, she, a widow, brought four more children into the marriage, and then she and Pierre had three more. Étienne must have felt that there was literally little room for him at home anymore. He did not know it at the time, but when he left on a voyage to the Caribbean in 1773—as a twenty-three-year-old newly licensed captain—he left for good. He sold the goods he had taken on credit at a loss, and did not return to Bordeaux for fear of his creditors. Étienne kept in touch with his family, but for the most part only through direct contact with his younger brother Jean.[2]

The young sea captain spent the next two years sailing between French ports in the Caribbean, New York, and New Orleans. He began to realize the importance of shipping mid-Atlantic wheat and beef to islands devoted almost solely to sugar plantations. But he came to Philadelphia by accident. During a voyage northward in the spring of 1776, high winds and waves damaged his ship and three of four hogsheads of water were swept overboard. His crew was concerned, and so, at the end of May 1776, Girard cut the trip short and put into the Delaware River.[3]

The city's population was still concentrated in the half dozen blocks along the Delaware. The best houses, like those of Deborah Logan's mother, Mary Norris, or the Galloways, had gardens surrounded by brick walls. The spires of Christ Church and the State House could be seen from the river, but public buildings were still few. For merchants, the main gathering place was the London Coffee House at Front and Market Streets. There sea captains returning from foreign ports would share maritime news; a book was kept for them to note items of general interest. Newspapers from several cities were available, and merchants seeking or offering cargo space would post notices there. Girard, like other merchant sea captains, would naturally go to the coffee house for news. Unlike Charles Peale or Debby Norris, however, the French mariner took no notice of the declaring of independence in front of the State House that July; he was too busy repairing his ship. But with wartime shipping hampered by the British blockade, he soon settled in the city as a minor merchant and shopkeeper. His stock of simple wares served as a hedge against the inflation and currency deflation brought on by the war.[4]

Stephen was living at a waterfront boardinghouse when a serving girl, young Mary Lum, caught his attention. She was the orphaned daughter of a poor shipbuilder from the Northern Liberties. But she was also a black-haired, creamy-complexioned beauty with a lovely figure and smile, and the chunky five-foot-six, one-eyed and red-haired Frenchman was smitten. What happened next happened fast. Stephen always did things his own way, and so the twenty-seven-year-old duly married the eighteen-year-old three weeks after meeting her, in June 1777 at St. Paul's Church (on Third Street south of Walnut)—but only after a trial four-day tryst in the countryside. Such an order of things was likely facilitated by her fatherlessness. The Girard family was cool to this union when they were first told of it, perhaps because of Mary's humble background. But Stephen's brother Jean changed his tune immediately after meeting and being charmed by Mary in 1781. The two exchanged many friendly letters and gifts thereafter.[5]

During the British occupation of Philadelphia from the fall of 1777 to the summer of 1778, the Girards, like many others, left town. They moved to and kept shop in Mt. Holly, New Jersey. (The house still stands, at 211 Mill Street.) Upon their return, Stephen rented a house and shop in Water Street just north of High (Market). That fall, in order to do business in the city, and likely heartened by the new American alliance with France, he went to the Philadelphia Court of Common Pleas at the State House/Independence Hall to swear allegiance and become a citizen of the new Commonwealth of Pennsylvania. Although he thus placed his bet on the colonies' winning their independence, Girard cannot be said to have become a warm patriot. He did not participate much in the war. He tried a little privateering, but it did not pan out well. Beyond that he was content to pay the periodic two-pound fine for not responding to the call to join the militia.[6]

Unlike many others, Girard did not suffer financially during the war, but his profits were modest. In early 1779, he wrote to his father that he had amassed some $6,500 in capital, along with the Mt. Holly house, an enslaved boy, and part ownership of two ships. This was a bit exaggerated—he was writing to his father, after all. He also wrote that he loved Mary despite her lack of fortune and was living very happily. Girard continued to make economic progress despite an unfortunate four-year trading partnership with Polish officer Joseph Baldesqui. Baldesqui spent more time chasing women than business, and so Girard ended the partnership. He operated independently for a few years, often cooperating with his brother Jean, now headquartered in St. Domingue. In 1783, the war over, Jean came for a long visit to Philadelphia. He and Stephen became partners for a few years. The brothers were only two years apart in age and could be very close and confiding. When apart, they wrote often. But theirs was a complicated relationship with dramatic ups and downs.[7]

Despite occasional reverses, Girard drove himself in his work and did very well in the 1780s. Indeed, the more easygoing Jean was frustrated with Stephen's ambition, telling him, "You will always be the same—never content." Stephen developed an uncanny ability to anticipate what goods would be in demand where and at what price. He smuggled goods into St. Domingue and got shipments of food to France during a period of famine. He also proved adept at overcoming inconvenient tariff barriers. In the case of one ship, for example, he provided the captain with a set of papers claiming French ownership under Jean's partner in St. Domingue and another set claiming the ship was American and owned by Stephen Girard. The captain was instructed to use whichever set made the ship duty-free in a given port.[8]

Whatever the exact proportions of hard work, ambition, ability, and willingness to take risks (including that of dodging laws) account for Girard's success, it cannot be said to have been a formula available to or equally efficacious for other Philadelphia merchants. There were some, like Girard, who came to the city with little and prospered. But there were many more who failed or only succeeded on a much more modest scale.[9]

Wealth did not guarantee happiness for Girard since he was soon having difficulty at home. Life with Mary became difficult after 1785, when she began having violent tantrums. Girard tried to be stoical at first, telling his brother "no one can live in this world without having some troubles." He sought medical help and curative trips to the countryside, but nothing worked. Neighbors witnessed the sounds of her screaming and breaking furniture and assumed she had turned to drink. Jean attributed her supposed mental illness to her disappointment at remaining childless. Both explanations are plausible, and surely Girard himself was disappointed by the lack of children. But Mary was probably unhappy at Stephen's obsession with work as well. In any case, Stephen soon began seeking companionship outside his turbulent marriage. In 1787, he took a mistress, a young and pretty Quaker tailor named Sally Bickham. She moved into his home as his housekeeper.[10]

Sally's portrait testifies to her good looks. We do not have a picture from life of Girard (one was painted soon after his death), but know that he was of average height and sturdy build. At age thirty-seven, he wore his hair in a queue and powdered, though this would become unnecessary as he grayed naturally. His descendants insist he was handsome, but, given his unfunctioning right eye and the infrequency with which he smiled, this may be doubted. He was neat and well-groomed, but cared little about his clothing. Like wealthy Quakers, he opted for quality fabrics but simplicity of style. An enduring monument to his frugality, moreover, can be seen in the pairs of darned and re-darned socks on display today at Girard College.[11]

Sally's company notwithstanding, Stephen still felt a need to get away from Mary. She now slept all day and raged all night, depriving him of rest. At this point he claimed to hate her, and with doctors' help began to give her opium to calm her down. He also asked Jean, now his partner, to take over his business in Philadelphia for a while in 1787 so he could make a trip to Charleston and France, his last to the country of his birth. He did not visit his family in Bordeaux, for fear of meeting old creditors, and so he did not hear of his father's recent death until he returned to Philadelphia. Much to the dismay of Pierre's other children, the father's will named Stephen his primary heir. He did not inherit much in the end; most of his share went to satisfy his Bordeaux creditors. But in the struggle over the estate his relations (and many would-be relations) learned of his own wealth. They would pester him ever after for assistance. He rarely replied. He did become thoughtful about wills and estates.[12]

Returning to Philadelphia after the trip to France meant returning to the problem of Mary. He tried sending her to Mt. Holly with her mother and sister and then set her up in a series of Philadelphia boardinghouses, but nothing worked. Her erratic behavior and loud complaints continued. And yet Stephen hesitated to send her to live at Pennsylvania Hospital, at Eighth and Pine Streets. If he did that, he would not be able to divorce her and start a new family, since her lunacy would be deemed incurable, and the law forbade divorce under those circumstances. He would thus continue without the prospect of a legitimate child and heir. These considerations give the lie to the few speculations, then and since, that Mary was not really mentally ill when Girard had her committed. But those who knew her scoffed at this idea. Girard had run out of options for her care and had her committed in 1790, with the approval of three of Philadelphia's most prominent physicians. Girard was lucky that the nation's first hospital was just a mile away from his home. Conditions at Pennsylvania Hospital were not great, but the physicians and Girard concurred in wishing to use as few restraints as possible at a time when chains and straitjackets were the norm for unruly patients. She was allowed to move about the hospital grounds, at least initially. A big surprise occurred when the previously childless Mary gave birth to a daughter in March 1791, six months after her admission. Stephen insisted that he was not the father. It is not clear who was, but Mary was likely impregnated in the months before her admission when she was roaming waterfront taverns. Baptized Mary and sent out to nurse, the baby girl died at five months (a not uncommon result of wet-nursing). Her mother lived on at the hospital in what are known today as the East Wing and West Wing of the Pine Building until her death in 1815, at fifty-six. Girard saw to her care to the end (he was also the hospital's largest benefactor), although he did try, unsuccessfully, to obtain a divorce. Mary Lum Girard is buried on the hospital grounds, under one of the current buildings.[13]

The wife- and childless man got some comfort from the upgraded housekeeping of Sally Bickham and the presence of her appreciative younger brother, Martin, who became his protegé. But he probably did not give much comfort in return. He callously described Sally to his brother as someone "with whom I amuse myself at very little expense and when I have the time." He may have kept Sally at an emotional arm's length; at the very least there was his obsession with work. The young woman had to content herself with spending his money, decorating his home, enhancing his meals, and improving his wardrobe. A visitor took note of her household authority, writing, "She seems to be very much obeyed, for everything she said was a law." Later, when her brother moved out of the house to start his own firm with Stephen's help, she may have been lonely. She knew that Girard could not marry her. So she found a new man and married him. Girard did not reveal any jealousy or disappointment. Instead, he paid for her trousseau. But he did not feel any long-term obligation either. Later, when she was a poor widow, he refused to help her.[14]

If Stephen Girard showed only modest warmth within his own household, we can imagine how he behaved with his business associates. At a time when a man's reputation was generally crucial to mercantile success, his lack of an easy sense of humor, or even a store of small talk, was at the least a handicap. Indeed, at the time that he had Mary taken to the hospital, it is hard to imagine that his Philadelphia neighbors held the taciturn Frenchman with the unorthodox domestic situation in much esteem. Rival merchants did not like his exacting ways. They probably envied his success. Some contemporaries simply noted his lack of refinement and indifference to high society. A lack of fluency with English was probably long a social barrier. One merchant said that Girard retained his "peculiar French accent" to his death. Whatever the cause, he rarely socialized with other Philadelphians of his class. To the extent that he entertained, it was generally other Frenchmen. He must have been more relaxed among speakers of his native tongue. Other Philadelphians could only speculate about him. Thus, for a long time, any good that Girard did went unnoticed by his peers. Few knew or appreciated, for example, how many young men (from France, New Orleans, and St. Domingue) he trained, housed, or educated. Often unhappy, he buried himself in work.[15]

The first boost to his reputation occurred when, in 1793, he aided many refugees from the Haitian Revolution. It was further buoyed soon after, when yellow fever struck Philadelphia. The fever broke out among poor dock workers in Water Street, about a block away from his home. As it spread, citizens panicked. Most Philadelphians with the means to flee the city—about a third of the population—did so. Girard instead responded to Mayor Matthew Clarkson's call for volunteers to meet at City Hall. Most officials of the federal and state governments had decamped. The scenes of death and abandonment were appalling. Girard rolled up his sleeves and volunteered for the worst job of all, that of cleaning up and staffing the improvised hospital out at Bush Hill, an unoccupied mansion located in the area between Sixteenth and Nineteenth Streets, between Spring Garden and Fairmount Avenues. When associates reproached him for neglecting their business, he replied that "it seems to me that the condition of our city offers a sufficient excuse for the neglect under which the affairs entrusted to me have suffered lately." He assured his correspondents that his own affairs suffered too, and that any spare moments were spent looking after their concerns.[16]

It is hard to know what motivated Girard in this crisis. He may have been exorcizing grief or guilt over his handling of Mary, or simply lonely for human connection. According to him, it was to "have the satisfaction of having performed a duty which we owe to one another." It was also characteristic of Girard in stubbornly going his own way. He had little faith in doctors and disagreed with their idea that the fever was contagious. Nor did he like their dramatic treatments of bloodletting and purging. He once asserted that "I object to employing doctors, not from motives of economy, but to preserve the health of patients." And yet, judging from his later acts, he may also have wanted the esteem of fellow Philadelphians that he could never win with personal charm. In any case, he applied his passion for work to bringing order out of the chaos that he and his partner, Peter Helm, found at Bush Hill.[17]

Girard also recruited a young French doctor, Jean Dévèze, who shared his skepticism about the theories of the Philadelphia medical establishment and his alternative ideas about the need for cleanliness and a simple diet. When other doctors refused to work with Dévèze, Girard stuck by him. The team performed miracles at the hospital in terms of efficient and fairly effective treatment at minimal cost. Girard personally attended many of the sick and dying, finding no task too offensive. Dévèze described how he went from bed to bed, administering care, only stopping to grab a bite of food when necessary and then rushing back to his work. When a patient got sick on him, he calmly cleaned him up, administered his medicine, straightened his bed, and went on to the next sufferer. Another witness described him half-carrying one of the stricken out of a house "in . . . the very hotbed of the pestilence," to take him to the hospital. That winter, the epidemic over, the city thanked them. Dévèze thought the thanks inadequate. Nevertheless, Girard volunteered again in the yellow fever epidemics of 1797 and 1798.[18]

Girard's heroism in 1793 made him known in Philadelphia, and he continued to be active in public life thereafter. Only now he became interested in politics, especially foreign affairs. Britain and Revolutionary France were at war and both sides wrought havoc with American shipping. As the stronger naval power, Britain's interruptions of American commerce were greater, and Girard remained loyal to his native country. He therefore chaired a public meeting at the State House yard (behind Independence Hall) in March 1794 to demonstrate against British depredations and demand a government response. Six thousand people turned out, but their resolutions were only partly heeded. Congress did begin to build a navy to protect American shipping, but President Washington pursued a treaty with the British instead of a more aggressive approach. The infamous—because too conciliatory—Jay Treaty that resulted prompted another public protest meeting. Girard was again among the leaders. These efforts prompted the Democratic-Republicans (the Jeffersonian party that was emerging in opposition to Washington and John Adams's Federalist administrations) to nominate Girard for a local office, a seat on Philadelphia's Select Council. He did not prevail the first time, but did so in 1802, two years after Jefferson won the presidency. He sat on the council until 1819. He also served as a port warden for twenty years, and invested in the waterworks at Center Square, where City Hall stands today. Thus, his managerial and business acumen were of great value to the growing city as Girard gained a deeper connection with his adopted town.[19]

Girard may have felt grateful to Philadelphia, for the reality was that he had grown rich there. In the early 1790s he experienced losses as Britain and France harassed and confiscated American ships, but after British supremacy became clear, Girard was more careful and prospered as a neutral trader. Some say the secret to his success lay in a combination "of caution with boldness in action." It cannot be denied that, given the complexity of his increasingly far-flung trading—among India, China, the European continent, and the Americas—Girard's hard work and scrupulous attention to detail were essential to his success. This was at a time when transatlantic voyages took weeks or months, and merchants sent multiple copies of their letters and orders on different ships, in hopes of one reaching its destination in timely fashion. He was well served by the carefully chosen agents in foreign ports who kept him informed of both economic and political conditions, and the well-trained apprentices whom he entrusted with his ship's cargoes. It must be added, however, that, when necessary, he used gifts to obtain favors in port. And he engaged in the illegal but highly profitable sale of opium to China. Whatever the means, he was undeniably successful. Already by 1794, when he converted his bookkeeping from pounds to dollars, he was worth approximately $200,000, and his wealth kept multiplying thereafter. The forty-five-year-old immigrant from France had clearly "made it." In 1795, he built a substantial five-story brick home with an adjoining countinghouse-store on Water Street.[20]

The brick house was not fancy, but it was substantial. Its location, on the east side of Water Street just north of Market, was very close to his old dwelling on Water Street, only even more convenient to his business, as it practically backed on to the one-hundred-foot-long wharf he built. This area is covered today by Interstate 95 and Columbus Boulevard (formerly Delaware Avenue). But a model of the house, as well as Girard's furniture, his two-wheeled gig, and other belongings, are all on view at Girard College. The first floor consisted of a private office, center hall, dining room, and kitchen. The hall and dining room were paved with black and white marble in a diamond pattern, which made them cool in the summer. In winter, an oriental rug was laid in the dining room. The drawing rooms upstairs were furnished with simple but elegant imported chairs and tables and decorated with marble statues. Girard's simply furnished bedroom was on the third floor, with other family bedrooms on the fourth. Servants and apprentices slept in the attics.[21]

Sally Bickham was there for the building of the mansion, but after she left, the housekeeping and mistress role went to laundress Polly Kenton. She decorated the house in her turn and took Stephen to a new level of luxury in his standard of living. Like Sally Bickham, Polly exerted considerable authority over the household. Of course, there were limits to the degree of luxury that Girard would allow. While hundreds of other wealthy Philadelphians rode in four-wheeled, enclosed carriages, for example, Girard drove himself about in a two-wheeled "gig," "the plainest and least comfortable" one in the city, according to an observer. And even then, he mostly walked. Still, he must have appreciated Polly's efforts on his behalf since he reciprocated with gifts of jewelry—although others have speculated that he did so because he appreciated her sexual favors, or because she ceased asking for wages. She must have treated him well, for he tolerated the presence of her four sisters and two nieces in his home.[22]

The household expanded again in 1803 when, after Jean died, at fifty-two, Stephen took in his brother's three young daughters. Their mother, whom Stephen detested, had become an alcoholic. The girls were aged nine, six, and four when they arrived. Polly helped take care of them, but they did not remain long. Girard sent them off to school. Overall, he took his responsibilities as guardian uncle very seriously, and the girls were well provided for.[23]

In addition to the diversions supplied by Polly and others in his household, Girard always made time for books. Although his formal education had ended early, he had a lifelong habit of self-education, probably nurtured by long months at sea. He especially enjoyed reading the Enlightenment philosophers, and had a complete set of the writings of Voltaire, his favorite. He also was a regular borrower of books from the Library Company, of which he was a member. So the library at Fifth and Library Streets, across from Philosophical Hall, must be added to his circuit.[24]

Another important comfort in Girard's life at this time takes us to a more distant point three miles southwest of his Water Street home that was nevertheless on his daily route. This was his farm, "the Place," in Passyunk (present-day Girard Park, at Twenty-First and Shunk Streets). This was not the country retreat of a gentleman of leisure. The land, at that time well south of the city limit and situated near the confluence of the Schuylkill and Delaware Rivers, was fertile. It allowed the savvy businessman to exploit the opportunities for truck farming presented by Philadelphia's market stalls; at the same time, it allowed the French native to grow some of the quality fruits and vegetables and raise some of the prize beef and chickens that were hard to find in his adopted home. After failing to secure a competent farm manager, Girard took over himself, putting in long hours of work after mornings in his counting house. Girard loved working on the farm; late in life he proclaimed it his only amusement. He was proud of the praise he received from the Horticultural Society of Pennsylvania. He even grew a profusion of flowers. The farmhouse, still standing, was built in 1750, and Girard added the middle and west sections in 1800 and 1825. He had two stalls in the South Second Street market (Newmarket), where his excellent produce always enjoyed a rapid sale.[25]

British and French harassment of American shipping having continued and previous measures failing to stop them, President Jefferson secured passage of the Embargo Act in 1807. It was widely hated for cutting off all U.S. overseas trade. Since the foreign trade that had made Girard rich was now stifled, he, like many other American merchants, began seeking additional investment opportunities at home. Girard also began to "domesticate" his foreign holdings, withdrawing his funds from the Baring Brothers firm in London, since he feared losing them if the United States went to war with Britain. He might have invested in early industrial enterprises such as textile mills that other Americans were pursuing, but he was too cautious. Instead, despite his strong pro-Jeffersonian Republican loyalties, he rejected his party's principled opposition to Alexander Hamilton's Bank of the United States and invested his Baring funds in that institution's stock. This move that made public his great wealth.

There was even a plot to kidnap him for ransom, but it was discovered and thwarted.[26]

By 1811 Girard had accumulated most of the stock of the First Bank of the United States, headquartered at Third and Chestnut Streets. This put him in a position to become sole proprietor when, despite his best efforts, the Republican-controlled Congress allowed its charter to expire. He quickly bought the bank building with all its furnishings. He hired George Simpson, its cashier, along with other members of its officers and staff. Nine days later, on May 18, 1812, the firm reopened as Girard's Bank. Now the world was astounded to learn exactly how wealthy he was.[27]

Girard ended up a principal source of government credit for the War of 1812. After the government failed to sell enough bonds to finance the war, Girard joined with European financier David Parish and John Jacob Astor to buy bonds at favorable rates, thereby saving the country from financial disaster. He also tried to use this opportunity to secure the protection of the Treasury Department from the machinations of rival Pennsylvania banks, but he was not successful. He lent the money anyway, and at a rate similar to that charged to the smallest investor.[28]

Girard remained involved in worldwide trade, but from this point on, banking would be his main business. He was now, at sixty-three, the richest man in America, and the first multimillionaire, with property worth $2,250,000. That he was as concerned about sound banking as personal profit is made clear in his support of a new national bank, the Second Bank of the United States, in 1816. He became one of its largest stockholders, purchasing $1.5 million worth of stocks, when public subscriptions once again proved inadequate. He was also one of the directors. He helped get the remaining stock sold but he thought the other directors corrupt or incompetent so he only agreed to serve for two years. He was more interested in his own practice, which favored spreading the risk by lending small sums to many borrowers (mostly of modest means) over risking large sums on a few. Not only did he favor lending to the workingman; he remained one himself. His subordinates recounted how early morning bank customers would often see him before they entered the building, at work pruning and weeding in the garden attached to the bank.[29]

Although the banks were the primary way Girard served himself and his country at the same time, they were not the only way. By buying stock and lending money, he backed other important ventures such as the Schuylkill Navigation Company, the Chesapeake and Delaware Canal, and several railroads. He thus played a role in the transportation revolution that was transforming the country and the economy. In 1829, he bailed out the state of Pennsylvania with an emergency loan. That he was public-spirited did not prevent him from being forward-looking in his investments. He got out of foreign trade and into banking at a good time.[30]

Then, after 1815, he pivoted again, and increasingly invested bank profits in real estate. He continued to do so until his death in 1831. In his final year, for example, he bought land in western Pennsylvania that later returned big profits in timber and coal. This was a characteristically savvy move, as others did not appreciate as much as he did at this point that coal was the fuel of the future. These acres would sustain his estate after he died, just as he planned. He also bought a number of houses and properties in Philadelphia, including many of the best properties throughout Society Hill. In addition, he acquired the block between Market and Chestnut Streets and Eleventh and Twelfth. It is still owned by his estate. Much to the relief of those who were sick of Philadelphia's reliance on brick, the row of houses Girard built on Chestnut between Eleventh and Twelfth had marble fronts and pillars.[31]

Girard had been engaged in building from the time he arrived in Philadelphia. Among many others, he had erected rows of three- and four-story brick houses, complete with baths and water closets, of which handsome examples still exist on the south side of Spruce Street between Third and Fourth. These were among the first block-long rows of houses, planned and constructed as a unit. Fashioned after British examples, they nonetheless became known in this country as "Philadelphia Rows." They contributed to the enormous growth in residential and commercial building in Philadelphia in the 1820s. By 1830, gentleman diarist Samuel Breck wrote admiringly that the eighty-four-year-old Girard had been "embellishing the city year after year by the erection of blocks of houses four stories high, built in the most substantial manner. He projects and executes schemes with the courage and ardour of a young man." Deborah Logan noted of a visit the same year that "it was likewise a satisfaction to see the improvement and prosperity of our city, a great many houses building, both in its extension, and new ones erecting where old and decayed ones have stood." She credited Girard for "employing some of his ample means in the latter case."[32]

After 1817, Girard's own house began to see more company, and his social life improved. Following Napoleon's defeat at Waterloo, the emperor's brother Joseph Bonaparte and other French exiles came to Philadelphia. They often came to Girard's for Sunday dinner, and Joseph, a popular bon vivant, has been credited with softening Girard's customary asperity. The mechanical organ he gave Girard may have helped, since it supplied Girard's drawing room with a variety of tunes. Joseph built a lavish estate in New Jersey, but also rented a house from Girard in Philadelphia, at Twelfth and Market Streets.[33]

Girard also began to show more fondness for children, although none lived with him at this point. Polly's sisters and nieces had moved out of the house, and Girard's nieces—Antoinette, Caroline, and Harriet—now in their late teens and early twenties—were growing up and finding husbands. Girard remained close with Jean's daughters even though they had mostly lived at school or in Mme. Grelaud's Philadelphia boardinghouse. When Antoinette married Wilmington merchant John Hemphill, Girard refused to provide a dowry, but he did not withhold consent or gifts. He was more generous in providing for the marriage of Harriet with his friend and Napoleon's artillerist General Henri Lallemand. He was least generous with Caroline, and refused her entreaties to employ her husband, John Haslam, though he sent some assistance during the short life of their baby son. Girard was evidently a frustrated great-uncle. He wanted a male Girard successor to his business, and Jean's daughters only produced girls. The Girard girls' marriages are a reminder of how small Philadelphia still was in the 1820s, despite its growth. Antoinette's husband was very likely a cousin to Joseph Hemphill of the next chapter. And after John Haslam died, Caroline married Charles Willson Peale's son Franklin.[34]

Why Stephen himself did not marry Polly at this point—since Mary had died in 1815—is not clear. Although she was twenty-six years younger than him, he may well have been convinced at this point that he was not capable of fathering a child with her. If he did marry her, and she outlived him, she would inherit part of his estate. It would then be liable to dispersal among her relatives. He was already formulating other plans for the wealth he would leave behind.[35]

In the meantime, his money drew entreaties for assistance from family near and far. Fellow merchant Thomas Cope begged him to support his indigent mother-in-law Mrs. Lum (Mary's mother). He refused. His French relations constantly begged for help; he generally resisted, but, desirous of perpetuating the Girard family line, he arranged to adopt his younger half-brother Étienne's two sons. Otherwise he steered clear of his feuding siblings. He was especially vexed when two sisters showed up in Philadelphia. He asked a subordinate to meet them, "find a boardinghouse" for them, and assure them "that I do not wish to see" them. He promised only to pay for their passage back to France. Girard's bark was worse than his bite, however, for he ended up giving thousands to most of his close Girard relatives, and this was despite their failure to show any evidence of actually caring for him. Once his half-nephews arrived in Philadelphia, Girard found Étienne's eldest son, Fabricius, nearly as demanding as his father, but Girard sent him to school, arranged an apprenticeship with another merchant, and was generally forbearing. Fabricius was not a conscientious student or worker and embezzled various amounts of cash. He spoiled things for his brother as well as himself, for Girard eventually gave up on his hopes of making an heir out of one of his nephews. He shipped both boys back to France.[36]

Not only did Girard give a good deal of money to family members, he was also constantly dipping into his pockets to help Philadelphia's poor. He regularly gave small sums to beggars on the streets, especially the handicapped. In winter, the poor were welcome to take firewood from his lumberyard. He told certain doctors to let him know of any deserving sick persons in need. He gave to groups and institutions as well: the volunteer fire companies, a school for Blacks, a female orphanage, a Sunday school, a widows' asylum, and the Magdalen Society for the rehabilitation of prostitutes. (His attention to widows and poor girls is noteworthy given his later endowing of a school for orphan boys.) He helped many young men who had impressed him by their industry to get a start in life.[37]

Girard received hundreds of appeals for help. He was particularly generous toward schools, and supported Joseph Lancaster's new system of mass education in Philadelphia. He also helped Peter Gallaudet establish his pioneering school for the deaf. William White was a founder of the institution as well as the Magdalen Society, so Girard likely had contact with him in these causes. Colleges and universities were not so lucky; though most asked him for money, Girard was only interested in practical education. He also had little concern for the arts, despite pleas from Charles Willson Peale to subsidize local artists and donate land for museums. Churches fared better, for contrary to gossip, Girard was not irreligious. He mistrusted clergymen, hated sectarian conflict, and ceased churchgoing after his forties, but he never renounced his natal Catholicism and sometimes paid for a pew in St. Augustine's Church. Indeed, churches from all over the country asked him for assistance, and he often gave, while encouraging local congregations to help themselves.[38]

Countless strangers offered Girard unsolicited advice as to how he should use his wealth—to liberate enslaved people, aid seamen, build a canal, educate men for the ministry, support missionaries, and so on. One helpful person, pointing out that "Washington, Penn, Franklin and Rittenhouse" all had pretty parks named after them in Philadelphia, suggested that Girard should add his name to the list by making another. Perhaps it was this constant stream of suggestions that made him so curt with those who tried to tell him what to do with his money. Many young people of both sexes, some boys named for him, offered themselves as candidates for his charity or even for adoption. He took in his former employee and Sally Bickham's brother Martin Bickham's son, Stephen Girard Bickham, for a time, hoping that he might succeed him. But the young man disappointed. His lack of children, compounded by Polly's defection from the household in 1827, possibly owing to illness, made Girard a lonely man in his later years. He had other housekeepers, but it is not clear that they were mistresses like Sally and Polly had been. Now in his late seventies, he withdrew from public activity. But he did not stop working. He divided his time between his office, his bank, and his farm. He simplified his lifestyle and became a vegetarian.[39]

Although the change in diet, his customary moderation in regard to alcohol, and his lifetime of activity helped Girard withstand and overcome illness, they could not prevent encroaching deafness and blindness in his good eye or protect him from accidents. In December 1830, crossing Second Street at High (Market) at dusk, he was run down by a horse-drawn wagon and suffered a severe laceration of his head. He was bedridden for two months and never fully recovered. Still, he retained his business acumen. It was at this time that he purchased the lands in the Pennsylvania interior that would earn his estate millions in coal profits, as well as more real estate in Philadelphia. He insisted to a business associate who visited that he was still minding his affairs. But subordinates reported memory lapses and slower movement. He was less cautious in policy with his own bank, and, although still involved with the Second Bank of the United States, he was less able to help it stay on a sound course. His eyesight declined further. He was in a good deal of pain. His once sturdy body wasted. He was therefore vulnerable when an influenza epidemic swept Philadelphia in December 1831. Stubborn to the end about his mistrust of doctors, he refused to consult them. He died the day after Christmas.[40]

After the largest funeral procession the city had seen to that point, Girard was buried in the vault he had built for the Baron Henri Lallemand, husband of his niece Harriet, at Holy Trinity Cathedral Cemetery, at Sixth and Spruce. (He was reinterred years later at Girard College.) Almost immediately after his death, newspapers around the country printed the news of his passing and obituaries. There was also a great deal of speculation about the fate of his estate. Girard's extended family was especially curious. One of Girard's nephews insisted that the will be read the day after his death, on the pretext that the family needed to know what Stephen's wishes were as to funeral arrangements. Girard's lawyer, William J. Duane, assured the family that the will contained no such details, but the family prevailed. Duane began to read the thirty-seven page will aloud to them.[41]

The family was stunned at what it revealed. Philadelphia would be amazed and delighted. The first bequest was to Pennsylvania Hospital, with an annuity to be paid out of those funds to the first individual mentioned in his will—Hannah, whom he had enslaved. Hannah had worked for him ever since his brother Jean had brought her to Philadelphia from St. Domingue in the 1780s. It is unclear why she was not manumitted by Pennsylvania's Gradual Abolition Act of 1780, but Girard freed her in his will, and provided an income for the rest of her life. The family waited for Duane to continue, and their disappointment grew. Given the size of his fortune, Girard made only modest bequests to his relatives, although all were quite generous in terms of monetary value at the time. He left gifts of $5,000 each to his French siblings and their children and gifts and bequests for trust funds running from $10,000 to $50,000 (depending on the number of their children) for each of his Philadelphia nieces. Family members and their spouses should not have been surprised at these figures, as Girard had always said that large legacies would only spoil relatives by placing them "above the honorable pursuits of needful industry." He left annuities of $300 to $500 to his housekeepers and current apprentices, and gifts of $1,500 to each of his three longest-serving ship captains. He granted sums between $10,000 and $30,000 to various Philadelphia institutions—besides Pennsylvania Hospital, these included the School for the Deaf, the Orphan Asylum, Philadelphia's public schools, the Society for the Relief of Poor Shipmasters, the Masonic Order, and a few others. Yet although all of these gifts were more than Girard ever said he would leave to any of these people or institutions, they only amounted to about 6 percent of his estate of more than $7 million. The rest went to public purposes. Family members, expecting much more, could not bear to hear any more.[42]

Lawyer Duane, however, tipped off the city organizations about the contents of the will to ensure a suitable memorial procession. Deborah Logan reported the immediate response: "We found the conversation in town turned very much on the demise and bequests of Girard. The citizens are proud and happy in his benefactions to them, and discourse of his character very favourably. His funeral is to take place tomorrow. And a great attendance, no doubt, will go with his remains to the silent tomb." Duane and Logan bet right. The turnout was the largest the city had ever seen. Twenty thousand people lined the snowy streets as a procession of three thousand mourners, including family members, civic officials, and representatives of his favored institutions, made the one-mile trip from Girard's house to Holy Trinity Church in carriages or on foot. Most of the onlookers were not intimates mourning Girard as a friend or relative, but citizens curious about or grateful for his public benefactions. Funeral arrangements themselves were still confused. The delighted Freemasons, whom Girard had joined years before, and whose debts were now forgiven, attended with their aprons on and proceeded to conduct a service, prompting Roman Catholic bishop Francis Kenrick to refuse to say a mass although he allowed the burial.[43]

The public clamored to know the details of the will and the newspapers soon obliged. They learned that Girard had left substantial legacies to the city of New Orleans, to the state of Pennsylvania (for canals and the Port of Philadelphia), and to his hometown. Some of the income from the money for Philadelphia was to be used for specific projects. The city was to construct a broad avenue along the river—Delaware Avenue. It was to tear down all remaining wooden structures within the city limits, and to prohibit the building of any in the future. It was to widen and pave Water Street. To ensure that these tasks be completed, Girard made his bequest to the state contingent on its passing laws requiring Philadelphia to complete them. The state legislature got right on it.[44]

These grants to local governments were unprecedented, yet the bulk of Girard's estate was intended to establish a school for poor white orphan boys. Girard explained in his will that he had "been for a long time impressed with the importance of educating the poor, and of placing them, by the early cultivation of their minds and development of their moral principles, above the many temptations to which, through poverty and ignorance, they are exposed." He left detailed plans to ensure the building of a solid edifice for at least three hundred students on the site where Girard College still operates, at Girard and Corinthian Avenues. One of his specifications was to ensure that the building was fireproof: "no wood may be used except for doors, windows, and shutters." The project was thus a boon to the region's marble masons. One result was that, by the time of its completion in 1846, the college was the nation's second most expensive building after the U.S. Capitol.[45]

As for the curriculum, Girard indicated his preference for a practical over a classical education and urged the inculcation of patriotism and reverence for republican institutions. Although he insisted on moral education and did not forbid the teaching of religion, he did ban any ministers from setting foot on college grounds. This was because he feared the effect of "clashing doctrines and sectarian controversy" on "the tender minds of the orphans." Otherwise, he left the direction of the institution to the wisdom of Philadelphia's elected officials. It was an impressive and unique gift to a city that had as yet no univer-

Figure 16. Girard College. Lithograph by Smith Brothers & Co., ca. 1850. Library of Congress.

sal free public school system and only rudimentary provisions for educating the poor. Most Philadelphians were delighted and began to publish belated encomiums to the departed benefactor. Strikingly, by 1833, the entire will and a brief biography of Girard were printed in the back of the city directory. It was as if, from then on, one could not grasp Philadelphia without understanding Girard's role.[46]

Family members did not care. Egged on by the French branch, they filed suit to break the will. They challenged its legality on a number of fronts and appealed the case all the way to the U.S. Supreme Court. Others, including William White, took a cue from and joined lawyer Daniel Webster's attack on Girard's barring of ministers from the school, but Girard was not the atheist they claimed. Early on, Girard's disgruntled relatives achieved a minor settlement from lands acquired after the will was written, but they lost the larger case against the will. Girard's legacy was secure.[47]

But what exactly was Girard's legacy? He is estimated to have been the fourth richest American of all time. What drove him to accumulate such wealth, to the degree that he never slackened his pace or retired from work? Some said that he chased riches not for their own sake, but as a means to exert power over his society. This explanation seems consistent with his public actions, especially regarding banking, as well as the lack of conspicuous consumption in his private life. But there were other factors. He seemed driven to prove himself; first, to his father, and then, to his fellow citizens—but always on his own terms. He was as stubborn as he was ambitious. And the specifications for what would be named, not by his request, Girard College show that his own terms were resolutely in line with the republican principles of his adopted United States.[48]

The city came to hold him in awe for his bequests, the largest sums a private U.S. citizen had ever left for public good. But Stephen Girard was never beloved, not in life or even after death. This was surely owing to his personality, which, like his public life, was complicated. Unfortunately, he kept his good side as carefully under wraps as his good works. He was said to love children and animals, and delighted in coaxing the caged canaries in his office to sing with the aid of a bird organ, a device he had imported from France for that purpose. He supported many young men in their careers and certainly provided well for the children of his siblings. But he had little patience for the lazy, whether among his siblings, their children, or his employees. In this, at least, he was consistent, as he worked very hard himself, into his eighties.[49]

In fact, it seems that work was the main thing that made Girard happy. Once, when his brother Jean cautioned him against some risky business, Stephen thanked him, but replied "my love of work, the only pleasure I have on this globe, will not permit me to entertain these prudent considerations." He rarely took a day off and claimed to labor as hard as he did so that he could sleep at night. So although Girard occasionally complained about work, his lifelong diligence and his correspondence suggest that he took a genuine pleasure in the risky business of commerce. And yet, he suggested to colleagues that family and an honest fortune were the key to real happiness, and that, by these lights, their circumstances were "a thousand times preferable to mine." Given his facial deformity, his long trial with Mary, and his childlessness, one cannot help but hear a certain sadness in his words. Surely he felt happier at some times than others. But his success at work, even though—or perhaps because—it required unremitting attention was a constant balm.[50]

While he was far more generous to family members and the needy than he got credit for, Girard was not a demonstrative man. He had the self-control of the successful businessman, in that he was able to participate in commercial dealings without revealing his interests. He had advised Jean to "use on every occasion a great deal of secret observation and coolness." And yet when angry at the mistakes of subordinates, his temper flared. He was not a humorous man, but could let loose a biting wit when antagonized. For example, when rival businessman Jacob Ridgway once chided him for his superciliousness, saying, "Friend Girard, thee assumes too much pride in thy dealings; I can both buy thee and sell thee." Girard immediately retorted, "And I, Friend Ridgway, can buy thee, but I do not think I could sell thee again!"[51]

And yet, although Girard was proud and sometimes exaggerated details of his life, he did not toot his own horn publicly and declined opportunities to allow others to. He always refused to sit for a portrait, even though he knew the Peales, as demonstrated not only through his niece's marriage to Franklin Peale, but also by a letter of introduction he wrote for Rembrandt Peale when he went to France. He also refused to cooperate with those who wished to write his biography. He told one of them, the son of his former bank cashier, "My actions must make my life. I have no information to give; when I am dead that will speak for itself." In fact, Girard's actions fairly shout to anyone exploring Philadelphia even today. The city is dotted with memorials in brick and stone.[52]

CHAPTER 9

Joseph Hemphill

> Mr. Hemphill was more distinguished for sound judgment, cool perception, and an almost unerring knowledge of men, than for brilliancy or splendor.
>
> —Obituary, *North American and Daily Advertiser*

Like most of the other men whose stories this book tells, Joseph Hemphill was not born in Philadelphia. But he did not come from far. He was a precursor to the countless young men of the nineteenth century who came to American cities from the countryside to seek their fortunes. Hemphill was born in in 1770 in Thornbury Township, then part of Chester County, one of the four counties that ring Philadelphia. His father was an immigrant of Scottish extraction from Northern Ireland. The Scotch-Irish were second only to the Germans in numbers disembarking at Philadelphia in the mid- and later 1700s.

Hemphill was not, like the other men we have followed, so important in his time as to be well known to historians today. Yet he participated in key changes in politics and the economy, from the Missouri Compromise to the conflicts over banking and Indian Removal, to the internal improvements that made the "transportation revolution," to the development of Philadelphia as a capital of industry. Moreover, born as he was on the eve of the American Revolution, he was witness to a period of rapid transformation and serves as a bridge to the next generation of Philadelphians that we will meet. His story also intersects with some of the places we have visited, and some others worth adding to the tour.

In terms of personality, Hemphill falls between Charles Willson Peale's boyish enthusiasm and Stephen Girard's fierce ambition. He, like William White, was known for his "bland manners," though in a positive sense. He was a very affable person and got along well with all. With his pleasant demeanor and gracious hospitality, he was almost the antithesis of Girard, and more ur-

Figure 17. Joseph Hemphill (1770–1842). Engraving by Max Rosenthal (1833–1918). Harvard Law School Library, Harvard University.

bane than Benezet, Muhlenberg, or Peale. These characteristics may explain both his rise and its limits.

Joseph Hemphill's father, also Joseph, had come to Philadelphia as a boy, around 1740, with his father, Alexander, his brother, James, and his sister, Mary. Their mother may have died during the voyage. Alexander Hemphill came from "Ulster," the County Donegal area around Londonderry where, three generations before, three Hemphill brothers had come from Ayrshire in the Scottish Lowlands to serve in Queen Elizabeth's forces pacifying northern Ireland. Unlike the many Scotch-Irish who disembarked at Philadelphia, they did not move west into the Pennsylvania interior, but settled in the countryside just southwest of the city. Soon Joseph and James married sisters Ann and Elizabeth Wills, and acquired and settled on adjacent farms. Joseph's Sweetwater Farm was substantial, and may still be visited today.[1]

Our Joseph was the fifth of Joseph and Ann Wills Hemphill's nine children. Born in 1770, he may have been just old enough to remember his father serving as a scout for the American forces in their Brandywine neighborhood and his mother telling off the British who ransacked their farm. His father had purchased Sweetwater in 1758 and added acres as the farm prospered. It is likely that Joseph intended to follow in his footsteps, as he did not begin to prepare for college at a school in the nearby county seat of West Chester until 1788. And since Hemphill was reported soon after to have a frail constitution, it is probable that the family concluded that he was not suited for manual labor. By this point his father was doing very well and older son Alexander had died in his twenties. So Joseph Sr. could afford to educate his namesake. Young Joseph doubtless showed the requisite intellectual ability as well, as another older brother, Wills, was not sent to school. Joseph must have prepared rapidly and well, since he took two rather than the customary three years to graduate from the University of Pennsylvania in 1791.[2]

It must have been exciting for the nineteen-year-old to travel from the farm to the city in 1789. He was on the older side, as the age at entrance of students varied widely in the late eighteenth century, and well-to-do city boys like William White often began in their mid-teens. But Joseph was old enough to appreciate some independence. Since the 1750s, the college had been centrally located at Fourth and Arch Streets, in the so-called New Building. This huge edifice was originally built to accommodate the crowds that gathered for popular itinerant George Whitefield's sermons, but had been adapted for the college. Hemphill may have lived in the building added next door in 1763, which had classrooms for the academy on the first floor and dormitories on the upper floors, or in an approved boardinghouse. His classes were even closer to the center of action, since the University of Pennsylvania had decamped for the two years Joseph attended to Philosophical Hall at Fifth and Chestnut Streets (before Peale's museum occupied the space). There he shared in the routine of exercises in Latin, Greek, and mathematics, which alternated with lectures on natural philosophy (what we would call science), moral philosophy (a combination of ethics, logic, rhetoric, and history), and geography. The college students also took turns "declaiming" each week, which gave them experience in public speaking.[3]

Little did Hemphill know then that, twenty years later, he would be presiding as a judge across the State House yard in Congress Hall, and living across the street in one of the beautiful townhouses of Norris Row. Yet Hemphill's commencement oration of 1791 was telling of his future interest in the law and basically humanitarian disposition, for in it he decried the policy of imprisonment for debt. That, too, raises a question of proximity, as the city's debtors' prison at Sixth and Spruce (then Prune) was just a couple of blocks away from his classrooms. Newly incarcerated there, and frequently visited by his friend George Washington, was William White's brother-in-law, Revolutionary War financier Robert Morris. Indeed, it could have been Morris's shocking fall that inspired Hemphill's thesis.[4]

After graduating, Hemphill moved back to Chester County and commenced training to be a lawyer in the way that was customary at the time, by "reading law" in the office of attorney Thomas Ross of West Chester. When Ross proposed Hemphill's admission to the bar in 1793, a contemporary observed that "it was a frail young man who rose to take the oath of fidelity to court and client." Yet by personality and preparation, Joseph was poised to do well. It was remarked that "his manner introduced him and his learning supported the introduction." Although he had only just started out when his father died without a will in 1793, Joseph felt sufficiently confident in his future prospects and concerned about his siblings (two brothers and five sisters remained to be provided for) to renounce any share in the estate. He said the cost of his education was enough of an inheritance.[5]

Hemphill was as ambitious as he was confident. In addition to practicing law, he entered into public life. In 1796, he joined the Pennsylvania Abolition Society. From 1797 to 1800, he represented Chester County in the state legislature. There, he was involved in the final adjustment of the "Wyoming controversy," concerning competing land claims with the state of Connecticut to the northeastern portion of present-day Pennsylvania. He also got authorization for the building of a poorhouse in Chester County, the first such approval from the state. He showed his Federalist political leanings in 1798, when he served as secretary of a Chester County committee gathered to condemn the perfidy of the French in the XYZ Affair. The group met in a tavern to compose a memorial to the U.S. Congress to that effect and to pledge their support for the Adams administration.[6]

By 1801, Hemphill was headed to Washington to represent Chester and Delaware Counties in the Seventh Congress. The Democratic-Republicans had just won the presidency for Jefferson, and Federalist Hemphill jumped right into the fray. He gave a speech opposing the Republican move to repeal the Judiciary Act of 1801, under which lame duck president John Adams had appointed a batch of new federal judges. Hemphill argued that Congress did not have the power to remove judges, who were to serve for "good behavior," that is, as long as they acted within the law. This was an important constitutional principle, crucial to judicial independence. The episode would soon be the basis of Chief Justice John Marshall's establishing another constitutional principle, that of judicial review, in the case of *Marbury v. Madison*. Hemphill objected to the removal of Adams's "midnight" appointees for fear of patronage in the judiciary—that "it will become as much a matter of course to remove the judges as the heads of departments, and in bad times the judges would be no better than a sword in the hands of the party." His speech was much admired, but as it was the only one he gave before that particular Congress, and he did not serve again for some years, his friends jokingly called him "Single-Speech Hemphill," after a British politician with that nickname.[7]

His term over, Hemphill moved from West Chester to Philadelphia, and was returned to the state legislature from the city. He was elected by a coalition of Federalists and a third party called the "Defenders of the Pennsylvania State Constitution." When time permitted, he continued his law practice. He did well, and was known for uniting a clear and persuasive style of argument with a candid and winning manner. He was still a Federalist, but found friends and clients among many Democratic-Republicans.[8]

Now in his mid-thirties and embarked on a promising legal and political career, Hemphill was ready to start a family. He courted and won the hand of twenty-eight-year-old Margaret Coleman, the beautiful eldest daughter of prominent Lancaster County iron manufacturer Robert Coleman. Robert Coleman was another early American success story, having arrived from Ireland with a few shillings in his pocket and then worked his way up as an employee in several Pennsylvania forges to become the most important ironmaster of his day. He served as an officer in the Revolution while also directing the production of cannonballs, musket balls, and the chain bar used to keep British ships from coming up the Delaware River. After the war, he served twenty-five years as a Lancaster County judge. He was a man of consequence, and Hemphill was lucky to win his daughter's hand. Joseph and Margaret married in 1806, and their union was soon blessed with the birth of two sons, Robert Coleman Hemphill in 1809 and Alexander Wills Hemphill in 1811.[9]

Owing to his "genial, urbane, tactful and generally agreeable" character, Hemphill was asked to join many Philadelphia institutions. He was involved in Girard's Bank and the Bank of the United States, the American Philosophical Society, the Dancing Assembly, and the Academy of Fine Arts. He also served on the vestries of three different churches. In the course of these activities, he met and worked with Stephen Girard, Charles Willson Peale, and William White. The latter officiated at the marriage of Hemphill's son Robert in 1834.[10]

Although few of Hemphill's personal papers survive, the newspapers bear witness to his political career in their listings of election results, judicial appointments, and the meetings of various political groups. In March 1808, for example, *Poulson's American Daily Advertiser* carried the notice of the endorsement of a gubernatorial candidate by a meeting of "Federal Republicans" of Philadelphia, at which Hemphill served as secretary. The same group endorsed Hemphill's run for Congress that fall. Hemphill did not win that election, which left him free to accept a commission in 1811 as the first presiding judge of the new District Court for the city and county of Philadelphia. It was charged with handling civil cases concerning amounts over $100. This was a political coup, since the appointment came from the Democratic-Republican governor, Simon Snyder, and hence from a member of the opposing political party. Hemphill served at the high salary of $2,000, and was recommissioned in 1817. He resigned in 1819, pleading delicate health and weak eyes.[11]

Owing to this appointment, Hemphill held court on the first floor of Congress Hall, on the southeast corner of Chestnut and Sixth Streets. This building, erected in 1787–1789, had initially served as the Philadelphia County Courthouse, but had hosted the federal Congress when Philadelphia was the nation's capital. When Congress moved to Washington in 1800, the building had reverted to its old function. Hemphill almost witnessed the demolition of the State House/Independence Hall next door, since the state legislature, now moved to Harrisburg, had come close to tearing down the old building and selling the land. Most Philadelphians did not care too much about the city's old buildings—Ben Franklin's home had already been razed, for example, and the land subdivided for sale by his descendants. But a few folks, who, like John Watson and Deborah Logan, did care about the past, protested the demolition of the building where the nation's founding had occurred, and the public alarm of newspaper publisher William Duane in particular led to a change in plans. The city of Philadelphia purchased the building and converted it into office space.[12]

Hemphill held court every day for most of eight years. The post may have tired him, but at least he did not have a long commute, as he soon moved to a townhouse on Chestnut Street at Fifth Street, just a block from the court. This home was one of the fashionable set of adjoining brick houses called "Norris Row," built in the early 1790s. These elegant rowhouses for the affluent, modeled on antecedents in London, were built on the southwest corner of the former Norris mansion garden. There Deborah Norris had sat on the wall listening to the reading of the Declaration of Independence.[13]

While certainly convenient, the Hemphill home was also the site of a tragedy. For it was there that, in December 1819, Hemphill's sister-in-law Ann Caroline Coleman died young—and mysteriously. Twenty-three-year-old Ann was Margaret's high-strung but attractive younger sister. She had become engaged the previous summer to rising Lancaster attorney and politician (and future U.S. president) James Buchanan. With her dark eyes and hair and the family's wealth and status, she was as much a catch for Buchanan as her elder sister had been for Joseph Hemphill. Buchanan's origins were modest, but the ambitious six-footer was clearly on the rise. Ann's friends described her as alternately quiet and sensitive or giddy and impetuous, however, which may mean that she suffered from what we would today call a mood disorder. Ann naturally wished for James's attention that fall, but the time was not propitious. The Panic of 1819 had prompted a flurry of land sales that kept the young lawyer busy. At the same time, the Missouri crisis was brewing on the national front, and Buchanan was busy trying to keep the local Federalist Party from falling apart. As politics caused him to neglect Ann, the local gossips got to work and suggested that he was only interested in her family's wealth. She wrote him to protest his neglect and voice the community's suspicions. He, hurt and not sure how to respond without making things worse, replied by protesting his innocence, but without apologizing. The relationship survived this exchange. Then Buchanan made an unwitting and perhaps fatal error. When visiting a close male friend upon returning from a trip out of town, he happened to socialize with another young woman before he had been to see Ann. The sensitive and impetuous fiancée, jealous and perhaps embarrassed from the gossip, broke off the engagement.[14]

Because Ann was so distraught, her mother thought a visit to the city would distract her and persuaded her to visit Margaret and Joseph in Philadelphia. A new series of plays at the theater might take her mind off the failed romance. Ann left Lancaster on December 4. Five days later, a messenger raced back to Lancaster with the shocking news that she had died the night before. A Philadelphia judge who knew the family left an account of the calamity in his diary. Judge Thomas Kittera marveled that he had "met this young lady on the street, in the vigour of health" at noon on the very day of her death. He heard that she was upset over the broken engagement and that "in the afternoon she was laboring under a fit of hysterics." But she had been well enough in the evening for Margaret to feel comfortable going out to the theater. That night, however, Ann "was attacked with strong hysterical convulsions." Doctors were called in. The convulsions soon subsided as they predicted, but Ann's pulse grew weaker, "until midnight, when she died." The doctor attending said "it was the first instance he ever knew of hysteria producing death," but historians think she must have died from an overdose of the opiate laudanum. What we cannot know, even though her neighbors wondered about it, is whether Ann's death was a suicide. Perhaps Buchanan wondered too.[15]

Two days later Joseph and Margaret brought the body to Lancaster for the funeral. Buchanan wrote to the family asking to take part; the letter was returned unopened. Apparently the family, along with her friends, had come to "look upon him as her Murderer." Distraught, he secluded himself for a few days and then fled Lancaster to be with his family in Mercersburg. They helped him recover emotionally, but any prospect of future love was over. When anyone ever broached the subject, Buchanan always replied that "marry he could not, for his affections were buried in the grave." He never did wed, later becoming the United States' only bachelor president. He almost never mentioned Ann, either, for the rest of his life. Yet he kept her letters tied up in a pink ribbon, with instructions that they be burnt when he was gone. His executors fulfilled his request.[16]

While the Colemans cast Buchanan out, Joseph Hemphill had to call upon all his diplomatic skills to deal with him, as they found themselves together in Washington in the next Congress and for most of the decade following. Buchanan's friends, seeking a way forward for him, secured his nomination for Congress in 1820. Despite having resigned his judgeship owing to poor health and eyesight, Hemphill had been elected as a Federalist from Philadelphia in 1818 and again in 1820. Apparently, he was driven to serve even though his eyes continued to plague him. He wrote a friend back home in January 1820 that he had a persistent "inflammation in one of my Eyes—I cant use it as yet and can see but very imperfectly with the other. I however attend in the house."[17]

Buchanan and Hemphill sometimes found themselves on the same side of an issue, as in 1826, when Hemphill introduced and Buchanan supported a bill providing pensions for officers of the Revolutionary War. The pension measure was relatively uncontroversial, especially in the fiftieth anniversary year of independence. But both men had to figure out what to do as their party dissolved. Going into the presidential election of 1824, Hemphill was initially a supporter of Henry Clay but switched, along with many Pennsylvania Federalists, to support Andrew Jackson when the contest narrowed to one between Jackson and John Quincy Adams. Election returns show his partisan evolution, as he was elected to the Eighteenth Congress as a Federalist in 1822, but reelected in 1824 as a Jacksonian. And yet, even as he tried to vote with the majority of the Pennsylvania representatives, Hemphill never became a true Jacksonian Democrat in terms of his policy preferences on the most important issues of the day. That is, he was strongly antislavery, he supported internal improvements and the U.S. bank, and he opposed Jackson's version of Indian Removal. He was not covert or underhanded about these stands. It was said of him that "in politics he was mild but without disguise or concealment."[18]

During the first session of his second term in Congress, in 1819, Hemphill was elected chairman of the Committee on the Slave Trade. This allowed him to serve a cause important to him. In particular, it enabled him to play a role in the debate over the admission of Missouri as a slave state. From his chair, Hemphill attacked Missouri's discrimination against free Blacks and biracial individuals as unconstitutional. In response to claims that "slaves are as happy as the lower class of white people," he remarked that if was so, "it must be in consequence of the degradation to which they are reduced; their faculties are not allowed that expansion which nature intended; they are kept in darkness, and are unacquainted with their true situation." Hemphill opposed slavery in Missouri for political reasons too, noting that the existing balance of power between states where slavery was legal and those where it was not, or was being gradually abolished, would be disturbed by the admission of Missouri as a slave state.[19]

Hemphill voiced his antislavery sentiments again in 1821, when he coauthored a report with Charles Mercer of Virginia on the enormities of the African slave trade. He must have been gratified by the favorable support it received in England, which was more advanced in the cause at this time. The report was lauded in the House of Commons and the *Edinburgh Review*, as well as in a letter from William Wilberforce, the leading antislavery member of Parliament, to William Lowndes of South Carolina.[20]

But Hemphill, true to his temperament, was not a radical in this or any other cause. Like many antislavery whites in the 1820s, he supported the idea of colonizing freed Blacks elsewhere as a supposed means of improving their condition. This was giving in to the racism of the nation at the time, or at least deeming it invincible. But some prominent Black leaders also supported colonization at first and for the same reason. Even those opposed (as the majority of African Americans quickly came to be) acknowledged the benevolent motives of the early colonizationists. Hemphill also sometimes expressed the opinion that northern attempts to force emancipation on the South were futile, given constitutional protections. He was criticized, for example, when he failed to support an 1827 measure calling for the abolition of slavery in the District of Columbia.[21]

Although he became a Jacksonian, Hemphill's antislavery stance went a bit against that party's grain. So did his strong support for Henry Clay's policy of federal assistance for internal improvements such as roads, bridges, and canals. Like other Pennsylvanians, he saw the value of such national support, especially for development in the West. Early in his political career he made an impassioned speech about the future rise of cities in the trans-Appalachian west. Many at the time thought his vision incredible and yet they lived to see it happen. Jacksonian Democrats, like the Jeffersonian Republicans from whom they claimed ideological descent, were generally opposed to such national schemes; this would also be part of their opposition to the Bank of the United States.[22]

As chair of the House Committee on Roads and Canals, Hemphill steadfastly pushed for the federal aid for internal improvement that grew increasingly popular as the nation recovered from the Panic of 1819. Improvers' efforts were stalemated, however, by those who wished to maintain "states' rights" in the face of the power of the national government. It was the same strict-construction versus loose-construction debate over the powers granted to the national government by the Constitution that had troubled the nation since the 1790s. President Monroe vetoed a Cumberland Road bill, saying that while he approved its object, Congress needed to pass an amendment to the Constitution to enable the federal government to engage in such a project. Given states-rights opposition, the improvers did not wish to risk such a campaign. A loss might set a precedent for an even further reduced national government. Hemphill's specific contribution to internal improvements measures was the recommendation that students at West Point undertake a general survey in order to help Congress decide wisely on specific improvement projects. This would strengthen the army, give students experience, get the job done cheaply, and bypass local interests. Political stalemate had killed other improvement bills between 1818 and 1822, but popular support grew to the point that the general survey bill finally passed in 1823. As its author, Hemphill had revised it so as to avoid the need for a constitutional amendment—surely Congress and the president could give orders to the army!—and left specific projects out of it that might sway the representatives of specific states.[23]

Hemphill continued to push for internal improvements legislation into the early 1830s. In 1825, he gave a long and impassioned speech promoting congressional support for the completion of the canal connecting the Chesapeake Bay and Delaware River. He pointed out the national benefits of this project, including military advantages, and pleaded for federal investment. As if to confirm his frequent claim that he was not just a supporter of projects close to home, Hemphill (now chair of the Committee on Internal Improvements) gave an even longer speech in 1830, advocating construction of a road from Buffalo, New York, to New Orleans. Again he pointed out that some projects were too big for individual states to undertake, but were nevertheless essential for military security, economic progress, and national unity. After 1831 Hemphill pursued these goals on the state level, as when he, Mathew Carey, and some other prominent Philadelphians of the Pennsylvania Society for the Promotion of Internal Improvements in the Commonwealth published an "Essay on Roads" in 1833 for "the consideration of their fellow citizens."[24]

As had been true of Stephen Girard, Hemphill's position on banking was also antithetical to that of his party, or at least its head. Jackson was against the national bank from the start, deeming it a dangerous monopoly. But Hemphill sided with those who regarded the bank as essential to national economic growth and regulation of state banks. He served on the Board of Directors of the Second Bank of the United States between 1823 and 1825, while representing Philadelphia in Congress. Hemphill's bank appointment comes as no surprise. As congressman, he was an important ally, and was immediately useful in introducing calls for banking legislation in Congress and corresponding with bank president and fellow Philadelphian Nicholas Biddle on various measures. In 1831, no longer in Congress, Hemphill attended a stockholders' meeting chaired by Girard, and was chosen to serve on a committee to respond to the report of the board of directors. The committee duly approved of Biddle's good management.[25]

Doubtless Hemphill was considered one of the "minions" of the bank when it came to the fight over its recharter in the election year of 1832. Jackson's antibank supporters claimed that the bank funneled loans to the powerful. They were right; it did. But even opponents had to admit to Biddle's competence in running the institution. One Washington editor who applied for a loan through Hemphill indicated that, of course, his newspaper's negative position on the bank would remain the same. Biddle instructed Hemphill to reply that the loan would nevertheless receive impartial consideration, that he cherished freedom of the press, and would expect the paper to speak its mind on the bank as freely as it had done before. Jackson won the bank war, of course. He was reelected and managed to have the charter renewal bill defeated, and then began to withdraw federal deposits from the Bank of the United States. Hemphill was faithful to the bank to the end, serving as secretary to a stockholders' meeting in 1834 that continued to express confidence in Biddle's direction. In 1837, when New York and Baltimore banks suspended specie payments, he was one of the organizers of a great public meeting at the Merchants' Exchange urging Philadelphians "not to give up the ship" by panicking.[26]

Hemphill had resigned from Congress in 1826, likely owing to ill health. He embarked on a trip to Europe, and returned from Liverpool in September 1827, reportedly "in excellent health." He ran for Congress again in the fall of 1827, but was defeated. He won a seat the next year, as a Jacksonian. Upon hearing the results, a crowd greeted him outside his home, still on the corner of Fifth and Chestnut Streets. Hemphill addressed those assembled, acknowledging that the triumph was not his, but Andrew Jackson's, and extolling the merits of the presidential candidate. So Hemphill returned to Washington in March 1829 as part of the wave that swept Jackson into the White House. Yet although he tried to work and vote along with the rest of the Pennsylvania delegation, and be a "sincere" friend of the administration, he was not a fully committed Jacksonian. In addition to continuing to press for support for internal improvements and the Bank of the United States, Hemphill had to assuage his own misgivings and those of Philadelphia's Quakers and other humanitarians about Jackson's Indian Removal program.[27]

In a sense, Indian Removal was simply the culmination of two centuries of fraudulent Euro-American dispossession of Native Americans in the East. The standard pattern from the colonial period was for Europeans to press on the Indians a treaty confirming land acquisition, either as a result of nominal purchase or conquest, while promising to respect Indian sovereignty and land rights beyond what had been relinquished. Shortly thereafter, Euro-American land thirst unquenched, the Indians would be pressed for another land cession. All of these takings revealed an underlying conviction on the part of Europeans that they could not share the land with Native Americans. The new United States proved no different from the British authorities in the colonies in this respect, despite some lip service to a "civilization" program on the part of the Washington administration. Of the groups who mobilized to resist European incursion by embracing civilization, the Cherokee nation went furthest. Adopting European-style literacy and government, they hoped to hold onto their lands. A Supreme Court decision, *Worcester v. Georgia*, gave them hope by upholding their sovereign rights. But Andrew Jackson claimed that the best way to protect southeastern Indians from the depredations of local Euro-American settlers and squatters was to remove them to lands beyond the Mississippi. Hence the controversial Indian Removal bill of 1830.[28]

Hemphill did not wish to defy the president, but he was troubled by the lack of detail in terms of how the removal would be carried out. His concerns were threefold; that the Indians to be moved had not been adequately consulted, that the lands they were to be removed to had not been adequately assessed, and that the government planned to negotiate with individuals about the properties they were leaving, rather than collectively as tribal entities. And so he offered suggestions to address these shortcomings in a substitute bill that he hoped would advance procedures more "in the spirit of William Penn." Hemphill recommended that three neutral commissioners (that is, white men from states that were not involved) be appointed "who should go through the Indian tribes east of the Mississippi, and ascertain their disposition to emigrate." He proposed that the commissioners then go "explore the country west of the Mississippi, and ascertain the quality and extent of the country which could be offered to the Indians in exchange for their lands east of the river." Hemphill outlined questions the commissioners could help answer. What about the Indians already there? Had their titles been extinguished, as the bill specified? In any case, "we do not know . . . whether they may be willing to leave their hunting ground peaceably." Would the land envisioned actually accommodate the seventy thousand to one hundred thousand Indians the government contemplated moving? Should the government purchase additional or better land? Was the government, in its promise to protect the eastern Indians, thereby promising to participate in future wars among Native peoples?[29]

Hemphill also questioned the contradiction between one part of the bill, which said that only the decision of whole tribes "in their national capacity" should be respected in the matter, while another mandated that individuals would be paid for improvements on the property left behind. Did this mean "if consent is not given by the tribe or nation, is it intended to go to individuals, and purchase from A, B, and C? If this is the intent of the bill, it ought to be plainly stated." Finally, Congress needed to know exactly how much removal would cost. Accurately foretelling the bleak future of the Indians of the Southeast, Hemphill argued that "it would be inhuman to expose them to the forests or the prairies; a third or fourth part of their number would be apt to perish." All these inadequacies induced him to recommend a year's moratorium on the policy, so that the commission could do its work and report back to Congress.[30]

Hemphill addressed the politics of the situation, asserting that the question was too important to be addressed "on party grounds," as "it deeply involves both the political and moral character of the country." He insisted that the Jacksonians who supported his amendment did so with great respect for the president, and in fact, were his sincerest friends in suggesting these improvements to his bill. Hemphill protested that the object of his amendment was simply "to obtain information before we act." Almost despite himself, he ended with an emotional appeal: "I feel a consciousness of my incapacity to give any glowing description of Indian wrongs. Against the aborigines who once possessed this fair country, what complaint have we to make? In what degree are their scalping knives and tomahawks to be compared to our instruments of death by which we have overthrown their powerful kingdoms, and reduced the whole fabric of their societies, with their kings and queens, to their present miserable condition?" Hemphill's speech reflected the romantic and humanitarian but inaccurate ideas of many eastern whites in concluding that "their fate, we all know, is irrevocably sealed" and "their extermination is certain." Nonetheless, "as a generous nation, we ought to act towards them with the strictest fairness, and attend to their glimmering existence with more than ordinary humanity." Apparently his arguments were persuasive, and addressed the concerns of other representatives. When a proponent of Jackson's bill called for a vote on the "previous question"—which, if successful, would sideline Hemphill's amendment—the vote was a tie, only broken by the affirmative vote of the speaker of the house. Jackson's unamended Indian Removal bill then squeaked through on a vote of 102 for and 97 opposed.[31]

So Hemphill did not oppose Jackson's policy outright. He was a born compromiser. But his doubts, and the degree to which they were shared, are an indication of Jackson's forcefulness as president. Hemphill was actually arguing that Congress should take more responsibility for crafting the removal law, which the president would then execute. But just as Jackson had been undeterred by reports that the Second Bank was functioning well, he had made up his mind on Indian Removal, and pushed his agenda through. And yet, one wonders how much pain and death might have been avoided on the infamous Trail of Tears if Hemphill's more humane approach had been adopted. Clearly white America was not united behind this project. Its execution only raised more doubts and sympathy for the Indians. In the years following, even some of those who had opposed Hemphill's amendment admitted that Jackson's policy was hastily and poorly administered and called for investigatory commissions similar to the one Hemphill had proposed in 1830.[32]

After this session in Congress, with Hemphill perhaps exhausted by the fight over Indian Removal, his interests shifted back home. He served as a state representative in 1831–1832, and then retired from legislative work for good. He had moved to a new house at Ninth and Walnut Streets in 1830, near the Walnut Street Theater. In addition to their Philadelphia townhouses, Joseph and Margaret had also enjoyed, since 1821, the respite of a summer home on the banks of the Schuylkill River. This was Strawberry Mansion, still standing today in Fairmount Park. The history of the place is a good example of the intertwining networks of Philadelphians discovered among these biographies. Before the Revolution the spot was the site of Somerton, the home of Secretary to the Continental Congress Charles Thompson. Thompson had worked with Anthony Benezet as a member of the Friendly Association. He was married to Deborah Norris Logan's cousin Hannah Norris, and Deborah grew extremely fond of him after the war. Alas, by that time the British had burned Somerton down.[33]

Figure 18. Strawberry Mansion, 2450 Strawberry Mansion Drive, Philadelphia, Pennsylvania (built ca. 1783). Wikimedia Commons.

The house Hemphill acquired, Summerville, was built around what was left of the old place starting around 1783, by Judge William Lewis. This was Grace Growden Galloway's "Lawyer Lewis," who had become president judge of the Supreme Court of Pennsylvania. He had also written Pennsylvania's law gradually abolishing slavery in 1780 (and was advised in so doing by Anthony Benezet). Like Hemphill, Lewis hailed from Chester County. Both Margaret Hemphill and her husband had often visited the Lewises at Summerville, so they knew the house well. It was perfect for the fashionable entertaining the Hemphills wished to undertake.[34]

Margaret, an avid horsewoman, and the Hemphill boys enjoyed the place immensely. It would appear that Margaret and Joseph spoiled their sons, for neither applied himself much to schooling or preparing for a career. Robert did go to Princeton at age seventeen in 1826, but left after a year owing to ill health. He then spent several years touring Europe. Robert shared his mother's love of horses and eventually built a racetrack near the home. He also bred dalmatians, then fashionable coach dogs and cultivated the strawberries (originally imported from Chile) that later gave the house its name. Family tradition is that, when the Hemphills took a trip to Europe in 1827 (likely taking Robert), Alexander, ambitious to entertain and join the fashionable First City Troop, built a ballroom at the south end of the house. His parents, appalled upon their return to discover the defacement of the home, built the two wings on either side of the original house in an attempt to hide the damage and restore the mansion's symmetry. Robert did go on to become an officer of the troop; Alexander went on to drink.[35]

Joseph Hemphill at least had more time to enjoy Summerville once he did not have to travel to Washington. His interests shifted from politics to industry. In 1831, he became a capitalist, by providing financial backing for the Tucker China Manufactory, the first sustained venture in fine china production in the United States. Hemphill remained involved with what became known as the Tucker and Hemphill Company until retiring in 1837. The company folded soon after, in 1838, following the devastating financial Panic of 1837. Its story is a good example of the difficult struggle for survival against European competition and the boom and bust cycles of early American industrial capitalism.[36]

Tucker china originated in the shop of Philadelphia Quaker china importer Benjamin Tucker, which operated between 1816 and 1827 at 324 High (now Market) Street between Ninth and Tenth Streets. Tucker built a small kiln in the back of the shop where his son William, earlier a teacher and then an engraver, began decorating and firing imported white china. William then started experimenting with the production of china itself, using clays obtained from around the city and then finding sources and trying different proportions of the other ingredients necessary to make good porcelain until at length he succeeded. In 1825, the twenty-five-year-old William went into business, building kilns in an old waterworks at Twenty-Third and Chestnut Streets that he purchased from the city. At his father's insistence, he took on his younger brother Thomas as an apprentice. Thomas Tucker, who became a talented artist, later described the frustrating succession of failures involved in developing their product, an experience worsened by the brothers' discovery of a worker—employed by English competitors—who sabotaged their efforts. They kept finding handles that had dropped off items being fired at the bottom of the kilns, until a hearing-impaired employee made it known that he had seen this man running a knife around items as he placed them in the kiln.[37]

The keen international competition illustrated by this crime made it difficult for William Tucker to make any profit from his venture. Benjamin Tucker had lent several thousand dollars to his son, and a few other investors came and went, but more help was needed. The Tuckers turned to enlisting then-Congressman Hemphill in their effort to get a government subsidy to aid the infant industry. They even sent President Jackson samples of their product, but they did not succeed in winning his support (although he kept the china). International competition also caused William to write in January 1831 to Senator Isaac Barnard, begging him not to join efforts to reduce the tariff on imported china, as dropping it would destroy his fledgling business. In the course of his plea, Tucker mentioned an October 1830 letter from an American gentleman in Paris to a friend in Chester County, noting French admiration for Philadelphia porcelain. Before leaving Congress, Hemphill helped to defeat the tariff reduction bill in the House. Back home, at the fall 1831 and spring 1832 meetings of the Friends of American Industry in the Musical Fund Hall, Hemphill was elected president of that protariff organization. He also served on a committee appointed by the New York Tariff Convention of 1831 to urge Congress to support import duties for the protection of American industry.[38]

Hemphill had become interested in porcelain during his 1827 trip to Europe. He, like Benjamin Tucker, was also looking for opportunities to set up his sons. Alexander, in particular, needed "direction" or at least distraction from drinking, horse racing, and otherwise spending his father's money. Far better to invest $7,000 in the china enterprise; maybe Alexander would rise to the challenge.[39]

William Tucker died in August 1832; the following February Hemphill bought out the Tuckers' interest in the business. Thomas Tucker stayed on as superintendent. Despite the passing of the enterprising pioneer, it was the period of Hemphill's control that was the best for Tucker china in terms of style; pieces from 1832–1837 are often mistaken for French Sevres porcelain. Before William Tucker died the two men had purchased a property at the southwest corner of Seventeenth and Chestnut Streets and had a large factory built, which allowed greatly increased production. Hemphill brought artisans and artists over from Germany, England, and France to work on the china, and it became very popular among the wealthy. Many families in Pennsylvania and New Jersey had pieces or whole services made and decorated to order. Newspaper articles lauded Tucker's experimentation and determination and Hemphill's investment in the enterprise. The company proudly exhibited its wares at exhibitions of the Franklin Institute and the American Institute of New York and won both praise and prizes. Many different pieces were produced, from pitchers, vases, urns, coffee pots, and teapots to dishes, bowls, fruit baskets, and other tableware, to picture frames, lamps, and cologne and smelling-salt bottles. The decoration often consisted of painted flowers and gold trim, but also landscapes and buildings and sometimes copies of portraits of famous men. The company's pattern books are preserved at the Philadelphia Museum of Art, which has a large collection of the ware.[40]

Hemphill's efforts to engage Alexander in the china business did not succeed. The son did not take to the work or reform his wayward habits and died, according to family tradition, a drunkard in November 1834. He was buried in Christ Church graveyard. This must have been a trying year at Summerville, for Joseph's mother, Ann, also died there, although she had attained the good old age of ninety-five. Hemphill's older son, Robert, had been taken into the business in 1833, but he was not very interested either. Effectively, the company was run by Joseph and Thomas Tucker. But no sooner had Hemphill bought into the business than the bank failure of 1833 hit him hard. He had to take out a mortgage on Summerville. His ownership of the china company was not to last much longer. When Joseph Hemphill finally retired from the business in 1837, Thomas Tucker leased the factory and continued to make porcelain for about a year, until he had enough stock to fill a store on Chestnut Street above Seventh. He then stopped making china but continued to import it from Europe. In 1841 he sold his entire stock at auction, and turned to other ventures. The china factory was sold at a sheriff's sale in April 1842.[41]

A month later, on May 29, Joseph Hemphill died. He was seventy-three and had been quite ill at the end. He was buried very near to Summerville at Laurel Hill Cemetery. Hemphill had led a busy and varied life. He had seen both success and failure but had the satisfaction of being involved in the important issues of his day. His obituary asserted that "few men have occupied until within a few years past, so large a share of the public notice of the citizens of Philadelphia." The author went so far as to argue that "to his personal popularity rather than to any other cause, may the early triumph of the Jackson party in this city be attributed." And yet the writer was precise in his evaluation, noting that "Mr. Hemphill was more distinguished for sound judgment, cool perception, and an almost unerring knowledge of men, than for brilliancy or splendor." In April 1844, Summerville was sold at auction. Margaret moved to West Chester with her son Robert and his family. While later generations of Hemphills would follow Joseph's path from West Chester to Philadelphia, this generation's sojourn in the city was at an end.[42]

PART IV

Pursuing an Inclusive America: Three Aspiring Antebellum Lives

Prologue

While Philadelphia, like the new nation writ large, was opening the door of opportunity for aspiring white men, it also closed the door of advancement on others. Nonetheless, some Philadelphians on the margins knocked for entry, both for themselves and for their brothers and sisters. The three figures featured in this part fought for the cause of inclusion in the young nation. In this they were representative of their city, for Philadelphia took the lead in nearly every variety of antebellum benevolence and reform. Each of these three individuals was born into disadvantageous positions (by merit of limits imposed by race, gender, and class); their lives show how both old hierarchies and rising divisiveness could dim the American promise in the decades approaching the Civil War. As Philadelphia approached midcentury, its reputation as a leader in advancing human rights would be tarnished.[1]

Philadelphia's social reform record owed much to its Quaker roots. While Quaker religious practice had become more routinized and settled over time, Friends' peace testimony and their faith in the Inner Light still proved a wellspring for social activism. Even as their proportion of the population declined, they had an outsized influence on social issues, particularly the cause of ending slavery. Following in the anti slavery footsteps of Anthony Benezet, in 1775 Quakers were the majority of founders of the Pennsylvania Abolition Society, the country's first. Philadelphia also proved a host to emerging independent Black churches. Richard Allen and Absalom Jones helped establish the African Methodist Episcopal Church in 1787, the first autonomous Black Protestant church in the country. Soon thereafter in 1792, an independent African American Episcopal Church would be established at St. Thomas. It should not be surprising that such churches would become an important early support for Francis Johnson, the subject of Chapter 10. In the early nineteenth century Johnson became Philadelphia's most famous bandleader. Being welcomed into the homes and churches of whites and Blacks alike, Johnson would eventually be invited to play for the queen of England, who awarded him a silver bugle. Thus, the cause of Philadelphia freedom was advanced as much by religious institutions as by the famed political documents drafted in the city.

But if religion helped support social change, it also yielded growing social conflict. Evangelicalism, in particular, proved polarizing. Leading the evangelical charge was Presbyterian revivalist James Patterson, whose Northern Liberties pastorate had swelled to a thousand congregants by 1827, making it the largest church in Philadelphia. Revival religion, with its emphasis on free will, carried within it the seeds of social activism. Patterson's Northern Liberties district became a major focus for temperance reformers, who attacked alcohol consumption as a sin. More radical revivalists would also join the call for the immediate abolition of slavery, helping to deepen a religious divide that would split the Presbyterian Church in two. In 1836 at the General Assembly in Philadelphia, the Old School Presbyterians cast aside the New School party that had become so enmeshed in revivalism and in nationwide reform causes.[2]

The rising polarization within Presbyterianism presaged the rising polarization of the city and nation. For reformers, there was no retreat. Sarah Thorn Tyndale, the subject of Chapter 11, would join an array of social causes. Having quickly turned her husband's business around in widowhood, Tyndale was able to use her newfound privilege to pursue a life of benevolence. Her causes included assisting prostitutes, abolitionism, and women's rights. She reached close to the outer boundaries of social experimentation, joining and helping found a Fourierist commune in New Jersey. Similarly, William Darrah Kelley, the subject of Chapter 12, was largely consumed with attacking a series of social evils, pushing for restrictions on banks, capital punishment, and alcohol. As midcentury approached, he became increasingly interested in the more radical causes of women's rights and abolitionism.

But if social radicalism was gaining steam, there was an equally strong conservative reaction, darkening Philadelphia's skies with smoke. Two mob action fires punctuated the turn: the burning of Pennsylvania Hall in 1838 and the torching of St. Augustine's Catholic Church in 1844. Pennsylvania Hall had been built by the Pennsylvania Anti-Slavery Society (established in 1838 and not to be confused with the older Pennsylvania Abolition Society). Its founders included both prominent Quakers and white and Black evangelicals. The society also advanced the cause of female activism, featuring such reformers as Angelina Grimké Weld and Abby Kelley, who spoke to mixed crowds. This would prove combustible material. The hall stood for less than a week. White rioters and their supporters justified their act of arson, by pointing to the "promiscuous audience" of Black and white women and men, seen leaving the hall arm in arm. A Philadelphia grand jury agreed, exonerating the rioters for their behavior.[3]

Meanwhile, growing nativism would spark riots in the working-class suburbs of Kensington and Southwark. While Catholicism had gained notable acceptance in the ecumenical years following the American Revolution, by the 1820s suspicions about its incompatibility with American values grew when the radical priest William Hogan failed in his efforts to democratize the Catholic Church in the United States. Growing fear of Irish immigrants helped drive further anti-Catholic sentiment in the city. When Bishop Francis Kenrick asked that Catholic children be allowed to read the Catholic Douay Bible in public schools (in place of the Protestant King James Version), it set off a series of heated public disputes that eventually spilled into the streets. Nativists and the Irish Catholic residents of Kensington and Southwark locked in pitched battles, exchanging gunfire. A group of homes and institutions, including St. Michael's Catholic Church, were set on fire in Kensington. While nativists in Kensington carried out this rampage, others burned the Philadelphia Catholic Church of St. Augustine's at Fourth and Vine. As rioters and residents watched, the church was consumed by flames.[4]

Many of the rioters were working-class white men. Taking pride in their whiteness and English identity, they attacked Irish workers who seemed to threaten their livelihood. While Irish immigration did serve to depress wages, it was the larger forces of capitalism and the deskilling of labor that undermined the standing of all workingmen in society. President Andrew Jackson had seemed to offer hope to workingmen with his war on the Second Bank of the United States (which operated in Philadelphia from 1816 to 1836), but his promises proved illusory. With the economy in a tailspin after the Panic of 1837, nativist workingmen found it easier to scapegoat the alien Irish immigrants for their economic woes. Thus, conservative backlash gripped antebellum Philadelphia, expressed in antiabolitionism, nativism, and the silencing of women.[5]

The lives of Johnson, Tyndale, and Kelley show how Philadelphians navigated these cultural crosswinds. Impressive success, even if not on terms entirely of their own choosing, was won by some African Americans, women, and working-class white men. Francis Johnson was readily accepted into the homes of white patrons. He nevertheless was constantly reminded of his inferior racial status by newspaper columnists, jeering crowds, and even white students. His ascent was necessarily negotiated. His concerts aimed more to entertain than edify. While often invited to perform at the Musical Fund Society, he was never offered membership in that prestigious organization.

Early in life Sarah Thorn Tyndale endured the hard lot of many ordinary women. As a wife to an Irish immigrant and china importer, she supported her

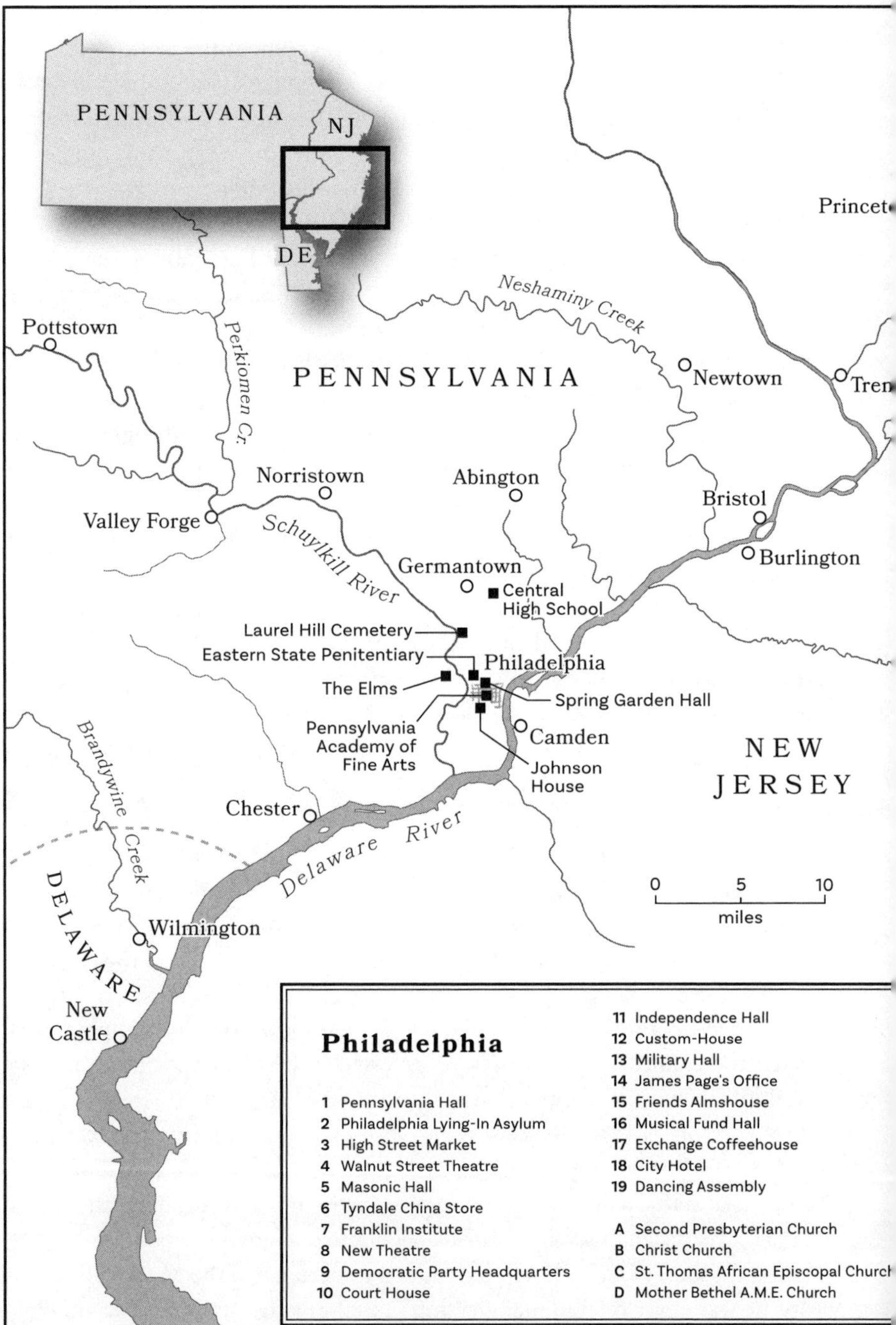

Map 4. People and Their Places: Three Aspiring Antebellum Lives.

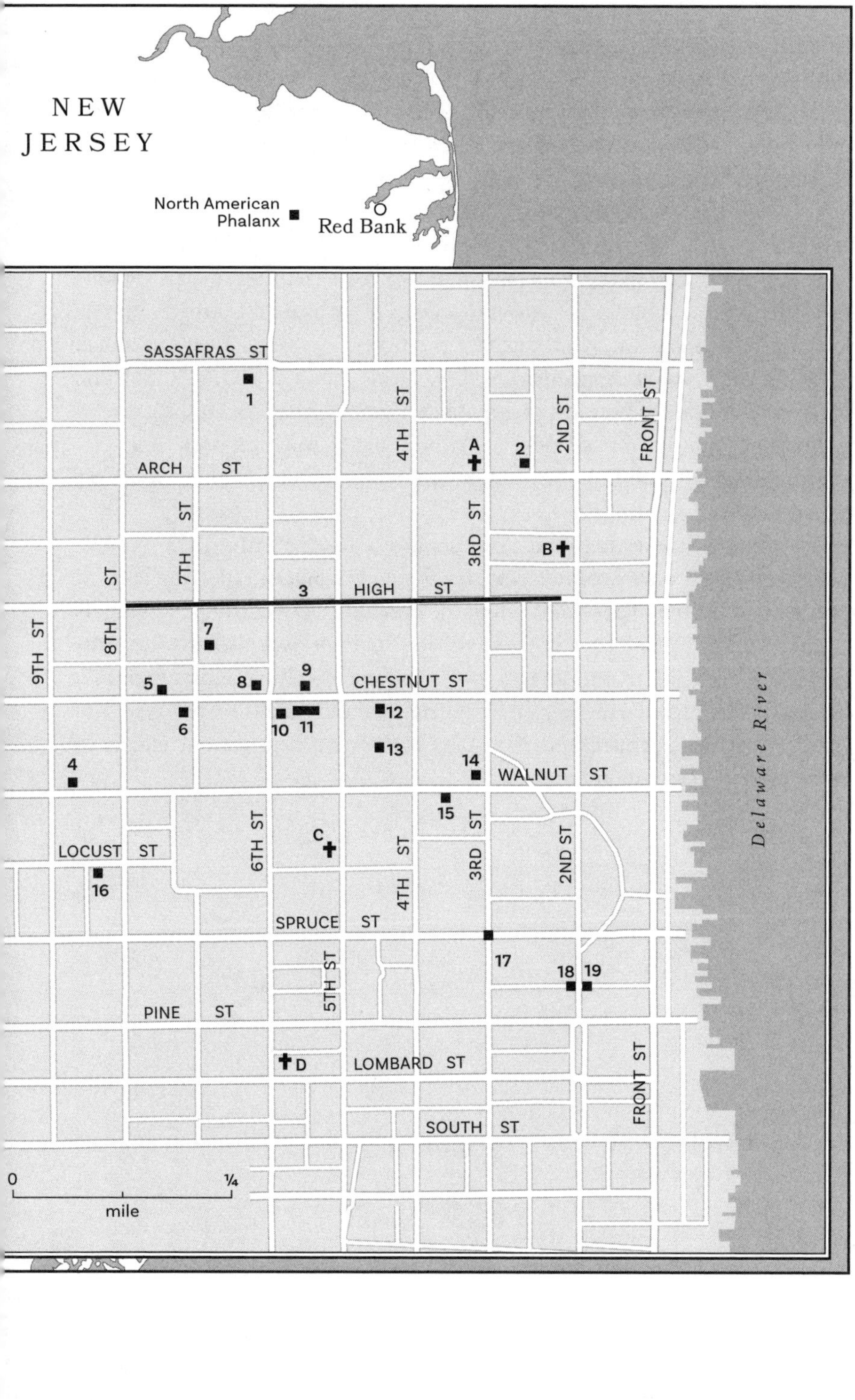
NEW JERSEY
North American Phalanx
Red Bank
SASSAFRAS ST
ARCH ST
HIGH ST
CHESTNUT ST
WALNUT ST
LOCUST ST
SPRUCE ST
PINE ST
LOMBARD ST
SOUTH ST
9TH ST
8TH ST
7TH ST
6TH ST
5TH ST
4TH ST
3RD ST
2ND ST
FRONT ST
Delaware River
1
2
3
4
5
6
7
8
9
10
11
12
13
14
15
16
17
18
19
A
B
C
D
0
¼
mile

husband's business while bearing ten children. The second stage of her adult life began in widowhood. Widows had the advantage of property acquisition denied most married women. Inheriting a bankrupt business from her husband, in four short years she was able to retire on a handsome fortune. But her larger reform dreams would die with her. Her pacifist principles would be deeply violated as America descended into the Civil War.

William Darrah Kelley also beat the odds. Raised by his widowed mother, by age eleven he entered the workforce and two years later became an apprentice jeweler. His passion for the law and politics drew him on a journey of self-education, which eventually produced a prominent career as a lawyer, judge, and politician. Measured against his early ideals, however, Kelley's later life would represent one of political pragmatism. He never abandoned the cause of the working man, but his strident calls for equality softened over time. His signature issue became trade protectionism, which earned him the moniker "Pig Iron Kelley."

The stories of these three individuals suggest an alternative nation in the making, one built on the promise of social equality and alternative forms of community. Like the lives of the men in the previous section, these individuals supported and informed one another's efforts. But their lives also provide testimony to the obstacles to building an inclusive America. Their efforts in nation making would be stalled and tested by riot actions and then the Civil War. The hierarchies of race, gender, and class they confronted still test our efforts to reach a more perfect union today.

CHAPTER 10

Francis Johnson

In fine, he is the leader of the band.

—Robert Waln

Francis Johnson was famous in his time. He should be better known today. He published two hundred pieces of music and probably composed over three hundred. His band played at hundreds of events. His popularity, especially in Philadelphia, was all the more remarkable because he was a Black man in a racially divided city. He was the first African American to publish sheet music. He played for Black and white audiences; he played with Black and white musicians. Occasionally, especially outside the city, his band was attacked by racists; regularly, in the city, he experienced racist snubs. But his band played on. As it did, Johnson's troupe demonstrated that African Americans could and would participate in the making of American excellence in art, music, and literature.[1]

This was important, for most white Americans associated Blackness with bondage. During much of Johnson's lifetime, roughly 90 percent of African Americans were enslaved, mostly in the South. But Johnson grew up in Philadelphia, which was home to the largest free Black community in the United States. Johnson was born in 1792, a moment of promise in the Quaker State. He was a biracial child in a state that preached liberty and equality and had passed a Gradual Abolition Act in 1780. As he matured, and as hundreds remained enslaved under the protracted terms of that act, Philadelphia's abolitionist promise faded. In fact, in the decade before Johnson's death in 1844, Philadelphia's Black community would suffer mob violence and disfranchisement. Nonetheless, the Black community grew, remaining around 10 percent of the city's rapidly expanding population. And Philadelphia's free Blacks built benevolent, religious, and cultural institutions to sustain the community. Philadelphia's whites mostly opposed any advances by Philadelphia's Blacks, which only made the embattled minority group redouble its self-defense efforts. It was a vicious cycle. Some of the institutions Black Philadelphians built carry on today, reminders of past struggles and sources of sustenance still. Through it all, Francis Johnson has remained an emblem of Black pride and uplift.[2]

Though some scholars believed he had Caribbean roots, we now know that Johnson was born free in Philadelphia and baptized at St. Paul's Church. This was not typical. The majority of free Blacks in early national Philadelphia had flocked to the city after leaving slavery elsewhere. According to abolitionist census work, there were about twenty-five hundred African Americans in Philadelphia in the early 1790s. Although Blacks faced discrimination—especially during the yellow fever epidemic—there was a sense of optimism among many African Americans. As Johnson's contemporary James Forten would observe, Pennsylvania remained one of the few places in the Union where Blacks and whites felt that a spirit of egalitarianism reigned—at least in theory.[3]

Johnson was the child of an interracial union, but nothing more is known of his family. We do know that he displayed musical talent early. By the age of fifteen, he could play multiple instruments, including the flute, piccolo, bugle, violin, and piano. How did this happen? John Cromwell, a Black scholar who grew up in Philadelphia in the 1850s and heard stories about the celebrated bandleader, asserted that Johnson "had received from a French musician a thorough course of instruction." Perhaps his parents originally hailed from St. Domingue, a prosperous French colony in the midst of a slave revolution that would soon overthrow bondage and proclaim the independent republic of Haiti. Or perhaps they came from another French colony.[4]

However he was nurtured and came by his musical talent, by January 1807, the fifteen-year-old was engaged to play the fiddle at dances in what was to be the new Exchange Coffeehouse at Third and Spruce Streets (formerly known as the Mansion House Hotel). He continued to do so for the next three years, thereby mastering the repertoire of popular music of his day, and becoming quite popular himself. Soon Philadelphia music publisher George Willig encouraged the teenager to compose something for him. The first result was "Bingham's Cotillion," published in 1810. Johnson was eighteen. He named the piece in honor of his first place of employment, since the hotel was formerly the mansion of William and Ann Bingham, famous society figures of the Revolutionary era.[5]

So Johnson was playing for dancers where Nancy Shippen had danced a generation before. But his was likely the first American cotillion, that is, music for a dance like the lively French square dance called the quadrille. The dancing assembly soon moved to the City Hotel at Second and Union Streets, where it lasted until 1815. Johnson was off to a solid start. He was lucky. Job opportunities for Blacks were narrowing as maritime commerce began to give way to manufacturing and industry, sectors from which they were often excluded. Many Black Philadelphians turned to self-employment: they worked as fisherman and oystermen, ran small dry-goods stores, and sold various wares on street corners. Johnson was fortunate to find success in music at a young age. It would afford him a place in the city's small but influential Black middle class.[6]

In addition to mastering old tunes and composing new songs, Johnson picked up new instruments. In 1815, the "keyed horn" "or keyed bugle" was introduced in the United States by Robert Willis, who became the bandleader at West Point. This was a notable improvement over earlier brass horns, allowing musicians to play more notes and horns to carry a melody on their own. Johnson got one and was among the first Americans to be proficient on it. He credited Willis with teaching him. Johnson's talent with the horn was crucial because the antebellum music scene, influenced by the local militias established during the War of 1812 (and very socially active thereafter), centered on military bands. By the end of 1814, possibly with the aid of George Willig, the twenty-two-year-old Johnson and three other young Black players were appointed as the band of the Washington Guards. Soon Johnson began publishing popular march tunes with Willig and another Philadelphia music publisher, George Blake. These men were at the top of the industry in the nation's foremost music publishing city. Through them, Johnson put an indelible stamp on early American martial music.[7]

Although Johnson played for and was patronized by white Philadelphians, he was and remained part of the free Black community. He lived in the heart of that community at 261 Spruce Street. In his twenties, he joined two of its central institutions, the First African Lodge of Free Masons (where he was initiated by the grand master, longtime Philadelphia religious leader Absalom Jones) and the African Episcopal Church of St. Thomas (which Jones had founded in 1792). Johnson recruited and trained a number of talented Black musicians. In the 1820s he formed the African Harmonic Society and began to lead it in sacred music concerts in New York and Philadelphia.[8]

Johnson's experience as a young artist was similar in many ways to that of his friend Robert Douglass Jr., the son of St. Thomas's pastor, William Douglass. Young Douglass was a gifted painter. Both Douglass and Johnson would be snubbed by the city's artistic elite. Both would go to Europe to refine their craft and stretch their wings. Yet while he was clearly sympathetic to abolitionism and racial justice, Johnson was not as overtly political as Douglass, who became more formally involved in Black protest causes. Not only did these

Figure 19. Francis Johnson (1792–1844). Lithograph of daguerreotype by Robert Douglas, Jr. Historical Society of Pennsylvania.

men demonstrate the growth of Philadelphia's Black middle class, then, they also illustrated its varied character. There was more than one way to deal with a racist world. Douglass admired Johnson. He gave the eulogy after his death, and published a lithograph of a daguerreotype he had taken of the musician. The image memorialized Johnson's respectability and success, which abetted the abolitionist cause.[9]

Johnson focused increasingly on his music. As a young bandleader, he was at the forefront of a number of musical developments. He was clearly an innovator as a composer. He took liberties with different genres and improvised to please his audience, mainly by converting popular melodies into danceable tunes. He also played a role in the evolving nineteenth-century social scene. In January 1818, for example, his band played at the first open (that is open to anyone who could pay the price of admission) cotillion party held at the new gaslit Masonic Hall on Chestnut Street.[10]

Even at these events, Johnson could not escape the specter of race. Indeed, the racial divide was clear—Blacks were present only in service capacities. While Johnson and his band played the music, Robert Bogle, who was also Black, catered the event. Still, white Philadelphians lauded the talents and artistry of these men (especially Johnson), since they loved to dance to their tunes. One white devotee of the Masonic Hall cotillions made this clear: "You observe the leader of the band. He is a descendant of Africa, and possesses a most respectable share of musical talents.—Among other follies of our young ladies, it is quite a fashionable one, to be 'enchanted' with this fiddler. He is indeed a prominent character in the gay world. . . . In fine, he is leader of the band at all balls, public and private; sole director of all serenades." Nicholas Biddle, head of the Second Bank of the United States and one of Philadelphia's foremost business leaders, expressed the fondness of the white elite in a humorous poem—his "Ode to Bogle"—that commemorated both Johnson and the caterer. Johnson returned thanks to the community for its support in an October notice in the city's most-read newspaper, *Poulson's Daily Advertiser*.[11]

Despite this adulation, Johnson remained firmly rooted, by necessity or by choice, in the Black community. In March 1819, in a ceremony at Christ Church, the twenty-seven-year-old married eighteen-year-old Helen Appo, the eldest daughter of a recently deceased confectioner originally from Saint Domingue (Haiti). He moved into her family home at 65 South Fourth Street. A few years later they moved to their own house at the southwest corner of Pine between Fifth and Sixth Streets. Eventually known as Cedar Ward, this neighborhood was the heart of Black life in Philadelphia. Just around the corner from the Johnson home was the already famous African Methodist Episcopal Church ("Mother Bethel"), founded by Richard Allen in 1794. The Johnsons did not have children but became the guardians of Helen's three teenaged siblings when her mother died in 1825. In addition to looking after her brothers and sister, Helen built a successful business as a seamstress, and then formed a tailoring business with John B. Sammons that served both Black and white elites.[12]

Meanwhile, Francis's career took off, in part because he had gained a fan at the pinnacle of white society. In October 1819 he played at the wedding of Phoebe Ridgeway Rush, who had followed him since she was sixteen. With her patronage, "Frank" Johnson—as fond clients called him—became the foremost bandleader for Philadelphia's leading families. That Johnson also worked for a couple of dancing masters suggests that this, too, was a means of capturing a following among rich Philadelphia teenagers. In 1820, Johnson and his band followed the movements of elite families by making the first of many summer trips to the resort at Saratoga Springs, New York. There they played at balls in the foremost hotels, adding members of high society beyond Philadelphia to their list of fans.[13]

The rest of the year the band was busy playing for several militia units. Johnson did not need to solicit their business; they came to him. His society engagements had spread his fame throughout elite Philadelphia. In the fall of 1821, for example, Democratic politician and attorney James Page sought him out to play with the State Fencibles. Johnson agreed to a nonexclusive contract. When the Fencibles' white fife and drum musicians resigned over this retention of an African American band, Page ignored them, and Johnson's band paraded with the troop. Johnson quickly showed his appreciation by composing the "Captain Page Quickstep." Engagement by the First City Troop and the Washington Grays followed in 1822. Over time, Johnson added instruments to the military bands, first fife and drums to the original woodwinds, French horn, and percussion. Later, as brass instruments became prominent, the group evolved into a brass band.[14]

A sure sign of Johnson's stature in the Philadelphia social and cultural scene was his commission to compose music for the premier event of 1824, the visit of Revolutionary War hero General Lafayette. Johnson's band played as the First City Troop escorted the Marquis de Lafayette and city leaders (including Stephen Girard, who organized the celebrations) to various events, including the visit to Independence Hall where Lafayette's moving reunion with Charles Peale took place. The band also played at the grand ball at the New Theatre on Chestnut Street. Johnson had composed many new musical pieces for these occasions as well as for a new circus theatrical event, a grand spectacle at the still-extant Walnut Street Theater called "the Cataract of the Ganges" or "the Rajah's Daughter."[15]

To top off the busy year, Johnson's band played in a future landmark, the Musical Fund Hall, which opened on the 800 block of Locust Street, and, converted to an apartment building, still stands today. This structure was designed by William Strickland, who used some of the materials of the Fifth Presbyte-

Figure 20. Musical Fund Hall, 808 Locust Street, Philadelphia, Pennsylvania (built 1824). Library Company of Philadelphia.

rian Church that had occupied the site previously. The old pew backs, for example, were used in the platform for the orchestra and proved to vibrate well. In fact, the space had the best acoustics in the city before the completion of the Academy of Music in 1857. Johnson played in the new hall for Lafayette and then many times thereafter.[16]

The latter half of the 1820s must have seemed full of paradox to Francis and Helen Appo Johnson. He was in constant demand, and his band quadrupled in size (it now included his two Appo brothers-in-law, William and Joseph). His talent was clearly recognized, applauded, and rewarded. And yet Philadelphia remained a deeply divided city in racial terms, and the Johnsons were not immune to ugly slights. Any achievements on the part of Philadelphia's Black bourgeoisie met with ugly ridicule in Edward Clay's popular caricature series, "Life in Philadelphia." The series, which lampooned Black uplift, circulated widely and was available in various Philadelphia shops. Moreover, Johnson's compositions were soon joined in the marketplace by minstrel music composed to accompany "Jim Crow" performances, an explosively popular genre of blackface music created by Thomas Dartmouth Rice. Though minstrelsy borrowed from Black musical traditions, it mocked African American dialect, dress, and dance styles in an effort to marginalize Blacks culturally and politically. In 1828, the newspapers joined in, ridiculing Black balls, failing to condemn the white ruffians who assaulted some of those attending, and even slighting "Mrs. Appo"—either Johnson's wife or sister-in-law Ann, who was the organist at St. Thomas Church. African American newspapers, including *Freedom's Journal* (launched in New York City in 1827 with Samuel Cornish, who had been educated in Philadelphia, serving as an editor), would respond with indignation and outrage; still, the stabs must have hurt Johnson. Family pain must have soared with the deaths of young Joseph and Ann Appo in 1829.[17]

And yet, through these trials, Johnson's popularity grew. His prominence was chronicled in the diary of Philadelphia politician Samuel Breck. In January 1826 Breck accompanied his wife and daughter to a dancing assembly conducted by Johnson at the Masonic Hall. In 1828, he praised Johnson's band (and Bogle's catering) at a "grand ball" at General Thomas Cadwalader's home and at a gala costume ball of the revived City Dancing Assembly. In 1829, he noted Johnson's band at a Phoebe Ridgeway Rush house party, in her home across the street from Independence Hall. "A propos of Johnson," he commented, "This *Black* musician is a man of taste, and even science in his vocation. He has organized a large band, and gives lessons upon various instruments; and what is still more useful and certainly more singular is the talent he has of turning every lively tune in the new operas to his purpose by adapting to it a Quadrille or Cotillion of his own composing which he introduces at the parties in Philada. and then gets engraved and circulated thro' the union; thus becoming the author of all novelty in dancing."[18]

In the meantime, Johnson was highly visible on parade with the State Fencibles, which performed at events ranging from the anniversary of Andrew Jackson's 1815 victory in the Battle of New Orleans to George Washington's birthday. The Fencibles took their show on the road in the summer of 1828 with an excursion to New York City, footing the bill for Johnson and eighteen musicians. Johnson was thus simultaneously conducting a military band and a cotillion band. He combined the two for big occasions.[19]

In 1830, the State Fencibles made "Military Hall" on the south side of Library Street between Fourth and Fifth its armory and meeting place. It was behind the Custom-House, formerly the Second Bank of the United States. It was here that Johnson practiced with his band. This means that Johnson and his musicians rehearsed on the spot that had been part of Deborah Norris Logan's childhood garden, the one her family shared with abolitionist Anthony

Benezet. The city had changed enormously in the intervening half century, although the old State house, now called Independence Hall, still stood around the corner.[20]

Johnson's popularity was reported in the newspapers. One story described his role in a daylong steamboat excursion in 1832, from Philadelphia to New Castle, Delaware, where near two hundred persons celebrated the opening of, and tried out, a new railroad line. "Johnson's fine band" played on the steamship, "pouring its rich heart-animating notes upon the ears of the company, and thrilling the hearts" of the many onlookers as the boat got under way. Then, lest the train ride occur without musical accompaniment, "there was a car hitched on expressly for the accommodation of our musical chief, Frank Johnson—and now and then the woods were made to resound to the airs which nobody can hear from Frank Johnson's band without being delighted." In April 1835 another paper praised his music at a costume ball.[21]

But local periodicals also mocked him. In a story in the popular women's magazine *Godey's Lady's Book*, a group of young men serenading young women were affronted at being asked to come in and play at a party because Frank Johnson was already engaged to perform. But "we are all gentlemen, madam," they protested, as the hostess proposed "to decide between the merits of your band and that of Mr. Francis Johnson." And a satirical account of the departure of a popular opera star noted that "Frank Johnson, that rara avis in terra, a civil darkey, had been engaged, with the whole of his black band, to give colour to the proceedings." How did Johnson feel about these disrespectful and quite public taunts? We can only guess. But it had to have caused pain, if not anger. Worse, racial injury was not confined to disrespect in these years. Mobs of whites attacked Black citizens and property in Johnson's immediate neighborhood in 1834, and then again in 1835 and 1838. We do not know if Johnson and his family were assaulted directly, but he was part of the Black bourgeoisie whose homes and institutions bore the brunt of the mob's fury.[22]

In this way, Johnson's life, if not his politics, became entangled in debates over racial identity and uplift. As a swath of Black Philadelphians rose in society, whites ridiculed them as pretentious transgressors of racial etiquette. By 1838, white politicians would formally disfranchise Pennsylvania's African Americans. Blacks fought back. Robert Purvis, a wealthy Black man who married James Forten's daughter and moved in some of the same circles as Johnson, published an angry pamphlet—*The Appeal of Forty Thousand Citizens, Threatened with Disfranchisement*—which demanded the return of voting rights for free Blacks in the Quaker State. Johnson may have thought that his music offered a similar rejoinder to the racist onslaught. But he found that this tactic did not work either.[23]

In fact, as Johnson's band traveled, it found that other locales replicated Philadelphia's worsening racial climate. Many excursions, such as an 1832 trip to Mount Vernon with the Washington Grays, were pleasant, but there was always fear of trouble. Virginians were particularly sensitive to the presence of a free Black band. Nat Turner's slave rebellion, which took place in August 1831 and killed fifty-five whites, had set the entire South on edge. Indeed, Virginia's General Assembly would soon debate a gradual emancipation plan that included the colonization of liberated Blacks, who whites saw as anathema to the state's social stability. One wonders what Johnson and his fellow musicians made of a white sergeant in their company calling "an old African, a servant of the General during the Revolution," one of the "curiosities" at Mount Vernon.[24]

Some trips held truly nasty surprises, such as a three-week excursion to Boston with the State Fencibles soon after Johnson's return from Mount Vernon. The *Inquirer* described the group's happy departure: "the officers and privates all appeared in splendid new uniforms, . . . and preceded by Johnson's celebrated band, presented a very creditable and military appearance." Their boat pulled away "amidst the cheers of the surrounding multitude," then "passed a short distance down the river and returned, the Fencibles presenting themselves in a line to their friends on the Philadelphia shore of the river." Everyone was "saluted with three cheers." At each stop on the trip, the group was greeted and hosted by local militia, and all went well until they got to Providence, Rhode Island. There, the white band of the local militia made it known that they would not play with "the d——d darkies." Colonel Page accordingly dismissed Johnson and the band to their hotel and paraded without them. When the troop got back to the hotel, Page called the band onto the porch. There, in their green uniforms trimmed with gold, before the large crowd that had gathered, and "still burning under the slight they had received," the band members got their revenge. According to Page, "Frank never got so much out of his bugle before." For three hours he and his bandmates "entirely captivated the Yankees, and were the victors." The Providence *Literary Subaltern,* which reported the incident, was ashamed and embarrassed, and urged the Fencibles not to blame the people of Providence. Fortunately, the rest of the trip passed without incident.[25]

The band endured a similar experience in the summer of 1838, when it accompanied the Fencibles on an excursion to Albany, returning via New York City. Both Albany and New York papers remarked on the race of the band members while praising their performances. Both papers noted with chagrin that a New York band refused to play with them. "Really," protested the *Albany Argus*, "this is carrying dignity a little too far. We think one drum major just as good as another drum major, especially on the 4th of July, provided always they perform equally good, and behave with decency." Johnson and his men kept their composure, as usual, while these northern whites warred among themselves over the meaning of the color line. As he grew older, Johnson saw that the nation's contradictions between its founding principles and racial injustice had only intensified.[26]

For those who knew his music, Johnson's artistry was paramount. When the band arrived at Saratoga in the summer of 1834, for example, it was greeted with a poem praising Johnson in the *Saratoga Sentinel*. It began:

> Hail thou potentate of Music!
> Welcome to the *healing springs*;
> Once again thy horn melodious,
> O'er my spirit sweetly rings.
> Many a sad and lonely minute,
> When blue ennui held her sway,
> Thy bugle had such magic in it,
> Chased the gloomy fiends away.

One hopes the verses themselves had healing powers to chase memories of racist fiends away.[27]

Perhaps the combination of praise punctured by racism inspired Johnson to embark on a European tour with his four best players in late 1837—the first by an American band. Judging from the discussion of this trip in the *Public Ledger*, white Philadelphians considered Johnson a major city asset. Appreciation of his artistry was framed in terms of white entitlement to his entertainment services, which would soon be lost. "The citizens of Philadelphia, the Lovers of martial music, [and] the softer . . . strains of the Ball Room are about to be deprived of the services of 'Old Frank,'" the paper announced when it learned of his plans. "What will our Military corps do for parade music? What will our dancers do without Frank's enlivening band?" The writer accepted Johnson's explanation that he was going only to "improve his musical capacity and knowledge, so as to be able in a much greater degree than formerly, to contribute to the gratification of the public." The paper sponsored a meeting of citizens to plan a benefit ball to raise funds for the trip, and then printed reminders for other planning meetings. Meanwhile, in several notices of his own, Johnson assured his clients that he was leaving management of remaining band members in capable hands, to supply Philadelphians with the dance music they required in his absence. A benefit concert at the Musical Fund Hall, the first of many, was a big success.[28]

In encouraging its readers to attend the concert and extend a "liberal patronage" in "remembrance of past services," the *Public Ledger* gave another hint as to why white Philadelphians appreciated this man: "A contributor to public amusement who makes but one Benefit appeal in so many years of assiduous devotion to his duties is . . . a manifestation from those for whom he has labored, that unassuming, unobtruding merit, when it does appeal, will be heard." Johnson's unfailing deference to his audience was paying off. Prominent Philadelphians went so far as to help assure the African American group's safety abroad by providing them—in this age before passports—with notarized and attested certificates of residency and U.S. citizenship. Yet even here there were indications of racial difference. We learn from Johnson's certificate that in October 1837, "Old Frank" was just forty-five years old; stood five feet four and a half inches tall; and had black eyes and hair, a broad nose, a small mouth, a round chin, and a "Sambo" complexion.[29]

His band ever popular with young people, it was during this tour that Johnson was presented with the silver bugle by the young Queen Victoria after a command performance. He apparently pitched his concerts to meet British expectations of the band, advertising it as "The American minstrels—First time in Europe of the self-taught men of Colour." His programs mixed selections from familiar operas, patriotic airs, and even a few minstrel pieces such as "Jim Crow," which British audiences might expect from Black entertainers. Johnson was navigating carefully. His European tour was an act of self-assertion, but to make it successful he catered a little to racist expectations. At home, newspapers followed his movements, first *Niles' National Register* and then the *Liberator* (published in Boston by William Lloyd Garrison). The latter, given its antislavery mission, stressed the positive impact of Johnson's troupe, reporting that his band was "giving concerts before the English nobility at the Argyle rooms, London," and that the "performances are highly spoken of," as, in general, they were. Before noted Black Americans would regularly travel to Europe to escape racism, Johnson's band made its mark as a trailblazer.[30]

Johnson did not actually learn much in the way of music in Europe. He found the same sort of tunes that he had been composing in vogue there too. He did bring home a great deal of new material, including new pieces he composed (such as "the Victoria Gallopade"). More important, he learned a key lesson in how to market his music. He was inspired by the "promenade concerts" invented by Philippe Musard in Paris and recently exported to London.

These were relatively inexpensive affairs, where large crowds could gather in an attractive space and sit and walk around between numbers and take refreshments. Today, we would call these programs light "classical" fare—operatic overtures and arrangements of arias, as well as quadrilles and, especially, Johann Strauss Sr.'s new waltzes. Johnson came home ready to imitate them by arranging and advertising similar concerts in Philadelphia. One of his advertisements made the French model clear: "Frank Johnson gives a musical soirée, similar to those at Musard's in Paris, this evening at 8 o'clock." Johnson was attempting to use elite Philadelphians' appetite for European fashion to wriggle out from the service role in which they had placed him. No longer would the band be dependent on society functions or militia engagements. They were ready to play on their own, with actual concerts, which they had never before attempted. Ironically they were trying to raise their status just as Pennsylvania decided to take the vote *away* from free Blacks. Instead of racial progress the band had returned to a regressive state of civil rights.[31]

Of course Philadelphia whites were not united in terms of racial attitudes. The city's active abolitionist community was composed of both Black and white reformers who undoubtedly appreciated Johnson's talent for what it was. At the other extreme were Philadelphia's many racists. These included whites of all classes, including southern slave owners who came to the city for school or marriage, and they were supplemented yearly by Irish and other immigrants who feared (groundlessly, given the color line in employment) Blacks' competition for jobs. It was Philadelphia's racists who burned down Pennsylvania Hall, built by abolitionists to hold peaceable meetings, just a week after its opening in May 1838. But in between abolitionists and violent racists were many who likely shared the *Public Ledger*'s more commonplace and complacent racism in recognizing Johnson's talent but describing him in the way a southern slave owner might describe a "prize cook."[32]

It was in this racial climate that Johnson made his gamble. By the end of 1838, he had called it quits with military bands and struck out on his own. He announced and advertised the programs for a series of "Musical Soirees" at the Philadelphia Museum. Besides his own compositions, he drew attention to the new waltzes of Strauss. As it turned out, his timing and advertising pitch, combined with his prior reputation, were just right: the band's varied programs drew overflow crowds. One visitor asserted that "not less than 3500 persons attended, for several evenings following . . . and on two occasions they were obliged to close the doors . . . to prevent the admission of more." Another event that drew much notice was the firemen's centennial ball in December 1838 at the Walnut Street Theater; an audio clip of the end of his famously innovative "Fireman's Cotillion" can be accessed online.[33]

Johnson's strategy worked, artistically and financially. Even before his trip to Europe, when he was living at 154 Pine Street, the 1837 abolitionist census had listed him as owning $2,000 worth of property, a not inconsiderable sum. But he was even more successful after his return (when he moved to 170 Pine Street, on the south side, above Sixth Street). In early 1839 the band was performing three to four nights a week at the museum, attracting crowds of between one thousand and three thousand, at an admission price of twenty-five cents. Johnson advertised the musical selections in the *Public Ledger* and used these programs to introduce several innovations, such as "The Voice Quadrilles." In these, the band members occasionally broke into laughter and song. Johnson also introduced trumpets and trombone and used these and other instruments to provide sound effects. The latter are suggested by his description of the "Sleigh waltzes":

> No. 1 As an introduction.
> No. 2. Bell solo.
> No. 3. Blacksmith making nails to shoe his horses.
> No. 4. Clock striking twelve, and watchman spring his rattle.
> No. 5. Sleighing party in an uproar, the horses supposed to be running away, with cracking of whips, jingling of bells, sound of post horns, etc.

This was totally new, and Philadelphians loved it. Although the crowds were more diverse than those at the society balls and parties, this did not prevent elite people from attending.[34]

Johnson's band kept up the grueling schedule into the spring of 1839, all the while continuing to play at private engagements for the likes of Phoebe Rush. So he did not give up society functions entirely. Interspersed with the promenade concerts and society parties were occasional benefit concerts at the Musical Fund Hall. By 1840, the ticket price for these had increased to fifty cents. Johnson's band also played in these years for at least eight events–such as medical school commencements and student exhibitions—hosted by the University of Pennsylvania, as well as at others at Princeton.[35]

In the summer of 1839, Johnson's band was invited to tour with the Buffalo City Guards. They were so well received on their stops in Buffalo, Detroit, Cleveland, and Toronto that the three former cities made them promise to return in the fall, which they did, to repeated praise. One paper observed that Johnson's talents won out over racial prejudice: "Our predictions are verified to the letter, that Johnson would surmount the prejudices got up against him, by an envious uncharitable few and come out 'right side up' after all. Is it not so?" The newspapers lauded the band again on their return, with one paper assuring readers that "any . . . piece by Frank is worth the price of the ticket." Another sign of increasingly national reputation and success was Johnson's continued popularity at Saratoga. "This fashionable place of resort is at present completely crammed with strangers from every point of the compass," the *Albany Microscope* observed that summer. "The Balls take place at the United States and Congress Hall, which are attended by all the beauty, fashion, and *elite* congregated here, and what renders the scene more gay and interesting, is the soul-thrilling, enchanting strains of the celebrated Frank Johnson's band."[36]

Despite his ever-increasing popularity, Johnson was still subject to that same old tune: racial prejudice. Likely the most hurtful was that from the very institutions that hosted his success. Despite the numerous successful benefit concerts and other performances at the Musical Fund Hall, for example, Johnson was never asked to join the Musical Fund Society, which one historian has called "the center of musical life until the Civil War." The institution was founded in 1820 to offer concerts and to raise money "for the relief and support of decayed musicians and their families." Johnson was well acquainted with its members, who included his publishers George Willig and George Blake. Whether his exclusion made him sad or angry or both we cannot know, but he must have felt the snub. He probably felt like his friend painter Robert Douglass did when he had a painting on exhibit in the Pennsylvania Academy of the Fine Arts but was not allowed to enter and see it! Johnson was not an abolitionist like Douglass, but he was not blind to racial issues. A few of his compositions addressed them, such as the music he composed for Sarah Forten's abolitionist poem "The Grave of the Slave" and the 1825 "Recognition March on the Independence of Hayti, . . . Composed expressly for the occasion and dedicated to President J. P. Boyer by his humble servant with every sentiment of respect."[37]

Johnson's band played for the Black community as well as white society, but these programs tended to the sacred and classical over popular dance numbers. This is not surprising, given the central place of the church in Black cultural life in antebellum Philadelphia. Johnson had been conducting the orchestra for sacred music concerts in New York and Philadelphia since the late 1820s. The programs included such composers as Handel, Haydn, Bellini, Mozart, Gluck, and Rossini. In late 1839, he conducted a sacred music concert at the renovated Saint Thomas Church. And in 1841, Johnson conducted a fifty-piece orchestra and over a hundred African American singers in the performance of Joseph

Haydn's oratorio "The Creation," later repeated for a white church. Johnson also volunteered the band that year for a concert to benefit the Philadelphia Library Company of Colored Persons (another manifestation of segregation in Philadelphia).[38]

These performances catered to elite Blacks, just as classical concerts at the Musical Fund Society did to wealthy whites. Was Johnson's ability to play formal classical music concerts without bells and whistles and outside of a party something white Philadelphia tried to ignore? Did whites only pay homage to his craft insofar as they could dance and be entertained, and refuse to credit him for mastery of "high art"? It was not that antebellum Americans drew hard and fast lines between "high" and "low" in their music or theater consumption. Both Shakespeare and opera were popular with all classes, and subject to parody as well. Johnson was able to shape a career more to his liking with his promenade concerts, which attracted all classes with its light classical fare. But white Philadelphia did not look to Johnson for Haydn.[39]

Johnson's career was, like that of many ambitious African Americans of his time and place, a compromise between unequal powers. He had always catered to white tastes. Like other African American composers of antebellum dance music, he stuck with European—rather than African-influenced—forms. This may have been a matter of personal preference as well as what he was mostly exposed to in a city where Blacks remained a minority. The Black churches of Philadelphia and New York did not regard spirituals and other clearly African-influenced forms as consistent with their campaigns for respectability and frowned on them, at least during formal services. Respectability required portrayals of African Americans as virtuous citizens whose fitness for freedom flowed from their mastery of fine arts, elevated political discourse, and other markers of cultural uplift. Needless to say, most of these things were defined by majority white culture. While some African Americans rebelled against such ideas, the Black elite felt strongly about them and embraced uplift initiatives. Johnson, ubiquitous at their sacred music concerts, might have felt the same way. It was also in his economic interest to play European composers to please white patrons.[40]

But why did those patrons prefer him above all others? It is hard to know how Johnson's music sounded since the sheet music only gives the skeleton. But it clearly was distinctive in some ways, especially his later combination of voice with music and sound effects. Some scholars have pointed further to the white observer who credited Johnson with "a remarkable taste in distorting a sentimental, simple, and beautiful song, into a reel, jig, or country-dance." Although the "distorting" was likely an infusion of African American rhythms, this cannot be proven. Johnson's sound might simply have been idiosyncratic. But then again, subtle African American influences might help explain why, in general, Black bands did most of the playing for white dancers in antebellum America.[41]

As we have seen, whites had already begun to show a taste for African American music in the mocking form of minstrelsy. Whether he was making a political statement or an artistic one, Johnson usually steered clear of that genre. In the late 1830s and early 1840s, his place in the array of musical offerings available to white Philadelphians showed this. Formal classical music concerts by white musicians aside, his "promenade concerts" were closer to the operas and concerts given by visiting European artists and bandmasters than they were to minstrel shows. He may have played a few minstrel tunes when abroad to meet the racist expectations of British aristocrats, but he did not repeat them in his Philadelphia programs. Whites accepted Johnson on their terms, for entertainment rather than culture, but he refused to cater to racism. It was not an arrangement between equal forces, but Johnson, again in his economic self-interest, always mixed genially and easily with whites, including the white musicians who occasionally played with him in the 1840s. To the extent that he was angry about racial injustice—and how could he not have been?—he kept it behind an impervious mask of civility.[42]

The diary of a young white man who sought Johnson out for violin lessons gives glimpses of Johnson's patient and polite interactions with whites. Eighteen-year-old Camden, New Jersey, resident Isaac Mickle described their meetings in the summer of 1841. Mickle was from a fairly affluent family and was reading law in the office of Johnson's State Fencibles employer James Page. Mickle's ancestors and mother were Quakers, and presumably opposed to slavery, but the uncle who raised him was openly racist. Mickle's descriptions of Johnson show his own more music-loving brand of racism.[43]

Mickle first met Johnson on a Delaware River boat excursion, where the company was entertained by "the famous Frank Johnson and his band." The two must have talked during a break, and one wonders what Johnson thought of the pompous young amateur: "Frank and I got pretty well acquainted and I found him to be pretty intelligent for a negro. He loves to talk about flats and sharps and naturals, and to tell of his visit to Europe, his reception in Paris, and his interview with Queen Victoria." Was Johnson defending himself from Mickle's racist condescension by reminding the boy of his accomplishments? In his diary Mickle alluded to gossip of bankruptcy on Johnson's part, probably overheard in the law office: "This musical genius has lately applied for the third time, I believe, for the benefit of the insolvent laws: from which it appears that however fast he may make money, he lives it away faster." But Mickle acknowledged the quality of Johnson's music, although again in a race-tinged way: "There were nine other Ethiopians with him to-day, whose music delighted the party in general and the ladies in particular." Mickle was neither the first nor the last white man to acknowledge Johnson's talent and then to diminish it by construing him as fashionable with the ladies.[44]

Mickle was impressed with Johnson, however, for less than two weeks later he became Johnson's student. His description of engaging Johnson reveals again his sense of racial superiority and that Johnson's color was always uppermost in his mind. It also reminds us that citizens could experience random encounters in what was still a "walking city": "I referred to the Directory this morning for the address of Frank Johnson, the famous black musician, and having ascertained it to be in South Eleventh Street, I sallied forth from the office . . . to engage him to give me lessons on the violin." But Mickle's walk was cut when, he bumped into Johnson near Independence Hall. The musician, he noted smugly, was "walking down the street with an air of great consequence and self-sufficiency." Mickle "accosted him," arranging to start his "pupilage on next Monday, for eighteen dollars a quarter." This arrangement did cause some grousing from Mickle's racist uncle. "When I came home and told my uncle what I had been doing," the young man reported, "I found that he did not altogether like the thought of my learning even to fiddle of a 'damned Negro.'"[45]

The following Monday, Mickle presented himself for the first lesson, his racism fully intact: "After a long walk down to Eleventh and Lombard Streets I found the residence of the sooty Apollo—a fine three-story house, with 'Francis Johnson' in capital letters on a stylish door-plate." At the ringing of the doorbell, he recalled, "a young darkee about thirteen years old" answered.

> "Is Mr. Johnson in?" I inquired.
>
> "No sah!" . . . .
>
> The young ape looked at me above half a minute with much earnestness, as if to see if I was on a dunning errand; then "Is you the gem'man what's goin' to take lessons on de violin?" asked he.
>
> "Yes."
>
> "O well den, I guess he is in—I'll see—walk up stairs sah."[46]

Mickle then proceeded to describe Johnson's home office. The level of detail and the tone confirms Black writer Joseph Willson's assertion in *Sketches of the Higher Classes of the Colored People of Philadelphia,* published to defend the Black bourgeoisie that same year, that whites would be surprised to find that the homes of the Black upper classes were equal to their own in taste and furnishings. Mickle wrote: "I was now introduced in to Frank's sanctum, a pleasant room on the second floor filled with articles of his profession." Among these, "immediately opposite to the door, and suspended in a gorgeous frame, was my visitee's portrait, representing him in his uniform with a bugle in his hand." Another portrait provided a glimpse of Johnson's political sentiments. Above the mantel hung a "likeness of Boyer, the President of Hayti, in whom all negroes so much glory." Mickle was noticeably taken with Johnson's trove of music and instruments: "The wall was covered with pictures and instruments of all kinds, and one side of the room was fixed with shelves whereon were thousands of musical compositions, constituting a valuable library." Looking down, Mickle found that "Bass drums, bass viols, bugles and trombones lay in admirable confusion on the floor." He even found direct evidence of Johnson's own work in progress, for "in one corner was an armed composing chair, with pen and inkhorn ready, and some gallopades and waltzes half finished." Undercutting his admiration of his holdings, Mickle mocked Johnson's entry into the room. "After I had taken a good look at all around me," he wrote, "Frank came in, yawning most gracefully after his afternoon nap, and dressed in fashionable dishabille which he sported with as much ease as ever beau Brummel himself could have done." Then Johnson "bow[ed] very politely . . . , rather than sat, into a chair" before getting down to business.[47]

As Mickle was leaving, Johnson gave him a report from the fashionable world, perhaps to reassure him, perhaps to repay his racism. "He promised to make me master of the instrument in three months, if I have any taste for music," Mickle reported. Johnson added that he had about "a dozen young men receiving instruction from him, and he says it is hardly respectable now to say you cannot perform on the divine violin." Playing to Mickle's snobbery, Johnson said that "the students he has are of the most decent families in the city, and the fashion of fiddling is soon to be one of the most universal of all fashions in the higher circles."[48]

Johnson was available to teach Isaac Mickle that summer because he did not go to Saratoga. He had asked for more money, and so the hotel managers replaced him. This might be taken as showing the limits of his popularity among whites, except that he was busy with other invitations to play—as far west as St. Louis—and was asked to come back to Saratoga in 1842. Moreover, at the end of that summer the band went on a ten-month-long tour through New York, Ohio, Indiana, Illinois, Missouri, Kentucky, Virginia, and Pennsylvania. This was unprecedented, since no other east coast American band had gone farther west than Cleveland or toured for so long.[49]

There were positive notices in the newspapers of his Cincinnati concerts. But racial incidents marred the band's concerts in St. Louis and Pittsburgh. Johnson and his band were arrested immediately after their arrival in St. Louis and fined ten dollars each "under the law which forbids free colored men to appear there without a license." The *Christian Secretary* reported that "some respectable citizens became bail, and the matter was carried to a higher court." The *New York Tribune* described the Pittsburgh debacle: "For several days past, the celebrated Frank Johnson, with his band, has been delighting the amateurs of our sister city Pittsburgh, with his delicious music." The act "has drawn full houses, and has been treated by the citizens generally in the most kind and cordial manner." Generally, but not universally; the paper explained that the local temperance society had hired Johnson to play at two benefit concerts to help it pay off the debt for the large hall the organization had just built for its meetings. Apparently some residents objected, and at the first concert "a large rabble of men and boys gathered around the doors and windows, and by their hooting and yelling did what they could to mar the pleasure of those within, who had . . . paid . . . for a rare musical treat." Not content to ruin the concert, the mob followed the band to their lodgings afterwards, "shouting '*nigger*' and other opprobrious epithets, and hurling brick-bats, stones and rotten eggs in great profusion." One of their targets received a serious head wound, his life preserved "no thanks to the mobocrats" who "hurled their missiles with murderous recklessness, if not with murderous intention." The reporter nonetheless insisted that "every well-disposed citizen deeply regretted the disgrace thus brought upon our city," and he called for justice.[50]

Their zest for travel surely dampened by this experience, Johnson and the band spent part of the summer of 1843 closer to home with concerts at the seaside resort of Cape May, New Jersey. In mid-July, Mickle found them there at Congress Hall, the best hotel in the crowded town. On his first night there, the band gave a concert in the dining room. Mickle pronounced the music "good" and the "audience quite brilliant." After some fireworks, the band supplied a midnight serenade. The next day, bored with the beach, Mickle appreciated the "change we had at Congress Hall, in what is technically called a 'hop,' that is a sociable dance, in the main saloon," which "lasted until midnight, longer than which not even Frank Johnson's admirable music could keep them together." Young white Philadelphians had to have Johnson for amusement, but this meant long hours for the band. And apparently it was not just Philadelphians who needed Johnson to spice up their days. The *New York Herald* reported from Saratoga a few days later that "Frank Johnson is expected here this week, to assist in enlivening the company with his inimitable strains."[51]

This incessant travel and work, with success and applause punctuated by racial attacks, must have worn Johnson out. At the end of March 1844 he fell sick and died within a fortnight, on April 6. The *Liberator* said he succumbed to bronchitis, but the death notice said the cause was "rupture of Aortal Aneurism." The newspapers also announced a funeral procession from the Johnson home to the Church of St. Thomas, where the service was held, William Douglass officiating. "The funeral of Frank Johnson, the colored musician, is said to have been the largest ever witnessed in Philadelphia," the newspapers reported. "The colored Masonic Lodges and Literary societies were in the procession," while "the band walked in silence with their instruments draped, and played a dirge at the grave." The silver bugle from Queen Victoria lay on the casket. Although the vast majority present in the church were fellow African Americans, some of Johnson's white fans and clients such as Colonel Page and Isaac Mickle may have been there, or among the very many Philadelphians gathered to watch the procession pass by.[52]

Management of the estate and the band passed to Helen Johnson. The household inventory showed all the marks of refinement and comfort that Mickle had described—mahogany furniture, pictures, carpet, and a mantel clock, in addition to musical instruments and considerable clothing—and yet its value was just sufficient to cover the family's debts. One hopes Helen's own business skills and continued management of the band brought in enough income to support her. She must have been sustained emotionally by the tributes that poured in, such as the long poem that Robert Douglass read at a musical celebration at St. Thomas in May. In one stanza Douglass paid tribute to Johnson's winning grace in the face of racial trials; in another, his generosity to his own community:

> And when with dire intent, men spurned the laws,
> He changed their purpose, gaining their applause.
> Who can forget his ever-winning smile,
> His jovial heart, his life so void of guile.
> His ready eagerness to serve a friend.
> Which gave a charm that nothing else can lend;
> And with what willingness he would impart
> To all a knowledge of his heavenly art?

The day after his burial, a group including Douglass that called itself the "Young Men of Philadelphia" had published another tribute in a resolution of condolence in three newspapers. Along with their deep regret, the young men also announced their conviction that "Captain Johnson" had "eminently and successfully proved that genius is sufficiently powerful to overcome *even prejudice*." Surely such a testimonial would have been music to his ears. So would have been the sound of his band, playing on.[53]

CHAPTER 11

Sarah Thorn Tyndale

> The kindliest piece of cumbrous candour and common sense
> I have happened to meet for a great while.
>
> —Bronson Alcott

Sarah Thorn's parents began life as British colonists, but she, born in the fall of 1792, was, like Frank Johnson, a child of the new nation. During her very full life, she participated with gusto in the various experiments of the fledgling democracy. After her share of family trials in young adulthood, she grabbed life with both hands when she reached her fifties and sixties. She turned around the family business as a widow, then retired and caught the era's fever for social reform. She sought to help prostitutes; she spoke up for women's rights; she supported antislavery causes; she became a pacifist; she lived in a socialist commune; she dabbled in spiritualism; and she promoted a distinct American culture by patronizing the poet Walt Whitman and a series of portrait painters. She gravitated to radical reform along with some other affluent northern liberals and was perhaps unusual in the extent of her activity. But as a mother and widowed businesswoman who joined "the great silent army" of reformers, she was representative of many middle-class women of her time. Still excluded from the polls, they found many other ways to shape their world. In all, she was like everyone—a unique individual and typical at the same time.

One could say Sarah Thorn had mission in her veins, since her father, William Biles Thorn, and her mother, Elizabeth Hutchins, were from successful Puritan and Quaker families, respectively. The Thorns had come to Massachusetts as part of the Puritan migration of the 1630s, moved with other Puritans to Long Island, and then came to Burlington, New Jersey, where Sarah was born. William's aunt, Sarah Biles, was the second wife of Lawrence Growden, the hated stepmother of whom Grace Growden Galloway spoke so meanly when

Figure 21. Sarah Tyndale (1792–1859). Oil portrait by John Neagle, n.d. Private collection.

"Mrs. Growden" was granted maintenance from her father's estate. Fortunately, negative attitudes towards stepparents were not universal at this time when earlier death made them so common. Sarah Thorn never showed any ill will to Sharon Carter, the man her mother married after William Thorn died at the age of thirty. Sharon Carter was probably the only father Sarah Thorn had ever really known, since William died when she was four, and her mother remarried when she was seven. It was not unusual that, although Sarah Thorn's two siblings had died young, she eventually gained seven half siblings after her mother's remarriage. Among them was her half sister Mary, who was born with the surname Carter, but who ended up as a Tyndale, when she married William Tyndale, the brother of Sarah's future husband, Robinson Tyndale. Sarah Thorn Tyndale and Mary Carter Tyndale would later share a home as older widows. Such were the combinations and recombinations of early American households—with families no less complicated than today's, though for a different reason, namely, death, rather than divorce.[1]

That Mary Carter married her half sister's husband's brother was not uncommon. Siblings often married siblings, especially at this time when new ideas about the importance of marriage for love and companionship still competed with older, more pragmatic, approaches to matchmaking—a shared connection through the retail market in china and glassware in this case. And proximity played a huge role. Sarah herself may have come to know Robinson Tyndale, an Irish immigrant who arrived in 1807, through her stepfather, who operated a china business in Philadelphia, located through the 1810s at 244–248 North Third Street. This was also likely where the family lived. Since Robinson was soon listed as a china merchant himself, Sarah may have met him at the store. The surviving evidence suggests economic interests, rather than romance, led to the wedding in 1812. There was a wide disparity in age: he was thirty-seven and she was twenty when they married. They were of different faiths: he was an Anglican (as their children would be), she a birthright Quaker. He came from a military family and had fought in Ireland. She was a pacifist. He waffled on the charitable activities that later meant so much to her. In 1831, Robinson told her that he was "forever disinclined to do more for mankind" (he was denying their daughter Elizabeth some money she had requested for a charitable purpose). Yet near death a decade later, he urged his children to "be ready to help the distressed." The retailing of china and glass seems Sarah and Robinson's only shared interest, but little survives to provide deeper insight into their courtship.[2]

Whether through personal inclination, because of the limitations of contemporary birth control technology, or in response to War of 1812–era injunctions to populate the new nation, they had ten children. Thus they did not follow the family-limitation trend starting among many other educated urban Quakers. The first baby, Elizabeth, arrived promptly, on Christmas Day, 1812. Sarah's mother's last child (Sarah's last Carter half sibling, Jacob) was born that same year, illustrating the unbroken round of childbearing from one generation to the next. Sarah bore her ten children over the next fifteen years, but stopped childbearing at the relatively early age of thirty-five. Given the persistence of high child mortality, perhaps Sarah was lucky that six of hers would survive her. Only one child died in infancy. Then little Mary died in an accident at four years of age. Son Troilus drowned in the Delaware River at twenty-one. And Julia died at twenty-nine. But Sarah must have been happy to see her other children reach adulthood and start their own families. Elizabeth, for example, was married to Edward Mitchell in February 1833. Bishop William White married the pair. And among their wedding gifts was a beautiful Tucker-Hemphill vase inscribed with Elizabeth's name. Despite great growth, Philadelphia remained a small world—at least for families like the Tyndales who were rooted by kinship, religion, or occupation; it was a less welcoming place for the transient poor or many recent immigrants.[3]

Although Sarah was lucky to finish out her life surrounded by adult children, the premature deaths of her father, siblings, and four of her offspring surely left scars. And because she would refer in later life to earlier trials, including the institutionalization of one child, perhaps these losses were compounded by difficulties in her marriage. It is hard to know; there are only hints of a less-than-warm relationship. What to make, for example, of a letter from Sarah to Robinson in 1830, when she was minding the store in Philadelphia and he was at the seashore in Cape May, New Jersey? She said she would join him and looked forward to the family being together. She hoped he would stay until she came, adding, "I could write as long as the time would allow me but you will not read it and shall therefore stop."[4]

One difficulty in the marriage was that Robinson was diagnosed with cancer sometime before 1822. His "protracted ill health" was noticed in the *Philadelphia Inquirer* not long before his death and may be the reason the firm's advertisement for "Christmas Fancy Goods" was not published until six days after Christmas in 1841, five months before his death. Robinson's earlier trip to the seashore could have been to "take the waters," since saltwater bathing and even drinking the ocean water were popularly believed by some to have nearly miraculous curative powers. Near the end of his life he consulted a cancer doctor, one of the self-proclaimed specialists considered quacks by the medical establishment. An advertisement touting the arrival of a practitioner in

Connecticut listed Robinson's name and address in Philadelphia along with a number of other Pennsylvanians who were supposedly able to provide personal testimony of the efficacy of William H. Norris's medical techniques. Some of the treatment protocols of cancer doctors were relatively benign and included herbs proscribed commonly at the time. Cancer doctors might also attempt to incise and cauterize the tumor, an extremely painful process. So the trials faced by Sarah included nursing a sick husband, educating a large family of children, and assisting in the family business. That the marriage may have lacked an emotional core would have multiplied the hardships faced, so it is perhaps not surprising that she did not remarry after her husband died.[5]

Robinson was a headstrong man of marked habits. He was fond of metaphysics and loved intellectual debate. What a daughter remembered, however, was how on Sunday nights he would hang a piece of cheese from the crane in the family's fireplace and catch the melting drips in a blue-and-white Chinese bowl. This habit annoyed the family's African American cook, whom the family called Betsy as if she were a child, one indication of the intense racial prejudices of the period, even among reformers. "Miss Elizabeth Tyler," as the cook insisted on being addressed on Sundays (when she also smoked a pipe), always criticized Robinson's method, while Sarah simply looked on from her cozy seat inside the huge hearth.[6]

City directories reveal the movements and continued domestic and business recombinations of Sarah Tyndale's family of origin and her family by marriage. They also show her living and working in the center of the city's retail cluster on Second and Third Streets just north of Market Street. As had always been the case, families generally lived above or behind the store. This residential pattern was changing in the early nineteenth century as manufacturing began to move from artisan shop to factory, making it difficult for married women with young children to continue to participate in the family business, but the mingling of home and work persisted for many in retail shops. Robinson was first listed as a china merchant at 201 North Second Street (opposite Christ Church Alley) in 1813, but by 1816—when he became a citizen—he was also listed as a partner with Sarah's stepfather, Sharon Carter, at 111 North Front Street. They conducted business together at this address through 1820, although by 1818 the Tyndales lived at 100 North Third Street, near Sarah's mother and siblings in the Carter family home at 244 North Third. It appears that Carter and Tyndale split in 1820. Carter worked on his own and for a glass company on High Street, while Robinson relocated his business and family to 10 North Third Street in 1821, then to 12 North Third in 1829. The Tyndales remained at that address through the 1830s, and thus it is there that Bishop White must have come to perform the marriage of their daughter Elizabeth in 1833.[7]

In 1829, Robinson was again listed with Sharon Carter at 21 North Third Street, but only for that year. Carter continued to operate a store there for the next couple of years with his daughter, Mary, Sarah's halfsister, until his death in 1831. Mary then disappears from the directories, only reappearing as "Mary Tyndale, china" at 46 South Second Street between 1847 and 1859. Presumably, she had lived and worked between 1835 and 1845 with her husband, Robinson's brother William, also a china merchant, at 26 North Third, and relocated to 46 North Second as a widow. That she was listed as a partner in her father's china shop before her marriage, and then again as proprietress of a china shop as a widow, strongly suggests that she was among the many married women performing "hidden market work" in antebellum cities. Married women were rarely listed in the directories.[8]

Alone or with his father-in-law, then, Robinson survived in the china business. As illustrated by his blue-and-white bowl for catching melted cheese, Canton and Nanking wares from the growing China trade were his specialty, but in addition he imported fashionable European items and encouraged American manufacturers of glass and ceramics. He also attempted a forward-looking investment in buying three six-hundred-acre parcels of land in the Republic of Texas in 1836. But he did not become wealthy. In fact, he fell victim to a real estate scam, investing the huge sum of $50,000 for two hundred thousand nonexistent acres in Wisconsin and Minnesota. Sarah Tyndale became a widow, a provider, and owner of a bankrupt business in 1842. Wholesaling and retailing were not easy paths for anyone at this time, especially given Robinson's ill health and the periodic market crashes and riots plaguing the city. We have seen the fate of the Tucker China Manufactory. Competition was intense. Already in 1811 the city directory listed sixteen china or china and glass retail shops, not counting china merchants or importers. Competition did not let up and was exacerbated by severe economic downturns such as the Panic of 1819–1823 and the recession of 1839–1843, so movement and combination continued in the firm's efforts to surmount the volatility of the market. In another tactic, in 1834 Robinson joined other businessmen in publishing a protest of "fancy fairs." The protest signers had no beef with the religious and charitable ends of these bazaars run by well-to-do women volunteers, but did object to the unfair competition, especially at Christmastime, of sellers with no overhead who undercut the prices of shopkeepers. He even sought and received Bishop White's endorsement of the protest, although the latter was mostly concerned about the fairs' inroads on the regular business of poor working women. Given Sarah's later roles as businesswoman, woman's rights advocate, and philanthropist, one wonders what she thought of Robinson's protest.[9]

The challenging economic conditions of the time required advertising and innovation as well as continued relocation. Newspapers indicate that the Tyndales tried all three. They publicized "the latest arrivals" in his stock. They gave notice of the relocation of the "Cheap China Glass and Queensware" wholesale and retail store from Front Street to Third Street in 1821. The firm frequently reminded customers that "persons wishing to save time can do so by purchasing in the evening," at the new store, opened in 1839 at Seventh and Chestnut Streets. This new store was designed as a major attraction—a consumer's palace—and, according to a front-page article in the *National Gazette*, "far exceeds in extent and splendor any similar establishment in this country or in England." The country may have been entering a major recession at that moment, but the Tyndales less often appealed to customers seeking cheap wares and focused instead on the well-to-do who still had money. Plate glass windows allowed pedestrians to view the stock in the great room and galleries while fifty gas lamps produced "a brilliant spectacle which crowds gaze upon." This store could stay open "till about 9 P.M. every night," thanks to these expensive investments in construction and lighting. Once Sarah took over, she appealed to the public snobberies and American insecurities by offering, for example, French glass "made expressly for this house, from old and beautiful patterns," and Spanish goblets "which with most persons of taste have always been preferred." The message was that American homes could be as sophisticated as European by shopping at select venues.[10]

Robinson and other family members also provided good service. In 1834 Deborah Logan wrote that she "went in the Carriage down 3d Street to Tyndale's store to get some articles exchanged that did not please [her], and found them very obliging." Andrew Jackson, perhaps to celebrate the approaching end of his second term as president, splurged on mantle ornaments, a jewelry box and toy tea set, and other luxury items as well as commonplace goods like mugs and chamber pots, spending in all the large sum of $108.37 in the fall of 1835. Daniel Webster must also have appreciated the store, as a Tyndale grandson remembered that he "always came in on his way to Congress." He "had good taste in china & glass" and "bought largely." Apparently he was extended liberal credit, because he "always said squarely he had no money but to catch him on his way home after Congress adjourned & before he had spent his pay."[11]

These measures could not protect the store from competition or economic booms and busts. Joseph Hemphill's partner Thomas Tucker himself operated a china shop in the same block of Chestnut Street after 1837. That Tucker sold out just three years later in 1841 confirms the difficulties, especially following the devastating Panic of 1837. Yet even had he met great success, Robinson Tyndale could not shield his family from the financial consequences of his death from cancer, at age sixty-six, in May 1842. He tried to prepare them, dictating from his deathbed a letter of advice to his youngest son and daughter, away at school in Maryland. When he succumbed, in great pain, Sarah had to take over. She was fifty. Five of her seven surviving children were under twenty-one; the youngest was fifteen.[12]

Of course she was not without experience. Sarah now headed the business that she had worked in her whole life, often on her own, judging from letters to Robinson at the seashore. But she had to acknowledge the change and step into a new role. She began by advertising that her late husband's business had not closed and that she was carrying it on; she asked the public for support. And she needed it, because the store was not doing well and may have been on the verge of bankruptcy. She soon reconfigured the space at Seventh and Chestnut Streets and looked for a small house to rent near the store. Perhaps aided by post-panic economic recovery, business improved. Just over a year after Robinson's death, Sarah's advertisements had a more confident and assertive tone: the store was open till nine, and carried the greatest variety of china and glassware in the United States, all at low prices, so the ads promised. Sarah also provided examples of American-manufactured glass for the Franklin Institute's annual competition. In just four years, by the summer of 1846, she was able to retire. She placed a notice in the *Public Ledger* that she had sold the business to her son Hector and son-in-law Edward Mitchell. But she did not do this until she had completely turned the business around. She retired a wealthy woman.[13]

In working in her stepfather's and husband's store, and then assuming control as a widow, Sarah had simply been following in the footsteps of many women before her, including her half sister Mary. Women had been fully involved in the urban economy in the eighteenth century and were still ubiquitous in Philadelphia shops, although male retail clerks were beginning to dominate in other cities. Women tended to have near monopolies in the manufacturing and service trades that most resembled their work at home (and, indeed, could be done in the home)—making women's and children's clothes and men's shirts, preparing food, doing laundry, or running boardinghouses, inns, and taverns, and so on. But they were also represented in many of the city's retail establishments. Through the 1810s, for example, roughly half of Philadelphia's china shops in the city directories were listed with female proprietors, but then china and glassware could be considered properly domestic spheres for women's engagement. The shopkeepers were probably mostly widows like Sarah and Mary Tyndale.[14]

And yet there were limits to women's place in business. Married women's lack of property rights had long constrained them. There had also always been contested gendered divisions of labor in commerce. For one thing, nineteenth-century women were less likely to be recognized among the city's wholesale merchants than they had been earlier. Robinson Tyndale had often been listed as a china merchant, but Sarah would not be, even though she took over all aspects of the business. And as businesses grew and left the owners' households, male store clerks often crowded women out of store positions.[15]

Further, these continuities and new developments were both consistent with the ideology that grew in the early nineteenth century that respectable white women worked only in the home after marriage. But these ideas were soon challenged by the few middle- and upper-class women who began the women's rights movement. They campaigned not only for the vote but to expand women's property rights. They were anxious to see women enter occupations that had been closed to them. Thus, for example, when two young Quakers, Elizabeth McClintock and Anna Southwick, told Elizabeth Cady Stanton that they wished to become silk importers, Stanton fired off a letter to her friend and ally Lucretia Mott in Philadelphia, enlisting her help. Mott raised the issue with her son-in-law, silk importer and progressive Edward M. Davis, who brought the proposal to employ them to his firm for consideration. The men hesitated, and then decided that the venture was too risky because the women lacked the requisite experience. It was also true that some of the male clerks just could not accept working with women. Davis recommended that the women gain experience by working in retail first. Stanton and the young women were miffed, but Mott thought the men's position reasonable. She wrote to Stanton that "all agree that for a beginning, a retail store would be preferable." She encouraged them to come to Philadelphia, where they would have "no difficulty" in finding positions. She then raised the example of Sarah Tyndale, who had "lately retired from the China business, with a handsome fortune" earned from "the largest & most handsome Porcelain store in this country."[16]

Tyndale's success was not just recognized by Mott. It was also pointed out by the popular women's magazine *Godey's Lady's Book*. A story called "Employment of Women in Cities: Shopkeeping" praised Sarah for her progressive employment of female salesclerks, all the while breathlessly touting the store itself. "We are at Tyndale's," the author exclaimed.

> You have heard of the establishment before; for it has even a European reputation for the exquisite taste in the selection and arrangement of the glass and china with which it is filled. And yet a woman founded this reputation by her energy, her tact, and industry; a woman planned the elegant hall, . . . and gathered together the large capital necessary to its construction, . . . where, instead of being received by a careless or obsequious clerk, a young girl comes forward, as a lady would receive in her own parlor, to know our commands. . . . It is a novelty to you, and you look to see how a woman in so exposed a position bears herself. With the strictest propriety and grace; for she . . . knows exactly what will suit her customers.[17]

Sarah's success thus attracted notice, but it also reveals the allegiance of *Godey's Lady's Book* over the preceding decades to the mission of preaching the gospel of domesticity to and for middle-class women: the store was likened to a parlor, the customers to houseguests. Tyndale's female clerks were remarkable for their ladylike propriety. These factors were promoted as enough to overcome the public exposure of these young women and illustrate how the Victorian emphasis on domesticity, usually so restrictive, might be used to open access to new occupations. In reality, women had maintained a persistent and significant presence in small business. Their activity was masked by marriage, and often by the small scale of their enterprises. And many women had succeeded in business as widows. Sarah Tyndale's success attracted notice because of its magnitude, because of her national reputation, and because some women were beginning to challenge the very idea that women's sphere was ideally confined to the home.[18]

That the editor of *Godey's* continued to single out Tyndale's among the businesses lauded in the mid-1850s indicates that the store's reputation persisted as did the close ties of the magazine editors and the Tyndales. In January 1855, the store was described as "a perfect receptacle of everything beautiful." The following December the editor contended "that a visit to this establishment by the lovers of the fine arts will well repay." Nowhere but in this "perfect gallery" could shoppers "find such an infinite variety of all kinds of fine and fancy china, statuettes, vases, busts, etc." The notice added that Tyndale's also carried more utilitarian wares and that were "very moderate in their prices." To cap it off, her shop had "on exhibition some beautiful specimens of china from Japan, brought over by an officer" on the Matthew Perry expedition. Tyndale's appeared again in the Christmas shopping scenes of a *Godey's* short story of 1858. These articles served to advertise the store while appearing to be travelogues or entertaining fiction—an early example of product placement. Desire for validation of taste through the consumption of goods was made to seem selfless by these ads stressing purchases of impractical gifts for family and friends and Christmas toys for children. Women could travel to these cathedrals of consumption and yet feel at home and properly domesticated. The emphasis on aesthetics, the cultivation of beauty, was made to seem a properly feminine sphere in shopping and the home. Sarah Tyndale had built the store into a fashionable and respectable Philadelphia institution before she handed it over to her sons, and they kept up her work.[19]

Why had she relinquished control? Sarah explained her decision at the women's rights convention at Worcester, Massachusetts, in 1850. She said that now "that her children had grown up to succeed her in business . . . she was employing her faculties for the good of others." As historian Mary P. Ryan has argued, middle-class reformers had "imperialistic pretentions." They thought they knew what was good for others, especially the poor and powerless, even if their own lives sometimes deviated from their professed ideals. Sarah had found that "her energies had been rendered greater and more active by attention to business and she desired still to be usefully employed." At this point, Sarah's friend and fellow Philadelphian Lucretia Mott "rose and said she must state what the modesty of her friend would not allow her to state." Sarah, Mott explained, "had with another friend visited all the houses of bad repute in Philadelphia; they had established a place of retreat for them, and had induced over three hundred young women to return to the path of virtue, and found homes and places of useful employment for them." Mott's tribute to Sarah's work among prostitutes moved the audience to applause and "was one of the most emotional moments of the entire two days."[20]

Prostitution was a major topic of discussion at the Worcester convention. Several leaders, male and female, gave speeches about it, including Unitarian minister William H. Channing of Massachusetts, the convention's vice-president and one of the stalwart male supporters of the infant women's rights movement. That a minister and, especially, respectable middle-class women—who were supposed to be ignorant of the trade—paid so much attention to prostitution was one of the most controversial aspects of the meeting. Various women's rights leaders were coming to see sex work as something that innocent young women were driven to by economic necessity or a lack of education and religious instruction. Survival, not sin, compelled them to it. Lucy Stone, Matilda Gage, and others would soon point out that, with so few economic options open to them, women's eagerness to marry to secure "the necessities of life" was not all that different from the prostitute's turning to the marketplace.[21]

Sarah had not lost any time embarking on this work after selling her business. In 1847 she and other Philadelphia women had formed the Rosine Society to help the prostitutes she visited. Their thinking anticipated that of the speakers at Worcester. They wished to assist "their fallen sisters" to a better way of life—that is, a domestic role as servant or wife. It was not that Philadelphians had neglected the plight of these women. Bishop White and other men had long since formed the Magdalen Society to reform prostitutes. But Tyndale and the others did not like the men's approach—or the fact that the society was "under the superintendence of men." They regarded the Magdalen home as a "prison." Unlike the men, they were not primarily interested in reforming the prostitutes' morals; they were determined not to pass judgment on "our sisters." Instead, they dedicated themselves to helping the women as peers to find "more dignified" work. Thus, they adopted the motto "You shall support yourself honestly by the labor of your own hands," and opened a home at 204 North Eighth Street.[22]

The Rosine Society organizers were not leading Philadelphians as were the men of the Magdalen Society. They were a mix of boardinghouse keepers, gentlewomen, and wives of small businessmen and clerks. The two societies continued for decades to differ in their leadership. Into the 1880s, virtually all the Rosine Society officers were female, including the physician (the only male officer was their lawyer), whereas the Magdalen Society officers and physicians were virtually all male (the only female officer was the matron). Sarah was heavily involved in the first six years, first serving on the board of managers and then, between 1850 and 1852, as vice president. From the beginning, the members of the Rosine Society worked hard, finding women who could teach trades to the women, visiting prostitutes in their homes, brothels, and Eastern State Penitentiary, opening a school and "Intelligence office" (employment agency), doing research on the problem nationally, and visiting similar homes and prisons in Boston and New York. They helped thousands of women, housing hundreds. Most of these did not wish to be "saved," and the published case histories show that some portion of those under the care of the association were not prostitutes at all but runaway teenagers, abandoned wives, petty criminals, or alcoholics. The women considered successes were placed as servants in domestic settings, returned to their parents, or married. Although they seem to have confined their efforts to helping white women, the members prided themselves on reaching Irish and German immigrants as well as women from all religions.[23]

Like the other members, Sarah was more interested in helping women than in chastising them. Her career could serve as an example, and her funds essential support. In addition, her business experience made her invaluable. In addition to her work for the Rosine Society, she soon became treasurer of the Philadelphia Lying-in Asylum at 229 Arch Street, a place for poor women to give birth. In an 1851 notice in Philadelphia's African American newspaper, the *Pennsylvania Freeman*, she solicited donations for that institution. The Lying-in Asylum was in turn connected to another sort of refuge for women rejected elsewhere: the new Female Medical College gave well-educated, middle-class women access to medical training and a professional career.[24]

Sarah did not just lend her energies to the plight of needy women when she gave up the store. She also became a peace activist. After Quaker women in Exeter, England, sent a "Friendly Address" on the subject to their American counterparts, she joined Lucretia Mott and others on July 4, 1846, in calling for a meeting of Philadelphians to reply. This call was part of a new form of "people diplomacy" in response to a threat of war between England and America over the Canadian border. The effort grew from two Quaker traditions: pacifism and the relative equality of women within the sect. At the Philadelphia meeting on July 17, Mott read an address explaining the committee's thinking. It effectively added to women's now customary responsibilities as moral mothers a new responsibility for political action: "We hold it to be the duty of women to look with an attentive eye, upon the great events which are transpiring around them." While poorer women were to be placed in domestic situations, these middle-class reformers encouraged their peers to turn their attention to international politics. Specifically, they should use the "force of their moral judgment against the iniquitous spirit of war," for "great is the responsibility of women in relation to this subject." Indeed, "the false love of glory . . . , the bloodthirsty ambition, swelling the breast of the soldier . . . are often but the ripened harvest, from the seed sown by his mother's hand, when in his childish hours, she gave him tiny weapons, and taught him how to mimic war's murderous game." Mott ended with a call for action: "Let us then, dear sisters, be unceasingly faithful in all our relations, . . . employing the mighty instances that cluster around the domestic hearth and . . . the pen and the press, in bearing testimony to the superiority of Christian love and forgiveness, over the law of physical force." It was a lesson that Sarah attempted to follow in her own family. Her son Hector "had a strong desire for military pursuits," like his father. At age sixteen he "was offered a cadetship at West Point, but at the persuasion of his mother declined it, and gave up his cherished wish." Nonetheless, he joined the Artillery Corps of Philadelphia and became increasingly involved in the military, despite his mother's influence.[25]

The Philadelphia women wanted to up the ante in responding to their English sisters. Not only did they urge women to use "the pen and the press" in a "more extended sphere" beyond the home. They added that, while it was heartening that Britain and the United States were resolving the border dispute, both sides still had work to do, since "your government" in Britain was currently waging war against India and "ours [in America] against Mexico." After the meeting, Sarah took the lead in quickly gathering 3,525 signatures to their petition, more than double the 1,623 gathered by the women of Exeter, and about 3 percent of Philadelphia's adult female population.[26]

Sarah's sights were thus lifted beyond Philadelphia, but it was women's rights, and her continued association with Lucretia Mott, that took her out of the city physically. Following on the example set by Mott, Cady Stanton, and others who launched the women's rights movement at Seneca Falls, New York, in 1848, Sarah was the first to sign the call for the first national women's rights convention, which met at Worcester, in October 1850. While many conservatives declined to support it, the 1850 meeting was endorsed by fifty other women and thirty men, including such luminaries as the famous philosopher Ralph Waldo Emerson and popular novelist Catharine Maria Sedgwick. Sarah served as a Pennsylvania delegate along with the Motts; she was also vice president of the convention along with William Channing.[27]

It was here that Lucretia Mott made her moving tribute to Sarah's work with prostitutes. Sarah had been introduced to the assembly as a prominent example of female commercial success and was speaking to encourage women about their capacity for business. The *New York Daily Tribune* reported that Mott interrupted Sarah soon after she began speaking, rising and stating "that Mrs. Tyndale was the proprietor of one of the largest and most beautiful China establishments in this country or the world." As Sarah resumed her speech, she hinted that she was more liberal than her grown children in her views of women's rights, exclaiming that "if they could see her standing up before such an audience, [they] would say, why, mother, how can you expose yourself so?" She said that she did it "for the encouragement of her sisters, and from a sense of duty," asserting that, accustomed to working, she could not now "remain idle and at ease." Then Mott rose again to describe Sarah's work with prostitutes. The reporter noted that Mrs. Tyndale's "remarks were delivered with great simplicity, natural eloquence and pathos." When she finished, Channing "rose to thank his sister for her noble conduct." Indeed, "if he were her son he should be proud of a mother who could stand up here and give such words of encouragement, and who had done such noble deeds." As one reporter observed, "here were not many dry eyes in the house."[28]

Boston physician Harriot Hunt described her excitement at meeting the Philadelphians at this convention: "Lucretia Mott . . . my ideal, stood embodied before me, the wife, the mother, the grandmother, the teacher of religion and of morals—her life unspotted." Of Tyndale, Hunt observed, "When left a widow with a family of children dependent on her exertions she continued her husband's business." Visitors to "the elegant glass and china store in Chestnut street Philadelphia ought to know that Sarah Tyndale built it, owned it, and having realized a handsome independence left the business to be prosecuted by her sons." When Lucy Stone praised Sarah's accomplishments at the 1855 convention in Cincinnati, Ohio, she went further, claiming that Sarah's husband had "died bankrupt," and that she herself drew the plan for her warehouse, drawing praise from architect and builder alike. Sarah was not at the 1855 convention, but Hunt recalled her speech in 1850: "Why was she there? That she might encourage every widow and raise her voice against the narrow sphere prescribed to woman." Sarah must herself have been thrilled in 1850 to hear the eloquent speeches of the likes of Frederick Douglass, William Lloyd Garrison, Sojourner Truth, Lucy Stone, Paulina Wright Davis, Abby Kelley Foster, and Ernestine Rose, among others, as well as that of Mott herself, who closed the three-day convention.[29]

Of course not all reporters were sympathetic. The *New York Herald* showed what the nascent woman's rights movement was up against in describing the convention rather differently:

> That motley gathering of fanatical mongrels, of old grannies, male and female, of fugitive slaves and fugitive lunatics, called the Woman's Rights Convention, after two day's discussion of the most horrible trash, has put forth its platform and adjourned. The sentiments and doctrines avowed, and the social revolution projected, involve all the most monstrous and disgusting principles of socialism, abolition, amalgamation, and infidelity. The full consummation of their diabolical projects would reduce society to . . . barbarism . . . ; and the most revolting familiarities of equality and licentiousness between whites and blacks, of both sexes, that lunatics and demons could invent.

And yet even this critical reporter could not think of anything really negative to say about Sarah Tyndale, describing her simply as a "merchant and general philanthropist," and noting that "Sarah Tyndale recommended the women to be encouraged, for it appeared that she herself had been remarkably successful in the crockery business." Mott and Tyndale, he continued, "had visited all the houses of bad repute in Philadelphia, and had established a retreat for the Mary Magdalenes [prostitutes], three hundred of whom she had reclaimed, and given useful employment." On the whole, he concluded, "Very good for Mrs. Tyndale." A more negative view was offered by the *Spirit of the Times*, which, recounting Sarah's query about what her children would say about her thus putting herself forward, rejoined "of course, the notion was received with derisive laughter; but a good many people will echo the cry of the little Tyndales."[30]

But Sarah's children were supportive of their beloved mother, as testified to in a speech on the history of the movement that Paulina Wright Davis gave at the twentieth anniversary celebration of its inauguration, at Apollo Hall, in New York City, on October 20, 1870. Sarah had died eleven years earlier, prompting Wright Davis to say that "From our midst another is missing: Mrs. Sarah Tyndale, of Philadelphia—one of the first to sign the call" for a convention on women's rights. According to Wright Davis, the national movement had its origins in a radicalized domestic space. "Indeed, the idea of such a convention had often been discussed in her home, more than two years before, a home where every progressive thought found a cordial welcome." Tyndale's "genuine earnestness" deserved "affectionate respect" for one who "was, perhaps, more widely known than any other woman of her time for her practical talents: having conducted one of the largest business houses in her native city for nearly a quarter of a century." But there were costs, according to Wright Davis. "Genial and largely hospitable, there was for her great social sacrifice in taking up a cause so unpopular; but she had no shrinking from duty." In all, she was remembered as embodying virtues both feminine and masculine. "Strong and grand as she was, in her womanly nature, she had nevertheless the largest and tenderest sympathies for the weak and erring." In all, "she was prescient, philosophical, just and generous." While she tended to a "large family" that "gathered around to honor and bless her, she had still room in her heart for the woes of the world, and the latter years of her life were given to earnest, philanthropic work." Wright Davis spoke for many when she lamented that "We miss today her sympathy, her wise counsel, her great, organizing power."[31]

Like many other women's rights advocates, Sarah Tyndale was also a staunch supporter of the antislavery cause. This is probably how Lucretia Mott had come to know her, for Mott wrote to Elizabeth Cady Stanton in 1849 that Sarah had "attended our late Anti S. Annual Mg. at Norristown, heard Garrison again & again, and became quite enthusiastic in the cause." Sarah was a latecomer to the movement; the Philadelphia Female Anti-Slavery Society had been active since 1833. But she soon was on board, and donated money to the Pennsylvania Anti-Slavery Society by 1851. In addition, Robinson Tyndale's earlier campaign against "fancy fairs" notwithstanding, that fall found her busy helping to organize the Sixteenth Philadelphia Anti-Slavery Fair, at this point the women's major activity and successful fund-raising scheme; between 1840 and 1860 the fair netted $32,000. These had become elaborate affairs, with needlework and farm produce for sale, speeches by antislavery notables, and music. Sarah was appointed a manager by the Philadelphia Female Anti-Slavery Society and therefore likely helped with some of the enormous amount of work involved, from advertising, to organizing sewing circles to produce goods for sale, to soliciting donations from merchants, to engaging speakers, to keeping the books.[32]

It is significant that Sarah did not engage in any of these activities before giving up the store even though Philadelphia women had been engaged in voluntary reform activity for decades. It is likely that the needs of her family and the shop had fully occupied her time. It seems that Robinson's death had freed her to express her personal, political, and philanthropic inclinations. In any case, Sarah could now follow her own passions. She could also choose where to make a home. Indeed, by 1853, if her children wanted to see her in the summer, they had to make their way to the North American Phalanx, a socialist commune near the shore at Red Bank, New Jersey. Its members believed that communal living would end both the isolation of married women in the home and the unending responsibility of male breadwinners for the family's economic welfare through the greater efficiencies of group living.

The North American Phalanx was the most successful of the nearly fifty Fourierist communities in the United States. This was one type of the hundreds of utopian experiments that sprang up in the years following the Panic of 1837. Reformers angry with the painful effects of unregulated capitalism desired to find better ways to organize families and economies. The socialist "phalanxes" were the creation of Frenchman Charles Fourier. While efforts to implement his ideas did not meet much success in his native country, they took root in the fertile soil of reform-minded antebellum America, although, like other communes then and since, few of the experiments existed very long. The North American Phalanx was one of the most successful, lasting from its founding in 1843 to 1854.[33]

We don't know when Sarah joined the community, but family papers begin to record her comings and goings between the phalanx and her children's homes in Philadelphia in November 1851. This leaving town for increasing periods was likely the cause for the subsidence of her active work with the

Figure 22. Main residential edifice of the North American Phalanx, Colts Neck Township, Monmouth County, New Jersey. U.S. National Park Service Historic American Buildings Survey.

Rosine Society and the Philadelphia Female Anti-Slavery Society. But it is unlikely that she was losing interest in her causes. At the phalanx she was surrounded by people who shared these concerns. From its beginnings, for example, the community professed strong support for women's rights, and some of its residents and supporters were active in the movement. It is possible that the expanded connections Sarah formed through her involvement in the national woman's rights convention of 1850 helped draw her attention to Fourierism. Perhaps this alternative community appealed to her as it did to others, as a way to address social problems wholesale by beginning anew. In any case, she was living at the North American by the fall of 1851 and apparently wintered there. It is indicative of the growing class divisions in America that while Sarah Tyndale was searching for alternatives to the nuclear, male-dominated household through political and economic reforms, she supported an organization that placed "reformed" prostitutes in just such an orthodox situation.[34]

At that time, the phalanx consisted of several large buildings built for the community. They offered comfortable lodgings. The main building included a large dining room, a couple of sitting rooms, a library, and spacious porches. The upper floors contained sleeping rooms of various sizes, with rents proportionate to their dimensions. References to excellent mattresses, abundant water supply, and the coming of steam heat suggest that the accommodations were modern. Dining was communal, since such an arrangement was thought best calculated to relieve women of domestic drudgery. The dining room accommodated two hundred diners at long tables. A bell rang to announce the meals. Residents generally sat at the same seats and one table was reserved for vegetarians. In 1851 a visitor described the food, served by young men and women, as plentiful, excellent, and wholesome, and noted that "an easy freedom and a harmonious feeling seemed to prevail." Such an atmosphere was impressive considering the diversity of the phalanx's inhabitants. Many had spent time in other communities and all had considered opinions on the many facets of the social experiment they were undertaking at this, one of the last surviving of such efforts. Progressive views of gender roles at least were widely shared. The 1851 guest described a group of people dancing in the dining room the evening he arrived and commented favorably on the bloomer costume worn by some of the young women. This outfit, essentially a skirt over trousers gathered at the ankles, had been designed by the reformer Amelia Bloomer to allow for freer movement by women. Viciously caricatured in contemporary newspapers, its appearance at the phalanx was a sure sign of the community's support of women's rights.[35]

Financial arrangements evolved over time, but were always designed with an eye to social justice. Everyone was supposed to work, and wages were paid according to the difficulty of the labor. Rent and board were deducted from residents' wages, and any profits left over at the end of the year were divided or reinvested. Community production was largely agricultural; most other activities were to meet the construction and supply needs of the phalanx. Although Fourier had originally envisioned a community of 1,640, the population at the phalanx ranged between 120 and 150.[36]

The combination of middle-class comforts and openness to reforms of all kind must have been appealing to the retired businesswoman from Philadelphia. Her family's equanimity about her residence there hints that, however radical or eccentric the ideas of the residents, these experiments were not regarded as far out of the bounds of mainstream society. While she had joined an alternative community, Sarah did not abandon her family in Philadelphia and they did not reject her. Her grandson James Mitchell recorded in his diary, for example, that "Grandma came home from the Phalanx" on April 9, 1852. He visited her at his aunt's house and she spent the day with his family early the next month, before her return to the commune in mid-May.[37]

And Sarah kept up a regular correspondence with her children while at the phalanx. In a letter to her son Hector in October 1852, she wrote that "I expect to go to Philad at Christmas it will be so delightful to see you all together again." A September 1852 letter to her daughter Clara, who was in a troubled marriage, reveals her maternal solicitude but also her religious inclinations in this period. First, she urged Clara to resume singing lessons at her expense, for she had a beautiful voice. As in her business, Sarah always combined a love of beauty with practical motivations, telling Clara (whose husband was both misbehaving and dying of tuberculosis) that "it is not right to let such a voice as yours be lost, besides you will have to educate your children yourself." Then Sarah spoke from the heart. Reflecting on her own past sorrows, she admitted, "You know Dearest that I have too much cause to know how to sympathize with you, with me tis past, and I trust that the young hearts agony was not in vain, but that the fire has burned the dross and left the spirit more free to receive the incomings of Divinity." She hoped her experience would teach a lesson. "Have I succeeded in imparting to you Dear a feeling of resignation to that which you can not avoid, or help, and at the same time an energy capable of enduring, faithfully to the end?" The comment says as much about her own experience in marriage as her daughter's.[38]

In the spring of 1853, the North American Phalanx was divided by conflict, and a new group called the Raritan Bay Union was formed in nearby Perth Amboy. Sarah was among the founders and trustees of the community, along with abolitionists Theodore Weld, Angelina Grimké Weld, and Sarah Grimké. According to one historian, "the White Hope of American Fourierism was too secular and extreme for some of its weightier and wealthier members." Sarah was both weighty (influential) and wealthy. The split was over two fundamental issues: religion and economics. The Raritan Bay members wanted more attention to both. Their efforts to provide more Christian religious teaching at the North American had run up against those who were resolutely opposed to any sectarian activity. The new group also thought the North American was too communistic in its economics; they were determined that those who did not work would not be paid. This led one observer to quip (referring to the Achilles' heel of all communes), "Whether they will drag the drones out, if they find any, and kill them as do the bees do in autumn . . . I can not say." The Raritan Bay Union also had a successful and progressive school—it was coeducational and interracial—run by the Welds; critics had noticed the want of education at the North American Phalanx. Sarah remained a trustee of the Raritan Bay Union until her death in 1859. Despite their greater inclination to share the wider world's principles of Christianity and private property, the Raritan Bay Union would not be immune to the dissensions of pluralism and challenges of communal living. It failed by 1860. The North American Phalanx, for its part, never recovered after a devastating fire in 1854 and had closed in 1856.[39]

Sarah was in Philadelphia in early February 1853, making the rounds among her children. She went to the Raritan Bay Union in early March and then came back to Philadelphia at the end of April. After a month of watchful concern over the declining health and then death of her daughter Julia Tyndale Milligan, Sarah returned to the Union in early June, accompanied by her daughter Elizabeth. Visits there from her children and grandchildren were common, as when the teenaged James accompanied his not-much-older aunt Clara on a visit that July. There they met up with Sarah's sons Sharon and Harold, and James echoed an earlier visitor's description of life at the phalanx when he noted that he "danced a little in the evening." Sarah was expecting another visit from daughter Clara and daughter-in-law Julia in January 1854.[40]

Indeed, visitors of all sorts were frequent at these communities, including most of the progressive reformers and literary figures of the day. Some had been involved in the shorter-lived commune of Brook Farm in Massachusetts, also organized according to Fourierist principles and still the most famous of these experiments because of the involvement of intellectuals Ralph Waldo Emerson, Bronson Alcott, and Henry David Thoreau. All three men visited and lectured at the Raritan Bay Union. Thoreau also surveyed the land. Sarah may have met Bronson Alcott on such a visit to the phalanx or she may only have met him in November 1856, when visiting friends in New York. In any case, it was Alcott who introduced her to her next cause, the poet Walt Whitman.

Sarah Tyndale and Alcott and Thoreau had all been visiting the family of merchant Richard Manning that month in Brooklyn. One evening, Alcott said, the talk was "spirited and talented." He had begun a conversation on divine, human, and savage attributes. He spoke for the divine, Sarah for the human, and Thoreau for the wild. Sarah and Alcott both preferred Thoreau's speech to each other's, but Alcott granted that Sarah "takes the woman's part to perfection . . . she being the kindliest piece of cumbrous candour and common sense I have happened to meet for a great while." When Alcott proposed to take Thoreau to meet Whitman the next day (Thoreau had recently published *Walden* and Whitman the first edition of *Leaves of Grass*), she simply tagged along "to whet her curiosity on the demigod." Alcott described how they visited Whitman at his mother's home in Brooklyn, and that, after a rather stilted and mutually wary conversation between the two writers in Whitman's attic bedroom, Sarah stayed to talk to him alone after they left. The scene must have been rather incongruous. The walls were covered with "pictures of well-muscled half-naked men—images of Hercules and Bacchus," the bed was unmade, and the chamber pot was in view. This tête-à-tête between Sarah and Whitman in his bedroom would have been considered scandalous if Tyndale was younger. She was a bohemian in soul and her solidly middle-class respectability allowed her a latitude that poorer women were not expected to have. She and the poet hit it off.[41]

Whitman had a number of friends among women's rights reformers, including Sarah's convention colleagues Paulina Wright Davis and Ernestine Rose, and he soon added her. They became correspondents. In a chatty letter of June 1857, for instance, Walt told her of his doings and his conversations with different people, including their mutual friend and Sarah's fellow woman's rights activist and New Jersey Fourierist Abby Price. Because he shared an interest with Sarah in Spiritualism, the then-popular consultation of spirit mediums who claimed to communicate with the dead (she had joined a Spiritualist circle in Philadelphia in 1852), he discussed the ideas of rival mediums. When he confessed to a want of politeness, she assured him that "where etiquette, or what is *called* refined and exquisite taste *predominate*, I never expect to find much originality of character." Sarah doubtless did much to solidify the friendship when she began helping Whitman financially. When he complained of ill treatment by his publisher Fowler and Wells and his desire to buy the plates of *Leaves of Grass* from them to bring out an expanded third edition, she promptly offered him fifty dollars to do so.[42]

But Sarah did not just let herself be, in the words of a New York gossip, "spunged from." She was candid with Whitman. When discussing a rumor that he was going to leave out some "objectionable parts" in the new edition of *Leaves of Grass*, she took the occasion to encourage him to do so. Her reasoning gives a glimpse of her ideas and personality, now in her mid-sixties: "I with all my ultra radicalism would be delighted if some of the expressions were left out, the pictures are too vivid in some instances, where it seems to me that common instinct seeks privacy," she wrote with some atypical Victorian reserve. But perhaps it was only her concern for reining in the poor and others who lacked self-control. She continued: "at the same time the entire nakedness of the intercourse is rather calculated to increase lubriciousness in weak minds, which Heaven knows is frightfully rampant." She was, perhaps, thinking of her visits to brothels, while she struggled to find the words to express herself. She "distrust[ed] the good effect of dwelling on the . . . indulgence of any of the appetites" and "detest[ed] drinking songs & poems on the delight of eating the most luxuriant food and always consider[ed] their votaries as mean sensualists," who should pause to consider the public effects of their actions on weak minds. In the same way, she criticized "an unnecessary expose of any personal enjoyment." Nonetheless, she "would have the freest social intercourse, men and women associating humanely in all the true brotherly relations of life, insensibly imparting the magnetism of humanity to each other" in order to "rectify the morbid condition of society on the great subject of procreation." This unsolicited advice to self-censor his poems notwithstanding, Whitman expressed appreciation of her liberal views on sexuality in one of his notebooks. Sarah's helping Whitman out was actually the culmination of a career as patron of the arts. She had long championed Philadelphia's young painters, commissioning portraits of herself, her children, and her grandchildren by Thomas Sully, John Neagle, and Thomas Buchanan Read. Her encouragement of Clara's singing was part of this appreciation for the arts. But Whitman's liberalism was very attractive to her as she settled into peaceful old age.[43]

And peaceful she was. In a January 1855 letter to Hector she had described being very happy at age sixty-two. Characteristically, she did not think just of herself, writing, "May all things conspire to make you as happy at 62 as is your own mother." That September, she visited Brooklyn and returned home with a Miss Addie Manning, perhaps her own experiment in "free social intercourse," who stayed with her until December. Sarah's grandson James described a number of evening visits by the two, with pleasant conversation and card games of euchre or whist. There was a family party on October 12 for Sarah's sixty-third birthday. A couple of days later, the more conservative but still admiring James reported that Sarah was feisty as ever: "[we] had quite a discussion about Tennyson, and how to read him. Uncle H. and I as usual agreed, in most points, and Grandma as usual differed." Three days later, "Grandma and Miss Manning took tea with us. . . . Miss M. and I beat Ma and Grandma five games of euchre." In January 1856, Sarah returned to the Raritan Bay Union for the winter.[44]

That spring, Sarah moved to "a very nice large house, corner of High and Main" Streets in Germantown, just west of the city, with her half sister Mary Carter Tyndale and Mary's two sons, William and Tecumseh. The young men worked for their mother at her china store, which she continued to operate at 42 South Second Street. But Sarah continued to move about. That November brought her visit to Brooklyn and meeting with Whitman. Her spirits continued high: "Thank God for the great influx of light, love, joy and beauty which is everywhere manifest," she exclaimed in a letter to him the following spring. "I can not help comparing the present with past eras of cruelty and carnage when men dare not express a thought outside the church inclosure." And yet, ever kindhearted, she hastened to add that she was "not blaming the good people who inflicted the tortures, if they thought they were sending a brother to Heaven thereby." She was "only rejoicing that the race is so expanded that each now (in this glorious land of the setting sun at least) dare to speak for himself."[45]

At the end of 1857, Sarah gave up her share of the Germantown house to another half sister, Hannah, and for the next two years, she made the rounds of her children's homes, visiting each for several weeks at a time. She was thus active until her death. She kept up with her grandchildren as well, even dispensing business advice during an illness, suggesting that James, now a fledgling lawyer, send some of his business cards to his uncle Harold. She was well in July 1859 but then got sick and declined rapidly. She died on August 18 and was buried, like her husband, at Laurel Hill Cemetery.[46]

By dying in August, Sarah just missed witnessing something that might have made her very proud or caused her distress. In December, her son Hector, soon to be a major in the Union Army, accompanied Mrs. John Brown to Virginia to witness her husband's execution for his raid on the Harper's Ferry Army Arsenal. John Brown hoped to ignite a rebellion of the enslaved that would end the institution for once and for all. Some prominent northerners such as Emerson and Thoreau abandoned pacifism and supported Brown. Hector, who supported antislavery causes, but who was, like his father, no pacifist, "did not approve." He was, nonetheless, concerned with maintaining order and agreed to bring home the body. Some of Hector's friends would refuse to speak to him for years afterward. And, despite being shot at himself at the execution, Hector took another risk when the coffin was delivered to Mrs. Brown. He had heard that some Virginians had promised to mutilate the body and to substitute that of an African American man. So he insisted the coffin be opened and the body identified before they proceeded. When Hector and another escort, J. Miller McKim, arrived with the casket at the Philadelphia train station, a crowd had gathered. Fearing a riot, the mayor would not allow the body to remain in the city. He got six policemen to carry an empty box out of the station and carefully put it on a wagon, which the crowd followed. Meanwhile, he had McKim take the real coffin forthwith to a boat at the wharf and then on to burial in New York. Hector quietly escorted Mrs. Brown through the crowd unnoticed.[47]

This coda suggests the hard barriers that Sarah Tyndale's hopes for social reform would encounter. How would she have reconciled the splintering of the confident, middle-class agenda of antislavery, pacifism, women's rights, communalism, and the arts that had once seemed so firmly interlinked? Her own expansive vision of human rights would soon be sorely tested in the crux of the Civil War.

CHAPTER 12

William Darrah Kelley

> I am "a solid, moving, mass of boiling fluids."
>
> —William Darrah Kelley

Like Frank Johnson and Sarah Tyndale, William Kelley had relatively humble beginnings. He was born in 1814, a generation after Tyndale and Johnson. His parents resided in the Northern Liberties, the working-class neighborhood just north of the city limits at the time. (It would become part of the city in 1854.) The Kelleys were of Scotch-Irish Presbyterian ancestry, but with deep colonial roots, their first American forebears having settled on the New Jersey side of the Delaware River in 1664, two decades before William Penn founded Philadelphia. His grandfather, Major John Kelley, served as an officer in the Continental Army throughout the Revolutionary War. Kelley also had Northern Irish roots, colonial forebears, and veterans of the Revolution on the side of his mother, Hannah Darrah.[1]

William's father, David, was a watchmaker and jeweler. The family—including William and three older sisters, Rebecca, Eliza Ann, and Martha Shaw—had lived comfortably at 227 North Second Street. They were neighbors to the Tyndales and other shopkeepers. But they were not doing well at the time of William's birth. David Kelley had made the generous but unfortunate mistake of endorsing a promissory note for his brother-in-law. When the latter defaulted on the loan, David Kelley was liable. Possibly owing to the stress, he collapsed in the street and died in 1816 from a heart attack or stroke. He was thirty-two; little William was two. Fortunately, William's mother was a strong woman who kept the family going. Hannah Kelley would have a lifelong influence on her son. Times must have been tough initially, as the family's belongings were seized in bankruptcy. Pennsylvania law did not protect a widow's inheritance from creditors. The Kelleys did benefit from the kind gesture of a

Figure 23. William Darrah Kelley (1814–1890). Library of Congress Prints and Photographs Division. Brady-Handy Photograph Collection.

quick-thinking Quaker neighbor. "Friend Scattergood" calmly filled two baskets with the family's silver and other valuable items at the sheriff's sale, pretending that they were her own, and walked off remarking aloud that "it seems strange that Friend Hannah Kelley should not have returned precious heirlooms." Apparently Mrs. Scattergood had sufficient gravitas and respectability to prevent any interference with her departure. She soon restored the items to the family. "Thee will have abundant use, Friend Kelley, for these belongings for thyself and thy children," she proclaimed. "I feel sure that thee has not misconstrued my good intention."[2]

Hannah Kelley supported her family as had many widows before and since, by running a boardinghouse. Among William Kelley's first memories was one of his sisters sweeping the steps at 102 High (Market) Street. He recalled her singing "at the top of her voice: There is a Fountain filled with blood drawn from Immanuel's veins," at which he ran "down the street calling back to her, 'I don't want to hear about blood.'" It was, his daughter Florence Kelley later asserted, his earliest "recorded protest in his long life of protest and dissent."[3]

Young William went to school at the Second Presbyterian Church, but not for long. He quit at eleven to help support his family, earning a dollar a week as an errand boy for a lottery office. Over the next two years he worked at a series of jobs: in a bookstore, for an umbrella maker, and as a copyboy for the printer of the *Philadelphia Inquirer.* The hours at the last job were so long (from dawn to dusk in the summer) that he had trouble keeping awake. At the advice of an older worker, he began to chew green tea leaves to stay alert. Kelley later attributed his lifelong stomach trouble and "nervous excitability" to the tea leaves and strain of those early years.[4]

When he turned thirteen, the family thought it time for him to learn a trade, and so, equipped with his father's tools, in 1828 he entered a seven-year apprenticeship as a jeweler for the firm of Rickards and Dubosq. As was customary, he lived with them. He also began to display the organizational and political energies that kept him going for the rest of his life. With other youth, he organized a library and lecture series for apprentices. At fourteen, he joined the State Fencibles, where he met Frank Johnson along with Democratic Party leader Colonel James Page. At sixteen, he joined one of the new workingmen's organizations and began to organize city laborers for the Democratic Party. There were no unions for jewelers, so he joined the carpenters union and became a member of the Mechanics Union of Trade Associations. He was promptly elected to office. Two years later, he encountered President Andrew Jackson when the State Fencibles escorted him during a visit to Philadelphia. The president assailed the Bank of the United States as contrary to the interests of workingmen. Young Kelley was persuaded. Not yet twenty, he became a politician.[5]

The 1830s were a heady time for Philadelphia workingmen. Organizing for the first time, they felt their political and economic power growing. In 1834, Kelley joined fellow workers in the first general strike—for the ten-hour workday. They won their goal in 1835. But Kelley's antibank activity got him into trouble with the city's conservative Whig party establishment. He lost his job and had difficulty finding another. After searching unsuccessfully for nine months, he moved to Boston, where one of his sisters now lived and where a former shop mate had found work. Kelley set up as a journeyman jeweler with his brother-in-law and gained a reputation as a skilled enameler. He even won an award from the Massachusetts Mechanics Association for a set of gold cups he had enameled for the imam of Muscat.[6]

Kelley did not like Boston's colder weather, but he did appreciate the city's intellectual climate. He later likened his time there to four years in college. This was self-education, and Kelley took advantage of every opportunity. He attended lyceums and lectures. He befriended Boston's intellectuals, including Orestes Brownson, Ralph Waldo Emerson, and William Ellery Channing. He became especially close to historian and Democratic politician George Bancroft, who offered him free use of his library and encouraged him to apply for a scholarship to Harvard. Kelley took advantage of the former, but he declined to do the latter. Kelley chose to advance on his own and was soon making a name for himself as a writer and speaker. His first major speech was in response to the burning of the Charlestown convent, but he really drew attention when he jumped on stage at a mass meeting at Faneuil Hall and introduced himself to the crowd. The six-footer was a striking presence with his dark eyes and hair and fair complexion. He had a certain charisma that attracted attention. And he thrived on attention.[7]

Kelley was also becoming a Locofoco Democrat under Bancroft's influence, gradually losing interest in the Workingman's Party. This switch of allegiance was not such a great jump as the Locofoco wing of the Democratic Party agreed with the Workingman's Party on several issues, particularly its opposition to paper money and most banks and its demand for a specie, or gold and silver, economy and monetary system. Kelley was concerned about special interests, and thought that commerce required more regulation. Kelley did not become an abolitionist, despite their presence in Boston. In fact, William Lloyd Garrison worked across the street. John Greenleaf Whittier's poems had converted Kelley to the larger antislavery cause, but he was put off by what he saw as Garrison's disdain for the masses and for politics and his use of inflammatory tactics rather than persuasion. Kelley believed that southern yeoman farmers would eventually overthrow the slaveholding aristocracy; it was all part of his vision of democracy.[8]

Although busy in Boston, Kelley did not lose touch with Philadelphia during these years. In addition to exchanging letters with his mother and sisters he continued to correspond with his Philadelphia friend Henry Patterson, a medical student at the University of Pennsylvania and another rising radical. Kelley subscribed to three Philadelphia newspapers and claimed to read five Pennsylvania papers, which allowed him to follow his home state's politics. In 1835, for example, he supported the candidacy of Henry Muhlenberg's grandson Henry A. P. Muhlenberg for the Pennsylvania governor's office.[9]

Kelley moved back to Philadelphia in 1839 at the suggestion of James Page, in order to read law in Page's office. He had tired of the life of an artisan, and doubtless thought the law would help him pursue politics. For that purpose, Page's office was the place to be. And politics were hot, as Philadelphia was a sharply divided city in 1839. Black and white antislavery forces were still smarting over the recent state disfranchisement of Blacks and the burning of Pennsylvania Hall. Philadelphia was also polarized on the bank issue. Kelley had long supported Andrew Jackson's antibank stance and was angry that Pennsylvania rechartered the old Bank of the United States after Jackson vetoed its renewal by the federal government. Kelley and other Democrats blamed the bank for the brutal Panic of 1837. He had also supported Jackson's Specie Circular and hard money policies. These divisions persisted under Jackson's successor, Martin Van Buren. Political contests between the Democrats and the anti-Jackson party, the Whigs, were sharply contested at both the state and national levels. All of this was fodder for discussion in Page's office.[10]

Page put Kelley to work immediately, and more on politics than the law. Kelley had arrived just in time for the 1840 presidential election campaign, and Page recognized his talent. They both addressed a Democratic rally in Salem, New Jersey, and another in front of the Democratic Party headquarters, across the street from Independence Hall. They had their work cut out for them because the Whigs, formerly the party of elites, on the one hand, and free Blacks, on the other, turned a new page and began to court the "common man" who had swept Jackson to the White House. They inaugurated their famous "log cabin and hard cider" campaign, painting their candidate, William Henry Harrison, as the frontier war hero who had vanquished the Indian leader "Old Tippecanoe." Harrison's birthplace was far from a log cabin, but no matter, the Whigs had learned to their pain of the efficacy of attributing humble roots to

Jackson. Philadelphia made a laudable contribution to this 1840 campaign when the E. C. Booz Distillery Company came out with whiskey bottles in the shape of log cabins. Needless to say, the name stuck, and "booze" has been a popular commodity ever since. With such powerful persuasion, the Whigs won the race. Kelley and Page and company did have some reason to be happy, however, since they won locally. They held on to the workers and immigrants who were their core constituency and in fact managed to increase the Democratic share of the vote in Philadelphia from 46.5 percent in 1836 to 50.3 percent in 1840.[11]

Isaac Mickle, the same diarist who gave us a glimpse of Frank Johnson at home, also provides a detailed eyewitness to the goings-on in Page's firm, once he began to read law there himself in 1841. Page's office was on Walnut Street near Third, opposite the old Friends Almshouse and a few doors over from William White's home. It was as much a Democratic Party headquarters as a law office, since "Colonel Page, being an active politician, has an army of friends, some of whom are stopping by for him at every minute." It was probably owing to this stream of political traffic that Page put Mickle "under the charge of Mr. Kell[e]y a young practitioner who occupies a part of the office." Kelley, now twenty-seven, had just passed the bar.[12]

So Mickle, too, was soon absorbed into the political activity, reporting during his first week that he "spent the day in reading Blackstone on the Parliament, and copying political notices for Mr. Kelley." Indeed, Kelley took it upon himself to educate Mickle in politics as well as the law, urging him to read a recent speech by radical Democrat Orestes Brownson. Kelley's friend Patterson, now an M.D. who nevertheless managed to be another daily visitor at the office, also shared his radical politics.[13]

Page did not. When Kelley was preparing to address a radical meeting in front of Independence Hall promoting a law intended to harm the hated banks by repudiating the state debt, the more moderate Page objected. Taking "a stand in the middle of the office," he "made a long and truly able speech in oppugnation to the wild schemes of Kelley, Patterson and their clique," who, he thought, threatened Democratic victory not only in the state but in the nation at large. Kelley did not dare to contradict his patron, and thus kept the peace for the time being. Mickle concluded that "Colonel Page has a great respect for the talents of Kelley, and it pains him that he should have adopted such fantastic notions."[14]

Young Mickle apparently absorbed Page's stance. His portrait of Kelley after two weeks was ambivalent: he was "too open to flattery, and too fond of displaying his powers," while "in religion and politics" he "was "too wild, radical, and theoretical; in his converse pointed and satirical." Still, he found him, "a very clever fellow withal." Kelly had "read law two years and passed his examination with flying colours, Mickle noted. "If he do not get too deeply into politics and theology, he may make an eminent lawyer; for his voice is deep, full and powerful, his apprehension quick, his gestures appropriate."[15]

It is possible that Kelley enjoyed shocking his young charge, as he continued to expose Mickle to radical thinkers. One day Kelley gave him a letter "which he received . . . from Edgar A. Poe, the poet and scholar." Mickle was disturbed to find that it revealed Poe was "a transcendentalist of the most ultra stamp" and not an orthodox Christian, but rather an "infidel." Mickle nevertheless admired Kelley sufficiently to engage him to give a couple of lectures across the river in his hometown of Camden, New Jersey. Mickle was nervous that they would not be well attended, and was sure Kelley was disappointed at the crowd of forty on the first occasion (the second crowd was ample). But he thought the audience was entranced at Kelley's oration. Mickle himself was impressed by "the originality, the pathos, [and] the variety of his eloquence" on the subjects of the American Revolution and the War of 1812.[16]

So despite his qualms about Kelley's radicalism, Mickle supported him. Although he thought Kelley's "Address to the Democrats of Philadelphia," delivered in the State House Yard behind Independence Hall, was a "Transcendental pamphlet," he was miffed when a Philadelphia newspaper sneered at Kelley's youth. The two men continued to work together, both giving antibank speeches in the State House Yard in August 1841. But Mickle expressed his disapproval of Kelley's wearing a fashionable loose blouse on that occasion, thinking it an appeal to the workingmen of Kensington and Southwark that would only backfire. Perhaps Mickle was jealous of the rising star. When he read an enthusiastic newspaper notice of a speech Kelley gave in Boston later that month, he wrote, "Mark my word—that man will be ruined by flattery."[17]

Mickle may have been biased, but clearly Kelley was feeling his oats. After reading a positive newspaper notice about his address to another large meeting in the State House Yard in September, Kelley broke out: "What are offices and public honours compared with the consciousness that I am in the front rank of those who are to regenerate the institutions of this commonwealth?" If he were "able to say 'I have done this,'" he "could live in the meanest garret contentedly." Mickle remained a bit skeptical, especially when Kelley began to engage in the production of "shinplasters," small-denomination bank notes to the back of which he and his friends had pasted anti-paper-money slogans. But Kelley himself was delighted to thus make "a missionary of every rag." And his activity and stature only grew. He gave a well-received public lecture on "The Philosophy of History" in Kensington in 1842. He was very active in the suspension-of-specie-payment crisis, when the city's banks refused to exchange the gold and silver in their vaults for the paper notes they had issued, which was a later phase of the bank war. An observer praised his "voice of unusual depth and power," remembering "standing at the northeast gate of Washington Square, and distinctly hearing him address a day-meeting at the other end of the State-House yard, notwithstanding the noises of the street." No wonder the *Spirit of the Times* called him "the tribune of the people." This must have made his heart swell. His popularity was likely an ingredient in his rapid success as a lawyer. He took in his own law student in February 1843.[18]

Mickle was usually impressed by the luminaries Kelley introduced him to. He met Orestes Brownson when the latter came to Philadelphia and stayed with Kelley. Mickle was happy to buy tickets to Brownson's lecture series, since he was curious about the famous radical and editor of the *Boston Quarterly Review*. The influence between Brownson and Kelley was mutual. Kelley was said to have made Brownson a Democrat and Brownson to have encouraged Kelley's advocacy of the working class and adoption of Unitarianism. Kelley admired this new liberal religious sect, although he was uncomfortable with its association with Boston aristocrats.[19]

In February 1843, Kelley took a wowed Mickle along on an hour-long visit to Ralph Waldo Emerson, then visiting Philadelphia on a lecture tour and staying at the United States Hotel. Mickle found Emerson's conversation "easy and unadorned" and enjoyed listening to his anecdotes of the European literary men he had met in his travels. On the other hand, Mickle noted that "it amused me not a little to hear Kelley trying to keep up with his host."[20]

Mickle was more cynical when Albert Brisbane, the main proponent of Fourierism in America, called on Kelley. When Kelley asked Brisbane what he was willing to invest in a communal society and the latter replied his "skills" rather than his labor, Mickle was not impressed. His doubts are interesting in that Mickle would soon marry Clara Tyndale, the daughter of avid Fourierist Sarah Tyndale.[21]

Regardless of his mixed feelings, Mickle regarded Kelley as a friend. They took tea and visited girls together several times in Camden. Mickle visited Kelley at his home in Southwark, an old neighborhood just south of the city's southern border, where the latter showed off his flower garden. In May 1843, the two young men went together to get their daguerreotypes taken. When Kelley relocated from the Southwark house to one at 14 Sansom Street, Isaac helped him move.[22]

Most significantly, when Kelley married Harriet Tenant, Page's orphaned Scottish niece, in August 1843, he took Mickle along with them on their two-week honeymoon trip to New England. It was not uncommon at this time for good friends to accompany newlyweds; the three were joined by another newly married couple. Together they attended parties with relatives and enjoyed the sights of New York, New Haven, and Boston. In the latter place Kelley gave Mickle a tour of historic sites. Kelley had also continued to pal around with his friend Henry Patterson in these years, attending theater and lectures and visiting the actress Fanny Kemble as well as other young women.[23]

Of course marriage short-circuited further bachelor activity. Kelley had already persuaded his mother to give up her boardinghouse and move in with him, and his sister Martha soon joined them as well. Thus, his household expanded in a short period, and doubtless kept him busy at home. Kelley liked living amid a group of women. He must have been happy when Harriet soon presented him with daughter Hannah. He was just as surely devastated, however, when Harriet died giving birth to a baby named Harriette in August 1847. Fortunately, his sister Martha took care of the little girls. In 1850, he moved his family of women to the Elms, the mansion he built in West Philadelphia.[24]

This was part of an important new development in Philadelphia, namely, its first suburbs. West Philadelphia was not subsumed within the city limits until 1854, so initially the Kelleys and other middle- and upper-class businesspeople and professionals who ventured west had moved outside the city when they crossed the Schuylkill River. Contemporaries extolled the "cottages and villas, surrounded by neat grounds" to be found there. Then as now, suburban properties were associated with "the good taste and the care and attention lavished on them" and the superior lifestyle they offered compared to the city's streets. The author of these particular comments, upper-class diarist Sidney George Fisher, concluded in 1859 that "fresh air, space, trees, flowers, privacy, a convenient & tasteful house, can now be had for the same expense as a narrow & confined dwelling on a pavement, surrounded by brick walls and all the unpleasant sights & sounds of a crowded town." According to Fisher, "the advantages are so obvious that this villa and cottage life has become quite a passion and is producing a complete revolution in our habits."[25]

Kelley loved the country atmosphere. He was able to afford his new home as his career had been coming along nicely. Indeed, the mansion was a way to make this clear to all. After stumping for the Democrats in the close presidential election that took James Polk to the White House in 1845, he had been appointed a Philadelphia deputy for the state attorney general. He earned general praise for his work as one of the two prosecutors for the city. In partic-

Figure 24. West Philadelphia when still suburban: University of Pennsylvania College Hall (built 1871–1872) and Hospital (built 1874). University of Pennsylvania Archives.

ular he conducted the high-profile case of the nativist "church-burners" of the "Bible riots" of 1844 "with skill, fearlessness and energy," and thereby won the support of Philadelphia's Irish Catholic community. Unfortunately, it earned him enmity among the Democrats' other constituents, native-born workingmen.[26]

These riots illustrated yet another way Philadelphia was divided in this era, as the influx of Irish immigrants who competed for jobs and turf with native-born white Protestant workers and African Americans led to violence. The immediate spur was a request by the Catholic bishop that students be allowed to study from Catholic Bibles in the schools. The school board's assent to this provided a spark to what had been a smoldering fire. It only took a few exchanges of affronts to lead to a nativist attack on Irish neighborhoods and churches in May 1844, and another in July. Newspapers of various persuasions offered different accounts of who started the tumult, but the wanton destruction of Irish property was undeniable. Prosecuting nativists sparked their electoral retribution, but Kelley won credit for defending the peace.[27]

Then, in 1846, Pennsylvania governor Francis Shunk appointed the thirty-two-year-old as judge of the Court of Common Pleas. It was as Judge Kelley, then, that he built his new suburban home and moved his family there. He may have been happy to retreat the four miles to West Philadelphia every evening—he could walk or take the train—since his courtroom in Independence Hall was directly over a dog kennel in the cellar. There it was his daily privilege to hear both cases and "the incessant howling of the imprisoned curs."[28]

It was not that Kelley was down on Philadelphia. Indeed, he thought his hometown was the most important city in the nation. Listen to his claims in a speech promoting railroads in 1851:

> What then is the position of Philadelphia? She is now, sir, in my humble judgment, the first American city. . . . In extent of territory; in the number of families occupying each its separate, distinct and comfortable home; in the skill of her workmen, and the extent, variety and perfection of the products of her workshops and factories; in the character of her merchants for integrity, steadiness of purpose, and persevering industry; in the pursuit of legitimate business; in the wide spread reputation of her bar, and the prosperous condition of her several medical schools; in far-reaching and generously endowed charities; in the means of religious instruction and worship; and, above all, in her grandly beneficent system of common schools and the regard paid by her citizens to the courtesies and genial duties of life, she is now the first city of the Union.

Kelley only grudgingly admitted that New York had now surpassed Philadelphia in population.[29]

Kelley was a town booster, but he knew that the city had ample problems because he had been engaged in trying to address them, and not only from the bench and bar. One would think that politics, the law, friendship, courtship, and family life would have provided a full plate for Kelley—but he had also become involved in a variety of campaigns for reform. He began with the anti-capital-punishment and temperance movements. He arranged a public debate on the former issue in 1842 and, along with Patterson, joined several anti-capital-punishment societies by 1844. Among the resolutions from his pen adopted by one meeting and reprinted in the *Public Ledger* were statements that capital punishment was "a relic of barbarism" and "by no means . . . efficacious in deterring men from the commission of crime—a fact, in proof of which we appeal to the history of the penal legislation of all countries and ages." He took his new wife and his friend Mickle to hear anti-capital-punishment speakers and made public addresses on the subject himself. During these same years, he gave speeches promoting temperance to residents of Camden as well as to Philadelphia Firemen, joined the Sons of Temperance, worked to reduce the number of liquor licenses in Pennsylvania, and became a teetotaler.[30]

When he joined the Unitarian Church in 1846, Kelley immersed himself in a veritable reform community. Led by the influential William Henry Furness, the Philadelphia Unitarian Church also saw the influx of Lucretia Mott and other former Hicksite Quakers who were heavily involved in antislavery and other reforms. Kelley soon befriended this group and may have followed their lead into prison reform and backing the first reformatory for Black juvenile delinquents. In his address at the "House of Refuge for Coloured Children" in December 1849, he spoke of "some of the means whereby the young are often led away, and the general character of the different gangs that congregate about our streets," as well as how, "by kindness, counsel and advice," the new institution would lead them back to the "paths of truth and rectitude." Kelley's talk was widely praised. Businessman Thomas Cope was impressed that he gave "an eloquent, appropriate speech occupying more than an hour . . . without notes."[31]

Above all, Kelley thought that every youth deserved an education. He placed great value on this, perhaps because his own self-education was so hard won. He insisted that "he who can read the language of Shakespeare and Milton, Johnson and Addison, Shelley and Wordsworth, has the collected wisdom of his race." Then would "the sages of the most remote past obey his call as counsellors and friends" and "Wisdom and Justice would make it the certain heritage of every child born into the commonwealth." In 1850, he compiled statistics on the near-universal lack of education of criminals incarcerated in Philadelphia, as well as the lack of criminal records among the graduates of Philadelphia's schools, and he lectured on the subject. He then worked with Philadelphia's Episcopal Bishop Alonzo Potter to establish night schools for apprentices; spoke at the cornerstone laying of the new Central High School, the city's first public high school; and helped with the establishment of the Female Medical College of Philadelphia.[32]

These efforts to promote education were praised by the ladies of the Rosine Society, who appreciated his help in furthering their cause as well. As a judge, he came into contact with the sort of young women they were trying to save, and sometimes communicated with the Rosines about them. In 1852, for example, he asked them to visit a fifteen-year-old girl in the prison. They did, and soon adopted her into their home.[33]

Kelley's association with the Motts and other adherents of the Unitarian Church surely boosted his interest in the antislavery movement, for which he became a powerful voice. His feelings on the issue had been growing for some time. He had not been without prejudice as a young man, but was shocked and converted to the cause by the burning of Pennsylvania Hall in 1838 and the various anti-Black riots of the 1830s and 1840s, especially that of October 1849. In 1844 he had already been elected to the council of the Pennsylvania Abolition Society.[34]

Perhaps this accelerating reform activity helped Kelley get over Harriet's premature death. His mother and sister were indispensable on the home front, which would have only made it harder when his mother Hannah Darrah Kelley died in 1852, just five years after his wife. This time Kelley tried a change of scene and traveled to Europe with Henry Patterson. He must have had friends to visit, as he had been, not surprisingly, an attentive supporter of the various failed democratic revolutions there in 1848. He had helped Hungarian patriot Louis Kossuth come to Philadelphia to raise support, for example, and in parting, Kossuth wrote a note of thanks "to the advocate of liberty in Philadelphia." Kelley had made several speeches in support of Kossuth—one at a banquet in the Musical Fund Hall, another on the revolution in France with a large demonstration of support—at the State House Yard.[35]

Back home after the European tour, Kelley's Unitarian Church connections provided additional comfort in 1854, when they were the means of his meeting Caroline Bonsall. She had been raised by Lucretia Mott's very close friends the Pughs of Germantown, after being orphaned in childhood. Kelley was a prominent man by this time. A magazine story of 1851 described him as "widely known as an active, energetic and radical member of the great Democratic Party . . . universally recognized as an ardent friend of humanity, a zealous collaborator in every effort for the elevation of the laboring community, and a helper in every good work." The writer even recommended him as an example to young men, owing to his rise by his own honorable effort and achievement of "reputation and fortune" "against all disadvantages." At least one young man was clearly open to his influence; Sarah Tyndale's eighteen-year-old grandson James Tyndale attended two Kelley lectures within a month in the fall of 1852, one at the Fourth Anniversary Celebration of the Forensic and Literary Circle at the Sansom Street Hall, and another at the Franklin Institute.[36]

Yet, upon meeting Carrie Bonsall, this paragon and city father acted like a boy himself. Smitten, Kelley wooed her with dispatch, and she must have worried about his impulsiveness. "So you smile at the energy with which I embark in a new work," he wrote her, admitting that he was "a solid, moving, mass of boiling fluids" and that "sometimes it excites the fears of my friends lest I endanger myself by rashness." He defended himself, however, insisting that "I am prepared to maintain that I am a cautious man requiring to understand things fully before I commit to them." Still, he acknowledged that, after "looking thoroughly beforehand, I do leap with some energy." Will and Carrie were married by Furness before the end of the year.[37]

Now that he was firmly ensconced in the Philadelphia antislavery network, national, state, and local politics began to drive Kelley away from the Democratic Party. In the late 1840s, he had supported Pennsylvania senator David Wilmot's proviso that no new state from the territories gained in the War with Mexico be permitted to allow slavery. He was disappointed when President James K. Polk, Pennsylvania senator James Buchanan, and other Democrats failed to join him. Then, because he handed down a decision unseating a fellow Democrat elected with fraudulent votes, the party did not renominate him for the judgeship. So he ran and was reelected in 1851 as an independent, winning handily despite strong attacks against him in the press. Kelley broke with Page and other Philadelphia Democrats over his opposition to the 1850 Fugitive Slave Act and support of the Christiana riot against its implementation. In 1854, Kelley gave a speech against "Slavery in the Territories" that received national attention. He formally quit the Democratic Party that year, after the Missouri Compromise was effectively repealed by the adoption of the Kansas-Nebraska Act.[38]

Influenced by Carrie Kelley's aunt Sarah Pugh, and Sarah Pugh's best friend, Lucretia Mott, Kelley's antislavery activity only continued to deepen. He became "an organizer and manager of the Philadelphia Female Anti-Slavery Society's annual fairs." He may have worked with Sarah Tyndale in this capacity. In 1855 he was a judge in the famous Jane Johnson fugitive slave case.[39]

Johnson and her two children had run away from her enslaver, Colonel John Wheeler, the American minister to Nicaragua, when their boat docked in Philadelphia on the way to New York. They had been advised to do so by William Still and Passmore Williamson, members of the Vigilance Committee of Philadelphia, a group active in the Underground Railroad. Still and Williamson informed Johnson that, according to the laws of Pennsylvania, no one could remain a slave on Pennsylvania soil. Wheeler saw to it that Williamson was jailed for contempt of court for refusing to reveal where Johnson was and brought charges against Still and several others for "forcible abduction." Kelley presided over the trial, in front of a room packed, as usual in fugitive slave cases, with members of the Vigilance Committee. The climactic moment came when, to the public's surprise, Jane herself appeared, escorted by Sarah Pugh and other members of the Philadelphia Female Anti-Slavery Society, and testified that she "went away of my own free will," thereby destroying the prosecution's case.[40]

Jane's appearance was risky since the district attorney and other officials had vowed that she would be apprehended and returned to her owner. But, flanked by Sarah Pugh and Lucretia Mott, Jane was able to leave the courtroom and was driven to safety. Kelley then advised the jury: "if you are satisfied that they [the defendants] only went to tell Jane she was free and conduct her to a place of safety, and acted peacefully, you cannot find them guilty." Still was acquitted. Kelley was later credited for assuring Jane's safety during and after the trial.[41]

By now a fervent advocate of the antislavery cause, Kelley was outraged along with other northerners at the news in May 1856 that Massachusetts senator Charles Sumner had been brutally beaten by South Carolina congressman Preston Brooks on the floor of the Senate. Brooks caned Sumner after the latter had insulted Brooks's uncle during his long and heated "Crime Against Kansas" speech. Sumner had vilified the bloody effects of Congress's leaving the issue of slavery in the Kansas territory up to "popular sovereignty" or popular referendum. This had only spurred pro- and antislavery forces in Kansas to go to war. Kelley was so upset at news of the caning that he suspended court business and held a protest meeting in his Independence Hall courtroom. When the severely injured Sumner arrived in Philadelphia to convalesce in William Furness's home, he was put under the care of renowned Dr. Caspar Wistar (then owner of Nancy Shippen's childhood home). Kelley's visits there with Sumner only stiffened his antislavery resolve.[42]

As Kelley's antislavery commitment deepened, so did his rift with James Page. When Page condemned the abolitionists after John Brown's failed raid in 1859, Kelley was included in the attack. Philadelphia had always had a large number of southern sympathizers, from southern medical students to elite families with southern branches, to businessmen with extensive commercial dealings with the South. Many, including politicians like Page, blamed the abolitionists for stirring things up. When John Brown's wife, Mary Ann, came to stay with the Motts before his trial, Philadelphians did not welcome her. But Kelley did, and he may have been the means by which Sarah Tyndale's son Hector was recruited to accompany Mrs. Brown to Virginia for the execution and to collect John Brown's body.[43]

Kelley may have met the Tyndales when his friend Isaac Mickle married Sarah's youngest daughter, Clara, in 1845. It is possible, however, that Sarah Tyndale had known him since he was a baby, when she, as a young mother herself, lived just down Second Street from David and Hannah Kelley. But it was likely shared liberal and reform inclinations that nurtured a friendship with Sarah and her son Hector in the 1850s. Sarah visited Kelley at the Elms with her daughter Elizabeth and son-in-law Edward Mitchell in June 1853, and her grandson James Mitchell, then studying at Harvard, saw him in Boston in May 1854. The friendship persisted after Kelley's second marriage, as James noted a visit in February 1855. His description gives a sense of the situation of the Elms, built on the edge of spreading suburban development. It was accessed by a corridor of streets directly west of the city center, or by a shortcut through undeveloped land: "After dinner Uncle Hector came up and we went . . . out to Judge Kelley's. Walked out by the railroad and then across the fields, but got very muddy. Found the Judge and Mrs. Kelley (Miss Caddie Bonsall) at home, and also little Harriet who is the most beautiful child I ever saw. After talking awhile we came home again through West Philadelphia and found the walking very much better."[44]

While Hector Tyndale was in Virginia with Mrs. Brown for John Brown's hanging, Kelley was among those in Philadelphia who attended pro-Brown speeches on December 2, the day of his execution. Feelings were high. When mixed-race abolitionist Robert Purvis went so far as to proclaim that "John Brown would be looked upon as the Jesus Christ of the nineteenth century," the southern medical students who had come to heckle rushed the stage. The scuffle was contained only by the police. A week later, Philadelphia was still simmering. Antiabolitionist leaders, including James Page, addressed a large meeting on December 7 to assure the South of Philadelphia's desire to preserve both states' rights and the Union. Then, on December 15, the two sides clashed on the occasion of a long-scheduled address by abolitionist George William Curtis on "The Present Aspect of the Slavery Question." After two other city leaders had refused, Kelley had consented "with alacrity" to introduce Curtis. An admiring witness later opined that Kelley "was perfectly fearless, and he enjoyed doing things that were a brave vindication of principle." Once again Mayor Alexander Henry feared a riot, and prominent citizens begged the sponsors to postpone the lecture. The latter opted to defend free speech. As many as six hundred policemen were called out to guard the hall. The atmosphere was tense. "Mr. Coffee, the District Attorney, sat on the platform with a loaded revolver in his pocket," the witness recalled, and "Judge Kelley had a billy, or small cudgel, up his sleeve." Kelley duly introduced the speaker "'upon the subject which God is pressing closer and closer upon us every day . . . the great question of slavery,'" and Curtis proceeded. There was no doubt the building itself would have been destroyed were it not for the police, so menacing was the antiabolitionist crowd that had gathered outside. As it was, the "mob made several charges upon the entrance," while "brickbats were thrown through the side windows," and "a bottle of vitriol was also thrown," blinding a member of the audience. Some protesters got inside, and a few "rough looking men jumped upon the benches and gave cheers for the Union, to drown the voice of the lecturer." They were promptly arrested. Philadelphia was not immune to the violence that was about to erupt in civil war.[45]

Antislavery commitment had been driving Kelley's politics for several years at this point. He missed the meetings to organize the new Republican Party and its first national convention at the Musical Fund Hall, because court was in session. But he helped organize Republicans in the city. In the fall of 1856, he also made an unsuccessful first run for Congress as a Fremont Republican and Free Soil candidate. In the course of campaigning, he delivered his first Republican speech, on "Slavery in the Territories," in Spring Garden Hall. James Mitchell and his uncle Harold Tyndale went to hear Kelley speak on another occasion "at the Fremont meeting at the corner of Sixteenth and Greene Sts." Kelley lost the election in part because he refused fusion with the anti-immigrant and nativist Know-Nothing Party. At this juncture, Kelley resigned his judgeship, perhaps embarrassed at the electoral defeat. But he was also bored with the bench. He resumed his law career. But he would not stay out of politics for long.[46]

The year 1860 saw Kelley in Chicago as a delegate to the Republican convention. He was an early supporter of Abraham Lincoln and made his confidence in the nominee known by a bet he made at a speech in Springfield. He wagered a ton of Pennsylvania coal against a barrel of Illinois wheat that Pennsylvania would give Lincoln a larger majority than Illinois would. Kelley stumped hard for Lincoln in Philadelphia. He was known as Lincoln's closest associate there. He was rewarded for his efforts when a barrel of wheat arrived from the Springfield Republicans.[47]

Many Philadelphians, however, were uneasy at Lincoln's election. Alarmed at the prospect of southern secession, they blamed people like Kelley for causing trouble. But the Confederates' firing on the last remaining federal fort in the South, Fort Sumter in Charleston harbor, changed things overnight. Most Philadelphians fell into line in support of the union. In the end, then, Kelley's campaigning for Lincoln served him well, as the Republicans would reign in Philadelphia (and elsewhere) for the next seventy years.[48]

In the short run Kelley's support for Lincoln got him the Republican nomination for congressman from the Fourth District. His antislavery friends departed from their tradition of eschewing electoral politics and actively campaigned for him. He himself campaigned with gusto. The contest was close, and Kelley awaited the results at the Elms with his accustomed anxiety. Of course the Republicans, and Kelley, won. He would serve the district for the next twenty-nine years, until his death in 1890.[49]

Kelley was sworn into the House of Representatives on July 4, 1861. He took his antislavery commitment with him to Washington and was one of the Republicans who consistently pushed Lincoln on the emancipation issue and the enlistment of Blacks in the military. He spoke, with Frederick Douglass and eloquent Republican orator Anna Dickinson, at the first meeting called to recruit Black troops in Philadelphia. As a member of Congress Kelley was exempt from military service, but he joined the reserves and went out when Pennsylvania was threatened in 1863. At war's end, he opposed Andrew Johnson's plans and later spoke in favor of his impeachment. He pushed for Radical Reconstruction and was attacked when he toured the South. Above all, he agitated for the vote for African Americans, secured by the Fifteenth Amendment.[50]

Kelley also wanted women to get the franchise. He had long been a friend of Susan B. Anthony and had spoken at women's rights conventions. He supported the Pennsylvania married women's property act proposed by Lucretia Mott. His speeches on suffrage and labor in the mid-1860s were the most widely circulated of the nineteenth century. His daughter, reformer Florence Kelley, attributed his interest in women's political and economic rights to the struggle of his widowed mother to raise her family.[51]

Kelley's continued pursuit of reform goals would be somewhat overshadowed in later years, however, by his economic policies. The devastating Panic of 1857 demolished his prior faith in free trade. His essential loyalties had not changed; as late as 1859 Lucretia Mott assumed that he and Carrie would want to meet with British industrial socialist Robert Dale Owen. He simply came to believe that protection of industry was necessary to help workers. Together with his desire to overthrow the southern "Slave Power," the depression had converted the former Democrat to the need for big, not small, government.[52]

Kelley's new big government stance also allowed him to support internal improvements. He had long been interested in them. An 1846 newspaper clip shows him advocating, along with James Page, congressional support for a railroad to the Pacific; another of 1851 shows him urging Philadelphians to invest in a railroad to the Great Lakes. An 1858 speech promoted the transatlantic telegraph cable. He also backed the first legislation to make Yellowstone a national park. But his chief legacy was protection for Pennsylvania's iron industry. This earned him the title "Pig Iron Kelley." His protracted tenure in office (he became the longest serving member of Congress up until that time and sat on many committees) allowed him to serve his constituents well.[53]

At one point Kelley was one of the richest men in Philadelphia. He later lost some money in bad investments, however, and was briefly touched by the Credit Mobilier scandal, though he was exonerated. He ended up leaving a rather modest estate of $30,000 at his death at age seventy-six in January 1890. It was in Washington, with his family at his bedside. He is buried at Laurel Hill Cemetery. He may have been ready to go, as he had suffered for years with a cancerous growth on his face, and surgical removal six years before had not lessened the pain.[54]

Kelley's daughter Florence, who became a famous settlement-house worker and Progressive reformer, later remembered her mother remonstrating when Kelley taught her to read as a child by using a gruesomely illustrated tract on the evils of child labor in the British factory system. He responded that privileged children needed to understand the facts of life of "their less fortunate contemporaries," if the world was ever going to be set right. Another thing her father told her in childhood made an equally deep impression. It was that "the duty of his generation was to build up great industries in America so that more wealth could be produced for the whole people. 'The duty of your generation,' he often said, 'will be to see that the product is distributed justly. The same generation cannot do both.'" It is fortunate for America that young Florence took these lessons to heart. But that, as her father said, is the story of another generation—and, we might add, another book.[55]

NOTES

Introduction

1. John Fanning Watson, *Annals of Philadelphia and Pennsylvania, in the Olden Time . . .*, 2 vols. (Philadelphia: J. B. Lippincott, 1870), 1:158–162; Thompson Westcott, *Historic Mansions and Buildings of Philadelphia* (Philadelphia: Porter and Coates, 1877), 11–36.

2. Watson, *Annals of Philadelphia,* 1:160. On changing views of historic sites in general, and on Penn Hall in particular, see Whitney Martinko, *Historic Real Estate: Market Morality and the Politics of Preservation in the Early United States* (Philadelphia: University of Pennsylvania Press, 2020), esp. 88–91.

3. See, for example, the digitized resources available through the Greater Philadelphia GeoHistory Network, http://www.philageohistory.org, accessed May 20, 2020. On the ways in which Philadelphians have collectively remembered and constructed their histories, see Gary B. Nash, *First City: Philadelphia and the Forging of Historical Memory* (Philadelphia: University of Pennsylvania Press, 2002).

4. Edward Lawler Jr., "The President's House in Philadelphia: The Rediscovery of a Lost Landmark," *Pennsylvania Magazine of History and Biography* 126, no. 1 (Jan. 2002), 5–95; special issue on "The President's House in Philadelphia," ibid., 129, no. 4 (Oct. 2005), 269–481; Erica Armstrong Dunbar, *Never Caught: The Washingtons' Relentless Pursuit of Their Runaway Slave, Ona Judge* (New York: 37 Ink/Atria, 2017).

Part I

1. Mary Maples Dunn, *William Penn: Politics and Conscience* (Princeton, N.J.: Princeton University Press, 1967); Andrew R. Murphy, *Liberty, Conscience, and Toleration: The Political Thought of William Penn* (New York: Oxford University Press, 2016).

2. Gottlieb Mittelberger, *Journey to Pennsylvania*, ed. and trans. Oscar Handlin and John Clive (Cambridge, Mass.: Harvard University Press, 1960), 41. For varied perspectives on these issues, see Michael Zuckerman, ed., *Friends and Neighbors: Group Life in America's First Plural Society* (Philadelphia: Temple University Press, 1982); Sally Schwartz, *"A Mixed Multitude": The Struggle for Toleration in Colonial Pennsylvania* (New York: New York University Press, 1987); A. G. Roeber, *Palatines, Liberty, and Property: German Lutherans in Colonial British America* (Baltimore: Johns Hopkins University Press, 1998); Patrick Griffin, *The People with No Name: Ulster Scots, America's Scots Irish, and the Creation of a British Atlantic World, 1689–1764* (Princeton, N.J.: Princeton

University Press, 2001); Peter Silver, *Our Savage Neighbors: How Indian War Transformed Early America* (New York: Norton, 2008); and Patrick Erben, *A Harmony of the Spirits: Translation and the Language of Community in Early Pennsylvania* (Chapel Hill: University of North Carolina Press, 2012).

3. Evan Haefeli, "Pennsylvania's Religious Freedom in Comparative Colonial Context," in Andrew R. Murphy and John Smolenski, eds., *Worlds of William Penn* (New Brunswick, N.J.: Rutgers University Press, 2019), 333–354.

4. John Smolenski, *Friends and Strangers: The Making of a Creole Culture in Colonial Pennsylvania* (Philadelphia: University of Pennsylvania Press, 2010); Jessica Choppin Roney, *Governed by a Spirit of Opposition: The Origins of American Political Practice in Colonial Philadelphia* (Baltimore: Johns Hopkins University Press, 2014), 1–2.

5. Roney, *Governed by a Spirit of Opposition*, 20–21, 29–30.

Chapter 1

Note to epigraph: Quoted in George S. Brookes, *Friend Anthony Benezet* (Philadelphia: University of Pennsylvania Press, 1937) 451. Brookes's volume is especially valuable for its extensive collection of transcribed correspondence.

1. Brookes, *Friend Anthony Benezet*, 16–17, 19, 456; Maurice Jackson, *Let This Voice Be Heard: Anthony Benezet, Father of Atlantic Abolitionism* (Philadelphia: University of Pennsylvania Press, 2009), 2–6. Jackson's is the best recent biography.

2. Brookes, *Friend Anthony Benezet*, 16, 19; Jackson, *Let This Voice*, 8–9.

3. For useful background on Philadelphia in this period, see Russell F. Weigley, ed., *Philadelphia: A 300-Year History* (New York: W. W. Norton, 1982), 33–40, 43–44, 57–62.

4. Brookes, *Friend Anthony Benezet*, 19–20; Nancy Slocum Hornick, "Anthony Benezet and the Africans' School: Toward a Theory of Full Equality," *Pennsylvania Magazine of History and Biography* 99, no. 4 (Oct. 1975), 401–402; Jackson, *Let This Voice*, 7–9.

5. John Smith, *Hannah Logan's Courtship: A True Narrative*, ed. Albert Cook Myers (Philadelphia: Ferris and Leach, 1904), 225–226, 304–305; Brookes, *Friend Anthony Benezet*, 405.

6. Brookes, *Friend Anthony Benezet*, 139, 278–279; Hornick, "Anthony Benezet and Africans' School," 401–402; Jackson, *Let This Voice*, 216.

7. Brookes, *Friend Anthony Benezet*, 207–208.

8. Jackson, *Let This Voice*, 18, 19, 21; Brookes, *Friend Anthony Benezet*, 27, 29, 31–35.

9. Brookes, *Friend Anthony Benezet*, 16, 26; Jackson, *Let This Voice*, 20.

10. Brookes, *Friend Anthony Benezet*, 34–35; Jackson, *Let This Voice*, 21.

11. John Fanning Watson, *Annals of Philadelphia and Pennsylvania, in the Olden Time . . .*, 2 vols. (Philadelphia, J. B. Lippincott, 1870), 1:373; Wilson Armistead, *Anthony Benezet, from the Original Memoir*, rev. ed. (London: A. W. Bennett, 1859), 132; Jackson, *Let This Voice*, 19–21. Donald Brooks Kelley considers Benezet's concern for animals part of a Quaker ecology that encompassed all his other concerns ("'A Tender Regard to the Whole Creation': Anthony Benezet and the Emergence of an Eighteenth-Century Quaker Ecology," *Pennsylvania Magazine of History and Biography* 106, no. 1 [Jan. 1982], 69–88).

12. Brookes, *Friend Anthony Benezet*, 32–33; Armistead, *Anthony Benezet*, 130.

13. Smith, *Hannah Logan's Courtship*, 50–51, 178, 198, 225–226, 243, 270; Brookes, *Friend Anthony Benezet*, 465.

14. Brookes, *Friend Anthony Benezet*, 149–151, 464–466; Armistead, *Anthony Benezet*, 116–117, 123.

15. Brookes, *Friend Anthony Benezet*, 153, 276.

16. Hornick, "Anthony Benezet and Africans' School," 399–404.

17. Brookes, *Friend Anthony Benezet*, 45; Weigley, *Philadelphia*, 85; Brookes, *Friend Anthony Benezet*, 49–50, 450, 452; Armistead, *Anthony Benezet*, 129; Jackson, *Let This Voice*, 20, 22.

18. Brookes, *Friend Anthony Benezet*, 37, 40–42, 466–467; Weigley, *Philadelphia*, 85; Mary Beth Norton, *Liberty's Daughters: The Revolutionary Experience of American Women, 1750–1800* (Boston: Little, Brown, 1980), 260.

19. Armistead, *Anthony Benezet*, 118–122; Brookes, *Friend Anthony Benezet*, 148–149, 471–472.

20. Armistead, *Anthony Benezet*, 24, 104; Brookes, *Friend Anthony Benezet*, 35, 38–39, 44; Jackson, *Let This Voice*, 21, 25.

21. Brookes, *Friend Anthony Benezet*, 54–55, 388–391; Roberts Vaux, *Memoirs of the Life of Anthony Benezet* (Philadelphia: James B. Parke, 1817), 16–18; Monica Kiefer, "Early American Childhood in the Middle Atlantic Area," *Pennsylvania Magazine of History and Biography* 68, no. 1 (Jan. 1944), 20–21.

22. Quoted in Kiefer, "Early American Childhood," 9–10, 16–17.

23. James Mease, *The Picture of Philadelphia* (Philadelphia: B. and T. Kite, 1811), 263; Brookes, *Friend Anthony Benezet*, 48–50, 159, 387; Hornick, "Anthony Benezet and Africans' School," 404–420; Jackson, *Let This Voice*, ix, 22–23, 24; David L. Crosby, ed., *The Complete Antislavery Writings of Anthony Benezet, 1754–1783* (Baton Rouge: Louisiana State University Press, 2013), 233.

24. Jackson, *Let This Voice*, ix, 206–207, 264n; Gary B. Nash, *Forging Freedom: The Formation of Philadelphia's Black Community, 1720–1840* (Cambridge, Mass.: Harvard University Press, 1988), 51, 96–101, 127–128; Hornick, "Anthony Benezet and Africans' School," 415.

25. Brookes, *Friend Anthony Benezet*, 84–85, 87–89, 90–93, 398; Jackson, *Let This Voice*, x–xiii, 31–56, 225.

26. Armistead, *Anthony Benezet*, 69; Brookes, *Friend Anthony Benezet*, 80–81; Jackson, *Let This Voice*, x, 14, 55–56; J. William Frost, ed., *The Quaker Origins of Antislavery* (Norwood, Pa.: Norwood Editions, 1980), 168; Jean R. Soderlund, *Quakers and Slavery: A Divided Spirit* (Princeton, N.J.: Princeton University Press, 1985), 153; Jonathan D. Sassi, "With a Little Help from the Friends: The Quaker and Tactical Contexts of Anthony Benezet's Abolitionist Publishing," *Pennsylvania Magazine of History and Biography* 135, no. 1 (Jan. 2011), 33–71.

27. Gary B. Nash and Jean R. Soderlund, *Freedom by Degrees: Emancipation in Pennsylvania and Its Aftermath* (New York: Oxford University Press, 1991), 14–18, 74–98; Jackson, *Let This Voice*, 14–17.

28. Jackson, *Let This Voice,* xii, 17, 207; Hornick, "Anthony Benezet and Africans' School," 419–420.

29. Jackson, *Let This Voice,* x, xii, 70, 72, 77, 80–88, 227.

30. Ibid., 32; G. J. Barker-Benfield, *Abigail Adams and John Adams: The Americanization of Sensibility* (Chicago: University of Chicago Press, 2010), 404.

31. Armistead, *Anthony Benezet,* 105; Brookes, *Friend Anthony Benezet,* 106; Jackson, *Let This Voice,* x, 215, 218–219.

32. Brookes, *Friend Anthony Benezet,* 397–399; Jackson, *Let This Voice,* 29–30, 219, 221.

33. Armistead, *Anthony Benezet,* 101–103; Brookes, *Friend Anthony Benezet,* 63–67, 70–75, 468; John Thomas Scharf and Thompson Westcott, *History of Philadelphia, 1609–1884,* 2 vols. (Philadelphia: L. H. Everts, 1884), 1:248–250; Jackson, *Let This Voice,* 26–27; Weigley, *Philadelphia,* 101.

34. Brookes, *Friend Anthony Benezet,* 237–238; Vaux, *Memoirs of Benezet,* 82–89.

35. Armistead, *Anthony Benezet,* 91, 95; Brookes, *Friend Anthony Benezet,* 112–113, 118–119, 479–483, 488–489; Jackson, *Let This Voice,* 27.

36. Brookes, *Friend Anthony Benezet,* 120–122; Peter Silver, *Our Savage Neighbors: How Indian War Transformed Early America* (New York: W. W. Norton, 2008), 100–101.

37. Brookes, *Friend Anthony Benezet,* 122–124, 378, 405; Jackson, *Let This Voice,* 130; Silver, *Our Savage Neighbors,* 294–295.

38. Jackson, *Let This Voice,* 27–28, 131–132, 226; Brookes, *Friend Anthony Benezet,* 134–135, 456; Benjamin Rush, *Essays, Literary, Moral and Philosophical* (Philadelphia: Thomas and William Bradford, 1806), 303.

39. Armistead, *Anthony Benezet,* 115, 133; Brookes, *Friend Anthony Benezet,* 134–136, 451.

40. Armistead, *Anthony Benezet,* 123–126; Eliza Cope Harrison, ed., *Philadelphia Merchant: The Diary of Thomas P. Cope, 1800–1851* (South Bend, Ind.: Gateway Editions, 1978), 285; Brookes, *Friend Anthony Benezet,* 146–148, 452, 465–466; Sassi, "With a Little Help," 37, 42, 62; Jackson, *Let This Voice,* 2.

41. Armistead, *Anthony Benezet,* 110–111; Brookes, *Friend Anthony Benezet,* 142–143, 146–147.

42. Brookes, *Friend Anthony Benezet,* 140–141.

43. Ibid., 154, 468; Thompson Westcott, *Historic Mansions and Buildings of Philadelphia* (Philadelphia: Porter and Coates, 1877), 402.

44. Armistead, *Anthony Benezet,* 130–131; Brookes, *Friend Anthony Benezet,* 154.

45. Armistead, *Anthony Benezet,* 135–137; Brookes, *Friend Anthony Benezet,* 458–463.

46. Watson, *Annals of Philadelphia,* 1:449; Armistead, *Anthony Benezet,* 137–138; Brookes, *Friend Anthony Benezet,* 161, 165–167.

47. Brookes, *Friend Anthony Benezet,* 461–462.

48. Armistead, *Anthony Benezet,* 111–112.

Chapter 2

Note to epigraph: Theodore G. Tappert and John W. Doberstein, trans., *The Journals of Henry Melchior Muhlenberg*, 3 vols. (Philadelphia: Evangelical Lutheran Ministerium of Pennsylvania and Fortress Press, 1942–1958), 1:94 (hereafter Muhlenberg, *Journals*).

1. Muhlenberg has been the focus of numerous biographies, including William J. Mann, *The Life and Times of Henry Melchior Muhlenberg* (Philadelphia: G. W. Frederick, 1887); William K. Frick, *Henry Melchior Muhlenberg: Patriarch of the Lutheran Church in America* (Philadelphia: Lutheran Publication Society, 1902); Paul A. W. Wallace, *The Muhlenbergs of Pennsylvania* (Philadelphia: University of Pennsylvania Press, 1950); Leonard Riforgiato, *Missionary of Moderation: Henry Melchior Muhlenberg and the Lutheran Church in English America* (Lewisburg, Pa.: Bucknell University Press, 1980); Lisa Minardi, *Pastors and Patriots: The Muhlenberg Family of Pennsylvania* (Collegeville, Pa.: Berman Museum of Art, 2011); Hermann Wellenreuther, Thomas Muller-Bahlke, and A. Gregg Roeber, eds., *The Transatlantic World of Heinrich Melchior Muhlenberg in the Eighteenth Century* (Halle, Germany: Franckeschen Stiftungen, 2013); Hermann Wellenreuther, *Heinrich Melchior Mühlenberg und die Deutschen Lutheraner in Nordamerika, 1742–1787* (Berlin: Lit Verlag, 2013).

2. Muhlenberg, *Journals*, 1:18–57, 60–61, 63–65.

3. Ibid., 63, 65–71.

4. Ibid., 69, 74, 83, 87, 75, 93–94.

5. Ibid., 75–82; See also John Fanning Watson, *Annals of Philadelphia and Pennsylvania in the Olden Time*, 3 vols. (Philadelphia: J. M. Stoddart, 1879), 3:324; John Thomas Scharf and Thompson Westcott, *History of Philadelphia, 1609–1884*, 2 vols. (Philadelphia: L. H. Everts, 1884), 2:1322–1323; Walter H. Wagner, *The Zinzendorf-Muhlenberg Encounter: A Controversy in Search of Understanding* (Bethlehem, Pa.: Moravian Historical Society, 2002). For a concise overview of Moravian activity in Pennsylvania at this time, see Aaron Fogleman, *Hopeful Journeys: German Immigration, Settlement, and Political Culture, 1717–1775* (Philadelphia: University of Pennsylvania Press, 1996), 117–119.

6. Muhlenberg, *Journals*, 1:1–4.

7. Ibid., 4–5, 7–8.

8. On German immigration to Pennsylvania, see Marianne S. Wokeck, *Trade in Strangers: The Beginnings of Mass Migration to North America* (University Park: Pennsylvania State University Press, 1999), esp. 37–58. On German clustering, see Fogleman, *Hopeful Journeys*, 80–82, 86. On Swedish Lutherans in early Pennsylvania, see Charles Glatfelter, *Pastors and People: German Lutheran and Reformed Churches in the Pennsylvania Field, 1717–1793*, 2 vols. (Breinigsville, Pa.: Pennsylvania German Society, 1980–1981), 1:126, 2:22–35; Thompson Westcott, *The Historic Mansions and Buildings of Philadelphia* (Philadelphia: Porter and Coates, 1877), 60–64; Scharf and Westcott, *History of Philadelphia*, 2:1418–1419. On the importance of the church, see Fogleman, *Hopeful Journeys*, 88–89.

9. Patrick Griffin, *The People with No Name: Ireland's Ulster Scots, America's Scots Irish, and the Creation of a British Atlantic World, 1689–1764* (Princeton, N.J.: Princeton

University Press, 2001); Watson, *Annals of Philadelphia*, 1:212, 236; Muhlenberg, *Journals*, 1:65.

10. Muhlenberg, *Journals*, 1:84–86, 91, 117–118, 499, 522.

11. Ibid., 93.

12. Ibid., 87, 94–95; Watson, *Annals of Philadelphia*, 1:451–452, 3:312; Westcott, *Historic Mansions*, 130–131.

13. Muhlenberg, *Journals*, 1:98, 103–104. On Brunnholtz, see Glatfelter, *Pastors and People*, 1:23.

14. Muhlenberg, *Journals*, 1:96–97, 102. Pyrlaeus complained to Weiser about Anna Maria marrying Muhlenberg, saying she could have done much better among Zinzendorf's flock (ibid., 103).

15. Ibid., 115, 180, 234.

16. Ibid., 194, 201–202, 215, 319–320. On Schlatter, see Glatfelter, *Pastors and People*, 1:117–119.

17. Alan Tully, "Englishmen and Germans: National-Group Contact in Colonial Pennsylvania, 1700–1755," *Pennsylvania History* 45, no. 3 (July 1978), 250–253; Ralph Frasca, "'To Rescue the Germans out of Sauer's Hands': Benjamin Franklin's German-Language Printing Partnerships," *Pennsylvania Magazine of History and Biography* 121, no. 4 (Oct. 1997), 345–346. Muhlenberg took the oath on September 15, 1754; see John B. Linn and W. H. Egle, eds., *Pennsylvania Archives*, 138 vols., 2nd Series, (Harrisburg, Pa.: 1896), 2:334.

18. Muhlenberg, *Journals*, 1:433–437, 453–471, 586, 2:69, 259. For a complete list of Muhlenberg's children and grandchildren, see Minardi, *Pastors and Patriots*, 85–86. On Handschuh, see Glatfelter, *Pastors and People*, 1:50–51.

19. Russell F. Weigley, ed., *Philadelphia: A 300-Year History* (New York: W. W. Norton, 1982), 68–69, 83, 86, 91.

20. Muhlenberg, *Journals*, 1:472, 489, 583, 2:303.

21. Ibid., 1:621, 623, 869, 2:89–90, 95, 268, 316–317, 359.

22. Ibid., 1:476–478, 2:48, 50, 90. The church trustees eventually admonished Handschuh, who promised reform (ibid., 1:479, 504, 598, 605–606).

23. Ibid., 1:480–485, 510–519, 540–541, 549–550, 554, 558, 561–563, 574, 627, 662, 713–715, 2:29.

24. On his perambulations, see, for example, ibid., 2:263; on parishioner visits, ibid. 1:587, 595, 668, 678, 702–703, 2:101, 108–109, 113, 121, 154, 156.

25. See, for example, ibid.,1:582. On Mary's views (from letters to her daughters) and activities (from the *Journals*), see Lisa Minardi, "Family and Domestic Life of Pennsylvania Germans in the Eighteenth Century: A Study of Henry Melchior Muhlenberg and His Family," undergraduate honors thesis (Ursinus College, 2004), 57, 64–65, 176, 186, 206.

26. Muhlenberg, *Journals*, 1:475–476, 499, 500, 501, 527, 2:142–143.

27. Ibid., 1:662, 2:5–6, 25, 57, 62, 81–82, 296–301, 304–305. Wescott, *Historic Mansions*, 135. In 1775, Muhlenberg petitioned the governor for land for a new cemetery, but was unsuccessful (Muhlenberg, *Journals*, 2:708–709). On Schulze, see Glatfelter, *Pastors and People*, 1:125–126.

28. Muhlenberg, *Journals*, 2:306–315, 318–332, 336, 341–349, 353–358, 369, 382, 384, 389–397, 413–429, 432–435, 443–444, 449–456, 460–463, 468–469, 493–500, 538–545, 556–668, 690–701.

29. Ibid., 360, 362, 378–379.

30. Ibid., 464–466, 473, 491, 503, 526. On Kunze, see Glatfelter, *Pastors and People*, 1:74–75. In 1770–1771 there was some back and forth as to whether Schulze should go to Tulpehocken (Muhlenberg, *Journals,* 2:466, 479, 481, 483–489). In 1772, Henry, concerned that he would die soon, wanted Schulze recalled to Philadelphia, but Schulze did not want to return. After finding out how competently Henry Jr. and Kunze took care of things in Philadelphia when he was away, however, Henry relaxed about the issue (Muhlenberg, *Journals,* 2:508–516, 519, 521–522, 526). On subsequent movements of Peter, Frederick, and Schulze, see Muhlenberg, *Journals*, 2:536–537, 548, 554–555.

31. Muhlenberg, *Journals,* 556–668, 688, 689, 702.

32. Ibid., 398, 400–403; Scharf and Westcott, *History of Philadelphia*, 2:1421.

33. Muhlenberg, *Journals,* 1:431, 463, 474, 476, 498, 502, 507, 526–527, 546, 549–550, 554, 567, 573, 574, 597, 602, 604, 669, 2:2, 4, 29, 46, 76, 139, 142, 154, 157–158, 230, 302–303, 360, 441, 3:620–627, 749.

34. Ibid., 1:562, 564–565, 648, 663, 669–671, 673, 675, 2:5–6, 50, 59, 3:411, 427–429, 502–503, 539–540; Glatfelter, *Pastors and People*, 2:264–272.

35. Muhlenberg, *Journals,* 1:631, 632, 2:54, 91, 103, 181.

36. Ibid., 1:654, 662, 668, 673–675, 700; 2:23, 50, 104, 125–126, 136, 137, 181, 230, 231, 433, 441–442.

37. Ibid., 1:650–655; 2:97–99, 104, 252.

38. Ibid., 1:560, 706–707.

39. Ibid., 2:84.

40. Tully, "Englishmen and Germans," 248; Muhlenberg, *Journals,* 1:604, 617; 2:69, 527. In part Muhlenberg's references to "the English" may reflect his journals' purpose as a report to his German Lutheran superiors. Still, the patterns are significant owing to the detail in which he reported his daily activities. On the legal manual, see Fogleman, *Hopeful Journeys*, 144. On the extent of Muhlenberg's cultural assimilation, see Minardi, "Family and Domestic Life," 209. On the *Gazette*, see Muhlenberg, *Journals,* 2:459, 552; on sauerkraut, 591.

41. Tully, "Englishmen and Germans," 242–243, 247; Alan Tully, "Ethnicity, Religion, and Politics in Early America," *Pennsylvania Magazine of History and Biography* 107, no. 4 (Oct. 1983), 512, 520; Fogleman, *Hopeful Journeys,* 139, 141–148; Muhlenberg, *Journals,* 2:90–92, 102–104.

42. Muhlenberg, *Journals,* 2:121–123, 208, 271, 273–275, 277; Tully, "Ethnicity, Religion and Politics," 521.

43. Muhlenberg, *Journals,* 2:57, 158, 213, 243.

44. Ibid., 1:58, 669, 721, 2:439, 637, 638–639.

45. Ibid., 1:641, 650–651, 671, 2:22–23, 54–55, 433, 437–438, 3:573.

46. Ibid., 2:746–747.

47. Ibid., 712–738, 740–743, 747–748, 763, 770–771, 3:3, 14, 19–20, 23, 25–29, 41–47, 67, 80.

48. Ibid., 3:55–56, 74, 82, 91–101, 103, 112, 121, 123–126, 139; Scharf and Westcott, *History of Philadelphia*, 2:1423.

49. Muhlenberg, *Journals*, 3:172, 176–177, 182, 199, 220, 227, 230–232, 234–247, 282, 286–289, 323.

50. Ibid., 317–320, 381–385, 426–431.

51. Ibid., 497, 517, 592–593, 596–597, 609, 620, 637–638, 640–641, 644–645, 652–653, 657, 659, 666, 670–673, 680, 701, 704, 714; Frick, *Henry Melchior Muhlenberg*,182.

52. Muhlenberg, *Journals*, 3:746, 749, 751; Frick, *Henry Melchior Muhlenberg*,187.

Chapter 3

Note to epigraph: Quoted in Bird Wilson, *Memoir of the Life of the Right Reverend William White, D.D, Bishop of the Protestant Episcopal Church in the State of Pennsylvania* (Philadelphia: James Kay, Jr., and Brother, 1839), 21.

1. Walter H. Stowe, ed., *The Life and Letters of Bishop William White* (New York: Morehouse, 1937), 3, 5–6, 9–10.

2. Wilson, *Memoir of William White*, 21; Stowe, *Life and Letters*, 10–11.

3. Wilson, *Memoir of William White*, 22–26, 270–271; Stowe, *Life and Letters*, 15–17.

4. Stowe, *Life and Letters*, 22–26; Russell F. Weigley, ed., *Philadelphia: A 300-Year History* (New York: W. W. Norton, 1982), 49, 84. An image and history of the building are at http://www.archives.upenn.edu/histy/features/campuses/campus1.html, accessed Dec. 14, 2016.

5. Stowe, *Life and Letters*, 17, 22.

6. G. B. Warden, "The Proprietary Group in Pennsylvania, 1754–64," *William and Mary Quarterly*, 3rd ser., 21 (July 1964), 374–375; Wilson, *Memoir of William White*, 27–28.

7. Wilson, *Memoir of William White*, 29–30; John Thomas Scharf and Thompson Westcott. *History of Philadelphia, 1609–1884*, 3 vols. (Philadelphia: L. H. Everts, 1884), 2:1332.

8. Stowe, *Life and Letters*, 23–24.

9. William Stevens Perry, "The Life, Times, and Correspondence of William White, D. D., First Bishop of Pennsylvania: Chapter II—Ordination and Early Ministry," *Church Review* 49 (Apr. 1887), 352–363.

10. Wilson, *Memoir of William White*, 30–34; Stowe, *Life and Letters*, 32–33; Scharf and Westcott, *History of Philadelphia*, 2:1332.

11. Julius Hammond Ward, *The Life and Times of Bishop White* (New York: Dodd, Mead, 1892), 77–79.

12. Anna Coxe Toogood, "Historic Resource Study, Independence Mall, the Eighteenth-Century Development, Block One, Chestnut to Market, Fifth to Sixth Streets" (2001), 33, http://www.npshistory.com/publications/inde/hrs-mall-block-one.pdf, accessed May 28, 2020; Wilson, *Memoir of William White*, 30, 46; Stowe, *Life and Letters*, 35–37; Scharf and Westcott, *History of Philadelphia*, 2:1332; Ward, *Life and Times*, 28.

13. Wilson, *Memoir of William White*, 46–48, 51; Ward, *Life and Times*, 28; Deborah Gough, *Christ Church, Philadelphia: The Nation's Church in a Changing City* (Philadelphia: University of Pennsylvania Press, 1995), 138; Scharf and Westcott, *History of Philadelphia*, 2:1333.

14. Wilson, *Memoir of William White*, 49–50.

15. Ibid., 50–51; Scharf and Westcott, *History of Philadelphia*, 2:1333.

16. Wilson, *Memoir of William White*, 54–56; Scharf and Westcott, *History of Philaadelphia*, 2:1333; Charles Henry Hart, "Mary White—Mrs. Robert Morris," *Pennsylvania Magazine of History and Biography* 2, no. 2 (1878), 160; Ward, *Life and Times*, 30–32; Gough, *Christ Church*, 128–129, 134–136, 141.

17. Wilson, *Memoir of William White*, 57, 58; Scharf and Westcott, *History of Philadelphia*, 2:1333; Gough, *Christ Church*, 131, 138–139.

18. Wilson, *Memoir of William White*, 59–60, 62–64; Scharf and Westcott, *History of Philadelphia*, 2:1333; Gough, *Christ Church*, 142–145.

19. Stowe, *Life and Letters*, 56; Wilson, *Memoir of William White*, 78–79.

20. Wilson, *Memoir of William White*, 66–77; Stowe, *Life and Letters*, 57–59, 62–63; Gough, *Christ Church*, 146.

21. Stowe, *Life and Letters*, 62. The school struggled with repeated closures and reopenings until 1846, when it was reconstituted as a classical academy and has operated continuously ever since. It proudly traces its origin to William White. See www.episcopalacademy.org/about-ea/history, accessed Dec. 14, 2016.

22. Toogood, "Historic Research Study," 58, 90.

23. Gough, *Christ Church*, 152–153, 159; Wilson, *Memoir of William White*, 79–80, 93–95; Stowe, *Life and Letters*, 83.

24. Wilson, *Memoir of William White*, 82–93, 96, 97–110, 157; Stowe, *Life and Letters*, 63. On the formation of church government and White's role in uniting the various factions, see Robert Prichard, *A History of the Episcopal Church*, rev. ed. (Harrisburg, Pa.: Morehouse, 1999), 84–98.

25. John F. Woolverton, "Philadelphia's William White: Episcopalian Distinctiveness and Accommodation in the Post Revolutionary Period," *Historical Magazine of the Protestant Episcopal Church* 43, no. 4 (Dec. 1974), 279–296; Wilson, *Memoir of William White*, 123; Gough, *Christ Church*, 153, 156.

26. *Account of the Meeting of the Descendants of Col. Thomas White of Maryland* (Philadelphia: n.p., 1879), 164–166.

27. Ibid.

28. Scharf and Westcott, *History of Philadelphia*, 2:1333.

29. See www.ushistory.org/tour/bishop-white.htm, accessed Dec. 14, 2016.

30. Thompson Westcott, *The Historic Mansions and Buildings of Philadelphia* (Philadelphia: Porter and Coates, 1877), 355, 375.

31. Wilson, *Memoir of William White*, 186, 428–430; *Account of the Meeting*, 158.

32. Ward, *Life and Times*, 78–79, 85, 153.

33. Weigley, *Philadelphia*, 50–51, 100; http://www.stpetersphila.org/about-st-peters/history/, accessed Dec. 14, 2016.

34. Wilson, *Memoir of William White,* 290–292; Stowe, *Life and Letters*, 184–185; Gough, *Christ Church*, 171.

35. Wilson, *Memoir of William White,* 270–271; Ward, *Life and Times*, 73; Gough, *Christ Church*, 169–170.

36. Wilson, *Memoir of William White,* 272–281; Gough, *Christ Church*, 169–170.

37. Wilson, *Memoir of William White,* 293–300; Gough, *Christ Church*, 173, 196.

38. James Taylor, "Memoir of Bishop White," ed. John D. Kilbourne, *Pennsylvania Magazine of History and Biography* 92, no. 1 (Jan. 1968), 52–53.

39. Ibid.; Wilson, *Memoir of William White,* 285.

40. Richard S. Newman, *Freedom's Prophet: Bishop Richard Allen, the AME Church, and the Black Founding Fathers* (New York: New York University Press, 2008), 183–208; Gary Nash, *Forging Freedom: The Formation of Philadelphia's Black Community, 1720–1840* (Cambridge, Mass.: Harvard University Press, 1988), 127–130, 234–242; Carol V. R. George, *Segregated Sabbaths: Richard Allen and the Rise of Independent Black Churches, 1760–1840* (New York: Oxford University Press, 1973), 62–63; "About The AECST: A History of St. Thomas," http://www.aecst.org/about.htm, accessed Apr. 15, 2020.

41. Angelo Repousis, "'The Cause of the Greeks': Philadelphia and the Greek War for Independence," *Pennsylvania Magazine of History and Biography* 123, no. 4 (Oct. 1999), 333–363; Anthony F. C. Wallace, *The Long, Bitter Trail: Andrew Jackson and the Indians* (New York: Hill and Wang, 1993); Richard Carwardine, *Evangelicals and Politics in Antebellum America* (New Haven, Conn.: Yale University Press, 1993), 57; John A. Andrew III, *From Revivals to Removal: Jeremiah Evarts, the Cherokee Nation, and the Search for the Soul of America* (Athens: University of Georgia Press. 1992); Gough, *Christ Church*, 203; Wilson, *Memoir of William White,* 283–287.

42. Weigley, *Philadelphia*, 204, 292; Wilson, *Memoir of William White,* 158–160, 187, 190–199. In 1799, White conducted funeral services for George Washington in what was still Philadelphia's most capacious church, Zion Lutheran.

43. Scharf and Westcott, *History of Philadelphia*, 2:1453–1454; Wilson, *Memoir of William White,* 289; Gough, *Christ Church*, 196–197.

44. Ward, *Life and Times*, 85–86.

45. Ibid., 126–130; Prichard, *History*, 114–123.

46. Ward, *Life and Times*, 128, 131–132.

47. Wilson, *Memoir of William White,* 215–216; Gough, *Christ Church*, 212–215.

48. Wilson, *Memoir of William White,* 211–212.

49. Ibid., 232–246; Gough, *Christ Church*, 174; *Vidal v. Girard's Executors*, 42 U.S. (2 How.) 127 (1844).

50. Wilson, *Memoir of William White,* 264–268; Stowe, *Life and Letters*, 185; Scharf and Westcott, *History*, 2:1335.

Part II

1. Merril D. Smith, *Breaking the Bonds: Marital Discord in Pennsylvania, 1730–1830* (New York: New York University Press, 1991), 10–43; Thomas R. Meehan, "'Not Made Out of Levity': Evolution of Divorce in Early Pennsylvania," *Pennsylvania Magazine of*

History and Biography 92, no. 4 (Oct. 1968), 441–464. Cruel treatment was originally considered only in "bed and board" divorces, the equivalent of legal separation: "An Act Concerning Divorces and Matrimony," "An Act Concerning Divorces and Alimony" (1785)," in James T. Mitchell and Henry Flanders, comps., *Statutes at Large of Pennsylvania, from 1682 to 1801*, 16 vols. (Harrisburg, Pa.: various publishers, 1896–1911), 12:94–99.

2. Marylynn Salmon, *Women and the Law of Property in Early America* (Chapel Hill: University of North Carolina Press, 1986), 81–119; Marylynn Salmon, "Equality or Submersion?: Feme Covert Status in Early Pennsylvania," in Carol Berkin and Mary Beth Norton, eds., *Women of America: A History* (Boston: Houghton Mifflin, 1979), 93–111; Linda K. Kerber, *Women of the Republic: Intellect and Ideology in Revolutionary America* (Chapel Hill: University of North Carolina Press, 1980), 119–149.

3. John D. Cushing, comp., *The First Laws of the Commonwealth of Pennsylvania* (Wilmington, Del.: M. Glazier, 1984), 98–110; William Henry Egle, ed., *Pennsylvania Archives*, 138 vols., 3rd ser. (Harrisburg, Pa.: Clarence M. Busch, 1896), 10:519–552; Wilbur Henry Siebert, *The Loyalists of Pennsylvania* (Boston: Gregg Press, 1972), 30; Kerber, *Women of the Republic*, 123–125. For examples of other women, patriot and loyalist, who remained behind to fight for their families' property when their loyalist husbands left Philadelphia, see Wayne Bodle, "Jane Bartram's 'Application,'" *Pennsylvania Magazine of History and Biography* 115, no. 2 (Apr. 1991), 185–220; Sarah Fatherly, *Gentlewomen and Learned Ladies: Women and Elite Formation in Eighteenth-Century Philadelphia* (Bethlehem, Pa.: Lehigh University Press, 2008), 174–179.

4. For more on women and domestic spaces, see Susan Stabile, *Memory's Daughters: The Material Culture of Remembrance in Eighteenth-Century America* (Ithaca, N.Y.: Cornell University Press, 2004), 23–27.

Chapter 4

Note to epigraph: Deborah Norris Logan, Diaries, 1815–1839, collection 380, 9:34, Historical Society of Pennsylvania, Philadelphia.

1. Raymond C. Werner, ed., "The Diary of Grace Growden Galloway, 1778–1779," *Pennsylvania Magazine of History and Biography* 55, no. 1 (1931), 32, hereafter cited as "Diary" (1931); J. Thomas Scharf and Thompson Westcott, *History of Philadelphia, 1609–1884*, 3 vols. (Philadelphia: L. H. Everts, 1884), 2:1505. Both poems are in the folder labeled "Grace Galloway Verses," Joseph Galloway Family Papers, 1743–1823, Library of Congress, hereafter cited as JGFP, LOC. Sarah Fatherly discusses how elite women wrote and exchanged poetry in the years before the Revolution in "'The Sweet Recourse of Reason': Elite Women's Education in Colonial Philadelphia," *Pennsylvania Magazine of History and Biography* 128, no. 3 (July 2004), 250.

2. "Diary" (1931), 32.

3. "Loyalist Women in the American Revolution," *History of American Women Blog*, http://www.womenhistoryblog.com/2009/06/grace-growden-galloway.html, accessed Mar. 3, 2011.

4. Because both Market and Sixth Sts. were widened when Independence Mall was created in the 1950s, part of the site of the Galloway mansion is now under Sixth St.;

Anna Coxe Toogood, "Historic Resource Study, Independence Mall, The Eighteenth-Century Development, Block One, Chestnut to Market, Fifth to Sixth Streets" (2001), viii, 29–31, appendixes C–D, http://www.npshistory.com/publications/inde/hrs-mall-block-one.pdf, accessed May 28, 2020; "Trevose Manor," http://www.livingplaces.com/PA/Bucks_County/Bensalem_Township/Trevose_Manor.html, accessed June 5, 2014.

5. Toogood, "Historic Resource Study," 55.

6. "Diary" (1931), 32; "Grace Galloway Verses," JGFP, LOC; Mary Beth Norton, *Liberty's Daughters: The Revolutionary Experience of American Women, 1750–1800* (Boston: Little, Brown, 1980), 44–45.

7. Norton, *Liberty's Daughters*, 44, 324n; G. J. Barker-Benfield, *Abigail and John Adams: The Americanization of Sensibility* (Chicago: University of Chicago Press, 2010), 180; "Diary" (1931), 33.

8. "Diary" (1931), 33.

9. Julian P. Boyd, "Joseph Galloway's Plans of Union for the British Empire, 1774–1788," *Pennsylvania Magazine of History and Biography* 64, no. 4 (Oct. 1940), 492–515.

10. James Galloway to Grace Growden Galloway (hereafter JG and GGG), undated; JG to GGG, Jan. 8, 1777; JG to GGG, undated; JG to GGG, Mar. 21, 1777; JG to GGG, Dec. 23, 1777, and other notes, all in folder JG to GGG, JGFP, LOC; Toogood, "Historic Resource Study," xi; "Diary" (1931), 33.

11. Scharf and Westcott, *History of Philadelphia,* 1:372; Toogood, "Historic Resource Study," 37. Joseph was less helpful to the British in the military arena; here he tried to interfere too much. He did try to organize local loyalists. For more on Joseph and the British, see Scharf and Westcott, *History of Philadelphia,* 1:274, 360, 366; and Russell F. Weigley, ed., *Philadelphia: A 300-Year History* (New York: W. W. Norton, 1982), 140–141.

12. Benjamin Irvin, *Clothed in the Robes of Sovereignty: The Continental Congress and the People Out of Doors* (New York: Oxford University Press, 2011), 157–160.

13. For more on actions against loyalists, see Scharf and Westcott, *History of Philadelphia*, 1:377; Weigley, *Philadelphia*, 144–145; "Diary (1931), 33, 34. For synopses of other women's similar struggles, see Sarah Fatherly, *Gentlewomen and Learned Ladies: Women and Elite Formation in Eighteenth-Century Philadelphia* (Bethlehem, Pa.: Lehigh University Press, 2008), 177–178.

14. "Diary" (1931), 36, 38; Toogood, "Historic Resource Study," xi.

15. "Diary" (1931), 36–37; Wendy Weston McLallen, "Affectionately Yours: Women's Correspondence Networks in Eighteenth Century British America" (Ph.D. diss., Florida State University, 2007), 45; Fatherly, *Gentlewomen and Learned Ladies*, 174–175; "Diary" (1931), 37–42, 46–47, 55–56.

16. "Diary" (1931), 38, 41, 46–47, 50, 53.

17. Ibid., 38–42, 60.

18. Ibid., 34; Toogood, "Historic Resource Study," 36–39.

19. "Diary" (1931), 39–40, 42, 44.

20. Ibid., 43, 45–46. On sending messages through lines to New York, see JG to GGG July 24, 1778, and others undated, folder JG to GGG, JGFP, LOC.

21. "Diary" (1931), 47–49, 51–52.

22. GGG to JG, Aug. 25, Aug. 30, 1778, JGFP, LOC; "Diary," (1931), 50.

23. GGG to JG, Aug. 25, Aug. 30, 1778, JGFP, LOC; "Diary" (1931), 152; JG to GGG, Apr. 1, 1779, JGFP, LOC.

24. JG to GGG Aug. 31, 1778, folder JG to GGG; GGG to JG, undated; GGG to JG Sept. 21, 1778, folder GGG—Letters to Husband and Daughter; Elisabeth Galloway (hereafter EG) to GGG, undated, folder Betsy Galloway—Correspondence of, JGFP, LOC; "Diary" (1931), 54.

25. JG to GGG, undated, folder JG to GGG, JGFP, LOC; EG to GGG, Oct. 9, 1778, Historical Society of Pennsylvania.

26. "Diary" (1931), 55–57, 60–62, 84; GGG to EG, Nov. 27, 1778, Letterbook of GGG 1778–1781 in GGG folder; EG to GGG, undated, folder Betsy Galloway Correspondence, JGFP, LOC. The property would eventually be numbered 118 S. Front St. Deborah Morris was one of the highly educated elite women in pre-Revolutionary Philadelphia discussed by Fatherly, "'Sweet Recourse to Reason,'" 254.

27. "Diary" (1931), 55–64; Raymond C. Werner, ed., "Diary of Grace Growden Galloway, Kept at Philadelphia, July 1, to September 30, 1779," *Pennsylvania Magazine of History and Biography* 58, no. 2 (1934), 153, hereafter cited as "Diary" (1934).

28. "Diary" (1931), 64–67, 69.

29. Ibid., 70–71, 74–75, 77–78, 81–82, 85; "Diary" (1934), 155–156, 160; JG to GGG, Jan. 5, Feb. 4, Apr. 2, 1779, folder JG to GGG; EG to GGG, undated, folder Betsy Galloway—Correspondence of, JGFP, LOC; "Grace Galloway Verses," JGFP, LOC. Linda Kerber argues that Grace Galloway "failed to recognize that her political gestures went beyond merely private behavior" (*Women of the Republic: Intellect and Ideology in Revolutionary America* [Chapel Hill: University of North Carolina Press, 1980], 76). On tirades against the British as tirades against Joseph, see Norton, *Liberty's Daughters,* 218. McLallen argues that Grace was increasingly isolated because of her politics ("Affectionately Yours," 48–49); I think, given her personality, that it is difficult to know whether estrangements were personal or political. On elite women's desire to preserve unity in the face of political division, see Fatherly, *Gentlewomen and Learned Ladies*, 167–168. For a discussion of Grace Galloway among several Philadelphia women disaffected with the war, see Judith Van Buskirk, "They Didn't Join the Band: Disaffected Women in Revolutionary Philadelphia," *Pennsylvania History* 62, no. 3 (Summer 1995), 306–329.

30. "Diary" (1931), 73–78, 81, 87; "Diary" (1934), 154–155, 157–159, 164–166, On women's dedication to visiting and tea taking in order to maintain elite social life, see Fatherly, *Gentlewomen and Learned Ladies*, 170–172.

31. "Diary" (1931), 72, 75–76, 79–80; "Diary" (1934), 156–157; GGG to EG, Mar. 11, 1780, folder GGG letters to husband and daughter, JGFP, LOC; Fatherly, *Gentlewomen and Learned Ladies*, 178. Beverly Baxter argues that Grace "slowly developed into a woman able to care for herself and able to survive" ("Grace Growden Galloway: Survival of a Loyalist," *Frontiers* 3, no. 1 [1978], 62–67). I see her evolution as more nuanced. I think she was less helpless to begin with and not unambiguously a survivor.

32. "Diary" (1931), 69; "Diary" (1934), 152, 156, 161–162, 164. On Quaker political and social neutrality, see Fatherly, *Gentlewomen and Learned Ladies,* 172.

33. McLallen, "Affectionately Yours," 46–50; "Diary" (1931), 79, 85. McLallen argues that the diminishment of her literary correspondence hurt Grace's health and that the diary shows the importance of literary sociability in her everyday life. But the diary itself makes only a few mentions of literary activity or sadness at the lack thereof. It does chronicle her feelings of social and political abandonment. Most mentions of writing are letters to Betsy ("Diary" [1931], 80–81). Other elite women were more successful in maintaining these activities, Fatherly, *Gentlewomen and Learned Ladies*, 170.

34. Scharf and Westcott, *History of Philadelphia*, 1:396–397; "Diary" (1931), 74, 86–88; "Diary" (1934), 152, 154, 171; "Trevose Manor."

35. "Diary" (1931), 84, 86; "Diary" (1934), 163–164, 166–167, 169–172. On material privilege and wartime survival, see Fatherly, *Gentlewomen and Learned Ladies*, 173–174.

36. "Diary" (1934), 171–183, 185–186.

37. Ibid., 175, 177–178.

38. Ibid., 182, 184–185, 187–189; GGG to JG, Jan. 25, 1780, folder GGG to JG, JGFP, LOC.

39. GGG to EG, Mar. 11, Apr. 5, 1780, folder GGG—Letters to Husband and Daughter, JGFP, LOC. EG wrote another loving letter to GGG, Sept. 1, 1789, LOC.

40. In addition to the letters in the preceding note, see GGG to JG, May 21–22, 1780, folder GGG—Letters to Husband and Daughter, JGFP, LOC.

41. GGG to EG, Nov. 5, [1780], folder GGG—Letters to Husband and Daughter, JGFP, LOC.

42. JG to GGG, received May 31, 1781; GGG to EG, Oct. 15, 1781; GGG to EG, Oct. 15, 1781, folder GGG—Letters to Husband and Daughter; Deborah Morris to EG, Nov. 20, 1781, folder Betsy Galloway, Correspondence of; GGG will, Dec. 20, 1781, JGFP, LOC.

43. Deborah Morris to EG, May 29,1782, folder Betsy Galloway, Correspondence of, JGFP, LOC.

44. Ibid.

45. Elizabeth Evans, *Weathering the Storm: Women of the American Revolution* (New York: Paragon House, 1975), 240–243; Weigley, *Philadelphia*, 171; JG to Miers Fisher, Aug. 20, 1792, JGFP, LOC; Evans, *Weathering the Storm*, 244.

Chapter 5

Note to epigraph: Quoted in Ethel Armes, comp. and ed., *Nancy Shippen: Her Journal Book* (Philadelphia: J. B. Lippincott, 1935), 156. I generally cite the Armes edition of the journal, because it is more accessible than the manuscript version. Comparison reveals it to be a nearly complete and accurate transcription. See Lorenza Gramegna, "The Journal of Anne Home Livingston (Nancy Shippen): A New Approach" (M.A. thesis, Illinois State University, 1991), 18, on the sort of things Armes left out.

1. On young people seizing control, see Robert Gross, *The Minutemen and Their World* (New York: Hill and Wang, 1976, 2001). On the cultural connections between antipatriarchal republican political and family relations, see Jay Fliegelman, *Prodigals and Pilgrims: The American Revolution Against Patriarchal Authority, 1750–1800* (New York: Cambridge University Press, 1982); Jan Lewis, "The Republican Wife: Virtue and Seduction in the Early Republic," *William and Mary Quarterly* 44, no. 4 (Oct. 1987), 689–721.

2. Armes, *Nancy Shippen*, 45–53, 55–56. On sibling survivors, see C. Dallett Hemphill, *Siblings: Brothers and Sisters in American History* (New York: Oxford University Press, 2011), 65–126.

3. Armes, *Nancy Shippen*, 21.

4. Mary Beth Norton, *Liberty's Daughters: The Revolutionary Experience of American Women* (Boston: Little, Brown, 1980), 180. Later, William Shippen was embroiled in controversy over allegations of grave robbing of human corpses for medical dissection. Gramegna, "Journal of Livingston," 14; Peggy Germano, "Nancy Shippen Livingston: 'The Consequences of My Unhappy Choice'" (M.S. thesis, University of Albany, State University of New York, 2000), 18–21. Ethel Armes, in contrast, gave a flattering description of William's army work, suggesting how the immediate family would have seen it (Armes, *Nancy Shippen*, 36–37).

5. Armes, *Nancy Shippen*, 21–22. Nancy did not mention the battle in her letters (ibid., 35–36).

6. Thomas Lee Shippen (hereafter TLS) to Anne Home Shippen (hereafter AHSL), Dec. 2, 1777, Shippen Family Papers (hereafter SFP), reel 3, box 4, Library of Congress, Washington, D.C. (hereafter LOC); also Armes, *Nancy Shippen*, 43, 44. For this and the next paragraph, see Alice Lee Shippen (hereafter ALS) to AHSL, Aug. 31, Sept. 22, Nov. 8, 1777, SFP, reel 3, box 4, LOC; also Armes, *Nancy Shippen*, 37, 39, 40–43, 72. On other elite women's goals for their daughters' education, see Sarah Fatherly, "'The Sweet Recourse of Reason': Elite Women's Education in Colonial Philadelphia," *Pennsylvania Magazine of History and Biography* 128, no. 3 (July 2004), 235–237, 242; Fatherly, *Gentlewomen and Learned Ladies: Women and Elite Formation in Eighteenth-Century Philadelphia* (Bethlehem, Pa.: Lehigh University Press, 2008), 169.

7. Armes, *Nancy Shippen*, 41–42.

8. William Shippen (hereafter WS) to AHSL, n.d., SFP, reel 3, box 4, LOC; Armes, *Nancy Shippen*, 71–72.

9. ALS to AHSL, June 3, 1779, SFP, reel 3, box 4, LOC; Armes, *Nancy Shippen*, 73–74.

10. Armes, *Nancy Shippen*, 75–78, 80–82.

11. Ibid., 81–83.

12. Ibid., 84, 87.

13. Ibid., 90–92, 94.

14. On novels and seduction, see Fliegelman, *Prodigals and Pilgrims*; Cathy Davidson, *Revolution and the Word: The Rise of the Novel in America* (New York: Oxford University Press, 1986); Lewis, "The Republican Wife," 697–698; Rodney Hessinger, *Seduced, Abandoned, and Reborn: Visions of Youth in the Early Republic, 1780–1850* (Philadelphia: University of Pennsylvania Press, 2005), 23–43.

15. Armes, *Nancy Shippen*, 9–97; WS to TLS, Jan. 14, 1781, SFP, reel 5, box 7, LOC.

16. Armes, *Nancy Shippen*, 98, 100.

17. WS to TLS, Jan. 27, 1781, SFP, reel 5, box 7, LOC; see also Armes, *Nancy Shippen*, 101–105. Germano points out that Alice Shippen, as an orphan, had been able to make her own marriage choice ("Nancy Shippen Livingston," 27, 30).

18. Louis Otto (hereafter LO) to AHSL, Mar. 1781, SFP, reel 3, box 4, LOC; also Armes, *Nancy Shippen,* 106–107.

19. Armes, *Nancy Shippen,* 108–109. On new ideas about marrying for love, see Lewis, "The Republican Wife," 694–695.

20. Armes, *Nancy Shippen,* 118–119. On Henry's conviction that Nancy's child was not his, see Germano, "Nancy Shippen Livingston," 9, 47–48.

21. Armes, *Nancy Shippen,* 119–120. On the duties of wives, see Lewis, "The Republican Wife," 711–714. Gramegna believes Nancy was a dreamer in thinking that she could change her husband ("Journal of Livingston," 41–42). I don't agree, given the contemporary cultural support for this tactic.

22. Armes, *Nancy Shippen,* 116–117; Germano, "Nancy Shippen Livingston," 42–45; Peter Force, comp., *American Archives,* ser. 4, 6 vols. (Washington, D.C.: M. St. Clair Clarke and Peter Force, 1837–1846), 2:91, 3:79.

23. AHSL to ALS, Oct. 4, 1781, SFP, reel 3, box 3, LOC; Armes, *Nancy Shippen,* 122–125.

24. Armes, *Nancy Shippen,* 125–126, 128–129. Gramegna ("Journal of Livingston," 41) and Germano ("Nancy Shippen Livingston," 9, 48–49) both suspect abuse.

25. Armes, *Nancy Shippen,* 169, 171. On the sentimental project of the Revolutionary generation, see Sarah Knott, *Sensibility and the American Revolution* (Chapel Hill: University of North Carolina Press, 2009), 109–111, 130–140. For an overlapping but slightly different analysis from that presented here, see Gramegna, "Journal of Livingston," 1, 18, 19–20, 39, 54, 57, 60, 66.

26. Armes, *Nancy Shippen,* 139–140. On parental advice in sentimental literature, see G. J. Barker-Benfield, *Abigail Adams and John Adams: The Americanization of Sensibility* (Chicago: University of Chicago Press, 2010), 134; Hessinger, *Seduced, Abandoned, and Reborn,* 38–41. Compare Gramegna, "Journal of Livingston," 40, 42; Germano, "Nancy Shippen Livingston," 23. Where Gramegna stresses naïve passivity, I see conscious choice of self-subordination to "duty."

27. Armes, *Nancy Shippen,* 139–140, 141, 142.

28. Ibid., 141–142.

29. Ibid., 143.

30. Ibid., 143–145.

31. Ibid., 145. On changing views of marriage, see Lewis, "The Republican Wife," 707.

32. Armes, *Nancy Shippen,* 145–146.

33. Ibid., 146–147. Prior studies of the journal have placed primary blame for their daughter's unhappiness on the Shippens and argued that Nancy did not perceive it. Gramegna mostly blames Nancy's fate on her father, but sometimes includes Alice in her indictment ("Journal of Livingston, 3, 15, 23, 24, 44). Germano generally blames both parents, although she sometimes draws back a little from their responsibility for the marriage choice and occasionally suggests that Alice wanted better for her daughter ("Nancy Shippen Livingston," 3, 10, 23, 30–33, 37–39, 66). I think this quote suggests that Nancy did blame her parents, even though she chose not to do so openly.

34. Armes, *Nancy Shippen,* 147, 148–149.

35. Ibid., 150–153, 156–160.

36. Ibid., 161; see also 167–168; Lewis, "The Republican Wife," 714–715, 718.

37. Armes, *Nancy Shippen*, 150, 170, 171–174, 182, 184; Bushrod Washington to AHSL, Apr. 1794, SFP, reel 3, box 4, LOC.

38. AHSL to Margaret Beekman Livingston (hereafter MBL), Sept. 1783, and MBL to AHSL, Sept. 10, 1783, SFP, reel 3, box 4, LOC. See also Armes, *Nancy Shippen*, 163–166.

39. Armes, *Nancy Shippen*, 167, 169, 173–178, 180–183, 185. Compare Henry Livingston (hereafter HBL) to AHSL, Jan. 5, 1784, SFP, reel 3, box 4, LOC; and Armes, *Nancy Shippen*, 170–171, with AHSL to HBL, June 1783; Armes, *Nancy Shippen* 157–159; and AHSL to HBL, July 1783, SFP, reel 3, box 4, container 3, LOC.

40. Armes, *Nancy Shippen*, 169, 172, 177–181, 183.

41. Ibid., 189–192, 195–202, 204–212. Whatever her illness, Alice Lee Shippen had recovered fully by the late 1790s, and lived until 1817 (Germano, "Nancy Shippen Livingston," 38–39).

42. Armes, *Nancy Shippen*, 203–204, 209.

43. Ibid., 177, 182, 213–214, 216–220, 222–224; LO to AHSL, Dec. 4, 1784, SFP, reel 3, box 4, LOC.

44. HBL to AHSL, Jan. 1785, SFP, reel 3, box 4, LOC; Armes, *Nancy Shippen*, 225–228; Germano, "Nancy Shippen Livingston," 49–50.

45. Armes, *Nancy Shippen*, 233–234; Germano, "Nancy Shippen Livingston," 50–52.

46. Armes, *Nancy Shippen*, 241–249; WS to TLS, Dec. 10, 1786, Feb. 1787, May 22, 1787 (quotation), SFP, reel 4, box 5, LOC; "Extracts from Washington's Diary, Kept While Attending the Constitutional Convention," *Pennsylvania Magazine of History and Biography* 11, no. 3 (1887), 301.

47. Armes, *Nancy Shippen*, 255–261.

48. Ibid., 267–268; Germano, "Nancy Shippen Livingston," 52–56. On Nancy's case as illustrative of the difficulties women had in obtaining divorces at this time, see Norton, *Liberty's Daughters*, 48–49; and Linda Kerber, *Women of the Republic: Intellect and Ideology in Revolutionary America* (Chapel Hill: University of North Carolina Press, 1980), 181–184.

49. MBL to AHSL, 1788 and 1789, SFP, reel 3, box 4, LOC; Armes, *Nancy Shippen*, 261–265, 268–271, 274; Germano, "Nancy Shippen Livingston," 37–38, 53, 55–57.

50. MBL to AHSL, Dec. 5, 1789, Mar. 16, 1790, Feb. 20, 1792; Peggy to AHSL, SFP, reel 3, box 4, LOC; Armes, *Nancy Shippen*, 277–279, 282–283.

51. Germano, "Nancy Shippen Livingston," 58.

52. Armes, *Nancy Shippen*, 292–294; Gramegna, "Journal of Livingston," 49.

53. MBL to AHSL, Feb. 20, 1792; HBL to AHSL, Dec. 7, 1792, SFP, reel 3, box 4; AHSL to MBL, letters from spring through fall of 1794; Peggy to MBL, SFP, reel 4, box 5; AHSL to TLS, n.d., SFP, reel 3, box 3, LOC; Armes, *Nancy Shippen*, 283–286, 289–291; Germano, "Nancy Shippen Livingston," 59–61.

54. Armes, *Nancy Shippen*, 295, 297, 299; Germano, "Nancy Shippen Livingston," 38, 61–62, 64; "Weekly Intelligence," *Weekly Visitor and Ladies' Museum* 6 (Nov. 9, 1822), 2. There is also a bill for a piano shipped from London in 1818, SFP, reel 4, box 5, LOC; Germano,

"Nancy Shippen Livingston," 63; Armes, *Nancy Shippen,* 300–301. Nancy and Peggy moved several times in the 1830s, living on the west side of Eleventh above Race St. in 1830, at Tenth and Shippen Sts. in 1832, and in Moyamensing, on Noble St. in the spring of 1833 (Peggy to William Shippen II and his wife, 1830, Nov. 17, 1832, and May 29, 1833, SFP, reel 4, box 5, LOC).

55. Gramegna, "Journal of Livingston," 3, 40–41, 50, 66. Gramegna argues that although Nancy showed progress through and with the help of her journal writing, she never broke through to attaining a full sense of herself, and ended a rather stunted person (ibid., 22, 29–32, 35–37, 43–50). I think that although bad parenting and misguided education contributed to prolonged immaturity, Nancy showed clear effort from the start to define and adhere to her duty as she saw it. As Gramegna admits, that included the assertive act of leaving Henry Beekman not long into their marriage (ibid., 4). It also included her turning to religion in the latter part of her life. In other words, I see more of a whole person in Nancy Shippen, from adolescence to old age. While she only occasionally bucked the system (as by leaving Henry), she also consciously chose and strove to live according to cultural tenets of the time that she adhered to, whether beliefs about marriage or filial duty or Christianity. While both her diary and letters can be construed as creative performances, Nancy is no less real for being their creator. The same person is evident throughout the different sources, and, moreover, is the one others—whether her parents, Otto, Henry, Margaret, or Peggy—responded to.

Chapter 6

Note to epigraph: Quoted in Susan Stabile, *Memory's Daughters: The Material Culture of Remembrance in Eighteenth-Century America* (Ithaca, N.Y.: Cornell University Press, 2004), 125.

1. Stabile, *Memory's Daughters*, 1–8, 229, 231.

2. Mrs. Owen J. Wister [Sarah Butler Wister] and Miss Agnes Irwin, eds., *Worthy Women of Our First Century* (Philadelphia: J. B. Lippincott, 1877), 282. On penmanship, see Deborah Norris Logan Diaries, 1815–1839, 17 vols., 16:230, Historical Society of Pennsylvania, Philadelphia (hereafter cited as DNL Diaries, HSP).

3. Of her mother, Mary Parker Norris, Deborah wrote, that she, an only child, "had received a much better education than was usually bestowed in daughters when she was young. Her mind was enriched by an acquaintance with the best authors" (Deborah Norris Logan Diary, 1808–1815, 35, Library Company of Philadelphia [hereafter cited as DNL Diary, LCP]; thanks to James Green for his assistance with this document). On the view from the parlor, see Stabile, *Memory's Daughters*, 228. Debby's brother, Isaac, was a frequent companion in her socializing, of him, she wrote: "Being very near of an age our infancy was passed together, and the most pleasing friendship commenced between us. Our studies, our company our amusements were the same, until an unfortunate bias in his mind, turned him from us, and made him desirous of seeking comfort in a Religious establishment in Europe. He stayd abroad until the approach of the Revolution in France obliged him to come Home"; Isaac returned a Catholic (DNL Diary, LCP, 41). For a glimpse at Debby's social circle, see Kathryn Zabelle Derounian, ed., "'A Dear, Dear

Friend': Six Letters from Deborah Norris to Sarah Wister, 1778–1779," *Pennsylvania Magazine of History and Biography* 108, no. 4 (Oct. 1984), 487–516; Albert Cook Myers, ed., *Sally Wister's Journal* (Philadelphia: Ferris and Leach, 1902), 203–205.

4. Debby's mother was loath to leave their fine home unprotected. It was probably a wise move, although they were not able to avoid having British troops quartered with them. See Barbara Jones, "Deborah Logan" (M.A. thesis, University of Delaware, 1964), 13; John T. Scharf and Thompson Westcott, *History of Philadelphia, 1609–1884*, 3 vols. (Philadelphia: L. H. Everts, 1884), 1:351. Sally's imagined dialogues give us her view of Debby's personality (Wister and Irwin, *Worthy Women*, 284–287; Myers, *Sally Wistar's Journal*, 13–15, 114–115, 123, 141, 143, 163, 167, 175, 179–180, 189–200).

5. John A. H. Sweeney, ed., *The Norris-Fisher Correspondence: A Circle of Friends, 1779–1782* (Wilmington: Historical Society of Delaware, 1955), 188, 192–193,199, 202. Deborah's old friend Mary Pleasants had married George's brother Charles in 1779, but Deborah doesn't mention George in describing them (they moved to Virginia). By November 1779, Deborah and this old friend Mary were estranged somehow, but they had been very friendly just a year before (ibid., 198n, 214–215). Altamont was a Genoese nobleman in the play, *The Fair Penitent*, as adapted for the stage by Nicholas Rowe (1674–1718). It was staged in Philadelphia on April 15, 1754, despite Quaker opposition. George Logan had traveled through England, France, Holland, Germany, and Italy after completing his studies at Edinburgh (Sweeney, *Norris-Fisher Correspondence*, 6, 215n, 219).

6. On the common use of romantic pseudonyms among courting couples, see Mary Beth Norton, *Liberty's Daughters: The Revolutionary Experience of American Women* (Boston: Little Brown, 1980), 52; Sweeney, *Norris-Fisher Correspondence*, 195, 204, 217. That these effusions were not part of Deborah's diary writing in middle and old age are an example of the rise and fall of her generation's cultural project of sensibility, as described by Sarah Knott in *Sensibility and the American Revolution* (Chapel Hill: University of North Carolina Press, 2009).

7. Sweeney, *Norris-Fisher Correspondence*, 217, 219n.

8. Ibid., 231n. The engagement may have been the subject of a long talk between Debby and Mary Pleasants Logan (the wife of George's brother Charles) that Debby reported to Sally Fisher in late 1780: "I had a most interesting conversation with her, it was twilight when we entered upon the subject & it lasted till near 10 Oclock, reserve was banish'd we spoke our sentiments freely, and parted mutually pleas'd (I believe) with Our Conference" (ibid., 209). In an earlier letter to Sally Fisher, Deborah wrote, "so I think we may as well be before hand with our destiny and agree upon living Old Maids, by the way, I think it is a situation that may be supported with great dignity; And I always thought it a striking impropriety for any person, especially one of our own Sex, to speak in that Contemptuous way of Old Maids which is sometimes common" (ibid., 203). See Jan Lewis, "The Republican Wife: Virtue and Seduction in the Early Republic," *William and Mary Quarterly*, 3rd ser., 44, no. 4 (Oct. 1987), 693–695; Norton, *Liberty's Daughters*, 41–44, 58–60. For an interesting discussion of another Quaker mother contemplating a daughter's marriage choice, see Susan Klepp and Karin Wulf, eds., *The Diary of Hannah*

Callender Sansom: Sense and Sensibility in the Age of the American Revolution (Ithaca, N.Y.: Cornell University Press, 2010), 275–278.

9. Lewis, "The Republican Wife," 697; Sweeney, *Norris-Fisher Correspondence*, 224; George S. Brookes, *Friend Anthony Benezet* (Philadelphia: University of Pennsylvania Press, 1937), 25; Myers, *Sally Wister's Journal*, 115–117n.

10. Deborah Norris Logan, *Memoir of Dr. George Logan*, ed. Frances A. Logan (Philadelphia: Historical Society of Pennsylvania, 1899), 121–122; Wister and Irwin, *Worthy Women*, 288, 290; Frederick B. Tolles, *George Logan of Philadelphia* (New York: Oxford University Press, 1953), 11, 13, 15, 17–18, 206.

11. Derounian, "'Dear, Dear Friend,'" 488, 498–500, 514–515; Sweeney, *Norris-Fisher Correspondence*, 198; see also Logan, *Memoir*, 31, 42; Tolles, *George Logan*, 11, 15, 18, 301. Jones says Deborah did not know George before his return ("Deborah Logan," 16); Wister and Irwin said she must have (*Worthy Women*, 288). On late eighteenth-century Quaker insularity, tribalism, and intermarriage, see Nancy Tomes, "The Quaker Connection: Visiting Patterns Among Women in the Philadelphia Society of Friends, 1750–1800," in Michael Zuckerman, ed., *Friends and Neighbors: Group Life in America's First Plural Society* (Philadelphia: Temple University Press, 1982), 174–195; Klepp and Wulf, *Diary of Hannah Callender Sansom*, 271–272. On the Norris–Logan family tree, see Laura C. Keim, *Logania: Stenton Collections Reassembled* (Philadelphia: National Society of Colonial Dames of America, 2014), 2; Sweeney, *Norris-Fisher Correspondence*, 192; Jones, "Deborah Logan," 64.

12. Jones, "Deborah Logan," 17; Logan, *Memoir*, 43, 44, 99; Tolles, *George Logan*, 43, 51, 53; Sally Fisher [Dawes] to Sally Fisher [Corbit], Aug. 1781, in Sweeney, *Norris-Fisher Correspondence*, 222; Jones, "Deborah Logan," 16; Wister and Irwin, *Worthy Women*, 294, 296–297. For Deborah Norris Logan's furniture, see Laura C. Keim, *Stenton: A Visitor's Guide to the Site, History, and Collections* (Philadelphia: National Society of the Colonial Dames of America, 2014), 50–52. It is tempting to conclude from the timing and size of their family (the three sons were born in the first ten years of the marriage; and Deborah had the last at age twenty-nine) that Deborah and George were part of the Revolutionary-era vanguard of couples who cooperated to limit the size of their family (Susan Klepp, *Revolutionary Conceptions: Women, Fertility, and Family Limitation in America, 1760–1820* [Chapel Hill: University of North Carolina Press, 2009]). Both Klepp and Mary Beth Norton interpret this as a sign of greater equality for women in marriage (Norton, *Liberty's Daughters*, 232, 234).

13. Jones, "Deborah Logan," 24, 31–36, 51, 53, 56–57, 59–60; Wister and Irwin, *Worthy Women*, 292–303; Anne Hollingsworth Wharton, *Salons Colonial and Republican* (Philadelphia: J. B. Lippincott, 1900), 163–167.

14. Stabile, *Memory's Daughters*, 38–45.

15. DNL Diaries, HSP, 3:105, 108–109, 114, 156; Stabile, *Memory's Daughters*, 228–229; Jones, "Deborah Logan," 31, 46, 47. As Deborah explained it, "my Brother has sold it and is about to give it up.—It would be unreasonable for me to blame him as he gets a large price, & has a large family to provide for, but it is an event that will affect me. And seeing it probably for the last time, was a melancholy consideration" (DNL Diaries, HSP, 3:109).

16. Logan, *Memoir*, 46–48.

17. Norton, *Liberty's Daughters*, 40; Terri Premo, "'Like a Being Who Does Not Belong': The Old Age of Deborah Norris Logan," *Pennsylvania Magazine of History and Biography* 107, no. 1 (Jan. 1983), 89; Lewis, "The Republican Wife," 707, 712–713; Rosemarie Zagarri, *A Woman's Dilemma: Mercy Otis Warren and the American Revolution*, 2nd. ed. (Hoboken, N.J.: Wiley, 2014); G. J. Barker-Benfield, *Abigail and John Adams: The Americanization of Sensibility* (Chicago: University of Chicago Press, 2010); Sheila Skemp, *Judith Sargent Murray: A Brief Biography with Documents* (Boston: Bedford, 1998), 61–62, 68–69, 72.

18. Lewis, "The Republican Wife," 699, 700; Rosemarie Zagarri, "Morals, Manners, and the Republican Mother," *American Quarterly* 44, no. 2 (June 1992), 192–215; Nancy Cott, *Public Vows: A History of Marriage and the Nation* (Cambridge, Mass.: Harvard University Press, 2000), 18–21; Derounian, "'Dear, Dear Friend,'" 501–502.

19. Lewis, "The Republican Wife," 689–721; Rodney Hessinger, *Seduced, Abandoned, and Reborn: Visions of Youth in Middle Class America, 1780–1850* (Philadelphia: University of Pennsylvania Press, 2005), 23–43; Cott, *Public Vows*, 17.

20. George Logan (hereafter GL) to Deborah Norris Logan (hereafter DNL), Sept. 19, 1785, Logan Family Papers, collection 379, box 7, Historical Society of Pennsylvania (hereafter cited as HSP379 B7), folder 8, p. 9; GL to DNL, June 1798, ibid., folder 31. In fact, George gave Debby power of attorney lest he be accused of treason on his mission to France and the property confiscated (Tolles, *George Logan*, 155).

21. GL to DNL, n.d., HSP379 B7, folder 40.

22. GL to DNL, July 1798, ibid., folder 32; see also GL to DL, July 26, 1798, ibid., folder 33; July 28, 1799, ibid., folder 34; GL to DNL, Dec. 12, 1799, ibid., folder 39.

23. GL to DNL, Apr. 5, 1783, ibid., folder 4, p. 5; GNL to DNL, Apr. 1783, ibid., folder 5, p. 6; GL to DNL, 1800, ibid., folder 41; Wister and Irwin, *Worthy Women*, 282. For other instructions, see GL to DNL, Feb. 20, 1805, HSP379 B7, folder 47; GL to DNL, Feb. 12, 1806(?), ibid., folder 49.

24. GL to DNL, 1802(?), HSP379 B7, folder 45; GL to DNL, Dec. 7, 1801, ibid., folder 43.

25. Logan, *Memoir*, 97–98, 101–103; Wister and Irwin, *Worthy Women*, 314; Jones, "Deborah Logan," 18. The eldest son, Albanus, accompanied George to Washington and then was sent to the College of William and Mary at the suggestion of Thomas Jefferson (GL to DNL, Dec. 7, 1801, HSP379 B7, folder 43. That we don't have much from Deborah on the birth and raising of her children is interesting, given Linda Kerber's influential argument that the nation embraced an enhanced "Republican Mother" role for women after the Revolution, to give them a quasi-political role in the new republic. Of course, for Deborah, as for other women, the periods of childbearing and rearing were intensely busy times. Deborah did not begin her diary until 1807, after her youngest son had reached the age of sixteen; other women's diaries also show gaps or sparer entries at these times; see, for example, Klepp and Wulf, *Diary of Hannah Callender Sansom*, vii, 1. And yet the lack of discussion of childrearing in letters or looking back might also indicate that motherhood was not yet endowed with the importance that it would come to have in the antebellum era. The Logan boys, like others among the affluent families who were

most likely to be affected by new ideas circulating in print, were off to boarding school at fairly young ages. Jan Lewis has argued that women strove to be republican wives before they came to focus on republican motherhood; perhaps this explains Deborah's lack of commentary on her sons' childhoods. See Lewis, "The Republican Wife."

26. Tolles, *George Logan*, 106–107, 129–130, 146–147, 154–156, 171. Tolles suggests that she did not think his behavior inconsistent and supported him (he imputes greater indifference to and ignorance of politics on Deborah's part than is warranted by his own evidence of her positions and concerns). See Logan, *Memoir*, 54; Wister and Irwin, *Worthy Women*, 305, 313; Logan, *Memoir*, 52–60; Jones, "Deborah Logan," 17, 65; Thompson Westcott, *The Historic Mansions and Buildings of Philadelphia*. Philadelphia: Porter and Coates, 1877), 152. For reaction to the venture, and Logan's law, see Logan, *Memoir*, 74–87; John Fanning Watson, *Annals of Philadelphia and Pennsylvania in the Olden Time*, 3 vols. (Philadelphia: J. M. Stoddart, 1879), 3:447.

27. Copy of GL to Thomas Jefferson and others (via DNL), HSP379 B7, folder 35; GL to DNL, Sept. 1798, ibid., folder 36; notes in DNL's hand, ibid., folder 37; Logan, *Memoir*, 58–60.

28. Wister and Irwin, *Worthy Women*, 304; Jones, "Deborah Logan," 38; Sarah Fatherly, *Gentlewomen and Learned Ladies: Women and Elite Formation in Eighteenth-Century Philadelphia* (Bethlehem, Pa.: Lehigh University Press, 2008), 133, 165. Deborah's interest in politics only increased as she got older; see, for example, DNL to Algernon Logan, Feb. 10, 1806, HSP379 B7, Folder 48; Premo, "'Like a Being Who Does Not Belong,'" 101–102, 105; Logan, *Memoir*, 82.

29. Logan, *Memoir*, 72, 75–76, 82; Wister and Irwin, *Worthy Women*, 309–310; Tolles, *George Logan*, 157, 170–172; Rosemarie Zagarri, *Revolutionary Backlash: Women and Politics in the Early American Republic* (Philadelphia: University of Pennsylvania Press, 2008), 106.

30. Westcott, *Historic Mansions*, 152; Abigail Adams to John Adams, Dec. 31, 1798, *Adams Family Papers: An Electronic Archive*, http://www.masshist.org/digitaladams/, accessed May 4, 2020. For others' mixed reports, see Tolles, *George Logan*, 206–207; Logan, *Memoir*, 115–117, 119; GL to DNL, Apr. 2, May 6, May 25, 1810, HSP379 B7, folders 56, 57, 58; Wister and Irwin, *Worthy Women*, 314, 316–317.

31. DNL to Maria D. Logan, Jan. 20, 1801, HSP379 B7, folder 59.

32. DNL Diary, LCP, quotes from Nov. 1814, Jan. 1815; Jones, "Deborah Logan," 92; Wister and Irwin, *Worthy Women*, 319–320; Westcott, *Historic Mansions*, 153; DNL Diaries, HSP, 2:17. That she copied letters to George from prominent political figures indicates again her continued interest in politics (DNL Diaries, HSP, 27–30, 31–42).

33. DNL Diaries, HSP, 3:148, 151.

34. Ibid., 61;

35. Ibid., 2:147, 3:35. Tolles quotes one of Logan's Senate colleagues, who judged that George Logan was "not a great man" and concludes that he "was not the wisest, the most prudent, the most consistent of men. He was naive, impulsive, humorless, often wrongheaded . . . but he had goodness" (*George Logan*, ix–xiii).

36. DNL Diaries, HSP, 2:128; Stabile, *Memory's Daughters*, 78. Deborah clearly thought unpleasant information should not be preserved. Of her brother Isaac's life after

his return home from France, for example, she wrote, "he came home unhappy and discontented, and a veil here must be drawn over events which succeeded" (DNL Diary, LCP, 42). In a marginal note of 1831, Debby explained why she cut out an ode she had written in 1815—it was "too unfavourable to Madison" (DNL Diaries, HSP, 1:8). On the "constructedness" of the diary, see Premo, "'Like a Being Who Does Not Belong,'" 88–89, 107–108.

37. DNL Diaries, HSP 4:12–17, 29–33, 36, 38; Premo, "'Like a Being Who Does Not Belong,'" 104, 109.

38. DNL Diaries, HSP, 4:46–50.

39. Ibid., 51–61, 63.

40. Ibid., 60–63. She further mourned, "and now that a week has elapsed since his interment . . . it seems like a frightful dream and that it cannot be that he is dead and that I shall never see him more. . . . But I have the great consolation to think that whilst he was here I made him happy, that his heart glowed with unbounded love towards me, [and that he has been saved]."

41. DNL Diaries, HSP, 4:65, 68, 70–71, 79, 81–82, 92.

42. Ibid., 94, 100, 102, 103, 107, 130.

43. Ibid.,104–105, 5:13; Jones, "Deborah Logan," 38, 112–113. On using the *Memoir* to create a George she could live with, see Premo, "'Like a Being Who Does Not Belong,'" 90.

44. Premo, "'Like a Being Who Does Not Belong,'" 92–94, 96–111; Jones, "Deborah Logan," 41. Premo points out that diary entries mentioning George "appeared much less frequently" during the 1830s and "ceased almost altogether" after 1835 (p. 90).

45. Jones, "Deborah Logan," 20–23, 92, 94–95, 107–113; Wister and Irwin, *Worthy Women*, 300, 319–320; Stabile, *Memory's Daughters*, 74–77, 79; Westcott, *Historic Mansions*, 153; Premo, "'Like a Being Who Does Not Belong,'" 88, 107–108.

46. Jones, "Deborah Logan," 115, 118–119, 121–124, 128; Wister and Irwin, *Worthy Women*, 322–327; Watson, *Annals of Philadelphia* 1:573–574. On the chair, see Keim, *Logania*, 11; on the box, see Keim, *Stenton*, 31.

47. Deborah often wrote poetry and published some anonymously in the *National Gazette*; she also published some newspaper articles and obituaries, again, anonymously. The *Memoir of George Logan* was only published after her death (Jones, "Deborah Logan," 94–95, 107, 114; Wister and Irwin, *Worthy Women*, 300; Logan, *Memoir*, 120–122). On her attachment to the past, see Premo, "'Like a Being Who Does Not Belong,'" 102–103.

48. Wister and Irwin, *Worthy Women*, 326; Westcott, *Historic Mansions*, 154; Jones, "Deborah Logan," 73; DNL Diaries, HSP 4:109.

49. DNL Diaries, HSP 13:11, 38, 14:10.

50. Ibid.,13:19, 21; Premo, "'Like a Being Who Does Not Belong,'" 90–91, 95.

51. Maria Dickinson Logan, "Obituary of Deborah Norris Logan," for the *Friend*, 1839, manuscript 14271, Logan box 8, folder 12, LCP. Premo makes the insightful observation that Deborah's struggle to achieve a sense of resignation late in life might have served to reconcile her to the disappointments of earthly constraints as well as to prepare her for death ("'Like a Being Who Does Not Belong,'" 99).

Part III

1. Sharon Salinger, *To Serve Well and Faithfully: Labor and Indentured Servants in Pennsylvania, 1682–1800* (Bowie, Md.: Heritage Books, 2000), 137–152.

2. David Waldstreicher, *Runaway America: Benjamin Franklin, Slavery, and the American Revolution* (New York: Hill and Wang, 2004); Lawrence Cremin, *American Education: The National Experience* (New York: Harper Colophon Books, 1980), 253–259. On Franklin's self-portrayals more broadly, see Edmund S. Morgan, *Benjamin Franklin* (New Haven, Conn.: Yale University Press, 2003).

3. Alexis de Tocqueville, *Democracy in America*, 2 vols. (New York: Vintage Books, 1945), 2:144. On Franklin's commitment to public service, see Morgan, *Benjamin Franklin*, 26–29, 55–70, 305–314.

4. The most influential statement of the mythological dimensions of nationalism is Benedict Anderson, *Imagined Communities: Reflections on the Origin and Spread of Nationalism* (New York: Verso, 1991).

Chapter 7

Note to epigraph: Lillian B. Miller et al., eds., *The Selected Papers of Charles Willson Peale and His Family*, 5 vols. (New Haven, Conn.: Yale University Press for the National Portrait Gallery of the Smithsonian Institution, 1983–1996), 5:415.

1. Miller et al., *Selected Papers of Peale*, 5:4.

2. Ibid., 6, 10.

3. Ibid., 7–9.

4. Ibid., 9.

5. Ibid., 10–13.

6. Ibid., 14–15.

7. Ibid., 14–17.

8. Ibid., 19–20, 23–25, 29–30, 32, 34; John Thomas Scharf and Thompson Westcott, *History of Philadelphia, 1609–1884*, 3 vols. (Philadelphia: L. H. Everts, 1884), 2:1035; Charles Coleman Sellers, *Charles Willson Peale* (New York: Charles Scribner's Sons, 1969), 48.

9. Miller et al., *Selected Papers of Peale*, 1:189–190; 5:39, 40, 41–42, 43; Sellers, *Charles Willson Peale*, 109.

10. John Adams to Abigail Adams, Aug. 21, 1776, *Adams Family Papers: An Electronic Archive*, http://www.masshist.org/digitaladams/, accessed May 4, 2020.

11. Miller et al., *Selected Papers of Peale*, 5:47–48, 50–53; Sellers, *Charles Willson Peale*, 124, 126.

12. Miller et al., *Selected Papers of Peale*, 5:55–57, 64, 67–69.

13. Ibid., 58–60, 69–71; Sellers, *Charles Willson Peale*, 164–165.

14. Sellers, *Charles Willson Peale*, 165, 175, 182–183; Miller et al., *Selected Papers of Peale*, 5:73–74, 75, 78–82.

15. Miller et al., *Selected Papers of Peale*, 5:84n; Sellers, *Charles Willson Peale*, 184, 256, 463n; Scharff and Westcott, *History of Philadelphia*, 2:1036. For discussions of Peale's work in the context of early American painting, see Margaretta Lovell, *Art in a Season of*

Revolution: Painters, Artisans, and Patrons in Early America (Philadelphia: University of Pennsylvania Press, 2005), 8–48, 141–183; Wendy Bellion, *Citizen Spectator: Art, Illusion, and Visual Perception in Early National America* (Chapel Hill: University of North Carolina Press, 2011).

16. Miller et al., *Selected Papers of Peale*, 5:83, 89–91; Sellers, *Charles Willson Peale*, 185, 188, 318.

17. Miller et al., *Selected Papers of Peale*, 5:91–93; Sellers, *Charles Willson Peale*, 194–199; Ethel Armes, comp. and ed., *Nancy Shippen: Her Journal Book* (Philadelphia: J. B. Lippincott, 1935), 175. This was not the last of his public art efforts. In the summer of 1788, for example, Peale was also involved in the planning and execution of the grand parade—including a thirty-foot-long "Federal Ship"—to celebrate the ratification of the Constitution in Philadelphia (Miller et al., *Selected Papers of Peale*, 5:129).

18. David Waldstreicher, *In the Midst of Perpetual Fetes: The Making of American Nationalism, 1776–1820* (Chapel Hill: University of North Carolina Press, 1997); Gary Nash, *First City: Philadelphia and the Forging of Historical Memory* (Philadelphia: University of Pennsylvania Press, 2001), 135.

19. Armes, *Nancy Shippen*, 142–143, 240; Sellers, *Charles Willson Peale*, 219; Nash, *First City*, 136; Miller et al., *Selected Papers of Peale*, 5:85–88, 93–94, 111. Nash stresses that Peale painted more of the Revolutionary era's conservative leadership than his old radical allies (*First City*, 95, 138, 140). But Peale clearly paid a price for his wartime radicalism in terms of losing commissions. His constant need to make money to support his growing family was doubtless the primary motive force in his pursuit of subjects. Moreover, with the growing power of conservatives in the late 1780s and early 1790s, the nation's leadership that he desired to display in his museum no longer included his old allies.

20. Miller et al., *Selected Papers of Peale*, 5:112.

21. Ibid., 113–117.

22. Ibid., 117–119, 130, 134–136.

23. Ibid., 160–161, 167, 216, 218–220.

24. Ibid., 128, 140, 192–195, 201, 205–206, 211, 214.

25. Ibid., 221–224; Sellers, *Charles Willson Peale*, 264–265. On the influence of the American Philosophical Society, see Myron Wehtje, "Charles Willson Peale and His Temple," *Pennsylvania History* 36, no. 2 (Apr. 1969), 164–165.

26. Miller et al., *Selected Papers of Peale*, 5:224–225.

27. Ibid., 226; Sellers, *Charles Willson Peale*, 266, 333.

28. Miller et al., *Selected Papers of Peale*, 5:234–244, 315–317. He did earn $500 from his fireplace patent. For more on Peale as an Enlightenment-inspired inventor, see Sidney Hart, "'To Encrease the Comforts of Life': Charles Willson Peale and the Mechanical Arts," *Pennsylvania Magazine of History and Biography* 110, no. 3 (July 1986), 323–357.

29. Miller et al., *Selected Papers of Peale*, 5:228–230, 257–263, 267; Sellers, *Charles Willson Peale*, 258–260.

30. Miller et al., *Selected Papers of Peale*, 5:271–272.

31. Ibid., 281, 284–287, 289–297, 303, 305–307.

32. Sellers, *Charles Willson Peale*, 303; Scharf and Westcott, *History of Philadelphia*, 1:514; Miller et al., *Selected Papers of Peale*, 5:269n, 309–310, 321. Peale also exhibited some of the musical instruments Hawkins invented and collaborated with him in improving the polygraph, or copying machine (Miller et al., *Selected Papers of Peale*, 5:310–315; Sellers, *Charles Willson Peale*, 306–307, 313). Information on Moses Williams's earnings from *Independence Hall*, brochure (N.p.: National Park Service, n.d).

33. This description follows Robert E. Schofield, "The Science Education of an Enlightened Entrepreneur: Charles Willson Peale and His Philadelphia Museum, 1784–1827," *American Studies* 30, no. 2 (Fall 1989), 29–30. Schofield stresses the museum's contributions to natural science. For more on the scientific engagement and education of visitors, see Bellion, *Citizen Spectator*, 36, 38, 41. For more detail on the evolution of the museum's layout, as well as operations and revenues, see Sellers, *Charles Willson Peale*, 335–337, 340–351.

34. Miller et al., *Selected Papers of Peale*, 5:323–325; Sellers, *Charles Willson Peale*, 258–260, 311, 341.

35. Miller et al., *Selected Papers of Peale*, 5:320n, 321.

36. Ibid., 321, 324, 326–327, 338–339, 342–343, 359–360, 385–386, 390–391, 420; Sellers, *Charles Willson Peale*, 239, 245.

37. Miller et al., *Selected Papers of Peale*, 5:334, 344, 346–349, 351–352, 354. Deborah Logan wrote the obituary when Hannah died in 1821 (Deborah Norris Logan, Diaries, 1815–1839, collection 380, Historical Society of Pennsylvania [hereafter DNL Diaries, HSP], 4:135); see Sellers, *Charles Willson Peale*, 319.

38. Miller et al., *Selected Papers of Peale*, 5:371–376, 379–383, 394–400, 424–425, 430; Sellers, *Charles Willson Peale*, 354–359, 391–392, 478n; DNL Diaries, HSP, 1:248, 3:123.

39. Miller et al., *Selected Papers of Peale*, 5:406, 424–428, 432; Scharf and Westcott, *History of Philadelphia*, 2:1037.

40. Miller et al., *Selected Papers of Peale*, 5:433–435; DNL Diaries, HSP, 4:126–127.

41. Miller et al., *Selected Papers of Peale*, 5:436–440, 442–443, 450, 472–473; DNL Diaries, HSP, 5:58, 7:124.

42. Miller et al., *Selected Papers of Peale*, 5:479–482, 488; Sellers, *Charles Willson Peale*, 415–418.

43. Miller et al., *Selected Papers of Peale*, 5:xix, 482, 484.

44. Ibid., xix, xxi; David C. Ward, *Charles Willson Peale: Art and Selfhood in the New Republic* (Berkeley: University of California Press, 2004), xvii–xviii. Some spot-checking of Miller et al., *Selected Papers of Peale*, vols. 1, 5, did not reveal discrepancies between Peale's letters and diaries and his autobiography.

45. Miller et al., *Selected Papers of Peale*, 5:xxiii; DNL Diaries, HSP, 9:34, 166.

46. DNL Diaries, HSP, 8:94–95, 160, 9:34.

47. Miller et al., *Selected Papers of Peale*, 5:488–489; Sellers, *Charles Willson Peale*, 424–427.

48. DNL Diaries, HSP, 11:13.

49. Miller et al., *Selected Papers of Peale*, 5:431; Sellers, *Charles Willson Peale*, 213.

50. Sellers, *Charles Willson Peale*, 432–433.

Chapter 8

Note to epigraph: Quoted in Stephen Simpson, *Biography of Stephen Girard* (Philadelphia: Thomas Bonsal, 1832), 157.

1. The voluminous Girard papers, in French and English, are available on six hundred reels of microfilm at Girard College and the American Philosophical Society, both in Philadelphia. This chapter is greatly indebted to the various biographies of Girard, each with its strengths and weaknesses. Simpson's *Biography of Girard* was the earliest, published just months after Girard's death. Because Simpson was an employee of Girard, he had the advantage of knowing the man close up. But the biography contains many inaccuracies, and some consider it tainted by Simpson's anger over not getting the job of his father, George, as chief cashier on the latter's death. Henry Atlee Ingram Jr.'s *The Life and Character of Stephen Girard*, 3rd ed. (Philadelphia: n.p, 1886), assails Simpson accordingly (vii–xv); but, as Ingram was a descendant of Girard's brother Jean, his own biography, while useful, can be faulted for its laudatory tone and lack of mention of Girard's mistresses. John Bach McMaster's *The Life and Times of Stephen Girard, Mariner and Merchant*, 2 vols. (Philadelphia: J. B. Lippincott, 1918), is the most comprehensive account of Girard's maritime and mercantile affairs, based on and with extensive quotation from his correspondence. Cheesman A. Herrick's *Stephen Girard, Founder* (Philadelphia: Girard College, 1923, 1945) is a good short account, geared for the use of Girard College. Harry Emerson Wildes's *Lonely Midas: The Story of Stephen Girard* (New York: Farrar & Rinehart, 1943) is a good read, frank about Girard's personal life, and based on substantial research in the Girard Papers. George Wilson's *Stephen Girard: The Life and Times of America's First Tycoon* (Conshohocken, Pa.: Signpost Books, 1995) is the latest full biography, and paints Girard as a "man of derring do" (15). Thomas J. DiFilippo's *Stephen Girard: The Man, His College and Estate*, 2nd ed. (1999), http://www.girardweb.com/girard/download.htm, accessed May 11, 2020, offers a useful account of Girard's papers and other effects. Brenna O'Rourke Holland, "Free Market Family: Gender, Capitalism and the Life of Stephen Girard" (Ph.D diss, Temple University, 2014), is the most recent scholarly treatment. On Bordeaux, see Wilson, *Stephen Girard*, 18, 49. Ingram claimed that the injury to Girard's eye was the result of an accident at age eight, but other biographers said it happened in infancy (Ingram, *Life and Character of Girard*, 20, 21; McMaster, *Life and Times of Girard*, 1:2; Herrick, *Stephen Girard, Founder,* 8; Wildes, *Lonely Midas,* 5, 7; DiFilippo, *Stephen Girard,* 2–4; Wilson, *Stephen Girard*, 16–19). Hereafter, where the various biographers (with their different perspectives and, to some degree, different sources) agree, all are cited to show consensus. Significant divergences between them are noted.

2. Ingram, *Life and Character of Girard*, 25–27, 29; Herrick, *Stephen Girard, Founder,* 16; Wildes, *Lonely Midas,* 5–10, 19; DiFilippo, *Stephen Girard*, 4; Wilson, *Stephen Girard*, 19–22, 26–27, 32, 36–40. McMaster, *Life and Times of Girard*, 1:4–5.

3. McMaster, *Life and Times of Girard*, 1:6–7, 10, 12.

4. Ingram, *Life and Character of Girard*, 30–32; Herrick, *Stephen Girard, Founder,* 55; Wildes, *Lonely Midas,* 22, 25–27, 323n; DiFilippo, *Stephen Girard*, 4–5; Wilson, *Stephen Girard*, 41–42, 44–48, 56, 59.

5. Ingram, *Life and Character of Girard*, 33–37, 40; Wildes, *Lonely Midas,* 28–30; DiFilippo, *Stephen Girard*, 5; Wilson, *Stephen Girard*, 63, 65, 67.

6. Ingram, *Life and Character of Girard*, 41; Herrick, *Stephen Girard, Founder,* 55; Wildes, *Lonely Midas,* 31, 33, 34, 39–41, 44–45; DiFilippo, *Stephen Girard*, 5; Wilson, *Stephen Girard*, 70–72, 75, 81–82; McMaster, *Life and Times of Girard,* 1:14–16, 21–23. Wilson alone thought that Girard "had impressive success in privateering" (*Stephen Girard*, 87).

7. McMaster, *Life and Times of Girard,* 1:19, 24–37, 75–80, 84, 104–105, 107–111, 114–116, 118–119, 150, 154; Wildes, *Lonely Midas,* 36, 42–44, 46, 59–61, 71–72; DiFilippo, *Stephen Girard*, 5; Wilson, *Stephen Girard*, 83–85, 88, 99; Thomas M. Doerflinger, *A Vigorous Spirit of Enterprise: Merchants and Economic Development in Revolutionary Philadelphia* (New York: Norton, 1986), 216–217; Ingram, *Life and Character of Girard*, 43, 45, 48–51; Herrick, *Stephen Girard, Founder,* 25–27, 56; Holland, "Free Market Family," 1–37.

8. McMaster, *Life and Times of Girard,* 1:61; Herrick, *Stephen Girard, Founder,* 77; Wildes, *Lonely Midas,* 64–67; Doerflinger, *Vigorous Spirit,* 11.

9. Doerflinger, *Vigorous Spirit,* 15.

10. Stephen Girard to Jean Girard, June 1, 1785, in McMaster, *Life and Times of Girard,* 1:65; Jean Girard to Stephen Girard, June 30, 1785, in Ingram, *Life and Character of Girard*, 45–46, 52; Herrick, *Stephen Girard, Founder,* 20–22; Wildes, *Lonely Midas,* 52–56, 73, 74; Wilson, *Stephen Girard*, 93–96.

11. DiFilippo, *Stephen Girard*, 5

12. McMaster, *Life and Times of Girard,* 1:84, 88; Wildes, *Lonely Midas,* 72–73, 75, 79, 81–83, 85–86; Wilson, *Stephen Girard*, 95, 97–101.

13. For contrasting accounts of Mary's living conditions at the hospital, see Ingram, *Life and Character of Girard*, 52–53, 59–61, 84–86; Herrick, *Stephen Girard, Founder,* 22–23; Wildes, *Lonely Midas,* 87–91; DiFilippo, *Stephen Girard*, 2; Wilson, *Stephen Girard*, 106–111, 290, 292–293.

14. Brenna O'Rourke Holland, "'Housekeeper, . . . Wife and All': Sally Bickham and Urban Women's Economic Strategy in Early National Philadelphia," paper presented at the annual meeting of the Society of Historians of the Early American Republic, Philadelphia, July 20, 2014; Wildes, *Lonely Midas,* 134–135, 138, 141–142, 145–147. Wilson asserts that Girard loved Sally and was hurt by her departure (*Stephen Girard*, 96–97, 102, 130, 173).

15. Ingram, *Life and Character of Girard*, 57; Wildes, *Lonely Midas,* 92–93, 95–96, 139; Wilson, *Stephen Girard*, 194; Eliza Harrison, ed., *Philadelphia Merchant: The Diary of Thomas P. Cope* (Philadelphia: Gateway, 1978), 394–395; Nicholas B. Wainwright, ed., "The Diary of Samuel Breck, 1827–1833," *Pennsylvania Magazine of History and Biography* 103, no. 2 (Apr. 1979), 233, 239.

16. Wildes, *Lonely Midas,* 117–123; Wilson, *Stephen Girard*, 114–115, 120–121; Ingram, *Life and Character of Girard*, 58, 61; McMaster, *Life and Times of Girard,* 1:215, 217; Herrick, *Stephen Girard, Founder,* 37–38, 40, 42; John T. Scharf and Thompson Westcott, *History of Philadelphia, 1609–1884*, 3 vols. (Philadelphia: L. H. Everts, 1884), 2:1605.

17. McMaster, *Life and Times of Girard,* 1:214; Herrick, *Stephen Girard, Founder,* 40–45, 47, 48–51; Wildes, *Lonely Midas,* 62–63, 120–124, 278–279; DiFilippo, *Stephen Girard,* 14; Wilson, *Stephen Girard*, 124–125, 129.

18. See J. H. Powell, *Bring Out Your Dead: The Great Plague of Yellow Fever in Philadelphia in 1793* (Philadelphia: University of Pennsylvania Press, 1949, 1993); Ingram, *Life and Character of Girard*, 67–70; Scharf and Westcott, *History of Philadelphia*, 2:1606; McMaster, *Life and Times of Girard,* 1:216, 222, 243, 374; Herrick, *Stephen Girard, Founder,* 46, 48; Wildes, *Lonely Midas,* 124–131; DiFilippo, *Stephen Girard*, 14; Wilson, *Stephen Girard*, 125–128, 132; Harrison, *Philadelphia Merchant*, 395.

19. McMaster, *Life and Times of Girard,* 1:241, 295, 305–306; Wildes, *Lonely Midas,* 152–156; Ingram, *Life and Character of Girard*, 69, 71; Herrick, *Stephen Girard, Founder,* 62–63, 114; DiFilippo, *Stephen Girard,* 21; Wilson, *Stephen Girard*, 136, 140–144, 146–150, 196.

20. McMaster, *Life and Times of Girard,* 1:9, 278; Herrick, *Stephen Girard, Founder,* 59–60, 62–72, 74, 76, 78–79; Wildes, *Lonely Midas,* 144, 152, 157, 159–171; DiFilippo, *Stephen Girard*, 6–9; Wilson, *Stephen Girard*, 98, 190–193; Thomas M. Doerflinger, "Capital Generation in the New Nation: How Stephen Girard Made His First $735,872," *William and Mary Quarterly*, 3rd ser., 72, no. 4 (Oct. 2015), 623–658.

21. Wilson, *Stephen Girard*, 170–171; Ingram, *Life and Character of Girard*, 123–127.

22. Wildes, *Lonely Midas,* 180–185; Wilson, *Stephen Girard*, 164, 174–177; Ingram, *Life and Character of Girard*, 116–117.

23. McMaster, *Life and Times of Girard,* 1:460–463; Wildes, *Lonely Midas,* 189–197; Wilson, *Stephen Girard*, 217, 294.

24. Wilson, *Stephen Girard*, 19–21, 105, 159.

25. Ingram, *Life and Character of Girard*, 119–121; McMaster, *Life and Times of Girard,* 2:410; Herrick, *Stephen Girard, Founder,* 101–107; Wildes, *Lonely Midas,* 201–205; DiFilippo, *Stephen Girard*, 12–13; Wilson, *Stephen Girard*, 178–180.

26. Ingram, *Life and Character of Girard*, 72, 75; Scharf and Westcott, *History of Philadelphia,* 1:551; McMaster, *Life and Times of Girard,* 2:73, 173, 205; Herrick, *Stephen Girard, Founder,* 84; Wildes, *Lonely Midas,* 206–209, 219–220; DiFilippo, *Stephen Girard*, 8, 9; Wilson, *Stephen Girard*, 227, 229, 234, 245, 246.

27. Ingram, *Life and Character of Girard*, 76; McMaster, *Life and Times of Girard,* 2:239–240, 244; Herrick, *Stephen Girard, Founder,* 85; Wildes, *Lonely Midas,* 210–211; DiFilippo, *Stephen Girard*, 8, 9; Wilson, *Stephen Girard*, 245–248.

28. Ingram, *Life and Character of Girard*, 82–83; McMaster, *Life and Times of Girard,* 2:246–256; Herrick, *Stephen Girard, Founder,* 91–95; Wildes, *Lonely Midas,* 214–216; DiFilippo, *Stephen Girard*, 9; Wilson, *Stephen Girard*, 263, 266, 274–276.

29. Wildes, *Lonely Midas,* 216, 220–222; DiFilippo, *Stephen Girard*, 9, 10; Ingram, *Life and Character of Girard*, 87–88; McMaster, *Life and Times of Girard,* 2:308–310, 313–314; Herrick, *Stephen Girard, Founder,* 95–97; Wilson, *Stephen Girard*, 230, 297–298, 300–302.

30. Ingram, *Life and Character of Girard*, 88–89, 90; McMaster, *Life and Times of Girard,* 2:202, 364, 409; Wildes, *Lonely Midas,* 273; Herrick, *Stephen Girard, Founder,* 130–133; DiFilippo, *Stephen Girard*, 10–12; Wilson, *Stephen Girard*, 303, 309–310, 317–318,

331; Russell F. Weigley, ed., *Philadelphia: A 300-Year History* (New York: W. W. Norton, 1982), 281. For a more critical view of Girard's business acumen, see Harrison, *Philadelphia Merchant*, 394–395.

31. McMaster, *Life and Times of Girard*, 2:202, 409; Herrick, *Stephen Girard, Founder*, 130–133; DiFilippo, *Stephen Girard*, 10–12; Wilson, *Stephen Girard*, 303, 309–310; Weigley, *Philadelphia*, 281.

32. Ingram, *Life and Character of Girard*, 121–122; Weigley, *Philadelphia*, 251, 281; Wilson, *Stephen Girard*, 225, 310–311; Wainwright, "Diary of Samuel Breck," 239; Deborah Norris Logan Diaries, 1815–1839, 17 vols., 13:16–17, Historical Society of Pennsylvania, Philadelphia (hereafter cited as DNL Diaries, HSP).

33. Ingram, *Life and Character of Girard*, 126, 127; Wildes, *Lonely Midas*, 241–242; Wilson, *Stephen Girard*, 173, 302–303.

34. Ingram, *Life and Character of Girard*, 113, 128; Wildes, *Lonely Midas*, 243–248, 258–261; Wilson, *Stephen Girard*, 303. John Hemphill was the son of William Hemphill, a merchant of Wilmington. William was born in County Donegal in Northern Ireland in 1743, and came to Wilmington in 1762. He married Elisabeth Allison in 1770 and died in 1823. He had sons James and John. William Hemphill corresponded in 1796 with his brother Curtis of Cadmus, Ireland. Thus John was a contemporary of Joseph Hemphill of the next chapter, and very likely a second cousin. Joseph's grandfather Alexander Hemphill emigrated from Cadmus around 1740 (genealogical notes in the Hemphill family possession). On Caroline Girard and Franklin Peale, see Wildes, *Lonely Midas*, 308.

35. Wilson, *Stephen Girard*, 295.

36. Harrison, *Philadelphia Merchant*, 395; Wildes, *Lonely Midas*, 224–240, 249–255; McMaster, *Life and Times of Girard*, 2:360–361.

37. Wildes, *Lonely Midas*, 263, 267–268, 271–272; Wilson, *Stephen Girard*, 164, 225.

38. McMaster, *Life and Times of Girard*, 2:362; Ingram, *Life and Character of Girard*, 138–139; Herrick, *Stephen Girard, Founder*, 118; Wildes, *Lonely Midas*, 264–267, 268, 269–270; DiFilippo, *Stephen Girard*, 2; Wilson, *Stephen Girard*, 161–162.

39. McMaster, *Life and Times of Girard*, 2:411, 431–432; Wildes, *Lonely Midas*, 282–285, 287; Harrison, *Philadelphia Merchant*, 394–395; Wilson, *Stephen Girard*, 314–317. For more on Girard's daily schedule and diet up to this point, see Ingram, *Life and Character of Girard*, 116–119.

40. Ingram, *Life and Character of Girard*, 91–93, 117–118; McMaster, *Life and Times of Girard*, 2:412–413, 429–430; Herrick, *Stephen Girard, Founder*, 10, 109–110; Wildes, *Lonely Midas*, 288–292; Wilson, *Stephen Girard*, 312–313, 319–320; Harrison, *Philadelphia Merchant*, 395.

41. McMaster, *Life and Times of Girard*, 2:444; Wildes, *Lonely Midas*, 292–294; DiFilippo, *Stephen Girard*, 2; Wilson, *Stephen Girard*, 323. In contrast to Wildes, Wilson asserts that Girard was loved as well as revered by Philadelphians before his death, but the newspaper tributes he cites all came after the leaking of the contents of the will (*Stephen Girard*, 325, 388n).

42. Ingram, *Life and Character of Girard*, 155–156; Scharf and Westcott, *History of Philadelphia*, 1:629; Wildes, *Lonely Midas*, 294–297; DiFilippo, *Stephen Girard*, 23–24;

Wilson, *Stephen Girard*, 30, 335–338. In response to criticism from family members, lawyer William Duane later reminded them of Girard's aversion to large inheritances. Duane insisted that his only influence on the will was, in response to a question from Girard, to encourage him to make extra provision for Antoinette Hemphill because of the number of her children. See Russell Duane and Daniel Webster, "Who Wrote Stephen Girard's Will?" *Pennsylvania Magazine of History and Biography* 54, no. 1 (1930), 25–27.

43. Herrick, *Stephen Girard, Founder*, 123, 159, 162; Wildes, *Lonely Midas*, 297–298; Wilson, *Stephen Girard*, 325–328; DNL Diaries, HSP, 13:332. The Girard biographies offer differing accounts of the size of the funeral procession and crowd; I quote from the most recent account in Gil Bunker, comp., "Biography of Stephen Girard," 2005, rev. 2006, Girard College, Philadelphia.

44. Wilson, *Stephen Girard*, 340–341.

45. Ingram, *Life and Character of Girard*, 155–163; Scharf and Westcott, *History of Philadelphia*, 1:629; McMaster, *Life and Times of Girard*, 2:452; Herrick, *Stephen Girard, Founder*, 124–125; Wildes, *Lonely Midas*, 298–301, 303; DiFilippo, *Stephen Girard*, 24–25; Wilson, *Stephen Girard*, 325, 354–358; Thomas DiFilippo and Gil Bunker, comps., "100 Facts About Founder's Hall and Its Relics," 2002, rev. 2006, Girard College, Philadelphia.

46. Ingram, *Life and Character of Girard*, 140–141, 167–171.

47. Ibid., 155–156; Scharf and Westcott, *History of Philadelphia*, 1:630; Herrick, *Stephen Girard, Founder*, 12, 15; Wildes, *Lonely Midas*, 301–304; DiFilippo, *Stephen Girard*, 27; Wilson, *Stephen Girard*, 343–350. The family lost several subsequent challenges in the latter part of the nineteenth century. On this and the setting aside of various provisions of the will after 1968 to allow nonwhite boys and girls as well as nonorphans to attend the school, see DiFilippo, *Stephen Girard*, 27–31.

48. Ingram, *Life and Character of Girard*, 150–152; Herrick, *Stephen Girard, Founder*, 111, 116. Girard's fourth-place ranking is as compared to gross domestic product; see Michael Klepper and Robert Gunther, *The Wealthy 100: From Benjamin Franklin to Bill Gates—a Ranking of the Richest Americans, Past and Present* (Secaucus, N.J.: Citadel Press, 1996), 26–28.

49. McMaster, *Life and Times of Girard*, 1:v; Ingram, *Life and Character of Girard*, 112–113, 124; Herrick, *Stephen Girard, Founder*, 15.

50. McMaster, *Life and Times of Girard*, 1:162–163; Ingram, *Life and Character of Girard*, 116–117, 150; Herrick, *Stephen Girard, Founder*, 108–109; Wilson, *Stephen Girard*, 155, 180–181, 184–185.

51. Wilson, *Stephen Girard*, 166; Harrison, *Philadelphia Merchant*, 394; Doerflinger, *Vigorous Spirit*, 11, 19. See Ingram, *Life and Character of Girard*, 138, for a different version.

52. Wildes, *Lonely Midas*, 277; Wilson, *Stephen Girard*, 307–308.

Chapter 9

Note to epigraph: *North American and Daily Advertiser*, May 30, 1842.

1. Genealogical notes in Hemphill family possession; J. Smith Futhey and Gilbert Cope, *History of Chester County, Pennsylvania* (Philadelphia: Louis H. Everts, 1881), 1657.

2. Genealogical notes in Hemphill family possession.

3. The college underwent some administrative turmoil in the decades leading up to Hemphill's arrival. Fearing that the College of Philadelphia was becoming too Anglican an institution, the Pennsylvania government of 1776 had revoked its charter and given one to the University of the State of Pennsylvania. The two branches were officially reunited as the University of Pennsylvania in 1791. See "Penn's First Campus, 1740–1801," and "The College: Curriculum," http://www.archives.upenn.edu/histy/features/1700s/college_curric.html, accessed July 25, 2014.

4. "Philadelphia Debtors Prison," http://teachingamericanhistory.org/static/convention/map/debtorsprison.html, accessed July 25, 2014.

5. Wilmer W. MacElree, *Side Lights on the Bench and Bar of Chester County* (West Chester, Pa.: n.p., 1918), 141; Futhey and Cope, *History of Chester County*, 1657; Gilbert Cope and Henry G. Ashmead, *Historic Homes and Institutions and Genealogical and Personal Memoirs of Chester and Delaware Counties, Pennsylvania*, 2 vols. (New York: Lewis, 1904), 1:110–111.

6. Futhey and Cope, *History of Chester County*, 1266, 1658; *Porcupine's Gazette*, May 5, 1798.

7. Futhey and Cope, *History of Chester County*, 1658. The speech was reprinted as "Columbian Eloquence: Speech of Mr. Hemphill," *Balance and Columbian Repository*, Mar. 16, 23, 1802. See also *Port-Folio*, Mar. 6, 1802.

8. Futhey and Cope, *History of Chester County*, 1658; Eliza Harrison, ed., *Philadelphia Merchant: The Diary of Thomas P. Cope, 1800–1851* (South Bend, Ind.: Gateway Editions, 1978), 187–189.

9. Mabel S. Ewer, unpublished genealogical note in Hemphill family possession; Sarah Dickson Lowrie, *Strawberry Mansion First Known as Somerton, the House of Many Masters* (Philadelphia: Harbor Press, 1941), 113. Robert was born in Philadelphia on Feb. 28, 1809. He was married on Oct. 2, 1834, to Martha Bryan. Martha Bryan Hemphill died in 1843 and Robert remarried a widow, Mary Guier Caldwell, in 1849. Robert had three children by each wife. Alexander Wills Hemphill was born on Apr. 8, 1811. He did not lead a long or happy life; a descendant recalled that "he was very intemperate and did little besides spend his father's money on liquor and fast horses. He was for a time with his father in the pottery business, but was not successful as a businessman. He died a victim of drink on Nov. 17, 1834, and is buried at Laurel Hill" (family history notes in Hemphill family possession).

10. Harold D. Eberlein and Cortlandt V. D. Hubbard, *Portrait of a Colonial City* (Philadelphia: J. B. Lippincott, 1939), 508.

11. *Poulson's American Daily Advertiser,* Mar. 8, Oct. 5, 1808. The associate judges were paid $500, and the not necessarily legally trained associate judges of the court of common pleas $400. See Futhey and Cope, *History of Chester County*, 1658; John Thomas Scharf and Thompson Westcott, *History of Philadelphia, 1609–1884*, 3 vols. (Philadelphia: L. H. Everts, 1884), 2:1572; James Mease, *Picture of Philadelphia for 1811,* in Thomas Wilson, *Picture of Philadelphia for 1824* (Philadelphia: Thomas Town, 1823), 99–100.

12. Charlene Mires, *Independence Hall in American Memory* (Philadelphia: University of Pennsylvania Press, 2002), 26, 57–58, 60–61; Gary B. Nash, *First City: Philadelphia*

and the Forging of Historical Memory (Philadelphia: University of Pennsylvania Press, 2002), 2.

13. Charles Belfoure and Mary Ellen Hayward, *The Baltimore Rowhouse* (Princeton, N.J.: Princeton Architectural Press, 1999), 16.

14. Philip S. Klein, *President James Buchanan: A Biography* (College Park: Pennsylvania State University Press, 1962), 27–31.

15. Ibid., 31–32. For an interesting partly fictional retelling of these events, see John Updike, *Memories of the Ford Administration* (New York: Knopf, 1992).

16. Klein, *President James Buchanan*, 32–33; Philip S. Klein, "The Lost Love of a Bachelor President," *American Heritage*, Dec. 1955, 20. The wrapper of the letter packet with Buchanan's instructions is held by the Historical Society of Pennsylvania, Philadelphia.

17. Klein, "Lost Love," 114. For election results, see *Franklin Gazette*, Oct. 14, 1818; *National Gazette*, Oct. 14, 1820.

18. *Niles' Weekly Register*, May 6, 1826; Futhey and Cope, *History of Chester County*, 1658; Andrew Burstein, *America's Jubilee* (New York: Random House, 2001), 232.

19. Margo Anderson, "The Missouri Debates, Slavery and Statistics of Race: Demography in Service of Politics," *Annales de Demographie Historique* 1, no. 1 (2003), 27.

20. "Hemphill, Joseph," *Biographical Dictionary of the United States Congress Online*, accessed May 11, 2020; *Edinburgh Review*, Oct. 1823; Futhey and Cope, *History of Chester County*, 1658; *Niles' Weekly Register*, Feb. 17, 1821.

21. Eric Burin, "Rethinking Northern White Support for the African Colonization Movement: The Pennsylvania Colonization Society as an Agent of Emancipation," *Pennsylvania Magazine of History and Biography* 127, no. 2 (Apr. 2003), 203–204. Hemphill served as a Pennsylvania delegate to American Colonization Society meetings in 1830 and 1831, which reviewed the progress of and worked to support the colony in Liberia. See "Annual meeting of the American Colonization Society," *Theological Repertory, and Churchman's Guide* 3 (Dec. 1830), 12; *Philadelphia Recorder*, Feb. 5, 1831; *Genius of Universal Emancipation*, Nov. 10, 1827.

22. Herman Hailperin, "Pro-Jackson Sentiment in Pennsylvania, 1820–1828," *Pennsylvania Magazine of History and Biography* 50, no. 3 (1926), 208; Futhey and Cope, *History of Chester County*, 1658.

23. John Lauriz Larson, *Internal Improvement: National Public Works and the Promise of Popular Government in the Early United States* (Chapel Hill: University of North Carolina Press, 2001), 138–142, 145; *Niles' Weekly Register*, May 4, 1822, Jan. 10, 1824; *Pilot*, Dec. 25, 1823; *National Government Journal, and Register of Official Papers*, May 1, 1824.

24. *Niles' Weekly Register*, Jan. 22, 1825, Jan. 16, 1830, Feb. 19, 1831; *Banner of the Constitution: Devoted to General Politics, Political Economy, State Papers . . .* , Apr. 24, Apr. 28, 1830; *Christian Advocate and Journal and Zion's Herald*, Jan. 29, 1830; *Hazard's Register of Pennsylvania, Devoted to the Preservation of Facts and Documents . . .* , May 4, 1833.

25. *Niles' Weekly Register*, Jan. 11, Mar. 8, 1823; *Cohen's Lottery Gazette and Register*, Jan. 23, 1824, Jan. 14, 1825.

26. *Niles' Weekly Register*, Sept. 10, 1831, June 23, 1832, Sept. 6, 1834, May 13, 1837.

27. Ibid., Oct. 14, 1826, Oct. 25, 1828; *Saturday Evening Post*, Sept. 29, 1827; *Genius of Universal Emancipation*, Oct. 20, 1827.

28. Ronald N. Satz, *American Indian Policy in the Jacksonian Era* (Norman: University of Oklahoma Press, 1975), 28–31. Hemphill seems to have mediated between historians as he did his colleagues, as both pro- and anti-Jackson discussions of Indian Removal give similar accounts of his role; see Robert Remini, *The Life of Andrew Jackson*, abr. ed. (New York: Harper and Row, 2011), 214; and Alfred Cave, "Abuse of Power: Andrew Jackson and the Indian Removal Act of 1830," *Historian* 65, no. 6 (Winter 2003), 1335–1336.

29. *Gales & Seaton's Register of Debates in Congress*, May 24, 1830, 1131–1133; *House Journal*, 21st Congress, 1830, 716.

30. *Gales & Seaton's Register of Debates in Congress*, May 24, 1830, 1131–1133.

31. Ibid.; *House Journal*, 21st Congress, 716.

32. Satz, *American Indian Policy*, 79, 134.

33. Lowrie, *Strawberry Mansion*, 22, 26, 48, 94–95, 104.

34. Gary B. Nash and Jean R. Soderlund, *Freedom by Degrees: Emancipation in Pennsylvania and Its Aftermath* (New York: Oxford University Press, 1991), 102.

35. Cope and Ashmead, *Historic Homes and Institutions*, 114; Lowrie, *Strawberry Mansion*, 127–131; Eberlein and Hubbard, *Portrait of a Colonial City*, 508; Beatrice Bronson Lippincott, "Strawberry Mansion," *Antiques* 82 (Nov. 1962), 529–530; *First Troop Philadelphia City Cavalry: The Military Magazine and Record of the Volunteers of the City and County of Philadelphia*, Mar. 1839.

36. Arthur E. James, "Tucker and Hemphill China," *American Antiques Journal* 2, no. 8 (Aug. 1947), 14–15; Ann Kilborn Cole, "Philadelphia Porcelain," *Philadelphia Inquirer Magazine*, Aug. 27, 1961, 29; Bill Barol, "American Made: Tucker Porcelain," *American Heritage*, May–June 1989, 28; Wendy Moonan, "A Potter's Dream: American Porcelain," *New York Times*, Jan. 28, 2005; Karla K. Albertson, "From Early 1800s Philadelphia, Striking Tucker Porcelain," *Philadelphia Inquirer*, Jan. 14, 2005.

37. Edwin A. Harder, "The Tucker and Hemphill Hard Porcelain Manufactory, Philadelphia, 1825–1838," *Bulletin of the Pennsylvania Museum of Art* 4, no. 14 (Apr. 1906), n.p.

38. Edwin A. Barber, *Marks of American Potters* (Philadelphia: Patterson & White, 1904), 18–19; James, "Tucker and Hemphill China," 15; Barol, "American Made," 28; *Hazard's Register of Pennsylvania*, Oct. 1, 1831, 14; *Banner of the Constitution*, Oct. 26, 1831; *New England Magazine*, Dec. 1831, June 2, 1832, 22.

39. Harder, "Tucker and Hemphill Porcelain," n.p.; James, "Tucker and Hemphill China," 15; Moonan, "A Potter's Dream."

40. Harder, "Tucker and Hemphill Porcelain," n.p.; Edwin A. Barber, *The Pottery and Porcelain of the United States* (New York: G. P. Putnam, 1909), 140–153, and plates following; James, "Tucker and Hemphill China," 15; Moonan, "A Potter's Dream." All of these works describe many pieces; the Philadelphia Museum of Art owns about five hundred of them. For press coverage, see *Philadelphia Album and Ladies' Literary Portfolio*, Aug. 24, 1833, 34; *Maine Farmer and Journal of the Useful Arts*, Aug. 10, 1833, 30; and *New-*

England Galaxy and United States Literary Advertiser, Nov. 30, 1833, 842. On exhibition prizes, see *Journal of the Franklin Institute*, Nov. 1, 1831, 5, Dec. 1, 1833, 6; *Niles' Weekly Register*, Nov. 2, 1833.

41. Harder, "Tucker and Hemphill Porcelain," n.p.; James, "Tucker and Hemphill China," 15; Cole, "Philadelphia Porcelain," 29; *North American and Daily Advertiser*, Apr. 4, 1842.

42. *North American and Daily Advertiser*, May 30, 1842.

Part IV

1. For a full view of the promises and problems in Philadelphia reform in this era, see Bruce Dorsey, *Reforming Men and Women: Gender in the Antebellum City* (Ithaca, N.Y.: Cornell University Press, 2002).

2. Rodney Hessinger, *Seduced, Abandoned, and Reborn: Visions of Youth in Middle-Class America, 1780–1850* (Philadelphia: University of Pennsylvania Press, 2005), 102–109; Dorsey, *Reforming Men and Women*, 114–115.

3. Dorsey, *Reforming Men and Women*, 153–154.

4. Rodney Hessinger, "'A Base and Unmanly Conspiracy': Catholicism and the Hogan Schism in the Gendered Religious Marketplace of Philadelphia," *Journal of the Early Republic* 31, no. 3 (Fall 2011), 357–396; Michael Feldberg, *The Philadelphia Riots of 1844: A Study of Ethnic Conflict* (Westport, Conn.: Greenwood Press, 1975).

5. Dorsey, *Reforming Men and Women*, 153–154, 195–240; Rosemarie Zagarri, *Revolutionary Backlash: Women and Politics in the Early American Republic* (Philadelphia: University of Pennsylvania Press, 2007); David Roediger, *The Wages of Whiteness: Race and the Making of the American Working Class* (New York: Verso Press, 2007).

Chapter 10

Note to epigraph: Peter Atall [Robert Waln], *The Hermit in America on a Visit to Philadelphia* (Philadelphia: Thomas, 1819), 155.

1. For a discussion of the "forgetting" of Francis Johnson in American music histories between the mid-nineteenth century and the mid-twentieth, see the work of his primary biographer—to which this chapter is greatly indebted—Charles Kelley Jones, *Francis Johnson (1792–1844): Chronicle of a Black Musician in Early Nineteenth-Century Philadelphia* (Bethlehem, Pa.: Lehigh University Press, 2006), 14–15. Jones's book is also a useful reference for Johnson's numerous compositions. On the European tour, see Eileen Southern, "Frank Johnson of Philadelphia and His Promenade Concerts," *Black Perspective in Music* 5, no. 1 (Spring 1977), 4. On Johnson's influence, see Eileen Southern, "Musical Practices in Black Churches of Philadelphia and New York, ca. 1800–1844," *Journal of the American Musicological Society* 30, no. 2 (Summer 1977), 298.

2. Gary B. Nash, *Forging Freedom: The Formation of Philadelphia's Black Community, 1720–1840* (Cambridge, Mass.: Harvard University Press, 1988), 2, 143. The Gradual Abolition Act took effect in March 1780 and required Pennsylvania masters to register enslaved people born after that date with a justice of the peace or other government authorities. When they reached the age of twenty-eight, enslaved people would be

liberated. People born before 1780 were not eligible for freedom, however. Nevertheless, the law was the first of its kind in the United States and thus a milestone. See Gary B. Nash and Jean R. Soderlund, *Freedom by Degrees: Emancipation in Pennsylvania and Its Aftermath* (New York: Oxford University Press, 1991); Emma Jones Lapsansky, "'Since They Got Those Separate Churches': Afro-Americans and Racism in Jacksonian Philadelphia," *American Quarterly* 32, no. 1 (Spring 1980), 54–78. According to the latest U.S. census estimates, Philadelphia's population is majority minority, with white residents accounting for roughly 41 percent of the population and nonwhite residents (African Americans, Native Americans, Latinos, and Asian Americans) accounting for over 50 percent (https://www.census.gov/quickfacts/fact/table/philadelphiacitypennsylvania, accessed May 12, 2020).

3. Jones, *Francis Johnson,* 9; Nash, *Forging Freedom,* 134–136, 151; James Forten, *Letters from a Man of Colour on a Late Bill Before the Senate of Pennsylvania* (Philadelphia: n.p., 1813), 1–4.

4. Jones, *Francis Johnson,* 32; John W. Cromwell, "Frank Johnson's Military Band," *Black Perspective in Music* 4, no. 2 (July 1976), 209.

5. Jones, *Francis Johnson,* 39; John Russell Young, ed., *Memorial History of the City of Philadelphia from Its First Settlement to the Year 1895*, 2 vols. (New York: New York History Company, 1895–1898), 2:135.

6. Jones, *Francis Johnson,* 41; Nash, *Forging Freedom,* 145–148, 152–153.

7. Robert E. Eliason, *Keyed Bugles in the United States* (Washington, D.C.: Smithsonian Institution Press, 1972), 5, 10; Cromwell, "Frank Johnson's Military Band," 208; Andy Gensler, "Francis Johnson," Oxford African American Studies Center, www.oxfordaasc.com, accessed Mar. 18, 2010; Jones, *Francis Johnson,* 44, 46, 47, 49; Dorothy Potter, *Food for Apollo: Cultivated Music in Antebellum Philadelphia* (Bethlehem, Pa.: Lehigh University Press, 2011), 102, 110, 121. Jones says the keyed bugle was introduced in 1811 and that Johnson had learned to play it by 1813 and had only met Willis a few times (*Francis Johnson,* 44, 50). Eliason thinks Johnson learned it a bit later, but certainly by 1821 (*Keyed Bugles*, 14, 15).

8. Jones, *Francis Johnson,* 47, 50, 104; Cromwell, "Frank Johnson's Military Band," 210; Southern, "Musical Practices in Black Churches," 306.

9. Aston Gonzalez, "The Art of Racial Politics: The Work of Robert Douglass, Jr., 1833–46," *Pennsylvania Magazine of History and Biography* 138, no. 1 (Jan. 2014), 5–37.

10. Gensler, "Francis Johnson."

11. Jones, *Francis Johnson,* 52–55; Atall, *The Hermit in America*, 154–155.

12. Jones, *Francis Johnson,* 56, 78, 99–100, 105. Cromwell wrote that the two brothers became members of Johnson's band ("Frank Johnson's Military Band," 210).

13. Jones, *Francis Johnson,* 57–60, 62, 66; Samuel A. Floyd Jr. and Marsha J. Reisser, "Social Dance Music of Black Composers in the Nineteenth Century and the Emergence of Classic Ragtime," *Black Perspective in Music* 8, no. 2 (Autumn 1980), 162. Cromwell wrote that he also played at the weddings of General George Cadwalader and the sister of militia leader and Democratic politician James Page ("Frank Johnson's Military Band," 210).

14. Jones, *Francis Johnson,* 67, 69–70, 72, 74, 118; Gensler, "Francis Johnson."

15. Jones, *Francis Johnson,* 86–87, 89–91, 94–95.

16. Potter, *Food for Apollo,* 58; Russel F. Weigley, ed., *Philadelphia: A 300-Year History* (New York: W. W. Norton, 1982), 251.

17. Jones, *Francis Johnson,* 101, 106–107, 114–115, 117; Gonzalez, "The Art of Racial Politics," 8–9.

18. Nicholas B. Wainwright, ed., "The Diary of Samuel Breck, 1827–1833," *Pennsylvania Magazine of History and Biography* 103, no. 2 (Apr. 1979), 225, emphasis in original; Jones, *Francis Johnson,* 110–111, 113. Until his death in 1844, Johnson continued to be the bandleader of choice among elite Philadelphians; for an enthusiastic description by diarist Sidney George Fisher of Johnson's music at a private ball in late 1838, see Jones, *Francis Johnson,* 178–181.

19. Jones, *Francis Johnson,* 101–103; Thomas Lanard, *One Hundred Years with the State Fencibles* (Philadelphia: Nields, 1913), 26–27, 37–39.

20. Lanard, *One Hundred Years with the State Fencibles,* 29; John Thomas Scharf and Thompson Westcott, *History of Philadelphia, 1609–1884,* 3 vols. (Philadelphia: L. H. Everts, 1884), 2:993, 1018. John Fanning Watson described Military Hall as "an old fashioned building . . . built in 1810 . . . for a printing-office." He claims that it was a tavern called "Union House," in 1832–1833, when the upper story was converted to an assembly room, and that it "afterward became the resort of military companies for a drill room, and was used by the State Fencibles." It became known as "Military Hall" in about 1834 or 1835 (*Annals of Philadelphia and Pennsylvania, in the Olden Time*, 3 vols. [Philadelphia: M. Stoddart, 1879], 3:305). See also (with an erroneous later date) Jones, *Francis Johnson,* 112.

21. *Hazard's Register of Pennsylvania*, Oct. 20, 1832, 287; *Atkinson's Saturday Evening Post,* Apr. 18, 1835. Johnson also played at the Princeton Commencement ball in 1837 (*Gentleman's Magazine*, Oct. 1837, 4, 292).

22. *Godey's Lady's Book*, Dec. 1835, 242; *Every Body's Album; A Humorous Collection of Tales, Quips, Quirks, Anecdotes, and Facetiae*, Sept. 1, 1836, 162. Johnson is featured more positively in newspaper advertisements for events at which he and his "celebrated . . . Band" were to play; see *Public Ledger*, Sept. 29, Oct. 2, 1837; W. E. B. DuBois, *The Philadelphia Negro* (Philadelphia: University of Pennsylvania Press, 1899), 27–31.

23. Robert Purvis, *The Appeal of Forty Thousand Citizens, Threatened with Disfranchisement* (Philadelphia: Merrihew and Gunn, 1838).

24. Jones, *Francis Johnson,* 132–134, 148; Lanard, *One Hundred Years with the State Fencibles,* 33. The latest study of the Turner uprising is Patrick H. Breen, *The Land Shall Be Deluged in Blood: A New History of the Nat Turner Revolt* (New York: Oxford University Press, 2016).

25. Jones, *Francis Johnson,* 135–139. Lanard, *One Hundred Years with the State Fencibles*, 39–44, which mistakenly says this happened in Boston.

26. Jones, *Francis Johnson,* 169–170.

27. Ibid., 149.

28. Ibid., 153–156; Potter, *Food for Apollo,* 75.

29. Southern, "Frank Johnson and His Promenade Concerts," 6; Jones, *Francis Johnson,* 157; Potter, *Food for Apollo,* 75. Black sailors often benefited from "protection papers," documents given to sailors and seamen after the American Revolution indicating their claims to citizenship; see R. Jeffrey Bolster, *Black Jacks: African American Seamen in the Age of Sail* (Cambridge, Mass.: Harvard University Press, 1998), 5.

30. *Niles' National Register,* Apr. 28, 1838; *Liberator,* May 18, 1838; Southern, "Frank Johnson and His Promenade Concerts," 7–8; Potter, *Food for Apollo,* 75; Cromwell, "Frank Johnson's Military Band," 211.

31. Southern, "Frank Johnson and His Promenade Concerts," 3, 4, 7–8, 10–11, 13; Jones, *Francis Johnson,* 168; "Amusements," *Atkinson's Saturday Evening Post,* Mar. 30, 1839.

32. Beverly H. Tomek, *Pennsylvania Hall: A "Legal Lynching" in the Shadow of the Liberty Bell* (New York: Oxford University Press, 2014).

33. Southern, "Frank Johnson and His Promenade Concerts," 15; Jones, *Francis Johnson,* 172–177. See also *Waldie's Select Circulating Library,* Jan. 1, 1841; *Boston Musical Gazette,* Oct. 31, 1838. For the clip, see "Francis Johnson: Music Master of Early Philadelphia," http://www.library.upenn.edu/exhibits/francisjohnson.html, accessed Jan. 6, 2011.

34. Jones, *Francis Johnson,* 171, 178–179, 202.

35. The band also continued to play at the anniversary celebration of the United Bowmen. Before "immense crowds," the archers, "in white pantaloons, green caps, and frock coats trimmed in gold," marched from target to target, "delivering their shafts with grace and precision to the music of Frank Johnson's band" (Jones, *Francis Johnson,* 181–183; Weigley, *Philadelphia,* 292). At the end of 1839, Johnson tried a new venue for his promenade concerts, at the Assembly Rooms on Library Street, opposite the Second Bank of the United States. This meant that he played in what had once been Deborah Norris's backyard, possibly in an edifice built over Anthony Benezet's old garden (Southern, "Frank Johnson and His Promenade Concerts," 15; Jones, *Francis Johnson,* 196; "Francis Johnson," http://www.archives.upenn.edu/people/1700s/johnson_fra.htm, accessed Jan. 6, 2011).

36. Jones, *Francis Johnson,* 183–187, 189–193.

37. Weigley, *Philadelphia,* 251; Potter, *Food for Apollo,* 63. Jones suggests Johnson remained optimistic that he would someday be asked to join (*Francis Johnson,* 95). On Douglass, see Gonzalez, "The Art of Racial Politics," 14; Gensler, "Francis Johnson."

38. Jones, *Francis Johnson,* 196, 200; Gensler, "Francis Johnson"; Cromwell, "Frank Johnson's Military Band," 211; Southern, "Musical Practices in Black Churches," 298, 306–307.

39. Potter, *Food for Apollo,* 63; Southern, "Frank Johnson and His Promenade Concerts," 13. On the way elite and mass culture often worked together in antebellum America, see Lawrence W. Levine, *Highbrow/Lowbrow: The Emergence of Cultural Hierarchy in America* (Cambridge, Mass.: Harvard University Press, 1990).

40. Southern, "Musical Practices in Black Churches," 301–304, 309, 311. Floyd and Reisser write that "it was not until after the Civil War that the published music of Black composers began to take on racial characteristics; only later would Black composers fuse

these European dance forms with Black folk elements to create such forms as ragtime" ("Social Dance Music," 162, 170–171).

41. Eileen Southern, *The Music of Black Americans: A History*, 3rd ed. (New York: Norton, 1997), 99, 110, 112–113; Shane White, "On Ownership and Value: Response," *Black Music Research Journal* 30, no. 2 (Fall 2010), 380.

42. Southern, "Frank Johnson and His Promenade Concerts," 7, 12, 16; Jones, *Francis Johnson*, 168; Potter, *Food for Apollo*, 61–62, 71.

43. Philip English Mackey, ed., *A Gentleman of Much Promise: The Diary of Isaac Mickle*, 1837–1845, 2 vols. (Philadelphia: University of Pennsylvania Press, 1977), 1:xiii–xxii.

44. Ibid., 1:186. See also Jones, *Francis Johnson*, 201–204.

45. Mackey, *Gentleman of Much Promise*. 1:194.

46. Ibid., 195–196.

47. Ibid.; [Joseph Willson], *Sketches of the Higher Classes of the Colored Society in Philadelphia, by a Southerner* (Philadelphia: Merihew and Thompson, 1841), 53, 56–57, 60.

48. Mackey, *Gentleman of Much Promise* 1:196.

49. Jones, *Francis Johnson*, 204–205; 211.

50. *New York Tribune*, May 23, 1843; *Philanthropist*, Apr. 26, 1843; *Christian Secretary*, Jan. 20, 1843; *Liberator*, June 9, 1843.

51. Mackey, *Gentleman of Much Promise*, 2:384; see also Jones, *Francis Johnson*, 229–230.

52. *Liberator*, Apr. 12, 19, 1844; Cromwell, "Frank Johnson's Military Band," 211; Jones, *Francis Johnson*, 242–245.

53. *Public Ledger*, Apr. 10, July 16, 1844; Jones, *Francis Johnson*, 246–248; Gonzalez, "The Art of Racial Politics," 32. For a brief discussion of the career of the band after Johnson's death, see Cromwell, "Frank Johnson's Military Band," 212.

Chapter 11

Note to epigraph: Odell Shepard, ed., *Journals of Bronson Alcott* (Boston: Little, Brown, 1938), 289.

1. Genealogical files in Hemphill family possession.

2. C. Dallett Hemphill, *Siblings: Brothers and Sisters in American History* (New York: Oxford University Press, 2011), 57, 89, 120; John M. McLaughlin, *A Memoir of Hector Tyndale* (Philadelphia: n.p., 1882), 5–6; Robinson Tyndale to Sarah Tyndale, July 6, 1831, in Hemphill family possession.

3. Nicole Eustace, *1812: War and the Passions of Patriotism* (Philadelphia: University of Pennsylvania Press, 2012); Susan Klepp, *Revolutionary Conceptions: Women, Fertility, and Family Limitation in America, 1760–1820* (Chapel Hill: University of North Carolina Press, 2009); genealogical files in Hemphill family possession.

4. Nancy Alexander, "Here's How I Found One Woman Missing from History," *Women's E-News*, Apr. 5, 2015; Sarah Thorne Tyndale to Robinson Tyndale, July 13, 1830, in Hemphill family possession.

5. *Philadelphia Inquirer,* Dec. 17, 1841; *North American*, Dec. 31, 1841; *Hartford Weekly Times*, May 27, 1848.

6. Personal communication and photographs of the bowl and notes from Rebecca Mickle Hemphill (1913) and Marjorie Hemphill Williamson (1930s) from Brenda Reuger, all in July 2011.

7. City directory information from the online collection provided by the Greater Philadelphia GeoHistory Network, http://www.philageohistory.org/rdic-images/index2.cfm, accessed various dates. On the reliability of city directories (from comparison with census data), see Claudia Goldin, "The Economic Status of Women in the Early Republic: Quantitative Evidence," *Journal of Interdisciplinary History* 16, no. 3 (Winter 1986), 375–404. On the Tyndale-Mitchell marriage, see Hampton L. Carson, "Honorable James Tyndale Mitchell," *Pennsylvania Magazine of History and Biography* 40, no. 1 (1916), 3. Robinson's brothers H (Harold or Hector?) and William Tyndale remained at 201 N. 2nd St. in 1817. H Tyndale was listed as an accountant in Webb's Alley between 1819 and 1822, at Loxley's Ct. in 1825, and at 34 Cherry St. in 1829–1830. Sharon Carter was listed at18 S. Front St. between 1823 and 1825 and as an agent for the New Jersey Glass Company at 281 High (Market) St. in 1828 and 1829.

8. City directory information from Greater Philadelphia GeoHistory Network; Goldin, "Economic Status of Women," 400–401; Susan Ingalls Lewis, "Beyond Horatia Alger: Breaking Through Gendered Assumptions About Business 'Success' in Mid-Nineteenth Century America," *Business and Economic History* 24, no. (Fall 1995), 101–102.

9. Carson, "Honorable James Tyndale Mitchell," 3; Texas deeds in Hemphill family possession; William Bradford Reed, *An Address to the Citizens of Philadelphia on the Subject of Fancy Fairs* (Philadelphia: Joseph and William Kite, 1834), 15; Alexander, "Here's How I Found One Woman" (Alexander is also a Tyndale descendant). On the volatility of the Philadelphia economy following the War of 1812, see Cathy Matson, "Mathew Carey's Learning Experience: Commerce, Manufacturing, and the Panic of 1819," *Early American Studies* 11, no. 3 (Fall 2013), 455–485.

10. *National Gazette*, Aug. 29, 1839; *North American,* Mar. 3, 1841, July 23, 1842. The Chestnut Street store had an annex that curved around to 18 S. 7th St. (*North American,* July 29, 1842).

11. Deborah Norris Logan Diaries, 1815–1839, 17 vols., 15:41–42, Historical Society of Pennsylvania, Philadelphia; Robinson Tyndale to Andrew Jackson, Sept. 1, 1835, Andrew Jackson Papers, Library of Congress, Washington, D.C.; James Tyndale Mitchell notes in Hemphill family possession.

12. Edwin A. Harder, "The Tucker and Hemphill Hard Porcelain Manufactory: Philadelphia, 1825–1838," *Bulletin of the Pennsylvania Museum* 4, no. 14 (Apr. 1906), n.p.; Robinson Tyndale to Harold Tyndale, Feb. 27, 1842, and Robinson Tyndale Death notice, May 25, 1842, in Hemphill family possession. His male friends were invited to his funeral, and to proceed from his house at 13 South Seventh St. to Laurel Hill Cemetery.

13. *North American*, Dec. 13, 1842, Sept. 22, Oct. 3, 1843; *Public Ledger,* Aug. 12, 1843, July 1846.

14. Goldin, "Economic Status of Women," 398–400; Sylvia Hoffert, "Female Self-Making in Mid-Nineteenth-Century America," *Journal of Women's History* 20, no. 3 (Fall 2008), 35–37; Patricia Cleary, "'She Will Be in the Shop': Women's Sphere of Trade in Eighteenth-Century Philadelphia and New York," *Pennsylvania Magazine of History and Biography* 119, no. 3 (July 1995), 181–202; Ellen Hartigan O'Connor, *The Ties That Buy: Women and Commerce in Revolutionary America* (Philadelphia: University of Pennsylvania Press, 2009); Beverly Wilson Palmer, ed., *Selected Letters of Lucretia Coffin Mott* (Chicago: University of Illinois Press, 2002), 189, 195. From 1790 to 1860, the largest group of employed female household heads in Philadelphia (approximately a third) were shopkeepers (Goldin, "Economic Status of Women," 396, 402; Wendy Gamber, "A Gendered Enterprise: Placing Nineteenth-Century Businesswomen in History," *Business History Review* 72, no. 2 [Summer 1998], 189–190, 204–205). For one less-than-respectable china shop owner, Ann Baker Carson, see Susan Branson, *Dangerous to Know: Women, Crime, and Notoriety in the Early Republic* (Philadelphia: University of Pennsylvania Press, 2008).

15. Gamber, "Gendered Enterprise," 209–210; Palmer, *Selected Letters of Mott*, 205. During the Stamp Act crisis in 1765, for example, at least six women signed a nonimportation agreement with their male counterparts (John T. Scharf and Thompson Westcott, *History of Philadelphia, 1609–1884*, 3 vols. [Philadelphia: L. H. Everts, 1884], 1:272–273).

16. Hoffert, "Female Self-Making," 34–59; Palmer, *Selected Letters of Mott*, 189.

17. *Godey's Lady's Book*, Oct. 1852.

18. Goldin, "Economic Status"; Gamber, "Gendered Enterprise"; Lewis, "Beyond Horatia Alger." On successful widows, see Lisa Wilson Waciega, "A 'Man of Business': The Widow of Means in Southeastern Pennsylvania, 1750–1850," *William and Mary Quarterly*, 3rd ser., 44, no. 1 (Jan. 1987), 40–64.

19. *Godey's Lady's Book and Magazine*, Jan. 1855, Dec. 1855, Dec. 1856. That Edward Mitchell was a friend of Louis Godey may also have helped secure positive notice in the magazine (Carson, "Honorable James Tyndale Mitchell," 4; *Godey's Lady's Book and Magazine*, Sept. 1858). The business continued to do well after Sarah's death. Diarist Sidney George Fisher noted that he "went to Tyndale's & selected a pair of pretty china vases . . . to give as a wedding present" ("The Diary of Sidney George Fisher," *Pennsylvania Magazine of History and Biography* 89, no. 3 [July 1965], 340).

20. Mary P. Ryan, *Mysteries of Sex: Tracing Women and Men Through American History* (Chapel Hill: University of North Carolina Press, 2006), 101; *Prisoner's Friend: A Monthly Magazine Devoted to Criminal Reform, Philosophy, Science, Literature*, July 1, 1851; "Caroline Wells (Healey) Dall to Paulina Wright Davis," *Worcester Women's History Project*, http://www.wwhp.org/Resources/cwh_dall_to_pw_davis.html, accessed Jan. 3, 2011; Rodney Hessinger, *Seduced, Abandoned, and Reborn: Visions of Youth in Middle-Class America, 1780–1850* (Philadelphia: University of Pennsylvania Press, 2005).

21. Nancy Isenberg, *Sex and Citizenship in Antebellum America* (Chapel Hill: University of North Carolina Press, 1998), 130–131.

22. *Reports and Realities from the Sketch-Book of a Manager of the Rosine Association* (Philadelphia: John DuRoss, 1855), 13, 17, 30; Isenberg, *Sex and Citizenship*, 130; Scharf

and Westcott, *History of Philadelphia*, 2:1454, 1468; Marcia Carlisle, "Disorderly City, Disorderly Women: Prostitution in Antebellum Philadelphia," *Pennsylvania Magazine of History and Biography* 110, no. 4 (Oct. 1986), 567.

23. *Reports and Realities*, 27, 37, 79, 133, 155, 177; Rodney Hessinger, "Victim of Seduction or Vicious Woman? Conceptions of the Prostitute at the Philadelphia Magdalen Society, 1800–1850," *Explorations in Early American Culture* 1 (1999), 201–222.

24. *Pennsylvania Freeman*, Mar. 6, 1851.

25. *Niles' National Register*, July 4, 1846; Wendy E. Chmielewski, "Women's Work Against War in 1846: The Transatlantic Peace Movement in Exeter and Philadelphia," paper delivered at the British International Studies Association Conference, University of Exeter, Dec. 2008; Isenberg, *Sex and Citizenship*; McLaughlin, *Memoir of Hector Tyndale*, 6–9.

26. *Niles' National Register*, July 4, 1846.

27. Elizabeth C. Stanton, Susan B. Anthony, and Matilda J. Gage, eds., *History of Woman Suffrage, 1848–1861*, 3 vols. (Salem, N.H.: Ayer, 1881), 1:221; Doris Weatherford, *A History of the American Suffragist Movement* (Santa Barbara, Calif.: ABC-CLIO, 1998), 44.

28. *New York Daily Tribune*, Oct. 26, 1850; *American Phrenological Journal*, Jan .1851; *Liberator*, Nov. 15, 1850; Stanton, Anthony, and Gage, *History of Woman Suffrage*, 1:224.

29. Harriot Hunt, *Glances and Glimpses; or, Fifty Years Social, Including Twenty Years Professional, Life* (Boston: John P. Jewett, 1856), 252; Stanton, Anthony, and Gage, *History of Woman Suffrage*, 1:166.

30. *New York Herald*, Oct. 28, 1850; *Spirit of the Times: A Chronicle of the Turf, Agriculture, Field Sports, Literature and the Stage*, Dec. 21, 1850.

31. Paulina W. Davis, comp., *A History of the National Woman's Rights Movement, for Twenty Years, with the Proceedings of the Decade Meeting Held at Apollo Hall, October 20, 1870* (New York: Journeymen Printers' Co-operative Association, 1871), 14–15. See also Stanton, Anthony, and Gage, *History of Woman Suffrage* 1:218.

32. Palmer, *Selected Letters of Mott*, 189; *Pennsylvania Freeman*, July 3, Sept. 25, Oct. 30, 1851; Jean R. Soderlund, "Priorities and Power: The Philadelphia Female Antislavery Society," in Jean Fagin Yellin and John C. Van Horne, eds., *The Abolitionist Sisterhood: Women's Political Culture in Antebellum America* (Ithaca, N.Y.: Cornell University Press, 1994), 80–82; Julie Roy Jeffrey, *The Great Silent Army of Abolitionism: Ordinary Women and the Antislavery Movement* (Chapel Hill: University of North Carolina Press, 1998), 108, 110–115, 120–121.

33. Federal Writers' Project, comp., *Stories of New Jersey: Its Significant Places, People and Activities* (New York: M. Barrows, 1938), 174–175.

34. Family history notes in Hemphill family possession; John Humphrey Noyes, *History of American Socialisms* (Philadelphia: J. B. Lippincott, 1870), 460.

35. Noyes, *History of American Socialisms*, 473–480.

36. Ibid., 463, 482–483; 500–506.

37. James Tyndale Mitchell Diary, Apr. 9, 13, May 12, 14, 1852, in Hemphill family possession.

38. Sarah Tyndale (hereafter STT) to Clara Tyndale Mickle, Sept. 29, 1852, from North American Phoenix; STT to Hector Tyndale (hereafter HT), North American Phoenix, all Oct. 11, 1852, Papers of Isaac Mickle, file 196, Camden County Historical Society, Camden, N.J.; James Tyndale Mitchell Diary, Dec. 14, 1852.

39. T. D. Seymour Bennett, "The Quakers and Communitarianism," *Bulletin of the Friends Historical Association* 43, no. 2 (1954), 98; Noyes, *History of American Socialisms*, 486–492, 495–496; Maud Honeyman Greene, "Raritan Bay Union, Eagleswood, New Jersey," *Proceedings of the New Jersey Historical Society* 68, no. 1 (Jan. 1950), 1–20. For an analysis of the community's failure, see Noyes, *History of American Socialisms*, 498–499, 510.

40. James Tyndale Mitchell Diary, Feb. 1, 12, Mar. 3, Apr. 22, 26, May 30, June, 4, 9, July. 28, 1853; STT to HT, Raritan Bay Union, Dec. 27, 1853, Papers of Isaac Mickle, file 196.

41. Shepard, *Journals of Bronson Alcott*, 289–291; Justin Kaplan, *Walt Whitman: A Life* (New York: Simon and Schuster, 1980), 218–220; Susan Cheever, *Louisa May Alcott: A Personal Biography* (New York: Simon and Schuster, 2010), 150; Peter Gibian, "Conversations with Whitman," *Mickle Street Review* 16 (n.d.), http://msr-archives.rutgers.edu/archives/Issue%2016/essays/gibianon.htm, accessed May 13, 2020.

42. Sherry Ceniza, review of Joyce E. Warren, *Fanny Fern: An Independent Woman* (New Brunswick, N.J.: Rutgers University Press, 1992), *Walt Whitman Quarterly Review* 11, no. 2 (Fall 1993), 90, 92–93; Edwin Haviland Miller, ed., *Walt Whitman: The Correspondence*, 7 vols. (New York: New York University Press, 1961–1977, 2007), 1:42–45; *Spiritual Instructions Received at the Meetings of One of the Circles Formed in Philadelphia, for the Purpose of Investigating the Philosophy of Spiritual Intercourse* (Philadelphia: n.p., 1852).

43. Ceniza, Review of *Fanny Fern*, 92; Sarah Tyndale to Walter Whitman, July 1, 1857, Charles E. Feinberg Collection of the Papers of Walt Whitman, 1834–1919, container 17, reel 10, Woodberry Library, Emory University, Atlanta, Ga.

44. Sarah Tyndale to Hector Tyndale, 1855, in Hemphill family possession; James Tyndale Mitchell Diary, Sept. 15, 23, 30, Oct. 12, 14, 17, Nov. 22, 30, Dec. 14, 1855, Jan. 5, Apr. 12, 1856.

45. Sarah Tyndale to Walter Whitman, June 2, 1857, Feinberg Collection, container 17, reel 10.

46. James Tyndale Mitchell Diary, Nov. 15, 1857, Jan. 2, 16, Apr. 8, 10, June 25, 1858, Jan. 25, July 13, Aug. 18, 22, 1859; James Tyndale Mitchell to Harold Tyndale, Jan. 31, 1859, in Hemphill family possession.

47. McLaughlin, *Memoir of Hector Tyndale*, 7–9; James Tyndale Mitchell Diary, Dec. 5 1859; *Public Ledger*, Dec. 14, 1902; James Grant Wilson and John Fiske, eds., *Appleton's Cyclopaedia of American Biography*, 6 vols. (New York: D. Appleton, 1887–1889), 6:202.

Chapter 12

Note to epigraph: Michael Robert Greco, "William Darrah Kelley: The Ante-Bellum Years" (Ph.D. diss., Johns Hopkins University, 1974), 223.

1. Greco, "William Darrah Kelley," 21, 26; L[inus] P[ierpont] Brockett, *Men of Our Day* (Philadelphia: Ziegler and McCurdy, 1872), 466–467. In addition to Brockett's there have been numerous short biographies of Kelley, including J. Donald Cameron, *Memorial Addresses on the Life and Character of William D. Kelley, Delivered in the House Of Representatives and in the Senate, Fifty-First Congress, First Session* (Washington, D.C.: Government Printing Office, 1890); Florence Kelley, "My Philadelphia," *Graphic,* Oct. 1, 1926. Information given without attribution below was found in multiple sources, including online biographies. Greco's thesis is the best source for the pre–Civil War years, especially regarding Kelley's antebellum political evolution. My goal is to show how his activities as a young man illustrated major trends of his time and were situated in place.

2. Greco, "William Darrah Kelley," 29–33; Kelley, "My Philadelphia," 10.

3. Kelley, "My Philadelphia," 10.

4. Ibid., 10–11; Greco, "William Darrah Kelley," 34.

5. Greco, "William Darrah Kelley," 36–38, 40, 42. Kelley served in the State Fencibles from 1829 to 1834 (Thomas S. Lanard, *One Hundred Years with the State Fencibles* [Philadelphia: Nields, 1913], 175).

6. Russell F. Weigely, ed., *Philadelphia: A 300-Year History* (New York: W. W. Norton, 1982), 280; Greco, "William Darrah Kelley," 40, 44–45, 48–49; Cameron, *Memorial Addresses on Kelley*; Philip English Mackey, ed., *A Gentleman of Much Promise: The Diary of Isaac Mickle, 1837–1845*, 2 vols. (Philadelphia: University of Pennsylvania Press, 1977), 2:392.

7. Greco, "William Darrah Kelley," 38. 48, 56, 58, 60, 62, 64; Cameron, *Memorial Addresses on Kelley,* 71.

8. Greco, "William Darrah Kelley," 50–53, 58, 71–73, 75–77, 79–81.

9. Ibid., 54; William D. Kelley to Henry Patterson, Aug. 23, 1835, Feb. 7, 1836, reel 3824-1, box 5, Kelley Family Papers, 1681–1936, Rare Book and Manuscript Library, Columbia University, New York.

10. Greco, "William Darrah Kelley," 81, 84–95.

11. Ibid., 97, 103–105; Mackey, *Gentleman of Much Promise,* 1:77.

12. Mackey, *Gentleman of Much Promise,* 1:154, 159.

13. Ibid., 161–162.

14. Ibid., 162–163.

15. Ibid., 168.

16. Ibid., 185, 190–192, 196–198, 242–243.

17. Ibid., 211–212.

18. Ibid., 228, 230; *United States Magazine, and Democratic Review,* June 1851; *Public Ledger,* Jan. 21, 1842; Cameron, *Memorial Addresses on Kelley,* 72; Greco, "William Darrah Kelley," 110, 114–115; Mackey, *Gentleman of Much Promise,* 2:354.

19. Mackey, *Gentleman of Much Promise,* 2:258–260; Greco, "William Darrah Kelley," 67–68, 70, 120.

20. Mackey, *Gentleman of Much Promise,* 2:353.

21. Ibid., 380.

22. Ibid., 1:190, 2:279, 322, 364, 373, 381, 398; Greco, "William Darrah Kelley," 118–119.

23. Mackey, *Gentleman of Much Promise,* 2:387–397; Greco, "William Darrah Kelley," 121–123.

24. Mackey, *Gentleman of Much Promise,* 2:471; Greco, "William Darrah Kelley," 123, 189–190.

25. Greco, "William Darrah Kelley," 191.

26. Cameron, *Memorial Addresses on Kelley,* 73; "The Prosecuting Attorneys of Philadelphia," *Pennsylvania Law Journal* 5, no. 2 (Dec. 1845), 54; *United States Magazine, and Democratic Review,* June 1851; Greco, "William Darrah Kelley," 136, 138, 141–142, 144–146; John T. Scharf and Thompson Westcott, *History of Philadelphia, 1609–1884,* 3 vols. (Philadelphia: L. H. Everts, 1884), 2:1574.

27. Greco, "William Darrah Kelley," 145–146.

28. Ibid. The courtroom was the first-floor west room of the center building of the State House (*Olwine's Law Journal,* Dec. 29, 1849, 8).

29. *American Railway Times,* Oct. 23, 1851.

30. Mackey, *Gentleman of Much Promise,* 2:279, 286, 339–340, 427; Albert Post, "Early Efforts to Abolish Capital Punishment in Pennsylvania," *Pennsylvania Magazine of History and Biography* 68, no. 1 (Jan. 1944), 49; *Public Ledger,* Dec. 19, 1844; *National Era,* May 17, 1849; Greco, "William Darrah Kelley," 153–154.

31. Greco, "William Darrah Kelley," 155, 156, 168, 171; *North American and United States Gazette,* Feb. 13, 1850; *Friend; a Religious and Literary Journal,* Jan. 26, 1850; Eliza Harrison, ed., *Philadelphia Merchant: The Diary of Thomas P. Cope, 1800–1851* (South Bend, Ind.: Gateway Editions, 1978), 588.

32. *United States Magazine, and Democratic Review,* June 1851; *Saturday Evening Post,* Mar. 9, 1850; Greco, "William Darrah Kelley," 152.

33. *Reports and Realities from the Sketch-Book of a Manager of the Rosine Association* (Philadelphia: John DuRoss, 1855), 121, 183.

34. Greco, "William Darrah Kelley," 160, 162, 165–166; *Public Ledger,* Dec. 26, 1844.

35. Greco, "William Darrah Kelley," 158–159, 192; Scharf and Westcott, *History of Philadelphia,* 1:686, 702–703; Louis Kossuth, note of thanks, n.d., Kelley Family Papers. Greco argues that Kelley's mother's death was harder on him than his wife's had been ("William Darrah Kelley," 192–193).

36. James Tyndale Mitchell Diary, Sept. 30, Oct. 29, 1852, in Hemphill family possession.

37. Greco, "William Darrah Kelley," 194–197, 223; *United States Magazine, and Democratic Review,* June 1851.

38. Greco, "William Darrah Kelley," 171–177, 185–189, 205–206, 226. A new Pennsylvania constitution had made his judicial position elective (Cameron, *Memorial Addresses on Kelley,* 73; Scharf and Westcott, *History of Philadelphia,* 1:722).

39. Greco, "William Darrah Kelley," 208–209.

40. Ibid., 209, 211.

41. *National Era*, Sept. 13, 1855; Greco, "William Darrah Kelley," 211–212.

42. Greco, "William Darrah Kelley," 213–215; Scharf and Westcott, *History of Philadelphia*, 1:722.

43. Greco, "William Darrah Kelley," 215–217. Page and Kelley must have reconciled after the war, as in 1872, Page (then age seventy-seven) presented Kelley with a certificate of honorary membership in the State Fencibles at a lavish celebration (Lanard, *One Hundred Years with the Fencibles*, 175–176).

44. James Tyndale Mitchell Diary, June 8, 1853, May 31, 1854, Feb. 18, Oct. 15, 1855.

45. Greco, "William Darrah Kelley," 217; Scharf and Westcott, *History of Philadelphia*, 1:732–733; *Public Ledger*, Dec. 14, 1902.

46. Greco, "William Darrah Kelley," 228–231, 232–235; Scharf and Westcott, *History of Philadelphia*, 1:722; Brockett, *Men of Our Day*, 471; James Tyndale Mitchell Diary, Sept. 5, 1856.

47. *Philadelphia Inquirer*, Dec. 7, 1860.

48. Greco, "William Darrah Kelley," 263, 267, 274–275, 292–295.

49. Ibid., 279–281.

50. Ibid., 298, 6–9, 13; Scharf and Westcott, *History of Philadelphia*, 2:1699; Ira V. Brown, "William D. Kelley and Radical Reconstruction," *Pennsylvania Magazine of History and Biography* 85, no. 3 (July 1961), 316–329.

51. Greco, "William Darrah Kelley," 18, 153; Kelley, "My Philadelphia," 10.

52. Greco, "William Darrah Kelley," 246–249, 252. On Owen, see Lucretia Mott to Caroline B. Kelley, Nov. 7, 1859, Kelley Family Papers.

53. *North American*, Dec. 24, 1846; *New York Evangelist*, Dec. 31, 1846; *American Railway Times*, Oct. 23, 1851; Scharf and Westcott, *History of Philadelphia*, 1:728.

54. *Altoona (Iowa) Rustler*, Jan. 17, 1890, cited in Find a Grave Memorial, http://www.findagrave.com, accessed Jan. 17, 2011.

55. Kelley, "My Philadelphia."

INDEX

ACKNOWLEDGMENTS

Only Dallett would have known whom to thank. We can only guess who helped her in the various libraries and archives. Regrettably, the notes will have to serve as the best recognition we can give to the institutions and people who retrieved items and provided leads to Dallett. After we chose to take over the manuscript, we experienced a swell of support from the historical community. We are particularly indebted to the individual chapter editors: Jean R. Soderlund, Lisa Minardi, Sarah Barringer Gordon, Judith L. Van Buskirk, Susan Branson, Nenette Luarca-Shoaf, Brenna O'Rourke Holland, Sarah K. Rodriguez, Richard S. Newman, Susan E. Klepp, and Andrew Shankman. Without their expertise, insights, and attention to detail, the project would never have come to completion. Toby Ditz and Jessica Roney provided expert editing advice on the entire manuscript. At the University of Pennsylvania Press, Bob Lockhart was a steady guide and able contributor. He enthusiastically assumed tasks that ordinarily would have fallen to the author or editors, helping particularly with procuring the images. John Carroll University came through for us with support for the publication costs.

For nearly three decades, Dallett was one of the key contributors to scholarly discussions at the McNeil Center for Early American Studies. We are in her debt, more than she in ours. But in reading her book, it is quite clear that she learned much from the many scholars who have been short- or long-term members of the center community. Just as we see the web of the early Philadelphia community in her chapters, the current-day community of Philadelphia is also clearly present in this book.

A final word of thanks must go to John Hill, Dallett's beloved husband. John was eager to help in any way he could, but also trusted us with his wife's legacy. We are grateful for the confidence he placed in us and hope we have earned it.